Edited with an Introduction by
Axel D. Steuer & James Wm. McClendon, Jr.

Abingdon
Nashville

Is God GOD?

Copyright © 1981 by Abingdon

Library of Congress Cataloging in Publication Data

Main entry under title:
Is God GOD?
  Bibliography: p.
  1. God—Addresses, essays, lectures.
  I. Steuer, Axel D. (Axel Detlef), 1943–
  II. McClendon, James William.
  BT102.A1I8   231   81-1927   AACR2

ISBN 0-687-19703-1

Scripture quotations noted RSV are from the Revised
Standard Version of the Bible, copyrighted 1946, 1952,
© 1971, 1973 by the Division of Christian Education of
the National Council of the Churches of Christ in
U.S.A., and are used by permission. Those noted TEV
are from The Bible in Today's English Version.
Copyright © American Bible Society 1966, 1971, 1976.
All others are from the King James Version.

The essay by Gordon D. Kaufman is an abridged
version of a chapter in his book, *The Theological
Imagination*, forthcoming from The Westminster
Press.

MANUFACTURED BY THE PARTHENON PRESS AT
NASHVILLE, TENNESSEE, UNITED STATES OF AMERICA

Contents

General Introduction................................7

I. THE AVAILABILITY OF GOD
  1. The Anonymity of God
    Thomas J. J. Altizer..................................17
  2. The Experience of God
    and the Search for Images
    Charles Davis......................................36
  3. Speaking of God
    Paul M. van Buren..................................55

II. IN SEARCH OF A GOD-CONCEPT
  4. The Supposed Incoherence
    of the Concept of God
    Axel D. Steuer......................................85
  5. Constructing the Concept of God
    Gordon D. Kaufman..............................108
  6. Can We Speak Literally of God?
    William P. Alston..................................144

III. GOD AND THE STORY
  7. The God of the Theologians
    and the God of Jesus Christ
    James Wm. McClendon, Jr......................181
  8. Stories of God: Why We Use Them
    and How We Judge Them
    David B. Burrell, C.S.C..........................206

IV. THE REALITY OF GOD
  9. The Holy Spirit As God
    Robert Neville......................................233
  10. The Buddhist Witness to God
    John B. Cobb, Jr..................................265

About the Contributors.............................287

General Introduction

The temper of our times is such that to mention God may be to suggest atheism—just as mention of virginity may suggest promiscuity and mention of tax returns may suggest fraud. The temper of our times—or human nature as such? Perhaps we cannot say. Yet we do know that for our times God is not the great and awesome Presence by which all things live; rather, to judge by the title of a recent book, God is a "problem"; the word "God" is at best mild profanity, and at worst a verbal fig leaf for pious fraud; belief in God is consigned to the past, or to the strange ones among us, or to the realm of the forlorn might-have-beens among our own deep convictions.

Why, then, a book about God?

Because, contrary to popular cultural assumptions, God is neither dead nor has the concept of God been captured by the culture for its own uses. Rather, some of the best minds in this land are God-obsessed; and some of the best work in modern theology, if little known, is unwaveringly focused on God as God. This is not a book about the popular culture, and it is not interested in the indubitably interesting socioreligious phenomena which sometimes use "God" as a conjuring word. In those phenomena, talk of God is a code for higher human aspirations. "God," it will be said, is "female, not male; black, not white." "God" is, for those who speak in this way and for those who oppose them, a counter in a human power struggle of epic proportions.

The contributors to the present volume are not unaware of or indifferent to those struggles, but our editorial focus here is on a different struggle. Not only may talk of God obliquely represent us humans and our world as we see it; it may be—and we will argue should be first of all, talk about *God*. And while admittedly our social, political, and religious outlooks affect our understanding of God, the tides also flow the other way: Our understanding of God as God is the very stream in which these others may find their course as well. Let God be God, then, is our motto. But which God? What is, who is, God? *That* is our concern.

Three sorts of questions about God have absorbed the attention of philosophers ancient and modern. The first, already alluded to, is the atheist's question: Is there a God? Does God exist? The second is the conceptual question just expressed: What is God? What is the (true, adequate, proper) concept of God? And the third is the apologetic question: What reasons undergird or justify belief in God? This book concentrates on the second question, confident that to answer it well will be to show the way to answer the first and the third; confident, that is, that adequate knowledge of God will furnish the best arguments for belief in God.

What, then, would constitute adequate knowledge of God? Here a certain confusion often grips us moderns. When Christians speak of "knowledge of God," do we mean knowing what other Christians traditionally have meant by their use of the same term (knowledge *that* "God" means one who is infinitely loving, all wise, etc., etc.)? Or do we by knowledge of God mean more the *skill* to use the word "God" in our own primary religious utterance—knowing *how* to pray, how to bear witness, how to question God and be questioned in terms of God and God's creation? Or do we mean most of all the personal *acquaintance with* the One of whom we do so speak and about whom we also know? In other words, is "knowledge of God" knowing that such and such is the case? Or knowing how such and such a Way is actually lived? Or knowing One whom we trust and obey and serve? Is knowledge of God more like knowledge of history (truths and facts) or knowledge of French (skills or know-how) or knowledge of your best friend (personal acquaintance)? While different theologians have concentrated on different aspects of knowledge of God (in the present volume, for example, Alston and Kaufman on our knowing *that,* Burrell and van Buren on our knowing *how,* and Cobb and Altizer on our knowing *One whom* . . .), the Christian approach to knowing God normally has involved all three models, so that to omit any of the three is to leave out something vital.

Yet there is another aspect of modern linguistic confusion which the preceding analysis has not cleared. When we speak of God, are we saying anything at all? Are we talking about something or someone other than ourselves and our own constructed world of thoughts and ideas? Is there really a God? Is God God? Does discussion of the *concept* of God (as in this book) simply ignore the real issue by confusing our own human concepts of a God with the real God (or with the lack of any real God)? This is one form of the atheistic question.

Modern philosophy, however, is teaching us that we must avoid a fallacy embedded in the question of the preceding paragraph. Wittgenstein and Austin, for example, have shown in different ways that this sort of question can deceive because it overlooks the context, the form of life, the place of the speaker who asks the question. That does not mean that the question about the relation between God and concepts of God (or about the relation between talk of God and God) is pointless; it does mean that to ask that question cogently we must specify a context for our concept or for our talk. One context (and the one presupposed by most contributors to the present volume) is that of the Christian community which (says that it) trusts God, worships God, prays "Our Father in heaven," and more. This community is the "form of life" in which our question can take shape.

For the Christian community not only calls upon and speaks of God but is also committed (as are other communities) to rationality and to morality. Some evidence to the contrary notwithstanding, Christians are *by definition* so committed. Thus we can acknowledge that we do trust, worship, and serve God and also can ask theologically, How is it rational and moral to do so? recognizing that the answer could be "in this way" or "in that sense"—but also conceivably could be, It's not! In the last case, though, something certainly would have to change.

As one of the editors of this book (Steuer) put the matter in a
1969 Harvard thesis: "It is rather obvious that Jews and
Christians have been worshiping and praying for many
centuries. To the object of their worship and prayer they have
given the proper name 'God.' I suggest that much light will be
shed on the theologian's dilemma in our day if we try to
understand *what it is* . . . that Christians [and Jews] have
referred to in using the name 'God.' The really interesting
question [for Christian theology] is whether 'God' refers to
God—that is, whether what Christians worship and pray to is
that which it is moral and rational to worship and pray to. I
further suggest that this sort of approach is much less
intractable than the way theologians usually approach the
problem of talking about God."

Let us follow Steuer's lead. For the question we wanted to
ask is exactly whether it is moral and rational (in liturgical
language, whether it is "meet and right") to trust, worship,
and serve God. To keep the question clear, let us call that
which Christians have traditionally intended to worship and
serve, "God." The word "God" thus will stand for the
Christian concept of deity, just as "Brahman" stands for a
Hindu concept of deity and "Jupiter" stood for a Roman
concept of deity. Now let us call that which morally and
rationally *ought* to be worshiped and served, GOD. Then not
only can we ask, Is Brahman GOD? and, Is Jupiter GOD?
(meaning, does that Hindu concept or term, or did that
Roman concept or term represent that which it is meet and
right to trust, worship, and serve?); we also can ask, Is God
GOD? (meaning, is what Christians have intended to trust,
worship, and serve, that which it is meet and right to trust,
worship, and serve? or if not, what [if anything] is?) In that
way, the conceptual question becomes the question about
atheism as well. As Steuer said in his thesis, "In other words,
this paper will attempt to deal with the question 'What is
God?' and with the cognate and for us theologically vital
question, 'Is it moral and rational to worship and pray to God?'
that is, is God GOD? That an answer to the first question is a
clear prerequisite to answering the second question should be
obvious upon reflection."

To raise the conceptual question in this way, then, has distinct advantages for theological thought. It shows that a *moral* question is involved. This means that we ask not, Is God moral? and far less, Is GOD moral? (questions to which the answers, in our tradition, have become analytic: yes); but rather our investigation obliges us to ask, Are *we* moral? That is, does our kind of Christian practice itself involve us in immorality—at the very least, the immorality of wasting precious time in prayer and worship that might be better spent in alleviating some of the world's suffering? And this applies whether we are ordinary Christians or (perhaps a rising breed) Christian atheists. In either case the question about God is self-involving as well. Nor does this question encourage us to slide off into a comfortable agnosticism. Indeed, it demands that we engage in the arduous struggle to think rightly about God.

Still, is this a struggle anyone really needs to engage in? Alasdair MacIntyre has argued that it is not. In a brilliant summation of the theistic debate of the 1960s (*The Religious Significance of Atheism*, with Paul Ricoeur [New York: Columbia University Press, 1969]), he has contended that the 1960s debate differed from the Victorian debate about God because the earlier represented a genuine cultural crisis. For the Victorians, God mattered, and if some of them ceased to believe in God, that mattered for their entire world-view, for their very lives. We have been saying that that is as it should have been—by definition, God matters. But MacIntyre argues that it is no longer so. As explanation, he says that both God and modern culture have been reconceived, so that God and religious belief in God are truly marginal with respect to modern culture.

This makes it possible to make clear in a fresh way the contribution of the death-of-God theologians, whose work converged in a momentary glare of publicity in the middle 1960s. It now may be seen that those theologians saw or sensed the irrelevance MacIntyre spoke of—and that they saw the incongruity, the utter irony, of such irrelevance. Consequently, they adopted a heroic course. Unlike the Victorian atheists, they did not leave the church. Instead they took up atheism as their own personal passion and theological burden *within* the community. Thereby they 'made' the debate relevant by internalizing it: The tension between God as they conceived (or were unable to conceive) God, and modern culture as they embodied it, was made explicit by their own Christian atheism.

It was a heroic step but not a sufficient one—a fact witnessed by the continuing development in the several lines of thought of those very theologians, some of whom (Altizer, van Buren—perhaps Davis?) have essays in the present collection.

Why was their original move insufficient? Logically, if one formerly has embraced both God and one's world, but comes to believe that they are utterly incompatible, there are five possible solutions. One can (a) reject God, as the death-of-God theologians did; that is called atheism. Or one can (b) reject contemporary culture; that may be called fundamentalism, but it is a heroic option too little investigated by academic theologians, though chosen by some of great integrity. Or one can attempt to reconstruct culture, either (c) along archaic lines (cf. T. S. Eliot) or (d) along futuristic lines (cf. Norman O. Brown). Or one can (e) reconstruct the concept of God, asking, as do several of the contributors to this volume, whether God as conceived by recent religion is indeed the GOD who is worthy of honor and faith.

A sixth option should be mentioned, theologically uninteresting though it may be, for it appears to be the path chosen by the American majority in our times. This is the trivialization of belief in God. In this option, we learn to believe in belief, or we believe with Robert Bellah in a religion "beyond belief"—a cultural piety or civil religion utterly unfalsifiable because its theistic content has been siphoned off. But MacIntyre warns of the false comfort this new cultural religion may offer. To be sure, 'God' and religion are now tolerated. Yet the comfort is false exactly because the religion has been trivialized; atheism has become uninteresting because theologians in their apologetic zeal (cf. Tillich) have made of God a smaller and smaller target, until the difference between belief and unbelief vanishes into "ultimate concern."

But the contributors to the present volume are not, as far as we can tell, engaged in such apologetics.

It might be an interesting exercise to figure out (a task we will leave to the reader) which of the five options, or which combination of these, has been taken by each contributor. In any case, it will be evident that the contributors have not collaborated; they do not share a common outlook. Rather, each essay has been solicited because it represents a distinct and alternative view of the concept of God. Yet in some way each vividly addresses the question *Is God GOD?* In the first grouping, The Availability of God, this is done by questioning whether our culture even can name the name God (Altizer) or symbolize it meaningfully (Davis)—at least without radically reconsidering our Judaic heritage (adds van Buren). In the second, In Search of a God-Concept, the focus is not upon the ultimate GOD but upon our concept or term "God." Is it coherent? (Steuer) Is it logical construct? (Kaufman) Is it a word we *can* use literally? (Alston) In the third grouping, God and the Story, two theologians argue that God cut off from the story of the Christian past (McClendon) or from the present Christian community (Burrell) cannot be GOD. And in the final part, two theologians point to ways to relocate The Reality of God—that is, to show how God *is* GOD—Neville via process thought, and Cob via a study of (nominally atheistic) Buddhism. So the writers come together, but strongly disagree.

Still, they are alike in this: Each cares passionately about the issues involved. If they sometimes seem to have hard words for one another, even naming names, this is because they see the final importance of the question at issue. Not all can be right. But by doing their own theological work in the public arena, they all contribute to the renewal of the discussion about God. Almost a generation has passed since the death-of-God controversy and its abortive termination. Now the conversation opens again, in a new key, with a new question at the center, and with renewed hope. There is a resurrection of God in American theology; there is a· *new* theism in our time.

Steuer and McClendon

I. THE AVAILABILITY
OF GOD

About Thomas J. J. Altizer's Essay

The problem of the identification of God, already
mentioned in the general introduction, is front and center
in the first essay in this collection. Thomas J. J. Altizer's
thought here shows both continuity and change as
compared to his *Gospel of Christian Atheism* (1966),
which constituted with a few other books and articles
the primary literature of the American God-is-dead
movement of the 1960s. That expression of radical
theology might be best understood as a cry of alarm,
announcing to itself and to us all that theology's business
could not continue as before; that a fundamental change
had made the old theological task impossible. In a way,
radical theology itself was only a more extreme expression
of the Barthian revolution against liberal Christianity,
acknowledging that 'God' no longer was *culturally*
available, so that (in the Barthian vision) only GOD could
disclose GOD; only God's self-revelation could make God
known. But for 1960s radicalism, not even revelation
worked; God was silent or absent or . . . nothing.

Altizer's present essay, however, is in continuity not so
much with neo-orthodoxy as with other strands of
modernity—the mystical vision of William Blake
(1757–1827), the dark disturbed sense of the world in
Franz Kafka (1883–1924) and Samuel Beckett (b. 1906),
and pervasively with the philosophical theology of G. W.
F. Hegel (1770–1831). Hegel saw the struggle to identify
God, or in his term Absolute Spirit, not merely as the
task of philosophy but as the very struggle of the cosmos
itself. The long evolutionary history of reality was the

17

effort of Absolute Spirit to become itself and to realize itself by means of its identification with the world. Thus in classical Christian terms God must incarnate himself in the world in order to realize himself as God. The summit of this self-awareness (and the ultimate form of religion) had come in philosophy—notably in Hegelian philosophy.

Altizer agrees with Hegel in seeing the actual history of cultural consciousness as being of ultimate theological importance. In art, in literature, in the spirit of the times, the only Spirit that matters undergoes historic change. But today's literature and *Zeitgeist* reflect two crucial facts: *God cannot be identified* (i.e., is anonymous); *neither can we be identified.* Both these facts seem false to some: They know their God; they know "who they are." But these popular opinions hardly matter. The real poets know the truth; so do the real philosophers.

The question is, What are we to make of this pervasive new cultural anonymity? Many a reader of these signs is led to existential despair. We are struck by the buoyant optimism which surges through Thomas Altizer's dark vision. We cannot name God—God *has* no name. We cannot name ourselves—ours is an unidentifiable modern existence. Nevertheless, the Spirit, the anonymous God, does what God the Spirit does, and there is our joyous hope. Identification of the old sort is gone for good, but that does not finally matter; beyond us, there is a new kind of identification of the Spirit.

One may wonder here whether such 'continuities' as these do not defeat our attempt to comprehend them and to relate them to other theological work. Surely if Altizer is right, some others in this book (including the editors) are quite wrong. Yet two considerations urge Altizer upon us: First, our humble recognition of the logical point that if he can be wrong, he also can be right—and we wrong. Second, the acknowledgment that maybe neither he nor any one of us has the matter just right; rather, the truth may lie beyond us, in ways to which both he and we point, though none yet can say aright.

1. The Anonymity of God

Thomas J. J. Altizer

Simply to speak of theology today is to raise a question, and that question is of the possibility of theology itself. Is theological speech possible in our world? Is it actually possible for us to speak of God? Can we speak of God and truly say anything at all? These questions and others are driving us to the realization that we can speak of God only by realizing a new identity of theology. One route to such an identity is the realization that what we once knew as theology has become a soliloquy, a narcissistic soliloquy in which the speaker speaks in total solitude. Thereby, too, the God which is evoked is the absolutely solitary God, the God which is only, insofar as it is solely and only itself. We can name that God only by way of total obedience, an obedience to the wholly other, and that other can be spoken only in the language of pure otherness. But a language of pure otherness can be spoken only in solitude, a solitude in which the speaker is only itself, for actually to speak of God which is only itself is to speak in a solitary and isolated speech. Finally that speech becomes isolated even from itself and thereby ceases to speak. Yet the silence of that cessation is not a simple ending of speech; it is rather a blockage of speech, an impotence of speech wherein a primal identity becomes unmanifest because unsaid.

Even poets and philosophers have ceased speaking of God, and while their silence has been heard as grace by many theologians, now it is more clearly evident that it has brought with it a wounding that perhaps only the theologian can address. For the theologian is a theologian only through his or her speech about God, and the ending of that speech would be quite simply the end of theology. Many fervently hope that

19

this end has occurred already, and they hope with good
reason, for if it has ended, therewith has ended the
speakability of the deepest ground of a purely solitary speech.
And if that which cannot be spoken is not real, or is not real for
us, then our inability to speak about God might well portend
the advent of a new and fuller humanity. Nevertheless, it is
manifest that an anonymous speech and identity abounds
among us, and perhaps never more so than today. Is there a
necessary and integral relationship between our new
anonymity and what we once spoke of as God? Is our
anonymity related to our previous speech about God? Or is
our failure or impotence of theological speech a decisive sign
of a new anonymity among and within us? One might begin to
address these questions by first questioning whether it is
really true that we no longer can speak either of or about God.
Perhaps we are speaking about God in ways that are hidden
even to ourselves. Perhaps it is theology itself that is truly
anonymous among us, and perhaps most anonymous to those
who identify themselves as theologians. For if to be a
theologian is to be bound to what once was manifest as
theology, this very vocation may obscure and darken
whatever actual theology exists and speaks today.

Theology as we know it came into existence as a
consequence of the movement of Christianity from its original
historical ground in Jewish apocalypticism into the "catholic"
world of hellenistic culture and society. Now theology is being
called to rebirth in the context of the movement of faith from
Christendom to a far more "catholic" world than ever was
envisioned in the Christian tradition. Rebirth occurs only
through death, and if a genuine rebirth is to occur here, we
must presume that it will occur only through the death of the
original form and identity of our theology. Indeed, this may
already have occurred, or be occurring, and if so, it is to be
expected that theology itself will now appear to be in crisis.
What many have hailed as the death of theology then could be
interpreted as its rebirth. In this situation, theology is seeking
its foundations, and not simply its historical foundations, but
its foundations in the very activity and identity of theology.

The real question of the identity of theology can be raised

only in the context of the impossibility of theology. As long as
theological forms are given and real, there can be no question
of their identity, if only because their life and activity will
preclude a questioning of their existence. Theology, like
anything else, cannot deeply question itself when it cannot
deeply doubt itself. This doubt occurs when the questions of
theology become unanswerable even to itself. Then God will
truly appear as a mystery, and as a theological mystery, a
mystery reflecting the groundlessness, or the apparent
groundlessness, of theology itself. Now the mystery of God in
this sense must be distinguished from what is commonly
known as the mystery of God. Commonly, we think of the
mystery of God as the unknowability of God. This can and has
gone hand in hand with a confident faith in God, and many
theologians have affirmed that true faith in God can be noted
by its realization of the pure or total unknowability of God.
Unknowability, in this sense, is the primary attribute of God
and the primary attribute for faith. Hence Kierkegaard could
insist that it is precisely the unknowability or mystery of God
that most fundamentally distinguishes faith from paganism,
and this Kierkegaardian thesis has been echoed widely in our
own century. Here mystery or unknowability is the primary
identity of God for us, and that mystery is the deepest source
of meaning and identity for us.

When the mystery of God appears in this form, it can be a
living ground of theology, and a ground reflecting the
knowledge of God in faith. Such a mystery of God is wholly
different from a mystery of God that reflects the disintegration
or transformation of theological thinking. For then it is the
very identity of God that is most deeply in question. If a
classical faith could claim the mystery or unknowability of God
as its deepest foundation, it is that unknowability which was
our source for the identity of God, and that identity is most
firm or secure in this pure unknowability. But this is exactly
the identity we have lost, and most deeply lost, so that one
could almost say that God is literally a mystery to us. We could
say it, that is, if it were possible to speak literally of mystery,
and perhaps in this one instance, we can. God is a mystery to
us if only because God is anonymous to us, and most clearly so

in contemporary theology. Here, too, we find a contrast between classical and contemporary theology. Classical theology could know God's name in his namelessness, in his transcendence. Contemporary theology knows God's namelessness as an anonymity wherein all concrete and actual identity is absent. It is only when God's name and identity is absent that theology can speak most naturally and spontaneously of God.

If we know ourselves only by knowing God, and this has been affirmed by Christians as diverse as Augustine and Descartes, to say nothing of Tertullian and Beckett or Paul and Blake, then to know the anonymity of God is to know the anonymity of selfhood, and the deeper our knowledge of God, the deeper our own anonymity will be. Surely this is one reason, and an "existential" reason, that Buddhism recently has become so real to so many Christians. From this perspective, that *anomie* so forcefully described by Durkheim and his followers could be interpreted theologically as a sign of the Christian identity of the modern world, assuming, that is, that it is faith which now knows the anonymity of God. Theologically, can we make that assumption? Is contemporary theology a reflection of faith, and of a contemporary and genuine faith? Or, to phrase it differently, we might ask if a truly contemporary theological statement could be a genuine reflection of faith. Is a statement that could be a theological statement for us also a statement that could be a reflection or embodiment of faith? And not of bad faith or false faith, but of genuine faith? Can we know the anonymity of God as the true identity of God?

First, we must inquire as to just what a theological understanding of anonymity might be. Recognizing that anonymity is not to be confused with unknowability, we might begin by employing a classical theological distinction, speaking of anonymity as a positive rather than as a negative attribute or symbol of God. It is so for us, if only because anonymity is virtually a living presence among us, and not only among us but deeply within us, a presence beyond which neither our artists nor our thinkers can penetrate. So pervasive is this presence, indeed, that we no longer can either imagine or conceive a region beyond such anonymity. All too naturally, many theologians have returned to a classical mystical language, and using such images as eclipse, the cloud of unknowing, and the dark night of the soul, to speak of our world and situation. But these no longer will do, if only because, in terms of their own language-worlds, each of these images presupposes and posits the presence, or the actuality, of its own contrary, or opposite. Eclipse, cloud, and night are meaningful only in terms of the potential and finally actual presence of their others or opposites and were employed by the mystics to speak of the preludes, or preparations, for union or coinherence. So also some of us are being forced to recognize that even 'death' carries with it a positive symbolic meaning which now lies behind us. Hence the attraction today of a radical iconoclasm, denying all images of either God or the divine presence.

Yet even inconoclasm presupposes the actuality of its opposite, as can be seen clearly in Buddhism, Yahwism, and Islam. Iconoclasm is a consequence of either faith or enlightenment and is meaningless apart from such a ground. A truly new iconoclasm may well be a possibility for us, but it is not so distant from a new enlightenment or a new faith. In any case, we cannot avoid our present dilemma by this means. We might note rather that the anonymity which we know is a total presence, a presence pervading all our modes of both speech and silence. Let us speak of it then as a totality. Images of totality pervade the history of religions and mythology, and these have been resurrected again and again by the modern imagination. Romanticism might be said to have begun with the image of the marriage of heaven and hell, and many would say that it has ended with their divorce and the consequent oblivion of heaven. In any case, if hell or nothingness now dominates the contemporary imagination, it does so by its presence as a total image. At one time this situation excited our Barthian theological mood, for such a nothingness seemed to present itself as the actual opposite of faith. Now we should realize that it cannot be so construed, if only because ours is a total nothingness, open to no possibility of an actual opposite other than itself. Most recently, this challenge has been taken up by attempts to identify our nothingness as a form of the Buddhist Sunnyata, or pure emptiness. But this tactic can succeed only by developing a theology of pure or total anonymity.

Is such a theology possible, and possible for us? Can we even imagine what it might mean? Can we speak of God as anonymous, and so anonymous that to speak the name of God is to evoke a pure and total anonymity? At the very least, this might be one way by which theology could preserve its role as speaker of ultimate depth and primal ground. It might be thought of also as a goal by which the breakdown of theology could be understood as the necessary and inevitable way to theology's own realization and resolution. Then that breakdown could be construed as a response to the divine presence, and to the divine presence within and among us. If it is true that for us, the divine presence is an anonymous presence, then a language speaking for that presence must inevitably speak against all our given ideas and images of God. And it would speak against them precisely by speaking of the divine presence, a presence not only embodying but evoking anonymity. When anonymity can be understood as an attribute or symbol of God, and as the primal or primary symbol for us, then anonymity itself will assume a new meaning and identity for us. Melville's Moby Dick has initiated us into such a possibility, for the whiteness of the whale can be readily construed as an overwhelmingly powerful image of the anonymity of God, and thereby we can also see that whiteness or anonymity can be realized as a polar power, equally and at once positive and negative. For too long the theologian has echoed Pascal by shuddering in the presence of the vast empty spaces opened by such an anonymity. Let us not forget that it was Newton himself who identified an all-too-modern space as the body of God.

One barrier to such a theological goal is the knowledge that we can realize it only by deepening our own anonymity. But we might more properly speak here of understanding our anonymity. We have long since come to understand that historically considered images of God are inseparable from both images and identities of selfhood. Augustine, who was most reponsible for the creation of our dominant theological idea of God, succeeded in this endeavor only by creating the literary genre of autobiography and thereby realizing a truly new and personal identity of selfhood. So also the new faith of the late Middle Ages and the Reformation was at last in part a consequence of a new and autonomous form of selfhood—a form culminating in the unique and solitary ego of the modern world and thereby giving birth to images of the absolute solitude of God. If this form of selfhood is collapsing in our midst, this collapse surely is not unrelated to the disintegration of our given ideas and images of God. And if a new and anonymous form of selfhood is succeeding our earlier forms of selfhood, then it would appear to be inevitable that this would be accompanied by a new and anonymous image of God. Indeed, such images already lie before us, as witness such writers as Kafka and Beckett; and one might go on to speak of Proust, Rilke, Joyce, and Stevens.

Further perspective for such an endeavor could be provided by casting a glance at painting. Far Eastern landscape painting initially startles us because we cannot readily identify the human presences that might be present within it. Soon we realize that these presences are enriched by their apparent disappearance and that our inability to see a singularly human form is precisely what makes possible our ability to see the fullness of a human identity which otherwise is invisible to us. So also the disappearance or radical transformation of the human face in abstract painting is not the consequence of a negative vision of the end of humanity, but rather a truly new and positive vision of an integral selfhood, organically united with time and space. Both God and man seem to be wholly absent from Monet's landscapes, but upon reflection one begins to suspect that the immense power of his later painting—most particularly his water lilies—derives from his success in actually seeing a total presence, a presence comprehending both the human and the divine. If God is present here, then that presence is anonymous, but the same could be said of man. And we are present here, and present by seeing the water lilies, even if that presence forecloses what we once saw ourselves to be. After all, if modern Western painting began with the union of sanctity and humanity in Giotto, it might well realize itself in an identity wherein everything we have known as God and man has disappeared.

Our understanding of iconoclasm itself would be deepened if we could conceive the possibility that the vision of God in our world is a vision of a total anonymity of nothingness, a plentitude of nothingness wherein the apparent absence of God is at bottom the fullness of God's presence. Then the Mahayana Buddhist symbol of Sunnyata would be for us a decisive clue to the identity of God, and the purely negative movement of iconoclasm once again could be understood as a way to the positivity or actuality of the divine identity and presence. Iconoclasm is clearly present in the higher and purer expressions of the modern imagination, and yet these negative movements of the imagination are manifestly expressions of religious or sacred or total vision. For example, Proust's vision of time recaptured is a vision of the presence of eternity in a real, concrete, and actual moment of time. But here time can be recaptured as eternity only when a concrete moment of time has passed through a process of oblivion; therein it is isolated from the vicissitudes of consciousness and preserved in a pure state by being forgotten, and thence it can be resurrected as eternity when a contingent and accidental event occurs, wherein there is a coincidence between a present and actual moment and the now-forgotten and pure, but once actual, moment. Yet this deeply modern presence of eternity can occur only as a consequence of the loss or disappearance of all the assurances and certainties of consciousness. Hence we find the paradox—that Proust's novel is at once the deepest orchestration of selfhood in modern fiction, even while that very orchestration is itself the very arena and avenue whereby and wherein our deepest selfhood passes into oblivion and, as selfhood, becomes wholly anonymous.

Iconoclasm cannot be genuine iconoclasm if it does not assault both the exterior and the interior forms of our given identities. And one way in which this assault occurs is through the interior realization of anonymity. This too is judgment, and not only judgment, but also self-judgment—perhaps the

most terrible form of judgment. Few theologians have taken
note of the biblical ground and source of that awesome guilt
and self-judgment which has so occupied the modern mind
and sensibility. Nowhere else is there such a clear link
between the biblical and the modern apocalyptic imagination.
We might note also that if Augustine created the literary genre
of autobiography, it was Blake who created the literary genre
of apocalypse. Just as the *Confessions* made possible a voyage
into the depths of selfhood, making manifest the genesis of
selfhood as the epiphany of the personal presence and identity
of God, then do *Milton* and *Jerusalem* make manifest a cosmic
and total self-judgment as the epiphany of the self-annihilation
of God. Here an ultimate self-judgment is finally the
self-negation of God, wherein an apocalyptic night of
judgment passes into an apocalyptic day of forgiveness and
joy. If a fully personal or self-conscious identity was spoken
first by Augustine, then it is in Blake that we may observe the
first modern expression of the self-negation of that identity.
Self-judgment lies at the very center of each of these
realizations of selfhood's identity, and each shatters and
transforms that given and established identity.

Historically, the genesis of what we know as self-
consciousness occurs in Paul's meditations upon guilt, in
which the actualization of self-judgment realizes the birth of a
fully personal self-consciousness. That consciousness knows
itself as fallen; thus self-consciousness is a guilty consciousness, or quite simply a bad conscience. That bad conscience
realizes its own interior identity in the Augustinian transformation of consciousness, and as a result of that transformation,
or self-transformation, previous forms of selfhood come to an
end. Then these forms of selfhood appear as anonymous, and
anonymous because only then is self-consciousness actually
absent. Apart from its realization, self-consciousness itself is
neither actually present nor actually absent. But once it is
present, it is irresistibly present, or is so until it fully realizes
itself. Not until Shakespeare will its depths and breadths be
fully celebrated or explored, but as that exploration and
self-exploration evolved, each earlier form and expression of
consciousness receded into a night of anonymity. From this

perspective, anonymity is a consequence of judgment and of
self-judgment—a self-judgment which is a self-negation. Not
surprisingly, it is the language of guilt that is the primary
language of self-consciousness, and this is true not only of
Augustine, Luther, and Kierkegaard, but also of Shakespeare,
Nietzsche, and Beckett. At no other point has our modern
imaginative language so fully returned to its biblical source.

If we could picture a line running from Paul to Beckett and
could understand this line as representing the movement of
self-consciousness, then we might be able to imagine that it
records the autobiography of self-consciousness, beginning
with its birth and culminating in its death. Both before and
after this line there is only anonymity, at least from the point of
view of self-consciousness. We might observe also that after
innumerable evolving cycles and gyrations, the line finally
returns to its initial form or configuration. For the same pure
nihilism which most Christians find in Beckett is found by
most non-Christians who respond to Paul. Certainly both are
apocalyptic visionaries and both are obsessed by chaos,
judgment, and guilt. Indeed, for both, the very form of
self-consciousness is identical with self-judgment. Yet in Paul,
self-consciousness initially comes into existence, and in
Beckett it seemingly comes to an end. True, Beckett's
contemporaries, or the great bulk of us, proceed as though
nothing has happened, but so also did Paul's. Indeed, Paul
knew that the end of a world was at hand, and so too does
Beckett—not only Beckett, but a host of modern visionaries.
If only for this reason, we understand such modern vision as
apocalyptic, but if it is truly apocalyptic, it cannot fail to record
a vision of God.

Most theologians would like to believe that this is exactly
what is absent from modern apocalyptic vision. But this vision
begins with Blake, and in no other visionary, not even Dante,
do we find a fuller or more comprehensive vision of God. And
in that vision we discover not only the self-annihilation of God,
but the disappearance of God, as God passes first into Satan
and then into that universal energy and life which the seer
names Jerusalem. Then God is truly anonymous, for no longer
can God be named as God, and therewith also perishes all

possibility of either a speech or a naming that is either a witness to or an expression of self-consciousness. Beckett might be interpreted as the climax of that speechlessness. If so, we then could interpret the absence of God in Beckett's language as a witness to the identity and presence of the anonymity of God. We also could entertain the possibility that the God that appears after and beyond self-consciousness will have wholly transcended self-consciousness, and it is for this very reason that God no longer can be named as God. The naming of God as God—a naming which itself forecloses an opening to the divine presence—then would become idolatry, since it would name God as that which God has ceased to be.

Nevertheless, we remain far removed from a theological understanding of the anonymity of God. Just as that vast region of consciousness lying in the pre-Abrahamic archaic world has become unreal to us, and unreal because of the historical realization of the naming of God, so also we might imagine that a world is now aborning wherein our world will become ever more fully unreal, and most unreal at just those points at which we have released and embodied self-consciousness. If so, we should be able to arrive at some sense of a truly new anonymity. If it is a new anonymity, and not simply a regression or return to an archaic and prehistoric state of consciousness, then it will not be identical with anything we can conceive or imagine as an archaic world. For that world, at least as we understand it, is not a purely anonymous world, since it named itself in what we know as myth and rite. Distant as the naming of the gods may be from the naming that is present to us as the activity of consciousness, it is a naming, nonetheless, and the very act of naming reverses anonymity. We know this all too well, because we have evolved a form of language that annuls or dissolves what once was present as naming, and this is true not only of our scientific, technological, and bureaucratic language, but of our poetic and conceptual language as well. Nevertheless, ours is not a simply or literally anonymous world. Indeed, it is not possible to imagine, even in fantasy, a literal anonymity. And we know all too well that identity of some kind, and of multiple kinds, is firmly established in our world. Our problem is that the deepest and most powerful identity in our world is incompatible with and alien to what we once knew and realized as identity.

Thus the theologian cannot say that God is literally anonymous, for this would be to say nothing at all. At most, to speak of the unknowability of God in contemporary language would be simply a rhetorical trick. Certainly the Christian theologian no longer can speak in good faith of the unknowability of God. For we have known God in knowing ourselves, and it is only through our naming of God that we have been able to speak and name ourselves. At this point, our theological problem derives from the brute historical fact that we have named God. That act is irreversible, and irreversible because we bear its imprint within ourselves—so much so that even our anonymous language continues despite itself to bear witness to God. So, far from being a literally anonymous language, our new language is inescapably and undeniably a consequence of our history, just as is our new consciousness, and it is for this reason that we know our new identity to be truly our own. But in knowing ourselves as a consequence of our history, we know ourselves to be a consequence of our naming of God; for what we have known and realized as our self-conscious identity is inescapably a consequence of what we have named and therefore known as God. To speak of the unknowability of God is to speak as though such a self-conscious identity never had been real. But we know it to be real, and we know it because we have now lost it, or are losing it. To speak of the unknowability of God is to speak as though nothing ever had happened ultimately in history, or nothing we can name. And it is also to speak as though we were not undergoing a catastrophic loss.

As Kafka has so profoundly taught us, we have lost irretrievably that innocence which makes possible the non-naming of God. So we cannot pretend that our anonymity says nothing about either ourselves or our world. We have not stumbled into the Garden of Eden, for we are not innocent, and therefore we are not simply anonymous. Accordingly, God is not and cannot be anonymous in this sense. The theologian is most tempted to speak of God as though God were not present in either our world or ourselves and thus not present in our desert and abyss. This is why it is now so tempting to speak of the unknowability of God and thereby to dissociate God from the actuality of our identity and condition. No, our anonymity does speak of God, and it speaks of God because it speaks of the loss of that which once was present only through the presence of God. That loss has created our anonymous language, and our anonymous consciousness, as well—a consciousness that is anonymous because it is no longer what it once was. In losing a consciousness that once was ours, and was ours because it was ourselves, we have not lost simply a source of our identity. We are losing our identity itself, and that identity is not merely absent or missing; it is coming to an end. And it is actually coming to an end; this is an actuality we know to be real because we speak it, and we speak it and live it when we are most actually ourselves. That is the mystery of our situation—that we actually speak our anonymity, and therein anonymity itself is realized not only in silence but also in language and voice.

Perhaps this is the most appropriate point at which the theologian now can speak of the mystery of God. We can speak truly of the mystery of God only in speaking of that which is most deeply a mystery to ourselves. And what could be more mysterious to us than the presence of speech and voice among us? Nor does such speech occur simply in response to our loss of identity. Our speech is a primary way by which we lose that identity, and this is true in all our modes and modalities of speech; true, that is, when our speech is most active and real, for only then is it most fully anonymous, and then anonymity is everywhere, but nowhere more than in the actual voice of speech. Then voice is another, but it is not simply another, for then all centers of identity cease to stand out and apart. Or rather, they cease to stand in themselves; losing all integral or interior identity, they cease to be what they once were or were named as being. Centers of identity flow into one another, and the voice of speech speaks both for all and for none. Now the source of speech is everywhere, and in being everywhere, it is nowhere—nowhere, that is, where it is singular or distinct. Voice itself then becomes unnameable, or unnameable in its singularity as a voice which is itself and no other. Then voice is itself by being another and is another by being itself. Only then is voice purely anonymous, and it is most fully anonymous when it is most fully present as itself.

In the presence of that voice, we cannot hear the voice which once was named as the voice of God. Nor can we hear the voice of conscience, or any voice whatsoever which speaks only itself. Does this mean that the voice of God is now silent? Surely it is, if we are forced to identify the voice of God with that voice we once heard. But God's voice need not be silent if it can be present in the voice of anonymity, even if while present therein it no longer can be named as the voice of God. Voices cease to be nameable when they are anonymous, or cease to be nameable as voices that are individual and unique. This need not mean that naming ceases, but only that a naming which can name anything whatsoever, which is itself and no other, vanishes. The paradox of our situation is that naming so fully occurs among us even if that naming names nothing that is uniquely and only itself. This could well mean that God is named in and by our speech, even if our speech says nothing of God. After all, we know that we name ourselves in our speech and are named by our speech, even if that speech says nothing that is only our own. For our speech is our most intimate identity, and is so even when we say and hear nothing we imagine to be our own. Certainly an anonymous speech means that which we are in the process of becoming, and we know all too well that it is we ourselves who both speak and are realized in that speech. If in some sense we are what we have lost or are losing, or are in continuity with what we are ceasing to be, then it is not impossible that God is now present in an anonymous form and identity, and therein is present as God.

But what could it mean to say this or something like it? Could this be genuine speech about God, or the only genuine speech about God that we can speak? If our anonymity truly speaks a loss of that which once was present only through the presence of God, then in speaking that loss of ourselves, we

speak of God, and therein voice that voice of God which once
we heard and spoke. Now that voice is a negative voice, a truly
and actually negative voice, a voice dissolving or reversing
what once was present as voice. Thus it is not an absent voice,
or an echo of an earlier and now distant voice, but a voice that
is present in a new form and identity. Even if we cannot speak
or name that voice as once we did, we name it or speak it in
speaking the loss of our identity, for that identity is
inseparable from that voice or identity we once named as God.
That naming occurred in us, and irreversibly occurred in
us—so irreversibly that it continues its occurrence even when
we do not and cannot speak that name which once was given us
as the name of God. Once we spoke that name, and that
naming cannot be undone, or cannot be undone as long as
voice continues to speak in continuity with that which voice
once said. If we recognize ourselves in a new and anonymous
voice and speech, and truly recognize our deepest and most
actual identity in that speech, then therein we must
inescapably recognize the identity of God, for that which once
most deeply and integrally was our own, was so only through
our naming of God.

Theologically, it is now most difficult for us to name a totally
and actually anonymous voice as the name and identity of
God. True, we can so recognize such a voice readily, if we can
identify it as a voice of judgment, and not simply of judgment,
but of total judgment. Perhaps self-judgment never has been
so fully present as it is in our world; certainly it never has been
so comprehensively present, and it is difficult if not impossible
to avoid or evade the theological conclusion that such
judgment can be only the judgment of God. For it is the
totality of that judgment that impels the theologian to speak of
God, and even if self-judgment now is realized most fully
through an anonymous consciousness and voice, it is
self-judgment nonetheless, an assault upon what once was
present to us as self-consciousness. If that self-consciousness is
now in process of being negated, then the theologian must be
open to the possibility that such negation is a transcending
negation, because the theologian as theologian cannot
dissociate judgment from grace. But if it is both an actual and a

transcending negation, a forward-moving actuality of negation, then the theologian can speak of the contemporary
actuality of grace and thus of the presence of God for us. Yet
this can be done only by speaking and naming the anonymity
of God, for it is precisely in anonymity that judgment and
self-judgment is now most actual and real. To continue to
speak of God as once we named God would be to evade and
refuse that anonymity and thus to refuse that one identity in
which the fullness of voice might be speaking now of God. For
a full and actual voice is now only an anonymous voice, and if
the theologian cannot speak of God in response to that voice,
then surely theology can no longer speak.

References

Altizer, Thomas J. J.
    1967. *The New Apocalypse: The Radical Christian Vision of
        William Blake.* East Lansing: Michigan State University Press.
    1977. *The Self-Embodiment of God.* New York: Harper & Row.
Barthes, Roland
    1974. *S/Z.* Trans. Richard Miller. New York: Hill & Wang.
Cassirer, Ernst
    1944. *An Essay on Man.* New Haven: Yale University Press.
Chipp, Herschel B.
    1968. *Theories of Modern Art.* Berkeley: University of California
        Press.
Cochrane, Charles Norris
    1944. *Christianity and Classical Culture.* Toronto: Oxford
        University Press.
Derrida, Jacques
    1974. *Of Grammotology.* Trans. Gaytri Chakravorty Spivak.
        Baltimore, Md.: The Johns Hopkins University Press.
Fabro, Cornelio
    1968. *God in Exile: Modern Atheism.* Trans. and ed. Arthur
        Gibson. Glen Rock, N.J.: Newman Press, Paulist Press.
Foucault, Michel
    1971. *The Order of Things: The Archeology of the Human
        Sciences.* Translation of *Les Mots et les choses.* New York:
        Pantheon Books.

Harnack, Adolph
    1961. *History of Dogma,* vol 5. Trans. Neil Buchanan. New York:
    Dover Publications.
Heidegger, Martin
    1973. *The End of Philosophy.* Trans. Joan Stambaugh. New York:
    Harper & Row.
Heller, Erich
    1965. *The Artist's Journey into the Interior.* New York: Random
    House.
Miller, J. Hillis
    1965. *Poets of Reality.* Cambridge, Mass.: Harvard University
    Press.
Poulet, George
    1956. *Studies in Human Time.* Trans. Elliott Coleman. Baltimore,
    Md.: Johns Hopkins University Press.

About Charles Davis' Essay

Charles Davis prefaces his discussion of the concept of God with descriptions of the state or condition of faith and the origin and function of the language of faith. Faith is not seen as a form of belief (e.g., believing on insufficient evidence or in spite of the evidence) but as a species of experience in which or through which one is given a sense of ultimate assurance in the face of the experience of nothingness. In turn, religious language ("the language of faith") is presented as having its origins in ordinary language. That is, religious language is ordinary language used in a symbolic way, a way that both articulates the experience of faith and functions to evoke that experience in others.

Davis' understanding of faith as a state of the self rooted in a transformative experience, an experience which religious language is intended both to express and to call forth, is by now familiar to readers of Friedrich Schleiermacher and the nineteenth- and twentieth-century liberal Protestant theologians who are Schleiermacher's offspring. However, Davis, whose theological roots are Catholic, notes that in the last quarter of the twentieth century, traditional religious language—in particular our talk about God—no longer serves the expressive and evocative function it once did. Davis traces the current ineffectiveness of religious language to recent changes in society which have cut this language off from its sources in ordinary experience. Thus a contemporary theologian such as Davis finds himself employing terms and concepts that no longer have a

finite reference or meaning which can be refined
or qualified in a manner that will allow them to be used
in a religiously meaningful way. In brief, contemporary
theologians have lost their linguistic starting point, even
though the experiential starting point is still intact.

But unlike those death-of-God theologians of a
generation ago, Davis does not conclude that his appraisal
of the current state of affairs in religion should lead him
to proclaim either the death of God or the end of
theology. God is not dead, because the faith experience
(or what amounts to the same thing, the experience of
God) is still a reality for many people, even if traditional
religious terms no longer properly serve to express or
evoke such an experience. The end of theology is not at
hand, because the theologian is well aware of the need of
a new comprehensive symbolism—a new set of linguistic
tools—which can function to "mediate God's felt
presence" to contemporaries. Rather, Davis awaits the
coming of poets, prophets, and mythmakers who will
point out or craft symbols that can communicate the faith
experience effectively. With these new symbols the
theologian will be enabled to construct a concept of God
for our time.

The reader certainly will want not only to reflect on
Davis' assumptions about the nature of faith and the
origins and function of religious language, but to consider
whether he is justified in his expectation that new
symbols are forthcoming and that the hope of theology
lies in their appearance. Furthermore, Davis' conviction
—that 'truth' in religious or theological matters is
determined by how well the terms employed serve the
symbolic function of communicating the faith experience
—raises some interesting questions about the status of
assertions that no longer serve this function. (E.g., Is
"God is good" now false for most people, or is it perhaps
true for some and false for others?) And finally, are we
like shepherds and wise men awaiting an unknown
appearance? Or are we like servants whose own master
will return after an indefinite absence in a far country?

2. The Experience of God and The Search for Images

Charles Davis

I

One must be lonely to know a sense of God. Deeply lonely. The loneliness where we find God is not the contingent loneliness that comes with the absence of friends and relatives, but the essential loneliness experienced inwardly even when we are surrounded by people we love who love us. We are essentially lonely because there is an emptiness at the heart of our existence. When we turn inward and confront what we are, we find vacancy, not plentitude. Our being fades off into nonbeing.

The experience I am attempting to identify is the experience of nothingness. If one reflects upon human thought and action, upon human achievement and hope, one finds that they end in nothingness. They are limited, but the final limit is not just a boundary marking off one action from another or one achievement from another. We are led to an absolute limit, beyond which is a void, empty of all human meaning. Human life is surrounded by darkness. We construct our world in interaction with nature; we create our human meanings, but we are like travelers lost in a vast desert, remaining within the circle of light cast by our campfire in the midst of an immense darkness.

The basic religious choice we face is not between atheism and theism, but between nihilism and faith. It is not simply that theism represents a particular conception of ultimate reality not shared universally by religious people. Even within the context of Western culture, the basic question is not about the existence of a personal God, but about the felt presence of a loving reality in the darkness that surrounds us.

It is possible to opt for nihilism. Then nothingness is indeed just that—at least as far as human existence is concerned. Whatever may be the nature of the whole of which we are part, it is finally meaningless to human beings and offers no satisfaction to our expectations and hopes. We must be content to create our fragile structures of human meanings, knowing that nothing we create, whether by thought or by deed, will last, but that everything human eventually will be submerged in the meaningless flux from which we momentarily arose. We must learn to live without consolation. There is no point in dwelling upon nothing; the emptiness at the heart of existence is best left without attention. There is more than enough to occupy our human lives. The finite does not lose its value even though it is limited and comes to an end.

The experience of nothingness may be instead the threshold of faith. Faith, when it is a personal act, arises from that inwardness where we confront the emptiness that swallows up our being. It is a response of loving trust or joyful assurance that has no apprehensible cause. The nothingness that meets us at the limits of our being is experienced as utterly real and the source of bliss and joy of a peculiar kind. As T. S. Eliot expressd it, "So the darkness shall be the light," though it remains darkness. There is no humanly apprehensible reality or a meaning that can be conceptualized directly. Faith is a feeling-response to the presence of mystery. The dark void bears down upon us as light beyond our vision and as "consolation without a cause" (Rahner, 1964:131 ff.).

> As a blind man, lifting a curtain, knows it is morning,
> I know this change:
> On one side of silence there is no smile;
> But when I breathe with the birds,
> The spirit of wrath becomes the spirit of blessing,
> And the dead begin from their dark to sing in my sleep.[1]

There is a similarity between the experience of faith and the experience of being affirmed by other persons. We all know that if a child is to grow with a sense of personal worth—an inward consciousness of being unique and lovable as a person—the child must be affirmed by its parents and by

other adults and its peers. There is a sense of basic fulfillment,
of being constituted as a person, that comes from being
affirmed by others. It is a response. It cannot be replaced by
self-affirmation, however intense. The experience, however,
of being affirmed intersubjectively cannot fill the essential
emptiness at the heart of human existence or remove the
essential loneliness of each person. It does not meet the basic
negativities of human life: finiteness and death; a sense of
estrangement from true being, compounded with guilt. Faith
is a sense of being affirmed at a deeper than human level, an
ultimate assurance, an inward sense of final worthwhileness.
The experience of faith is that of a response. Faith cannot be
had by gritting one's teeth and affirming meaning in the face of
unmeaning, any more than the sense of worthwhileness that
comes from being affirmed by others can be produced by
self-affirmation. The basic trust in reality and in the
worthwhileness of human existence, the sense of being
unconditionally affirmed as a person before ultimate reality,
the inward conviction that despite all the negativities of
existence—

> All shall be well, and
> All manner of thing shall be well,[2]

which is faith—is a response to the darkness that emcompasses us and draws us toward itself as toward the supremely
real. Not our doing, but a transcendent gift, faith is a
transformative experience, changing our despair at the
nothingness that envelops human existence into peace, joy,
and love, at the felt presence of mystery.

II

I will step back now from this account of faith as an
experience, to discuss the way I have been using language.

I have been using language to evoke the experience of faith.
I have been drawing attention to it as to an experience that
may be forgotten or overlooked or sometimes more or less
consciously evaded or refused. I have been attempting to
provide a way into an experience inaccessible by direct

description. It is true indeed of all language that I never understand what another person is saying unless in some way I share the experience underlying the content of the other's speech. But when we are talking about the observable world, we move smoothly to an understanding of the reports of others, even when they concern what we ourselves have not experienced personally. The language of faith does not simply add futher content to a common experience that all may be presumed to share but works to bring about a shift in the level of experience. Unless that shift occurs, what is said about faith will be taken as meaningless, or at best, interpreted as a hyperbolic expression of an experience that could be described in plain language.

To borrow from Ian Ramsey (1963), the function of religious language is to provoke the occurrence of a disclosure. I myself would explain the matter in this way: Faith is an intentional experience.[3] This means that faith is an experience of some reality; it intends a reality; it puts us into contact with what reveals itself in the experience as its term. Faith is not a merely subjective experience in the sense that the subject is enclosed within his or her own states without reaching any reality beyond them. Just as all consciousness as intentional is consciousness *of* something, so also faith as intentional is the experience *of* the reality felt in the darkness that surrounds human existence. But that formulation already points to the peculiarity of faith. The reality experienced in faith does not manifest itself as an object. It reveals itself as the term of a feeling-response, although remaining hidden from us, or unknown inasmuch as it does not appear to consciousness as an apprehensible object. I have expounded in some detail elsewhere (Davis, 1976) upon the nature of feeling as distinguished both from intellectual apprehension and from emotion. Briefly, feelings rest upon a oneness between the subject and what is felt. Unlike intellectual activity and emotional reaction, each of which, in its own way, is a partial, restricted response, feeling is a total response—that is, a response of our total being, mind and body, spiritual and material. Feelings are responses springing from what we are. They are the responses of our being as we meet reality. Our feeling-responses depend upon what we have become as beings, what we are as persons. Feelings are the resonance of reality upon human subjects; the arousal of our personal being through union with a reality present to us. In the case of religious feeling, the response of our spiritual affectivity to transcendent reality precedes knowledge and continues without any direct knowledge of a kind that would make the term of that response a known object. The reality that draws us to the point where our being falls off into nothingness—the reality that gives a sense of basic fulfillment at the center of our emptiness—remains outside our intellectual grasp. When we are dealing with known objects, the language we use conveys information about them to one another, and this information can be registered by the mind without any arousal of our personal being or any engagement of our spiritual affectivity. The language of faith concerning transcendent reality has no such information to convey. Therefore if the language does not evoke a personal response of faith, it remains language without any apparent reference and merely expresses a subjective state. Or to adopt another approach, its referent, with Feuerbach and Durkheim, may be taken as human reality or society, though cloaked by religious images. Hence if the language of faith is to communicate its true content, it must provoke a disclosure through the arousal of faith.

The language used to evoke the experience of faith also serves to articulate that experience. Any intentional experience is specified by its object. We define a state of consciousness by determining what it is a consciousness of. With faith, however, the term of the experience—that of which faith is a consciousness—remains unknown. The experience of faith therefore cannot be directly specified or described. Consequently, the language of faith is always metaphoric, in that wider sense in which metaphor is speaking of one thing in terms of another (Richards, 1965: 116-17), and tied to symbols—namely, to expressive elements (images, concepts, words, stories)—with a double intentionality, referring directly to one thing and through it indirectly, analogically, to another.

No more than any other form of language is the language of

faith an individual creation—it is a social product. Religious people depend upon a tradition. All our basic concepts and symbols come to us from tradition. We inherit them. They are socially formed by the cumulative experience, reflection, and interaction of generations of men and women. They arise in each of us as individuals, as we grow up into a particular tradition, are initiated into a way of experiencing and acting, and develop an ability to speak a language and use its symbolic and conceptual heritage. This is not to deny that tradition draws upon the creativity of individuals, particularly of those outstanding individuals who originate new and distinct traditions by selecting a new central symbol, thus altering the religious symbol system (Slater, 1978:28-46). But even the originative experience of religious founders takes place within the context of a previous tradition, and in some continuity with it.

I certainly would argue that religious maturity demands the coming to terms with an inherited religious tradition. To be brought up in a tradition would seem to be a condition of possibility for personal growth. A religious tradition indeed may block or distort growth by untruth or unfreedom in its content or manner or maintenance. To the extent to which it moves toward the extreme of an oppressive ideology, it is destructive of the personality, rather than edifying. But a religious tradition from which many people or even entire societies have lived never is a wholly negative factor. And it is better to struggle with, and perhaps out of a partly oppressive tradition than to remain unformed because of the absence of any tradition. Many young people today have not had transmitted to them any religious tradition or quasi-religious tradition—such as secular humanism or Marxism—clear, explicit, and comprehensive enough to evoke and ground a coherent way of living and of experiencing total reality. They fumble and stumble around like people whose vision is blurred. They are apt to seize upon and overestimate the importance of some contemporary opinion or movement. They have had no experience of living from an encompassing tradition, and therefore they tend not to grasp the difference in the level of discernment involved in choosing a religious

faith and in adopting a particular thesis in natural or social
science. Even when brilliant intellectually, they have a
learning disability in their spiritual faculty. A person without
tradition is like a plant without depth of soil. We might apply
to a different context Nietzsche's remark: "All that is good is
inherited: whatever is not inherited is imperfect, is a mere
beginning" ("Twilight of the Idols," Nietzsche, 1954:551).

The role given to tradition clearly implies that religious
experience is culturally specific. There is no raw experience
undetermined by a particular language, by its symbolic and
conceptual heritage, and by the social and historical context it
brings with it. Steen Katz argues this in relation to mystical
experience, stating rightly enough that in each tradition a
specific way is taught in order to reach a specific goal (Katz,
1978:22-74). At the same time, the peculiar way in which
religious language functions affects the manner in which it is
specific, and this, for me, modifies the pluralistic account of
mystical experience given by Katz.

To elaborate, then, on the functioning of religious language:
All religious images, concepts, words, statements, stories,
have a double intentionality, a double level of sense and
reference. As used religiously, they express and refer to
transcendent reality, or mystery. But because there is no
direct apprehension of the term of faith, which remains
unknown or hidden as mystery, their immediate level of
meaning and reference—that which provides all their
imaginative and ideational content—is within the world of
finite objects, the world of our everyday experience.
Language used religiously always is taken from some area of
our ordinary, nonreligious experience. Its usage becomes
religious when its immediate, secular sense and reference is
rendered inoperative by some device or other. Its direct
interpretation is made implausible or inconsequential, so that
the language must be either dismissed as meaningless and
empty of reference, or interpreted as having a deeper
meaning and pointing toward mystery. The immediate sense
and reference are not entirely removed; they remain as
functioning symbolically, as providing the content for an
indirect or symbolic expression of the directly inexpressible

mystery. Various procedures or devices are used to shift language from its immediate function to a symbolic function. I might mention Ricoeur's treatment of extravagance and intensification in parables and proverbs (1975:107-28) and Ian Ramsey's examination of qualifiers (1963:55-120). Something in the language or context prevents one from accepting an ordinary meaning and leads to a symbolic interpretation. For example, the language of ancient kingship is used in the Bible to refer to God. All the imaginative and ideational content comes from what was said about kings in those days, but which now is used in such an absolute and unlimited fashion as to be inapplicable to any earthly king. The hyperbole, for once, is to be taken seriously.

Religious language is culturally specific through its imaginative and ideational content—in other words, through the symbols it uses. The availability in a culture of particular elements that can be used symbolically, their culturally determined effectiveness as symbols, the social conditions and institutions for their ordering, development, and propagation—all this establishes the irreducible plurality of the experience of faith in different cultures. That does not prevent the diverse forms of religious experience from belonging to the same order of experience, as distinct, say, from experience of the observable world or from ordinary intersubjective experience. Moreover, precisely because the religious reference is indirect or symbolic, with the imaginative and ideational content of religious expression torn from its proper meaning to intimate a felt but inapprehensible reality, the final referent can be the same reality, though experienced in a different fashion in each tradition. On what ground can one assert an identity of referent, if religious experience is admitted to be diverse and not reducible to a single type or an underlying universal form? There is first the exclusive absoluteness of most religious experience. Christians and Jews and Muslims must understand their God as being the God of all men, including Buddhists, who do not recognize that God. Buddhists must see Nirvana as the one true goal appropriate for all men, even for Westerners who do not acknowledge that goal. Implicit in each form of religious experience is an absoluteness and universality which, if no longer interpreted as excluding the truth and legitimacy of every other form of religious experience, does at least indicate that the symbols mediate a relation to that which, as transcendent, is absolute and universal and thus one. Unless that much is granted, religious experience must be dismissed as deceptive. There is, in the second place, the equivalence of symbols. Within each tradition and sometimes across the traditions, the same religious people have used different sets of symbols and have not found them contradictory, even though the experience proper to each set differs (Johnson, 1970, 1971; Merton, 1968; Pannikar, 1961). It is indeed a general characteristic of symbolic expression that there can be multiplicity without contradiction.

III

Against the background of this account of the working of religious language, I will examine the concept of God. There is not, indeed, a single concept of God. When the word "God" is used as a descriptive term, it has a variable content of images, stories, and concepts. It is possible to reject one or more of the traditional elements without ceasing to be a theist. All the same, if we discount some popular distortions and some eccentric theories, the content given to the term "God" in the Christian tradition is sufficiently stable and coherent to allow it to be treated as a single conception.

I can agree with Gordon Kaufman (1975, *passim*) that the concept of God is an imaginative construct. It is not a concept drawn from an apprehension of God as an object, but put together from our knowledge of finite reality. On the other hand, I disagree with Kaufman's exclusion of any direct experience of God (1975:72, n. 22). Although in its content the concept of God is constructed entirely from previous conceptual elements, its religious function is to mediate the experience of faith as an effective union with the reality thus expressed. Consequently, the concept of God is not a mere regulative idea with the help of which we order our knowledge intramentally, but a mediating expression for an intentional experience terminating at the divine reality itself.

To look more closely at the process of constructing the concept of God, we must distinguish between the religious and the theological levels, while recognizing that they are in constant interaction.

At the religious level, we begin with images, sayings of different types, and stories. By several devices, as I have mentioned, these are twisted away from a literal sense and reference and thus made to point to a mysterious reality beyond. The concept of God arises from the convergence of all these expressions (Ricoeur, 1975:130) as the horizon, or limit, where they all meet and fall into silence because the reality beyond escapes them. As Ian Ramsey puts it, the word "God" presides over the rest of religious language and completes it (Ramsey, 1963:67). Since the principal biblical images and stories are drawn from social and historical life rather than from nature, the concept of God becomes clothed in various images of God as person, and God as the mysterious reality beyond is conceived as a person.

As a descriptive term, the word "God" at the religious level carries an imaginative rather than a conceptual content. In other words, the understanding of God remains largely inseparable from the images and stories and cannot, by abstraction, be formulated conceptually. Unless one enlists the aid of philosophy, the conceptual content as abstracted from the images and stories is little more than a concept of a transcendent personal reality upon which all the stories and images converge. However, once language at the religious level has evoked the experience of faith and thus by the response of faith has excluded the option of nihilism, it becomes possible to elaborate the concept of God with the help of philosophy. I want to stress the necessity of the religious context of the theological enterprise. Without faith, the nihilistic option is open and theology remains groundless.

The experience of faith as an ultimate assurance, giving a basic trust in reality, originates the conviction that reality is totally meaningful and good, even though our understanding of it is limited. That conviction grounds an affirmative theology. The general procedure of affirmative theology is to extend to God the basic categories used for the philosophical

understanding of finite reality. By a kind of extrapolation, and
with a qualification to indicate that they are being turned from
their proper meaning and reference, concepts drawn from
finite reality are applied to God. Thus those who hold an
objectivist metaphysics conceive God as First Cause, Prime
Mover, Supreme Being, and so on. The process philosophers
apply their process categories to God. Since Lonergan gave
primacy to cognitional theory and expresses metaphysics in
cognitional terms, he derives his theological categories from
the operations of the conscious subject (Lonergan, 1972:281-
93). In each case, the intelligibility that the philosopher has
grasped in finite reality is used to answer questions about
God, on the ground that the intelligibility immanent in finite
beings finds its prolongation, fulfillment, and source—not its
contradiction—in God.

The theological elaboration of the concept of God has its
religious dangers. The chief danger is that of idolatry. We
forget that we have no direct apprehension of mystery and that
all our concepts receive their ideational content from finite
reality and are extended to God by a kind of extrapolation.
God becomes an object, albeit the chief object among those
objects of our direct knowledge, and such a God is an idol. A
further danger is that the inadequacy or desuetude of a
particular philosophy may become a hindrance that blocks the
experience of faith. There is little need to dwell here upon the
difficulties created for Christian faith by the modern attack
upon metaphysics.

At the same time, the use of philosophy in developing the
conception of God is both unavoidable and religiously useful.
It is unavoidable because the theologian, in interpreting his
religious data, does so in a cultural context and therefore in
relation to a problematic set by the current philosophy. It is
religiously useful because it helps to integrate the experience
of faith into the world of human meaning and relate it to the
different areas of human thought and living.

To turn from this abstract account to the present concrete
situation, if I might venture a personal assessment, it is not
simply that the philosophy of God has run into difficulties, a
fact which is widely recognized, but that at the basic religious

level the traditional language of God no longer effectively functions. In attending Christian services—chiefly Catholic, but also of other Christian churches—I have increasingly felt the lack of any sense of the reality of God on the part of those present. The mention of God is a formality carrying with it little conviction or impact. A sense of reality is present, however, when reference is made to the community or to personal growth or to interpersonal relationships. Jesus is seen as a person who shared our existence and sufferings, and left us his teaching. As for God, his reality is assumed—no one denies it—but he is not a living presence. The atmosphere is not one of worship; indeed, the liturgy today spontaneously brings to my mind the remarks of Heidegger on *Gerede*— "idle chatter." Perhaps I am being unfair, but there is such incessant talk at every turn! It flows from an implicit recognition that, of themselves, the traditional images, symbols, and stories no longer work. We conceal this by ceaselessly assuring ourselves that all is well and that we are united in a helping community. The talk, of course, is about us, not about God. As my children—then ages nine and seven—said after attending an Advent catechetical course designed to prepare them for Christmas, "They told us how to be good, but they didn't tell us anything about God."[4]

I am agreeing, then, with Farley (1975:9) that the fundamental loss or diminution of reality has occurred not in the academic community of theologians, but in the concrete historical community of faith. The theological questioning of traditional beliefs has resulted from the loss of reality in the referent of its faith which has been experienced by the community of faith. Why has there been that loss?

When confronted with the statement that the traditional religious symbols no longer function effectively, some people retort that the fault does not lie with the symbols. What is lacking, they argue, is the experience that the symbols are intended to express. Since our secular culture suppresses or refuses transcendent experience, or overlooks or forgets it, it is not to be expected, they say, that the traditional religious symbols will be found meaningful. However, it is the function of the symbols to mediate the experience, and if as a general rule they fail to do so, it is reasonable to conclude that they have become inappropriate in the cultural context. Certainly, as Ian Ramsey remarks, "Whether the light breaks or not is something that we ourselves cannot entirely control." No matter how appropriate the models, "we can never guarantee that for a particular person the light will dawn at a particular point, or for that matter at any point in any story" (1963:90). This corresponds to the traditional teaching—that the initiative in any story must come from God. All the same, we are entitled to assess the appropriateness of particular symbols within a particular context. When, as at present, some who fully acknowledge the experience of faith, mediated to them by secondary rather than by the primary symbolic elements of the tradition, find the traditional language about God empty and largely distasteful, it is time to question its adequacy.

The imaginative and ideational content of the language of theism is drawn from social and political life. God is the ruler and supporter of the social group. The social order is projected onto the universe as the cosmic order, so that the cosmos is society writ large. God thus becomes the ruler and sustainer of the cosmic order. The language of theism puts to symbolic use the language of traditional, hierarchically organized society—a language therefore obsolete in its secular usage and without a starting point in living speech for its symbolic meaning. Consider even so simple and basic an expression of Christian theism as the Our Father—the Lord's Prayer. It presupposes a set of social relationships no longer ours today: Without patriarchy, fatherhood does not evoke transcendence; the name of rulers are not exalted, save in some survivals of archaic ceremonial; kingly rule, as such, is no longer a reality; society is not an affair of a single will, but of consensus; we consider we have a right to the necessities of life and do not need to ask for them as bounty; our "debts" in present society are not to persons, from whom we can beg remission, but from banks, which simply blacklist our credit cards; as for the last two petitions about not putting us to the test and saving us from evil (the Evil One?), they need a commentary before we can assign them any meaning.

The critique feminist writers have given of traditional

theism because of its reflection of patriarchy, its androcentrism, and its exclusion of female power and symbolism is, in my opinion, but one instance of a critique that can be directed against it from other directions. In brief, for its symbolism, theism deploys social relationships and social attitudes no longer acceptable today. The feminist critique makes it clear that this is not just a question of symbolic appropriateness, but of truth. Any ordered set of symbols express a structure of values and thus makes an assertion about reality; it calls for an assessment concerning its truth or falsity. The barrier that inhibits any deep immersion into traditional religious language, leaving it a ceremonial formality, is the unformulated sense of its untruth —an untruth that does not lie in the nonexistence of God as transcendent reality, but in the falsity of the symbolic material intended to mediate God's felt presence.

Political theology may be seen as an attempt to reform theism by relating it to a different conception of human society. Observing the attempt from the outside, Habermas wonders whether it can salvage the idea of a personal God, and he summarizes his perception of the new understanding of God now being put forward: "The idea of God is transformed [aufgehoben] into the concept of a Logos that determines the community of believers and the real name for a communicative structure that forces men, on pain of a loss of their humanity, to go beyond their accidental, empirical nature to encounter one another indirectly, that is, across an objective something that they themselves are not" (Habermas, 1976:121).

From within political theology, the most stimulating contribution has come from Peukert (1976:307-15), who links the biblical conception of God to Habermas' communicative theory of society. Habermas uses a theory of human communication—that is, an analysis of communicative action and its presuppositions—as the basis for his critical theory of society. Peukert points to a major aporia in the account of human communication, an insoluble difficulty pointing beyond the limits of human meaning and providing the point of insertion for the idea of God. This aporia arises from the death of the participants. Death threatens the very meaning of human communication, because it apparently renders impossible the kind of relationship sought with others. What are we to do when our partners in communication are annihilated? Erase them from our memory? That would be an evasion of reality. But can the meaning attached to human community remain intact if that community is conceived as passing eventually into nothingness, as a result of the continuous, successive annihilation of all its participants? Here Christians and Jews may recall that their God is a God of the living and of the dead and is a God who creates human community. They can conceive of God as the saving reality met with in all structures of human communication, as the ground of that communication.

That, of course, is only the briefest summary and cannot convey the force of the original exposition. Two remarks, however, immediately suggest themselves. First, if human society is radically reconceived in a fashion that treats human beings as free and equal subjects, and excludes domination, it is not clear that God, as the saving reality that grounds such community, still can be conceived on the basis of the traditional theistic imagery and language. Second, in any case, we have shifted our reflection from the religious to the theological level. But theological reconception of itself remains an empty exercise. If human community, as emancipated—that is, as a structure of human communication free from domination—is to provide the symbolic content for a reformed religious language, it must be lived out, at least as a practical hope, in concrete human experience. Social life in the wider society no longer is personally hierarchical, but impersonally bureaucratic. Social life within the churches is a faded throwback to traditional society, touched up with much talk about community. Both make theistic language unreal, but neither provides a rich enough experience to give rise to a new symbolic medium for the experience of faith.

We are in need of prophets, mythmakers, and poets, rather than theologians. Meanwhile, what? The account of the experience of faith with which I began this essay took as its starting point the human experience of loneliness and the need to be affirmed by others. I attempted to make that common experience symbolic—that is, evocative of tran-

scendence—by using qualifiers such as "essential," "ultimate," "absolute." The approach I adopted is similar to Peter
Berger's search for "signals of transcendence within the
empirically given human situation" (1969:65 ff.). It is valid
and often effective, but fragmentary and finally unsatisfactory.
An individual may stumble to faith on the fragments of human
experience, but the resulting religious language does not
contain enough meaning to build or transform a culture. For
that we need a comprehensive symbolism. A theologian can
note the need; he cannot fulfill it.

Notes

1. Extract from "Journey to the Interior" copyright © 1961 by Beatrice
   Roethke, Administratrix of the Estate of Theodore Roethke, from the book
   The Collected Poems of Theodore Roethke. Reprinted by permission of
   Doubleday & Company, Inc., and Faber & Faber Ltd., London.
2. Julian of Norwich (1975:98-100).
3. "Intentional" is used here in the Husserlian sense of intentionality, which
   Husserl himself borrowed from Brentano, who derived it from the
   Scholastic tradition.
4. By way of contrast, I recommend the marvelous little book, *Mister God,
   This Is Anna* (Fynn, 1974).

References

Berger, Peter
   1969. *A Rumor of Angels: Modern Society and the Rediscovery of
   the Supernatural.* Garden City, N.Y.: Doubleday & Co.

Davis, Charles
   1976. *Body as Spirit: The Nature of Religious Feeling.* New York:
   Seabury Press.

Farley, Edward
   1975. *Ecclesial Man: A Social Phenomenology of Faith and
   Reality.* Philadelphia: Fortress Press.

"Fynn"
   1974. *Mister God, This Is Anna.* London: Fontana Paperbacks,
   Collins Sons & Co.

Habermas, Jürgen
   1976. *Legitimation Crisis.* London: Heinemann.

Johnston, William
   1970. *The Still Point: Reflections on Zen and Christian Mysticism.*
   Bronx, N.Y.: Fordham University Press.
   1971. *Christian Zen.* New York: Harper & Row.

Julian of Norwich
   1975. *The Revelations of Divine Love of Julian of Norwich.* Trans.
   James Walsh, S.J. Religious Experience Series, 3. St. Meinrad,
   Ind.: Abbey Press.

Katz, Steven T.
   1978. "Language, Epistemology, and Mysticism." *Mysticism and
   Philosophical Analysis.* Studies in Philosophy and Religion, 5.
   London: Sheldon Press.

Kaufman, Gordon
   1975. *An Essay on Theological Method.* American Academy of
   Religion Studies in Religion, 11. Missoula, Mont.: Scholars
   Press.

Lonergan, Bernard
   1972. *Method in Theology.* New York: Herder & Herder.

Merton, Thomas
   1968. *Zen and the Birds of Appetite.* New York: New Directions.

Nietzsche, Friedrich
   1954. *The Portable Nietzsche.* Ed. W. Kaufmann. New York:
   Viking Press.

Pannikar, R.
   1964. *The Unknown Christ of Hinduism.* London: Darton,
   Longman & Todd.

Peukert, Helmut
   1976. *Wissenchaftstheorie—Handlungstheorie—Fundamentale
   Theologie: Analysen zu Ansatz und Status theologischer
   Theoriebildung.* Düsseldorf: Patmos.

Rahner, Karl
   1964. *The Dynamic Element in the Church.* Freibrug: Herder.

Ramsey, Ian T.
   1963. *Religious Language: An Empirical Placing of Theological
   Phrases.* New York: Macmillan Paperbacks.

Richards, I. A.
   1965. *The Philosophy of Rhetoric.* New York: Oxford University
   Press.

Ricoeur, Paul
   1975. "Biblical Hermeneutics," *Semeia* 4:29-148.

Slater, Peter
   1978. *The Dynamics of Religion: Meaning and Change in
   Religious Traditions.* San Francisco: Harper & Row.

About Paul M. van Buren's Essay

As much as any theologian represented here, Paul van Buren is on the move. His *Secular Meaning of the Gospel* (1963), regarded as a key work of the death-of-God movement of the 1960s, was meant to rescue Christians from a truly desperate predicament—linguistic analysis seemed to prove that one could not speak of God at all! But the result was a virtual theological atheism. Then in *The Edges of Language* (1972), a shift began. To speak of God was now said not to be impossible, but a limiting possibility; one speaks of God (or at least uses the word "God") when all other language fails. Now again there is a decisive shift. Speaking of God, awesome though it be, is not marginal but central to van Buren's current work.

The great difference has been made by a reassessment of the importance of contemporary Judaism to Christians. Two events, the genocidal death camps in Hitler's Germany (1933–1945) and the rebirth of the state of Israel (1949), force reconsideration of Judaism, a religion long treated by Christian theology as a meaningless fossil. Van Buren sees the mistreatment of Jews in the Christian era as the consequence of a fatal mistake in early Christianity: the rejection and subsequent neglect of the Jewish people.

This has meant that every Christian doctrine now must be reconsidered, examined for latent or patent anti-Jewishness, and reformed in the light of a new dialogue between the two traditions.

In this essay Paul van Buren makes three theological

moves of great intrinsic interest. In the first section, he
argues that the possibility of Christian speaking of God is
logically and historically tied to the church's responsibility to
the Jews. Auschwitz and the state of Israel demonstrate to
us that theodicy and our own morality are inseparably
linked. And he shows that the mainline churches, in recent
pronouncements, have been perceiving that link.

Section 2 is an attempt to face the moral difficulty—
Where was God at Auschwitz?—by a Judaic restatement of
the doctrines of creation, covenant, and redemption, putting
strong emphasis on the *logical* priority of creation over the
other two. In creating the world, God freely limited himself;
so now the course of the world is *our* responsibility.

In section 3, van Buren considers the resultant conception
of God—God is actually a person, and therefore actually is
(or has) a self and actually is (or has) a body. By the latter
he does not mean, as some theologians have taught, that the
world is God's body; rather, for van Buren, to think
theologically is necessarily to risk much more radical
solutions of old problems and consequent departures from
received tradition, both Christian and Jewish.

For a critical reader, of course, there will be radical
questions regarding these radical positions. Starting with the
last-mentioned thesis, are there logical problems in the
concept of God the Actual Person which simply cannot be
overcome? For example, what does or can *constitute* the
divine "body"? Second, does van Buren's "responsible"
reconception of the created world any longer require a God,
especially such a self-limited God?—and would such a God
be GOD, worthy of worship and trust and service? (It is
interesting that process theology also limits God and also
trades in the problem of evil on the problem of the deity of
its God.) Finally, is the proposed theological reconciliation
of Christianity with modern Judaism *sufficiently* radical to
call into question the long Constantinian involvement of the
church with Christendom—with "the powers that be"?
Might a post-Constantinian theology be also a more biblical
one?

3. Speaking of God

Paul M. van Buren

How should we speak of God after Auschwitz? Our traditional talk of God's providential love rings hollow in view of Hitler's ghastly "final solution of the Jewish question." The Holocaust, to be sure, does not stand quite alone: The pages of the history of the first three-quarters of this century are smeared with more than Jewish blood. The particular horror of Hitler's death camps is framed, before and after, by the Turkish massacre of the Armenians, the senseless slaughter of the First World War, the firebombing of Dresden, Hiroshima, Vietnam, and much more. Without denying this larger framework of violence and destruction, we may focus the theological question properly with reference to Auschwitz, for the Holocaust was an event of incalculable significance in the history of that people whose ancestors were the major protagonists in the Scriptures that the Christian church as well as Judaism holds sacred. The horrors of our age have touched profoundly the people whose existence is bound up theologically with that of the church, and this raises for Christian theology the question of God's relationship to our history. Indeed, the question is raised for any believer. But since Christians do still speak of God after Auschwitz, the special theological question is raised concerning the adequacy and consistency of what they say. Should the church go on speaking of God and his relationship to the world and human history as it has in the past, or should it speak in a different way?

In the first and foundational part of an answer to this question, I shall analyze the situation in which God is affirmed and the bearing of historical circumstances on that affirmation,

in order to clarify the relationship between historical events
and our understanding of God. The second part will sketch a
possible reconstruction of the major components of our
traditional understanding of God's relationship to the world,
and the last part will explore the consequences of that
reconstruction for our understanding of God as a person. The
three parts thus will help develop the thesis that there is solid
historical precedent for and sound theological reasons in
support of the reorienting effect on the church, which already
is being brought about by recent events in the history of the
Jewish people. The consequences of this reorientation will be
both a more temporally relational view of God's involvement
with this world than has characterized our theological
tradition and a franker confession that God is a person.

I. History As Revelation

As a matter for theological reflection, speaking or writing of
God does not just happen. It arises in the context of that
linguistic community that is the church. It arises in history and
as the result of history. We come to speak of God, usually,
because we have been brought up by parents who taught us to
pray to God. We learned, from them and from others of the
community, to trust in God. By earliest association with that
community, or in some cases by later voluntary affiliation, we
came to share in its linguistic character and so came to speak of
God. There is solid historical and sociological sense, then, in
Augustine's remark that without the church he would not have
believed in God. Apart from the fact of the Christian
community, whatever our individual reservations about one
or another aspect of it may be, it is unlikely that any of us
would speak of God.

To a large extent the language—and to some extent the
life—of that community has been shaped by the books it has
held sacred. The church has used these books as the basis of its
liturgical acts and of its preaching; and its members,
generation after generation, together and individually, have
read and pondered them in their homes. Had not the church
so preserved and used these books, its language surely would

have become something quite other, as would, presumably, its life. More important for the actual state of the church at present than the argument between fundamentalists and liberals, is that which unites them: However interpreted, read, and understood, it has been just these books to which the church has turned when in doubt or confusion. The church is a community fed on this diet, tarred with this brush. The church as we know it is incomprehensible apart from the Bible.

The Bible that has had this effect upon the language of the church consists of two literary collections, with varied histories over the past eighteen or nineteen centuries as different as the circumstances of their original composition and collection. The first and oldest collection, designated "the Scriptures" by the earliest Christian writers, was and remains, first of all, the book of the Jews. Among them it is known by the acronym "Tanach," for its three parts: Torah (the Pentateuch), Nabiim (the Prophets), and Chetuvim (the Writings). Of these, Torah, with the Talmud as its interpretation, carries the greatest weight, as the divine leading for the people given by Moses at Sinai. Torah, for Judaism, is God's gracious instruction for his people to practice already in an unredeemed world the first steps of the messianic age.

Read in a different way and under the different name "Old Testament," the Bible of the Jews also has been authoritative for the church. Since the word "old" can imply that it is worn out or only preliminary, there is much to be said for returning to the only title (in translation) by which the collection was known to Jesus and to his Jewish disciples—the Scriptures. To this, the church slowly added its own collection of Apostolic Writings, usually known as the New Testment. Again, to avoid the misunderstanding latent in the old/new comparison, it seems appropriate to give these writings a title that expresses the way their collectors viewed them: as the written testimony of Christ's chosen apostles. For our purposes, it is important to recall that each of these collections of writings came into existence through a historical process with formal simlarities which bear upon our present situation. In each

case, they were a product of the history of Israel, or more
specifically, of the Jews.

The Hebrew Scriptures came into being as a result of the
telling and retelling, the writing and rewriting of Israel's
tradition, understood broadly as the history of Israel with God
and of God with Israel. In the course of that long history,
which is thought to have begun with Abraham, down to Ezra's
reform, this tradition-bearing people was confronted again
and again with events which challenged that tradition and
jarred one or more of its members to reinterpret it so as to
account for the latest event. Nowhere is this more evident
than in the canon of Torah which Ezra brought back to
Jerusalem from Babylon. The canon closed with Moses and
the people not yet in the Land: The condition of Exile thereby
was set into the core of the tradition in such a way that the
recent events could be seen to be compatible with Israel's
ancient story (J. A. Sanders, 1975:esp. 45-53).

The tradition so reinterpreted, however, was itself the
product of earlier reinterpretations which reveal this same
pattern. The settlement of the land; the rise of the monarchy;
the centralization of government in Jerusalem; the struggle for
faithfulness to the God of Sinai in the face of innumerable cults
and practices linked to the gods of the land; foreign invasions
and national defeat—all were unanticipated new events with
reorienting effects, leading to successive new interpretations
of the received tradition. "You have heard it said of old . . .
but I say to you . . ." could stand as the recurring pattern in
the shaping and reshaping of Scripture.

The preaching of Jesus as presented in the Gospels was part
and parcel of this tradition of reshaping the tradition. Not one
jot or tittle of the story was to pass away; rather, it was to be
retold and lived in a new way in the light of the anticipated
new event of the beginning of the reign of God. For the band
of Jews who followed Jesus, the issue was brought to a head by
the undreamed-of events of Jesus' crucifixion and the Easter
appearances. If God had affirmed a crucified messiah, then
surely there was a need to search the tradition with new eyes
in order to discover how it could be that the God who was
involved in these latest events was no other than the God who

had been at work in the long history to which the tradition bore witness.

Then came the influx of Gentile converts to the Jesus movement and the disastrous Jewish war with Rome. The two occurrences together would appear to have had much to do with the break that came in the last part of the first century between the relatively few Jews who believed that something radically new had begun with the coming of Jesus, and the majority of Jews, who did not. Following the break, the two separate and different interpretations of Israel's tradition proceeded to develop. Most Jews followed the lead of the rabbis of Javneh and their successors, and over the next four centuries, what we call Rabbinic Judaism took shape. Some Jews and their Gentile converts began a movement, soon to become almost totally Gentile in makeup, which over the same period grew into what we call Catholic Christianity. Both movements, however, were one in at least this: They reinterpreted Israel's tradition in a way that took into account events in Jewish history which reoriented their thinking and led them to their views of how God was concerned with that history and how they were being called upon to respond to God. This is not to overlook the differences. Perhaps one could put it this way: The church put the emphasis on the former—God's *concern* with history; Judaism put the emphasis on the latter—the proper *response* to God's instruction.

In the course of this period, the church developed a way of reading and understanding Israel's tradition so as to include, by anticipation, the further history of the church and to exclude the further history of the Jews. The main lines of this reinterpretation soon could be found in Justin Martyr's *Dialogue with* (Monologue at!) *Trypho*. According to the *Dialogue,* the church is the true and only heir of the tradition, so the Scriptures now belong to the church, not to the Jews. The Jews only misunderstand what once had been their tradition. All that had been promised to them by God has been fulfilled in Christ and now is available only to those who believe in him. Christ is the final reorienting (revelational) event, after which there can come only the final unveiling of that which is already the last word in God's involvement with the world. As for the Jews (the church was so predominantly Gentile by Justin's time that the Jews had become "the other"—"you," "them"), they can be at best, as Barth, the last great voice of this tradition saw it, only a negative witness to Christ, witnessing against their will to an election they resist, and thus to the God whose final act of love they continue to reject. From Justin to Karl Barth, the church's image of the Jew often was worse then this, but never better.

And the church? If the destruction of Jerusalem was the confirmation of God's transfer of his election from the Jews to the Gentile church, so the eventual triumph of the church over the pagan empire confirmed that this reinterpretation of the tradition was correct. The exiled, despised, wandering condition of the Jewish people only confirmed this interpretation. That Judaism developed, matured, and flourished did not register on the mind of the church. It did not reflect on the fact of Jewish survival in spite of persecutions instigated by the church itself. Exciting new interpretations that developed in Judaism (e.g., Kabbalism out of the expulsion from Spain; Hassidism out of the pogroms in the East) were ignored. Instead, the church interpreted the conditions which it imposed on the Jews (dispossession, the Ghetto) as the direct work of the hand of God.

In the light of this tradition of eighteen centuries, the change in official statement about the Jews that has begun to take place during the past fifteen years is astounding. A minority position at the Amsterdam assembly of the World Council of Churches hinted at the change to come. The statements of Vatican II opened more possibilities, although carefully qualified. Since 1968, however, a series of increasingly clear pronouncements has been building, which frankly contradicts the interpretation of the past. It is as explicit in many of these statements as it is obvious from their historical context that this latest reinterpretation of our tradition is the consequence of the reorienting effect on the church of two major events in the recent history of the Jewish people—the Holocaust and the establishment of the state of Israel. The driving force behind this change in the church's teaching, be it noted, has not been any aspect of intellectual history. Neither Kant and the Enlightenment, nor Marxism, nor secularism, however important these may be, have done this work. Rather, the change appears to have been brought about by events of political and social history centering in the Jewish people: Hitler's death factories, and the state of Israel as a historical, political fact, won by "blood, sweat, and tears" against apparently insuperable material and numerical odds.

Since relatively few theologians have noticed this change, it will be useful to offer a few examples selected from a one-hundred-fifty-page collection of official Catholic and Protestant statements from 1965 through 1975 (Croner, 1977). By vote of the Pastoral Council of the Catholic Church in the Netherlands in 1970, Canon 1325, paragraph 3, promulgated in 1924, was declared null and void. That canon had asserted that "relations with Jews must be avoided, because this people is very estranged from the doctrine of the Cross of Christ. . . . Moreover the faithful must take care—according to the warning of Benedict XIV (Enc. *A quo primum,* 1751)—never to need the help or support of Jews." This action was based on the recommendations of the Vatican Council's Committee on Relations between Jews and Christians which included the statement, "The Jewish people must be seen as the people with whom God concluded His covenant *for all time*" (Emphasis added, here as in the following citations). The council also voted to encourage combined Catholic and Jewish study of the Scriptures and declared that "the Church has the duty to reflect on the entire history of the Jewish people before *and after* Christ and on *their* self-understanding." (Croner, 1977: 53-55; 48n.)

In 1973, the French Bishop's Committee for Relations with Jews said:

> We cannot consider the Jewish religion as we would any other now existing in the world. . . . Even though in Jesus Christ the covenant was renewed for *Christendom,* the Jewish people must not be looked at by Christians. . . . as the relic of a venerable and finished past but as a reality alive through the ages. . . . This vitality of the Jewish people. . . . poses questions to us Christians which touch on the heart of our faith. (Croner, 1977:60-66)

The Faith and Order Commission of the World Council of Churches, in its 1968 report, also noted the seriousness of the issue. Recognizing that there was a need for those who held the old view of Jews and those who had shifted to an affirmative view to deal with this difference, they said: "The conversation among us has only just begun and we realize that in this question the entire self-understanding of the Church is at stake" (Croner, 1977:79-80)

Again, in the United States, the National Council of Bishops in 1975 underscored the seriousness of the theological consequences: "The brief suggestions [on Catholic-Jewish relations] of the Council [Vatican II] has been taken up by some theologians, but their implications for theological renewal have not yet been fully explored." Indeed, they spoke of "a task incumbent on theologians, as yet hardly begun, to explore the continuing relationship of the Jewish people with God" (Croner, 1977:32-33).

Although the Catholic statements have on the whole gone farther in the new reinterpretation and probed it deeper than those of Protestant churches, one of the most suggestive proposals is to be found in the statement adopted by the synod of the Reformed Church in the Netherlands in 1970: "Jesus Christ has a fundamentally different function for the nations and for Israel. The Jews are called back by him to the God who bound himself to them from their beginning. But the Gentiles are not called back to their origins by Jesus Christ; rather, they are called to something which is radically new in their history" (Croner, 1977:98).

It is evident that an about-face on a matter touching the core of Christian doctrine is taking place. The trail was blazed by George Foote Moore's work on early Judaism and by James W. Parkes' work on the history of Jewish-Christian relations. More recently, scholars of Christian origins (e.g., E.P. Sanders, 1977) have opened a picture of first-century Judaism which contrasts markedly with that employed by the church throughout almost its whole life. Finally, as we have seen, episcopal conferences and church synods have turned the corner.[1] The cause or root of this most recent reinterpretation of our tradition lies, as I have said, in the impact of historical

events. A document on ecumenism of the Catholic archdio-
cese of Cincinnati in 1971 named them explicitly: "The Nazi
holocaust and the establishment of the State of Israel," which,
it said, together "force" and "challenge" the church to
reconsider its past positions (Croner, 1977:28). It would
appear, then, that once more the old pattern that shaped the
Scriptures, the Apostolic Writings, and so the theology of the
church, is reasserting itself. Our tradition, by which we had
understood God's relationship with his world, has been
challenged by new events in the history of the Jewish people,
which are leading us to reinterpret that tradition at a point that
touches every aspect of it—not least, our understanding of
God.

II. God's Involvement in History

That God is related to and involved in history and in the
world is a position that has been important for ancient Israel,
for Judaism, and for Christianity. In the light of what we have
said here, however, we have reason to be suspicious of the
generalized form of this statement. In fact, Jewish and
Christian concern about God usually has been far more
specifically about God in his relationship to this earth, and
especially about God in his relationship to the history of Israel.

In connection with this concern, there has arisen a
distinction between God in his relationship to our world and
our history, about which it has been claimed that we can have
some knowledge, and God in himself, about whom it has been
said that we can know nothing. This distinction, however,
appears to rest in large part upon a misuse of language. Can
one know any person or any thing "in itself"? As for persons
(and we shall return in the last section of this paper to consider
the appropriateness of this category), if I know you "in your
relationships," then I know *you*, unless you are a most
deceptive person. If I know you as a person—that is, *as
persons know persons* (as our life and language work in this
respect)—then I may have surprises in store for me, but the
possibility of novelty does not militate against my being able
properly to claim that I know you. I can know you extremely

well indeed and yet always come to know you better, if, that is, you will allow it. It is a serious misunderstanding of the workings of our language, however, if I say that I really can know only your external behavior—the outside of you, so to speak—but that the real you is, in principle, unknowable. As Wittgenstein observed, we do not see a person writhing in evident pain and yet say that his feelings are hidden from us. If we may say that we know God in his relationship to us (to history, to our world), then we may say that we know God as he is. God, we must believe, can be trusted to be himself, especially when and if he relates himself to us. We therefore cannot continue to make use of a distinction between God as he is related to or relates himself to us (perhaps a so-called available God) and God as he is "in himself" (the *real* God) (Kaufman, 1972:95 ff., 148 ff.). Since our knowledge of God is of the same sort as that with which persons know persons, however, we may recall our readiness to admit the inadequacy of our knowledge of one another, as well as of our knowledge of ourselves. As persons know persons, there is ever the possibility of discovery, of a deeper understanding. In that sense it will always be in order to say that God surpasses our understanding.

Traditionally, we have thought of God's involvement with us and with our history under three headings: Creation, Covenant, and Redemption. We shall review these briefly in that order, in the light of our preliminary considerations. Although historically the Creation stories of the first two chapters of Genesis are thought to have come later than, and to reflect the conviction of, God's relationship with Israel in the Exodus and at Sinai, it is proper nevertheless to give Creation a logical priority for theological reflection, for as it is presented in Scripture, it sets the stage for the relationship of God with Israel in the covenant. It is appropriate, therefore, to consider redemption last, as the completion of creation (I shall capitalize this word when referring to God's work of Creation and use lower case for the resultant object—that which has been created). Creation is, as it were, the logical presupposition of first the covenant and and then redemption. It therefore merits first consideration.

A. God's Creation

The scriptural story of Creation, as well as its further
treatment in the development of the scriptural tradition,
affirms a relationship between God and this world (between
God, we might say, and everything else) that is *sui generis*. In
affirming this story, we commit ourselves to say something
about God and something about the world, the latter being
understood generally as everything there is other than
God—*other* than God, for with its doctrine of Creation the
church has marked off God from all else and all else from God.
The attempt to think of God together with everything else as
"all that there is" undercuts precisely that which the doctrine
of Creation seeks to assert. God and everything else are
conceivable together, according to this doctrine, only in the
over-againstness of the Creator and his creation. The
world—everything there is other than God—is understood to
be *from* God, not a part or aspect of God, or a part of an "all" of
which God is the other part.[2] The world is itself, creation, and
it is that because God is himself, the Creator.

Creation has been properly thought to be the result of God's
love in action, since its existence can be the consequence only
of God's will that there be another than himself. Whether we
call Creation a necessary consequence of God's character
depends upon our perspective. If we consider it as an act of
God's freedom, then it would not be proper to call it a
necessary act. God did not *have* to create the world. On the
other hand, when we consider Creation as an act of God's love,
then it expresses God's eternal character, and what else could
we expect of One whom we know (after the fact) as loving, but
that he create an other to love? On both sides of the question,
the church has been consistent with Scripture in speaking of
God's relationship to creation in terms appropriate to the
relationship of persons to the things they make, a point to
which we shall return.

This double aspect of God's necessity to create in relation to
his own character (Rosenzweig, 1971:114-16) found one of its
most radical developments in Isaac Luria's concept of the
Tsimtsum, the Divine Contraction. According to Gershom

Scholem (1974:260 ff.), Luria answered the question about how the world possibly could have come to be, if God was already all in all, with the idea that God contracted himself in order to make room for creation. The act of Creation consequently is seen as one of self-limitation on God's part. One could say that creation, so conceived, *cost* God something, namely his being all in all. God sacrificed this in order that the world might be.

The merit in this idea that God, as it were, made himself less in order that there might be an other than himself—the world—is that it emphasizes the interrelationship between the world and God and thereby the radical reality of creation. Creation is real and it has its reality in the gift of its making. Creation is not a conditional act, as though the world depended on God's continuing to will its existence every moment. It *has been* created: Creation is a completed act, although what has been created is incomplete; creation is good, but it is not finished—it is a good start, a good beginning. The idea of God's continuing Creation is conceivable as his renewing and sustaining, his further development of that which *is*. Creation is presented in Scripture as an irreversible commitment on God's part, sealed with the rainbow.

Once begun, creation is a condition on God. God cannot withdraw from this commitment, from the genuine and independent reality of the world, and therefore from his having become the God who has given his world this independence. From the time of Creation, God must, by his own decision, live with the world he has created. From Creation until redemption, therefore, God's relationship with his creation makes him relative to creation's temporal dimension. By his own choice, God has involved himself in time and history for as long as creation endures.

The Creation stories of Genesis present human beings as the crown or center of creation. If Creation is an act of personal love conferring freedom, then it is appropriate to regard that part of creation which can respond personally—human beings—as its fullest development. (If the 'world' means everything there is other than God, then perhaps one should say that God's angels are that highest development; if on the other hand one takes the world to mean primarily the earth, then human beings are the crown of personal response.) But men and women are themselves part of the world, *adam* made out of *adamah*. Their ability to respond in love and trust to the Creator makes them creation's fullest expression of its own reality as creature. They therefore have no task other than to be creation's primary way to share with the Creator in caring for and completing creation. This entails the view that God shares with his creation the care for its completion. If the assertion that God created man and woman in his own image says something about us, then it also must say something about God! In creating the world, at the very least with respect to this earth, God has made men and women his co-workers in the enterprise to which he committed himself by having become the Creator of an earth on which he has brought forth human beings. How the earth is to develop in time is therefore a shared responsibility of God the Creator, and men and women, his creatures.

B. God's Covenant

God's temporality, his having made his own future subject to temporal development by having become the Creator of the world, becomes yet more evident when we consider God's covenants. Whether by his promises to Abraham (Gen. 15), Isaac (Gen. 26), and Jacob (Gen. 28; 35), or by his covenant with Moses and the people at Sinai, or by the covenant sworn before Joshua at Schechem (Josh. 24), renewed under Josiah (II Kings 23; II Chron. 34) and again under Ezra (10), the God worshiped by the Christian church is the same God who has committed himself to the historical people Israel and to whom they have committed themselves. God has bound himself to the history of this people, and again and again they have committed themselves to walk through history under the guidance of his Torah. Commitments were made on both sides, so that the history of Israel must be considered also God's history.

Relative to each other, Israel has had to take the active role in this history, with God taking a more passive part. More precisely, the history of the Jews—what they have done or failed to do and also what has happened to them—makes up the foreground of this mutual engagement in which they and their God have been involved, with God directing, warning, and enticing from the wings of the historical scene, as it were. The principal actors in this history, which is God's as well as Israel's, are a Moses and a pharaoh, a Joshua and a Jael, a Ruth and a David, and even a Cyrus. The story of the "mighty acts of God" is always a tale of the acts of Israelites or of those who acted upon them. According to the concluding verse of Torah (Deut. 34:10-12), it was *Moses* who wrought those "great and terrible deeds" in Egypt and "in the sight of all Israel."

So it was that Jesus is presented as having thought of God as One who left it to *him* to accept responsibility, to resist temptation, to forgive men their sins, and finally, to drink the cup of betrayal by a disciple and to suffer death at the hands of Pontius Pilate. At only one point did it seem that God stepped into history with no human intermediary: on Easter morning. But even this event, however it may be described, was seen by none. Only the results—the appearances of Jesus to his disciples and the gift of the Spirit—are reported, and then not as events in history in the usual sense that historians give to that expression, but certainly in that history in which God and his creatures are involved together.

Again, always as One who urges, coaxes, warns, and entices, God was said to be involved in the Gentile mission which resulted in a radically new situation, with Gentiles worshiping and serving the God of the Jews. Consequently, God came to be considered more clearly than ever before as also the God of (some) Gentiles. This was a Lord of history who evidently would not rule history as a potentate but only through men and women who would conduct themselves as if answerable to him.

In the light of these reflections, we can begin to see something of the nature of the problem when we ask what God was doing in the Holocaust. The question ignores the way God has been involved in the history of his people, implying that he ordinarily steps in when his creatures fail to act. In the light of that history, however, one is forced to say that the failure was that of men and women who did not act effectively to prevent that horror, a failure in which God had to share as well. We can risk saying, then, that in the Holocaust, God was doing what was consistent with all his doings: He was watching and suffering with each victim and agonizing over each oppressor, and also over all those millions who watched and did nothing or even failed to notice what was going on. In the Holocaust, as in the founding of the state of Israel and all that led up to it, the actors or agents in God's history were as ever his creatures. The proper theological question to ask of the Holocaust, therefore, as reflected in the collections of Halachic issues posed by those events, is not Where was God? but, Where were we? The history of God's creation has been given over to his creatures as *their* responsibility. If we Christians have not learned that fact from a sensitive knowledge of Jewish history before now, then it is time we learned it anew in our day. The age of Messiah, the time of righteousness and peace, the fulfillment of God's intended goal for his creation, depends upon our accepting responsibility for bringing it nearer, for clearing away the obstacles we are so busy erecting.

C. God's Redemption

The idea of redemption presents the final form of God's involvement with his creation. Redemption constitutes the fulfillment, the achievement, and so the completion of creation. Consequently, we must speak of redemption in the future tense; any reference to redemption in the past or present tense can refer only to anticipations or hints of what is to come. Its characteristic human response is hope. Jewish tradition provides a much needed corrective to the church's tendency to place redemption outside history and outside creation. The church's original reinterpretation of Israel's hope tended to speak of redemption both at the beginning of the history of the church, in connection with the coming of Jesus, and also at the end of or beyond history. The result was to evacuate continuing history, the one in which we live, of serious importance. Redemption at the end of time was conceived of as the uncovering, the manifestation of the event that already had come fully in principle.

A redemption "in principle" evidently cannot be in history. It leaves history behind, taking place on some other level—indeed, "in principle." But then redemption is no longer the fulfillment of God's original creative purpose. God the Redeemer is no longer or not necessarily God the Creator. Such a view of redemption lacks the cooperative feature which marks both creation and the covenants, but which is preserved in Jewish messianic hope. Jewish hope is for this world, for genuine creaturely peace and justice, to be realized when Messiah, a human figure, appears. The messianic age, however, will come about only when Israel prepares the way by living a life faithful to Torah.

Judaism also knows of a tradition of the world to come, evidently distinguished from the age of Messiah, which shares with the Christian tradition the conception of an end of history and so an end of this world as we know it. That is to conceive of reality without this world, which must mean, logically, without creation. Rosenzweig dared to take this thought to its logical conclusion and to affirm that redemption must mean ultimately the redemption of God, in that God will be redeemed from his history-with-his-creation! In proposing this radical conclusion, however, Rosenzweig did not omit the cooperative element: It is the prayers and acts of love of the faithful that bring the Day of Redemption nearer. In the end, with creation completed, God will be all in all.

From these three aspects or elements of God's involvement with the world, we can draw some conclusions about how we may speak of God. From Creation to Redemption, from speaking of God as Creator to speaking of him as Redeemer, we are speaking and can speak of God only as being consistently personal in relation to his creation. If we are to speak of the God of the Jews at all, and so of the only God confessed by the church, then we must say that from Creation to Redemption, this is how God is: God is in a personal relationship with creation. He relates to men and women and to human history as persons relate to persons, and he is related to the world of nature as persons are related to nature. Indeed, we must add, as persons *ought* to be related to persons and nature, for the concept of God is not simply personal; it is normatively personal, as the fact of worship implies.

If there is any sense in the idea of God's omnipotence, it must refer to the power of personal involvement. As Rosenzweig put it so well, "God is capable of all that he wills, but he wills only what he must will out of his essence" (1971:114). If God is essentially personal, we can interpret this to mean that God has all the power he needs in order to support and help his creation in a personal way and in cooperation with his human creatures.

Judaism has known throughout most of its history that what men and women do has an effect on God. The rabbis said frequently that God is increased or decreased, so to speak, by the faithfulness or unfaithfulness of his people. More recently, a few Christian theologians have, with the help of Whitehead's metaphysics, begun to say something similiar. One who saw this without the help of Whitehead was Bonhoeffer. Under the impact of the events of his time, he came to see that it is God himself who is forcing us to live in the world as if the God of the theological tradition, the One classically defined in Latin, were not here to do for us what he expects us to do for ourselves and for him. Had more Christians come to this realization earlier, perhaps millions murdered by Hitler before he got around to hanging Bonhoeffer might have been saved. Precisely the concept of the God who, as "the Absolute, relativizes all things finite," (Kaufman, 1975:53) is no longer, if it ever were, a morally defensible concept of God. The finite creature in his finite history is far too important to his creator to be so relativized. Rather, the finite is, if I may be excused the term, relationalized—that is, created so as to be open to relationship with a person—because God, by becoming the person's Creator, by entering into a covenant with him, and by calling the person to work together with Him for the world's redemption, has related Himself to his creature personally.

III. God As the Normative Person

From the beginning of this essay, we have consistently
followed the scriptural lead in speaking of God with the same
verbs, adjectives, and expressions that are characteristic of
our speaking of persons. As we speak of human beings
"willing," "doing," "intending," and the like, so we have
spoken of God. To put the matter sharply, we have been
speaking of God as a person, just as we speak of one another
(sometimes) as persons. In doing so, we have followed without
reserve the lead of Genesis 1:26-27, that man and woman were
created in the image and likeness of God, and also of
Colossians 1:15, in which Jesus is said to be the image of the
unseen God. Above all, we have had in mind Exodus 33:11,
where it is said that God spoke to Moses "face to face, as a man
speaks to his friend."

We have been speaking of God *as* a person, not as *if* he were
a person. We are not saying that we are using the model of a
person in speaking of God, any more than we would say that
we are using the model of a person to speak of one another. We
are not even saying that we are using "person" as an analogous
way in which to speak of God. No, quite directly, we are
saying that the scriptural language we are following requires
us to say that the God of whom we are speaking is and must be
a person. This is *not* to say that God and human beings are the
same—far from it. The scriptural literature and the traditions
of both synagogue and church make clear that they
understand God and man to be as different as Creator and
creature. After all, even among human beings, we do not say
that one person is the same as another—indeed, part of the
function of the concept of "person" is to preserve the
particularity, the individuality, of one so designated. To speak
of a human being as a person is to imply that we can ascribe to
him or her the values of individuality and expect from that
person a response and a responsibility that we do not expect
from beings other than personal. To say that God is a person,
then, is to say that those terms of worth or value that we
sometimes can ascribe to human beings, such as faithfulness,

reliability, sensitivity, and responsibility, are ascribed most
appropriately to God.

The biblical writings, our tradition, and especially the
Jewish tradition, are marked by a respectable reticence in
speaking of God, for God is that one person who is above all
and before all to be feared and loved. He is the one and only
person whom we adore and worship. He is, so to speak, the
normative person from whom our personhood comes by way
of creation. He has made us in his image, not the reverse (cf.
Eph. 3:14-15). Hence the Scriptures and our tradition of
worship have been cautious in speaking of God as a person,
lest we forget this priority in the one concept that links God
and human beings. God is not just a person, it seems right to
say, but rather God is always that one unique person by whom
we measure what it is for us to be persons.

The biblical reserve that is evident in speaking of God as a
person is the reserve of respect. It is not, so to speak, a logical
reserve. Bultmann's program of demythologizing rests on a
logical reserve which confuses matters and leads us into an
impossible undertaking. Mythological speaking and thinking,
according to Bultmann, consists of thinking and speaking of
the divine in terms of the finite or mundane. This views the
classical *finitum non capax infinitum* as a logical or
metaphysical assertion rather than as a personal and moral
reminder. If we speak of God at all, then we have no words to
use but our own. Either we shall speak of God in human terms
or we shall not speak of him at all. Since there is no linguistic
alternative, the distinction between mythological and non-
mythological talk of God fails to stand up. In fact it cannot even
get started. Human terms are all we have; the only issue
concerns which terms we shall use. We certainly have many
terms that are more abstract than those of personhood. Such
impersonal abstract terms as force, power, absolute, and
infinite, all have been tried. These terms are not less human,
even if they are more abstract. Why that fact should commend
them is hard to see. That they have been tried arises from
thinking that the creature's difficulty in speaking of the
Creator is a logical one, not a moral and personal one.

Whatever may have been its prehistoric origins, language

about God as we know it arises from a historical context. To speak of God is both to reflect one's association with a historical linguistic community that so speaks, and to take part in its way of speaking of reality. To speak of God is a complex move and this surely is one reason for reserve: On the one hand, we are affirming that reality is like the best we know of ourselves—it is the realm of personal relationships; on the other, the book that has shaped our language leads us to say that this book's image of the personal, the one we derive from its story, tells us what is best about us. To speak of God is, if one wants to put it that way, an imaginative construction of reality, but it is not one made up out of whole cloth. It is developed out of the scriptural story of the God of Abraham, Isaac, and Jacob, and of the men and women who engaged with that God in this historical process. To let the story have this normative role in our construction of reality is exactly what we mean when we speak of it as revelation. So also to allow historical events to orient our reading of that story is exactly what is at stake in speaking of history as revelation.

Is this a projection onto reality of our self-understanding as influenced by a complex interaction of a particular book and particular historical events? Are we reading our own experience into reality? Of course we are, but we do so in the unprovable conviction that we have it at least partly right. We know we are projecting, and this is sufficient reason for hesitation in speaking of God. We dare to take this risk, however, in the conviction that by the gift of our created personhood we have that in common with our Creator which makes it right and proper to speak of him as a person.

We could say that God is a person, surely the unique, normative person who is the judge of how we speak of and treat one another as persons; or we could adopt a more hesitant stance and say that God is personal, not less than a person. Hesitation here is fully in order: We are speaking of our Creator. But since the difference is not substantive, it seems more clear for the purposes of theology to opt for the former. The concept "person," then, will be our fundamental bridge-term which, by the grace of Creation and revelation, by the grace of having been made persons in the image of the

God who is normatively personal, crosses the gulf between the Creator and those of his creatures who have been called by him to cooperate in completing his work of Creation.

From this point, two consequences follow. If God is a person, the normative person, then his relations with his Creation properly ought to be conceived as personal. We then are to conceive of God as being related to the world as a person is related to the work of his or her hands, or more particularly, with respect to human beings, God is related to us as a person ought to be related to other human beings. This would exclude the possibility of speaking of God as if he were related to the world as a self is related to its body, for example (*contra* Ogden, 1966:175). I am persuaded that "the concept of person is logically prior to that of an individual consciousness" (Strawson, 1959:103). Logically then, if a person is an individual, the self is not another individual, but a way of speaking of the person, either when the person to whom I refer is myself, or when it is another person. So I can say that I do not think much of myself, or I can ask you if you could not put more of yourself into what you are doing. But to speak of the self as being in relationship with the body is to adopt a (Cartesian?) dualism of the person which is in conflict with the scriptural source of our manner of speech in the linguistic community called the church. The relationship that may be presumed to be between the self and the body is logical, not personal. If I cut myself, I can expect that blood will flow from my body. If I am aware of myself or if I am aware of my body, I am attending to the whole or to an aspect of my reality as a person. The concept of relationship that seems best able to do justice to all three traditions, the biblical, the Judaic, and the Christian, is the personal. It would seem best, then, to say that God relates himself to his creation as a person relates to what he has produced or to other persons.

The decision to say that God is a person has another consequence that is more difficult to think through. Apart from God—which hardly can be an adequate condition for theological reflection—the persons we know and relate to are human persons, and a feature of their personhood is that they are (or have) bodies. As the self is an aspect of the primary

concept "person," so is the body. We might say that human
beings, persons, are embodied selves, or enselved bodies. It
takes more than a body to make a person, but it never takes
less. In this understanding of the concept of person, the idea of
a disembodied person is self-contradictory. The connection
between this and the Jewish and Christian hope in the
resurrection is evident.

If persons have or are bodies—the alternative expressions
bring out the fact that "body," as far as our bodies are
concerned, is a sub-category under the primal category
"person"—and if this holds true for all created persons, and if
"person" is to be our prime bridge-term for speaking of God,
and then if God, properly speaking, also is a person (always the
normative person), it follows that God must be or must have a
body. It is consistent with this that the Scriptures speak freely
of God's finger, his hand and arm, his voice and mouth, his eye
and face. God is said to have talked to Moses face to face,
though at another time, Moses was allowed to see only God's
back. Isaiah claims to have seen the Lord sitting on a throne in
the temple. The scriptural conception of God as a person,
then, is not that of a disembodied person. It is of a person who
has that which goes with being and living and acting as a
person—namely, a body. As an embodied person, however,
God usually is unseen.

In the Scriptures, God never is said to be invisible. He
occasionally is said to hide himself or to hide his face (Ps. 10),
and it is said also that to see God face to face must result in
death (Moses on Sinai; Isaiah). With but the rarest exceptions,
God in fact is not seen. There is, however, no suggestion that
it is *logically* impossible to see God, only that in fact God does
not show himself or allow himself to be seen. The term used in
the Apostolic Writings (there is no term at all for it in the
Scriptures!) therefore is best translated "unseen" rather than
"invisible." It is not as though God is not seen because there is
nothing (no body) to see. Rather God is unseen because he
chooses to hide himself. His hiddenness is not a denial of his
personhood, and so not of his embodied personhood.

This line of reflection runs counter to the whole tradition. In
the Christian and also in the Jewish tradition, God is said to be

without body. Divine theophanies are interpreted as visions, accommodations to limited human imagination. But this reservation inevitably endangers the concept of God as person. To conceive of the world as God's body is no solution. That makes God visible apart from his choice, and more seriously, it makes the world the bridge-term between God and the world, which is a contradiction. If the world is God's creation, then God's body becomes the creation of—what? A divine self? Again, the concept of person is exploded.

The tradition's aversion to accepting the scriptural language of God's embodiment is easy to understand, being a reaction to a conception of the body as in some way imperfect, a prison of the soul. This is consistent with a soul/body distinction that places a low valuation on the body. It is as if we could conceive of being something more and thus other than persons—something more worthwhile or valuable or preferable, such as an abstraction, a disembodied spirit, or perhaps a mathematical point.

A support for such thinking can be provided by supposing the apostolic assertion "God is spirit" to be a definition of God's nature, rather than a definition of God's function or activity or purpose (Lampe, 1977:92, 210). If spirit is thought of as a state of being or a kind of being, in contrast to body or physical nature, then God is thought to be without body, and of course then the rest of the classical definition—without parts or passions—will follow. Whatever else may be said of such a God, "person" hardly could be appropriate. Without passions, without feelings, without hands to wring and eyes to weep?—what can such a God have to do with the Holocaust? Such a God—more appropriately "It" rather than "He"— cannot suffer with his children when they ignore his will, bringing unimaginable horror into his creation. Such a God— "It"—can be only a "steady state" condition of the world as it develops or unfolds its process, for the process here is conceived in impersonal terms.

The choice between thinking of God as disembodied (the classical tradition), or as having the world for a body, or as being embodied in a way that is hidden, is not easy, for there are serious difficulties with each. Let us consider them. (1) If

God is conceived as disembodied, then we are forced to abandon the concept of God as a person, or else conceive of him as a disembodied person, which contradicts our every notion of "person." God then would be the unique case of a person without body. How the logic of "person" can survive this exception is difficult to see. God then will be better conceived as a metaphysical principle—if not as first cause, then perhaps as the principle of creativity. Such a principle hardly could talk to Moses "face to face as a man with his friend." (2) If God has the world, or some aspect of it, for his body, then God can be a person, but he cannot be Creator. Then the world itself is a part of God, indeed his body, and so he cannot relate to it as a person, for now we must speak of God as a self, thereby dualistically breaking up the concept of person. The world itself then would be part of the total personhood of God, and the only possible interpersonal relationship that God could have would be with something outside his body. But since his body, on this theory, is the world (everything there is), this is impossible. The result is that the concept of God as person becomes vacuous. (3) The only alternative is to conceive of God as embodied with a body that is not the world, not part of creation, but which ordinarily is hidden, unseen by us. This will preserve God's personhood, but it has its own difficulties. God's visibility then will depend on his will. His body is not by definition invisible, but only as a matter of fact—except when he chooses to show himself. Further it will need to be a body that permits God to be present wherever and whenever he chooses. In a word, we shall be forced to use the word "body" in God's case in an almost utterly unique way, so that it can well be asked whether the word has any meaning here at all.

No matter which way we move, we are confronted with the fact that our words do not work well when we attempt to speak of God. If we opt for the concept of person as being fundamental for the concept of God, that leaves us with problems which I have no illusion of having solved. Yet it seems to be the least objectionable, especially when we speak of God after Auschwitz. The recent events in the history of Israel, the Holocaust and the founding of the state, are primarily historical events. The one represents a massive failure of human persons to fulfill the minimal requirements of our God-given and God-instructed personal existence. It was not God who failed at Auschwitz, but human beings. The only God who could be said to have failed at Auschwitz would be a *deus ex machina,* a potentate whose conditional creation still was totally his own responsibility and who had not given his creatures the full responsibility that goes with the genuine independence of a real creation. The God who failed at Auschwitz would be a god who does not risk a cooperative engagement with men and women to bring creation slowly along to its completion in righteousness and peace. The God who could be said to have failed at Auschwitz would be a god who did not deal with his creaturely persons as a person. Such a god, we may conclude, has not died; he has never been.

As for Israel, that state came into existence because men and women took action, risked their personal existence in doing so, and assumed personal responsibility for what they did. They did not wait upon a heavenly force, a creative principle, or a first cause, to accomplish what seemed right to do. No one else in heaven and earth offered them help. In the best covenantal tradition, like Abraham, Moses, and David, they got up and went; they provided the leadership; they became an army. Once more the hand of God appeared in history, in no form other than in the hands and feet of his people. Whether they shall so act as persons as to avoid falling under the judgment their prophets made upon their ancestors, remains to be seen. But surely the One who watches and agonizes with them over the way they are handling their situation is the person we call God.

Those two events in recent Jewish history took place in the framework of personal choice and action. In each event, the supreme question for each person is that of personal responsibility. Therefore the God with whom this history is being lived, reflected upon, and carried forward, seems best conceived as a person, with eyes that see and weep, with hands that comfort the suffering, and with a voice that whispers still, to those who have ears to hear.

Notes

1. The most important statement yet is the 1980 Confession of the Evangelical Church of the Rhineland. See Klappert and Stark (1980).
2. On this, Rosenzweig (1971) provides an important argument with which Christian theologians should be familiar.

References

Croner, Helga, ed.
  1977. *Stepping Stones to Further Jewish-Christian Relations: An Unabridged Collection of Christian Documents*. London: Stimulus Books.

Kaufman, Gordon D.
  1972. *God the Problem*. Cambridge, Mass: Harvard University Press.
  1975. *An Essay on Theological Method*. Missoula, Mont.: Scholars Press.

Klappert, B., and Stark, H., eds.
  1980. *Umkehr Und Erneuerung*. Neukirchen-Vloyn: Neukirchen Verlag.

Lampe, G. W. H.
  1977. *God as Spirit*. Oxford: Clarendon Press, Oxford University Press.

Ogden, Schubert M.
  1966. *The Reality of God*. New York: Harper & Row.

Rosenzweig, Franz
  1971. *The Star of Redemption*. Trans. Wm. Hallo. Boston: Beacon Press.

Sanders, E. P.
  1977. *Paul and Palestinian Judaism*. Philadelphia: Fortress Press.

Sanders, James A.
  1975. *Torah and Canon*. Philadelphia: Fortress Press.

Scholem, Gershon
  1974. *Major Trends in Jewish Mysticism*. New York: Schocken Books.

Strawson, P. F.
  1959. *Individuals*. London: Methuen & Co.

II. IN SEARCH OF A GOD-CONCEPT

About Axel D. Steuer's Essay

More directly than most of these essays, Axel Steuer's takes up the controversy between theistic belief and unbelief. It goes on the offensive, claiming that recent arguments against the coherence of traditional theism are themselves misguided, even incoherent. So this piece belongs to the genre of polemical philisophical theology.

This being the case, it displays stylistic qualities that distinguish it from some others in the present volume. Steuer does not ask here (as for example Altizer does) how the present *Zeitgeist* makes the concept of God possible or impossible, or (as for example Davis does) whether we require a new vision of God from our poets. He does not, for these are not the salients threatened by the antitheism Steuer engages—the antitheism represented by Kai Nielsen and J. M. Mackie. Rather Steuer asks whether it is indeed true that "God," as conceived by traditional Christian theism, is an incoherent or self-contradictory *idea*, and he answers no, it is not.

One value of such discussion about belief and disbelief is that it permits the reader to discover where the real issues lie. Even if Steuer's logic is sound, it does not follow that unbelief will surrender and turn into belief. Why not? Presumably because the deeper human motives at work in both belief and disbelief are not disturbed. This is not, however, to discount the relevance of Steuer's (and for that matter Nielsen's) arguments. For by showing us what, though true, may not persuade us, they free us to examine and test those deepest motives which otherwise might remain concealed and unexamined.

This may seem to assign a rather preliminary, pedagogical role to philosphical theology in general. Yet such pedagogy is not to be despised; indeed it could be argued that it is indispensable for a Christian approach to the doctrine of God. As long as Christian convictions are to be not only lived out but also thought out; as long, that is, as the Christian life is, among other things, a life of the mind, such work is indeed necessary. That it is not sufficient as well as necessary is hardly a criticism.

By way of appraisal, the reader might wish to compare this essay with that by Alston, where similar topics are addressed. There is in Steuer's argument a careful development reminiscent of G. E. Moore. His drive to set the matter straight can only delight the careful reader. McClendon (see his essay) well might ask Steuer whether the God here conceived is indeed the God of Jesus Christ or only the God of the theologians.

4. The Supposed Incoherence of the Concept of God[1]

Axel D. Steuer

Undoubtedly a number of religious believers, particularly theists, would agree with the observation that the sceptic or atheist serves a very useful function for the believer. Whether an Epicurus, a David Hume, or a Friedrich Nietzsche, the sceptic often expresses in a very clear manner what are perceived to be the primary weaknesses in the understanding of the religious thinkers of the day. The sceptic forces at least the more philosophically inclined religious believers to reexamine both the foundations of their beliefs and the arguments used to defend or support those beliefs. Thus, to paraphrase Plato, if an unexamined belief is not worth holding, then the sceptic does a peculiar service to believers by constantly prodding them to reflect upon their beliefs.

The most insightful and hence most helpful sceptics have a special gift for getting at the heart of the matter—that is, for so formulating their attacks on religious belief that they seem to undercut what a preceding or contemporary generation of philosophers and theologians has put forward as the firm foundation of such a basic belief as the reality of God. Thus Hume's attacks on religion focused on the common deistic assumption that belief in God was somehow natural, or at least reasonable, in light of the wonderful order we perceive in nature. In turn, Nietzsche's moral attack on religion was probably inspired or fostered largely by the popular Kantian notion that religion was a necessary presupposition of morality. In any event, as the history of religious thought bears out, sceptical attacks of the sort just described have generally served not so much to destroy religious belief as to push theologians and philosophical defenders of faith into a

87

creative rethinking of their positions. In light of this dialectical relationship between belief and unbelief, particularly between theism and atheism, it should not surprise the student of contemporary religious thought to find that during an era such as ours, in which a number of theologians can be found arguing for the wonderful incomprehensibility of God (often under the influence of neo-orthodoxy and religious existentialism as filtered through a crude Wittgensteinianism), many of today's sceptics address themselves to this claim and make the issue of God's incomprehensibility precisely the point of their attack.

An earlier version of this genre of scepticism is the philosophical movement that came to be known as logical positivism or logical empiricism. Although logical positivism is still perceived by many theologians as a force to be reckoned with, that movement and the sceptical arguments based on it lost much of their forcefulness when logical empiricism, at least in its most strident forms, was itself displaced from its position of philosophical respectability by the later Wittgenstein and the so-called ordinary language philosophy. In the face of attacks by the logical empiricists, many philosophically trained theologians of the 1950s and 1960s jumped on the Wittgensteinian bandwagon and espoused what Kai Nielsen has referred to as Wittgensteinian fideism. This should not be surprising to anyone familiar with the Kierkegaardian background of many of these converts to Wittgensteinianism and aware of Wittgenstein's own great respect for the Danish thinker. Although there is reason to doubt that Wittgenstein would have approved of the use many contemporary theologians make of his later writings, he seemed for awhile to grant theists the right to hold beliefs that stricter canons of meaning—for example, those employed by the logical positivists—would discount as worthless.

However, if Wittgenstein's later writings seemingly gave a new lease on life to the beliefs of some theists, they also provided a new generation of atheists with the tools, or basis, for a new attack on belief in God. The most vocal sceptics currently take their cue from the ordinary-language philosophy of the later Wittgenstein and his disciples, arguing that

the theist's use of our common language so distorts or
stretches linguistic meaning as to make assertions about God,
and indeed to make the very concept of God utterly senseless
or incomprehensible. Thus one frequently comes across
charges that the traditional concept of God is incoherent or
that some central element in that concept gives rise to
paradoxes that can be resolved only by ceasing to attribute
some essential property to God. It is maintained that careful
attention to the way theists use or misuse ordinary language
will show that their assertions contain fatal confusions.

It is this latest version of the antitheistic argument, found in
the writings of such philosophers as Antony Flew, Wallace
Matson, and Kai Nielsen, which calls for a response by the
theist and to which I briefly address myself in this essay.[2] I will
discuss the so-called paradoxes of omnipotence, omniscience,
and divine agency, with the intent of showing that the theist
who wishes to ascribe omnipotence, omniscience, and agency
to God is not thereby caught up in conceptual paradoxes or in
linguistic confusions.

II

In the major religious traditions of the West, the word
"God" commonly functions as the proper name for a personal
being conceived of (minimally) as the all-powerful, all-
knowing, infinitely good incorporeal creator and sustainer of
the universe. This definite description is thought to apply to
God alone and therefore serves to identify God. God,
furthermore, is viewed as a "God who acts," and his actions
are seen as revealing his nature and confirming that the
properties traditionally ascribed to God are truly descriptive
of him. Because divine agency serves as the ground or basis for
the ascription to God of all other properties, it is probably best
to begin with an examination of the frequently heard claim
that it is incoherent to ascribe agency to a being such as God.

Kai Nielsen's well-known essay "On Dining with the
Theologian" (Nielsen, 1971:112 ff.) attempts to speak also for a
number of his atheistic colleagues, defending some of them
against the theistic assaults of Donald Evans and D. H.

Hudson. In the present section therefore, I will limit myself to examining his arguments against theism, to see whether
the charge of incoherence—that the theist so distorts the
meaning of ordinary language as actually to engage in
self-contradiction—really is justified.

What Nielsen and his sceptical colleagues find especially
incoherent is the theist's notion of and talk about a
disembodied God—one who reveals himself through his
actions as a personal being, in spite of the fact that he has no
body through which or with which he can act in order to reveal
himself and his will. And belief in God's disembodied agency
clearly seems to be, as I have indicated, a core belief in the
Western theistic traditions, although some process theologians or panentheists might dispute this claim. Hence if the
notions of disembodied personhood and disembodied agency
are incoherent, Nielsen would seem to be justified in his
conclusion that there are "good grounds for thinking the
Judeao-Christian concept of God is an incoherent concept"
(Nielsen, 1971:128).

With regard to the notion of disembodied personhood, it
does not seem at all obvious that to talk about persons who are
not embodied is to use language in an incoherent way. If
indeed "person" meant "a certain kind of body," then to talk
about a certain kind of disembodied body certainly would
involve the speaker in making senseless utterances. However, I doubt that Nielsen would claim that this is the meaning
of the word "person." Perhaps the view Nielsen really holds is
that all human persons necessarily are embodied and that
human persons exhaust the category of, or candidates for,
personhood. In that case, to talk about disembodied persons,
or personal beings, would be to talk about a class of entities
that has no members and therefore would be incoherent in the
sense of being a waste of time, silly, and so on. However, even
this weaker claim, which does not lead to the really
disreputable sort of incoherence Nielsen would like to
attribute to the theist, has been challenged by such
philosophers as Peter Strawson and Jerome Shaffer, who
maintain that it is logically possible for human persons to exist

in a disembodied state—for instance, by surviving bodily death (Strawson, 1963; Shaffer, 1968).

Even if one grants that human persons are necessarily embodied, this in itself does not justify the claim that the concept of persons is exhausted by the concept of human persons. It may well be that there are nonhuman persons, even nonembodied persons such as God is said to be. Perhaps there are beings or entities that are not, compositionally speaking, material bodies in the way the human persons we know are composed of or identified with human bodies, but to whom we would ascribe a sufficient number of 'personal' predicates (*i.e.*, predicates of the sort applied only to persons), so that it would be quite appropriate to ascribe personhood to them. But if embodiment is neither a necessary condition for personhood (*contra* Nielsen) nor a sufficient one (a point most philosophers willingly grant), then whether there are such disembodied personal beings seems to be a question of fact and cannot be answered simply on the basis of any philosopher's feat of linguistic analysis.

Now, Nielsen builds his case against the coherence of talk about disembodied persons on the conviction that the *identification* of an entity as a person is not possible if that entity is disembodied (Nielsen, 1971:129). And it does seem that Nielsen and his sceptical colleagues have the right to ask the theologian to state some reasons for believing that there is such a disembodied, presumably divine, personal being. That is, the theologian should be able to state how he identifies this disembodied person, God, and furthermore, on what ground he asserts the continuity over time of this disembodied person. Put perhaps somewhat more crudely, but nonetheless to the point, the sceptic is entitled to ask the theist to write something like a biography of God, telling us about God's abilities and character (*i.e.*, in what way God is personal) and about the kind of person he is.

Obviously, if the theist maintains the traditional position that God is disembodied—that God has no body in the ordinary sense of the term "body," which assumes that bodies are experienced, at least indirectly, through human sense organs and hence are knowable in the empiricist's sense of "knowable"—then the theist cannot use bodily criteria of personal identity and continuity with respect to God. However, if we do not use criteria that are solely or even primarily bodily criteria in identifying entities as persons and as the sort of persons they are, but, as I would like to suggest, make such identifications on the basis of the *actions*, if any, that candidates for personhood have performed, then one might well be able to make a case for the claim that the list of actions ascribed to God both identifies God as a person and defines the sort of person he is. If, in other words, we can rightly lay claim to a peculiar or unique set of actions as being the acts of God, then by employing these criteria, we can legitimately claim that there exists a personal God who has a certain character and certain abilities that we can read from his actions—whatever his composition might be. For actions always point to a person or agent whose actions they are, and it is from their actions that we determine the character and abilities of the person or agent who performed them.

But this last suggestion brings us directly to what seems to be his real criticism of the theist, and that is that the theist invokes a truly incoherent notion when he asserts that God's personhood is revealed through disembodied actions. To quote Nielsen, "It is not that I doubt that agency can in fact occur in the absence of bodily movement, but I doubt the intelligibility of the sentence—and not simply on verifica- tionist grounds—'Agency can occur in the absence of bodily movements' " (Nielsen, 1971:124). The idea of a bodiless agent, or pure spirit, God for instance, is due to Platonic or Cartesian ways of conceptualizing, according to Nielsen, and ultimately is rooted in the "plain fact" that each of us has private experiences (Nielsen, 1971:126).

Although I have some qualms about the supposed experiential roots of the notion of bodiless agent, I believe that the best response to Nielsen is to examine briefly the model sentence he claims to find unintelligible. At the outset, we can grant that the sentence "Agency can occur in the absence of bodily movement" is, if not unintelligible, at least ambiguous. As it stands, it might be used with the intention of claiming any of several different things: That at least (a) some actions are not also (at least in part) bodily movements, (b) some actions do not result in or are not followed by the movement of some body or other, (c) some actions are not initiated by or preceded by some sort of bodily movement, (d) some actions are not also bodily movements, nor are they preceded by, nor result in the movement of some body or other. It seems to me that only the last interpretation of Nielsen's model sentence can plausibly be claimed to be necessarily false and in this sense, unintelligible, because if no observable changes or events have taken place, as it appears to imply, we have no grounds for saying that an action, which is a type of event, has been performed. But even this qualification does not apply to the agent's own mental acts. In any event, there is no reason the believer in disembodied agency should want to make a claim such as that expressed in the fourth interpretation of the model sentence, especially when talking about divine agency. In turn, the remaining three interpretations seem to me to be capable of being read as making arguable claims and therefore are not obviously incoherent or unintelligible. With respect to these first three interpretations, it can be said that each denies that bodily movements are somehow a necessary condition for agency and that for our present purposes, they differ primarily in the location of the bodily movement whose necessity for agency they deny—that is, whether it precedes, follows, or is part of the action.

Now, that actions are not reducible without loss to mere bodily movements of the agent, however complex, seems obvious in nonphilosophical settings. In fact it is often very important that we be able to distinguish between such mere bodily movements as accidentally pulling the trigger of a gun in response to a sudden noise and thereby causing someone's death, and the action of stalking a man and murdering him with a well-placed shot in the heart. In ordinary life, as well as in courts of law, we often distinguish between the mere bodily movements of a person and his responsible actions. Thus, at least in the very strongest sense in which bodily movement might be viewed as a necessary condition for agency (when actions are viewed as reducible to particular bodily movements), the denial of such a necessary condition seems to be justified. If the identity thesis were indeed correct—if it could be shown that all actions are reducible to or equivalent to bodily movements of the agent—Nielsen's model sentence would in fact be unintelligible, for then it would read, with appropriate substitutions, "Bodily movements can occur in the absence of bodily movements." But this assumption of identity does not appear to be warranted, and it clearly is not an assumption the theist needs to make in order to escape the charge that he is misusing our ordinary language.

Furthermore, even if the identity thesis is not maintained but it is claimed that actions require bodily movements in some 'weaker' sense, the theist's denial of such a claim by asserting Nielsen's model sentence (at least any of the first three interpretations of that sentence) is not obviously incoherent. For there are a number of important human actions which do not, in the process of performing the action, involve bodily movements as such on the part of the agent, or even the movement of objects in the world external to the agent. Certain mental actions—praying silently or solving a problem or memorizing a poem—do not require any noticeable bodily movements. Furthermore, as John L. Austin pointed out, a number of important human actions are performed as speech-acts rather than as bodily movements. Although speech-acts usually involve some bodily movement such as moving one's lips, exhaling air, or writing on paper, they clearly cannot be equated with such movements, nor do they require a particular form of bodily movement. The important thing is that the desired communication is achieved and that thereby we change our own or another's social, legal, emotional, informational, or some other state, status, or condition by uttering or writing certain words. At times, even the act of remaining silent can achieve drastic changes. The act of punishing by maintaining a frosty silence is a familiar example of an often effective action which does not involve bodily movements as such, either on the part of the agent or of objects in the world external to the agent.[3] These sorts of considerations should be sufficient to raise doubts concerning the claim that bodily movements are a necessary condition for agency and thereby to undercut Nielsen's *a priori* argument against the theist, based as it is on the supposed incoherence of the assertion "Agency can occur in the absence of bodily movement."

Nielsen's response might well be that the above considerations really are not relevant to his argument, since the kinds of actions that theists have traditionally ascribed to God and on the basis of which they have attributed to God a certain character and certain abilities—various personifying attributes—are not the kinds of mental and verbal actions we have just considered. Theists talk instead about God creating the world, leading Israel across the Sea of Reeds, or sending a Son to redeem mankind from sin. These purported actions imply that observable changes have taken place in the world or in human experience. And observable actions of this kind (the kind from which, by the way, we can best read the character and abilities of the agent) seem to require some sort of bodily movement on the part of the agent.

However, although acts of creating, leading, and sending, if performed by human agents, normally do require some bodily movement on the part of the agent, this seems to be more a function of the fact that they are being performed by human agents who are embodied, than a function of the meaning of the terms "creating," "leading," and "sending." There is nothing inherent in the notions of creating, leading, and sending that requires that these sorts of actions involve either a particular kind of bodily movement on the part of the agent or any bodily movement at all by the agent. At most, these concepts require that something be created, that someone or something be led or sent. And this, in turn, comes down to the requirement that the purported actions have been performed. No explicit or implicit reference is made to bodily movement on the part of the agent when we say that acts of creation, leading, or sending have been performed.

Speculating on the reasons Nielsen might have for assuming his particular stance with regard to disembodied actions, it appears that he takes such activities as going for a walk, skipping rope, and lying down as his paradigms for the concept of action. These are all performed with the body and hence obviously require some sort of bodily movement on the part of the agent. Other philosophers, perhaps most notably Roderick Chisholm, defend an agent-causation paradigm of actions; that is, they view actions as events caused by agents.[4] This latter perspective tends to dissociate the agent's bodily movements from the actions performed. However, it appears that the concept of action is broader or more inclusive than allowed for by either Nielsen's presumed paradigm or Chisholm's theory of agency. Clearly, going for a walk is a perfectly good example of an action, and it is the kind that Nielsen's view of action as involving bodily movement appropriately describes. It would certainly be peculiar to describe going for a walk as an agent causing his body to make certain moves. In turn, making someone happy is the sort of action that is difficult to describe on the basis of Nielsen's paradigm, although Chisholm's agent-causation view seems quite well suited for giving an account of it. In brief, the paradigms of both Nielsen and Chisholm properly apply to certain classes of actions. But since the concept of action is much broader than allowed for by a strict adherence to either perspective, neither paradigm is adequate as a general account of actions.

The upshot of all this is that a nonembodied being such as God could not logically perform actions such as taking a walk or skipping rope. However, the sorts of actions on which the agent-causation theory tends to focus are not actions that a disembodied being would be logically barred from performing. As long as a disembodied being effects changes in the world which properly can be described as the leading of someone or the creation of something, we can ascribe agency to that being, even though it does not achieve or cause such changes by moving its (nonexistent) body. Furthermore, such presumed actions, like all actions, can be the basis on which personhood is attributed to such a being; that is, character and abilities can be ascribed to the agent. That human beings do not ordinarily effect such actions without moving their bodies does not imply that bodily movement is somehow part of the concept of such actions, as it is, for example, of taking a walk. Though there are some actions that only embodied beings can perform, this does not entail that nonembodied beings can perform no actions.

I believe, then, that Nielsen's *a priori* argument against the theist, based on the latter's supposed confusion with respect to our understanding of the concept of action, does not hold up. Consequently, the theist's claims about the purported disembodied actions of God, and the resultant personhood of God that is revealed through such actions, must be examined one by one. The theist's position, as well as I can understand it, amounts to the claim that certain events that have occurred in the history of the universe, which, because they suggest power and intelligence of a divine (or at least superhuman) magnitude or quality, are appropriately viewed as divine actions precisely because there is no visibly embodied agent to whom they can be ascribed. Since they fall outside the usual causal order (of material causes and human agency), these 'actions' or their effects are often distinguished by the labels "providence" and "miracle." Furthermore, like all actions, they are read as revealing the character and abilities of the agent or personal being who performed them. And it is this disembodied agent that theists have traditionally named God. That the theist may, in the end, be mistaken as to the nature of the real cause of these purportedly divine actions—these providential and miraculous events that some have discerned in the world—is a fact of religious life.[5] What I have tried to indicate in this section of the essay is that, contrary to the opinion of Nielsen and his colleagues, such a theist is not making incoherent claims.

To summarize, this discussion of disembodied agency has assumed that actions are best understood as the subclass of events through which the character and abilities of persons are revealed to us. Since in our experience to be human is to be embodied, it appears that one cannot talk about human agency and the human personhood this reveals unless one admits that some bodily movement or other, or at least some bodily presence or existence on the agent's part, is involved. To this extent, therefore, human action cannot serve as a model for understanding the supposedly disembodied action of God. Yet if certain events are perceived as revealing a person's character and abilities to us, we are justified, or so at least it seems, in describing those events as actions. And since actions always point to an agent whose actions they are, whether or not that agent is presently perceived as having a given location in space and time, the occurrence of certain actionlike events justifies us in postulating an agent who caused those events. If an embodied being can be identified as the agent who is effecting such action-events, we appropriately ascribe agency and personhood to that embodied being. If, on the other hand, no such embodied being can be perceived, and furthermore, if all plausible embodied candidates for agency with respect to these supposed actions can be ruled out, it seems that one is as justified in ascribing the agency, and the personhood such agency reveals, to a nonembodied being (for instance, to God) as in denying that these actions actually occurred. Hume, of course, held that the occurrence of miracles is so unlikely that it is never rational to abandon the search for a natural, presumably embodied cause for such events. In any case, unless one stipulates that the term "action" can be applied only to character- and ability-revealing events ascribable to an embodied being (quite appropriate with respect to certain classes of actions such as taking a walk), there seems to be no *a priori* or conceptual reason for ruling out the possibility and therefore the coherence of God's disembodied agency.

III

The accusation that the traditional concept of God is incoherent in that it involves conceptual and linguistic confusions, has also been directed at certain specific attributes that have been viewed as essential to the description of God—specifically, his omnipotence and omniscience. The concept of an all-powerful and all-knowing personal being entails such paradoxes, it is sometimes claimed, that it is not possible to give a coherent account of the God of Western theism. Since it has traditionally been held that a personal being who is not omnipotent and omniscient is not God, and certainly not an appropriate object of prayer and worship, this

criticism of the concept of God would, if valid, undermine the
theist's position. Put another way, the abilities that God
supposedly has revealed to us through his actions, and which
have traditionally been summarized as omnipotence and
omniscience, are such that if God truly possesses them he
could not have a personal relationship with his creatures—
that is, there could not be a relationship with God that would
allow his creatures a certain degree of freedom and dignity.

As J. L. Mackie states the problem associated with ascribing
omnipotence to a supposedly personal God, "There is a
fundamental difficulty in the notion of an imnipotent God
creating man with a free will, for if men's wills are really free
this must mean that even God cannot control them, that is,
that God is no longer omnipotent" (Mackie, 1964:57). We
seem, in brief, to be caught in a paradox—whether we affirm
or deny that God can create such beings, we end by imposing
a limit to his power. The options for resolving this so-called
Paradox of Omnipotence seem to come down to either the
denial of divine omnipotence or the denial of human freedom
and dignity (and with the latter denial, we preclude any
personal relationship between God and man). Mackie, in
different essays, finds both 'escapes' appealing (cf. Mackie,
1962, 1964). However, I believe that there is yet another way
to resolve this supposed paradox, one which comes from a
better understanding of how, or in what sense, freely acting
human beings are beyond God's control.

An omnipotent God is able to do whatever he wants, short
of involving himself in self-contradiction. One of the things
he presumably wanted to accomplish, and in fact did, was
to create beings capable of a degree of self-control—or
freedom—sufficient for the forming of personal relationships.
And of course if these decisions of the free agents he created
actually are their own decisions, finding expression in free
actions, these decisions and actions may well not conform to
God's wishes.

Although this ability of a free human agent to control
choices, to engage in free actions, may seem to place a limit on
God's omnipotence, that really is not the case. For this
self-control, or freedom, is a property of the human agents

whom God chose to create and in no way reduces God's power to create, destroy, intervene, or in any other way to exert control over the lives of all his creatures. The suggestion that our understanding of God's omnipotence requires that he be able to control even more directly the mechanism of self-control that human agents are said to possess, seems to come down to the demand that God actually becomes identical with his creatures, for only in that case would he have immediate or absolute control over their free choices, their means of self-control. If one wants to make a distinction between God and finite free agents (a distinction which, in contrast to monism or pantheism, is fundamental to theism), God's control over these finite free agents can never be identical with or as immediate as the self-control, the power to make choices and to engage in free actions, which his human creatures are said to possess. Since this impossibility of God's determining the free decisions of agents other than himself is a logical impossibility, God's power is not diminished by the fact that human agents cannot be created both with a degree of self-control and lacking such self-control.

In summary, human beings cannot possess the sort of freedom of action required for a personal relationship with God and still remain absolutely under God's control, unless one maintains the identity of God and his creatures—a heresy condemned as ontologism. The one kind of control that God logically cannot have over free human agents is self-control. Thus, contrary to Mackie, it is not paradoxical that an omnipotent being cannot completely control another distinct being which has at least a certain degree of self-control, or freedom. The creation of such freely acting, or independent beings in no way limits God's power (indeed it might well be viewed as further testifying to that power), nor does the creation of such beings require any sort of self-limitation on God's part. God still can do whatever is logically do-able; in other words, he still is omnipotent, even though he freely creates beings over whose free choices he has, on logical grounds, no control.[6]

It should be noted that the above resolution of the paradox of omnipotence is rather distinct from the one Charles

Hartshorne has employed in several of his writings (cf. Hartshorne, 1941). Hartshorne seeks to assure human agents a "sphere of free activity" by arguing that there are things that finite beings can do that God cannot do, since some actions can be done only by finite beings. However, unless Hartshorne is limiting that 'sphere of free activity' for finite agents to things that for logical reasons only an embodied being can do—for instance, skip rope—it puts too severe a restriction on God's omnipotence to maintain that there are classes of actions performable only by finite beings. In contrast, our argument hinges on the logical point that God cannot perform the same action performed by another free agent. This logical limitation, however, does not imply a limitation on God's power to do whatever it is possible to do.

The problem of reconciling God's omniscience (particularly his reputed foreknowledge) with human freedom and dignity seems to be somewhat more complicated. The difficulty is that if God foreknows all that will happen, including the future free decisions of his creatures, and if God's knowledge is infallible, it would appear that the outcome of all human choices and actions is predetermined. Therefore, if the human freedom and dignity required for a personal relationship with God could cast doubt on God's omnipotence, God's omniscience seems to make human freedom logically impossible. Again, the theist's dilemma appears to be the following: Either he should give up the claim that human beings possess the sort of freedom requisite for a personal relationsip with God (and for making sense out of such religious activities as prayer and worship), or he must deny the traditional notion of God's omniscience.

Paralleling our argument with respect to the property of omnipotence, I would suggest that omniscience does not entail foreknowledge of the free choices of other persons, because such foreknowledge would be logically incompatible with the claim that those choices are in fact free. In spite of Augustine's claim that "one who does not foreknow the whole future is most certainly not God" (Augustine, 1958:108), I want to maintain that because it is logically impossible to have certain knowledge concerning which particular option a free agent will choose at some time in the future, even an omniscient being is not required to have such knowledge.

It seems obvious that as human beings reach higher or more sophisticated levels of personal development, as they develop ever greater capabilities to act freely, their actions are determined less and less by so-called external causes and become more directly a function or product of what might be called their personhood—their abilities, beliefs, experiences, and moral values. Therefore, if we focus only on the so-called physical events impinging upon such persons, we will become less and less able to accurately predict their actions as they grow in freedom.

Not surprisingly, therefore, in the early stages of personal development the behavior of such individuals is relatively unfree and predictable, given adequate information about the stimuli affecting them, because it is almost totally determined by causes beyond the agent's control. At later stages in this development, only knowledge of a person's past actions and such information about the developing character, capabilities, moral values, and beliefs as is revealed in those actions will allow us to make fairly accurate predictions about that person's future free actions. This, of course, accounts for the fact that a person's spouse often can predict what a person will choose to do "better than the person can." Thus maturity and growth in freedom do not entail unpredictability in behavior in the sense of increased capriciousness. Quite the contrary! A different kind of knowledge about a person is required in order to predict behavior with any accuracy as that person grows in freedom. Thus a certain degree of intimacy fostered by such things as shared experiences and common trials becomes a prerequisite for knowing "ahead of time" what decision a person will make. However, this means that unless we can somehow share totally in an individual's experiences, moral values, beliefs, and abilities, our predictions about that person's future decisions will never be certain or infallible. Even spouses can surprise each other! In brief, there seems to be a logical impossibility involved—knowing other persons as well as or in the same way that they know themselves—which keeps one person from making infallible predictions about the free actions of another. In contrast, at the very earliest and most predetermined stage of development, only our lack of knowledge of the various stimuli affecting an individual keeps us from making infallible predictions about that person's behavior.

All this means, of course, that the free actions of other agents cannot be predicted infallibly even by Deity (just as they cannot be predetermined), unless we assert the identity of those free agents with God—something theism necessarily denies. No one, even an all-knowing being such as God, can predict infallibly and therefore foreknow the outcome of a truly free choice of another agent, unless one is party to the other agent's total personhood out of which that decision comes. Clearly, no one could be in that position. Thus even God cannot foresee infallibly what a person will choose to do in any particular or open situation, although God undoubtedly comes closer to such foreknowledge than does any other being.

God does foresee infallibly, however, and this preserves his omniscience, the consequences of each free choice, including the further options it may open up or foreclose. In other words, God foresees all the options that will ever be available to all persons, under every combination and permutation of choices that are possible, and the consequences of each series of choices. He also knows all choices that have been made and all events, including all actions, that have ever taken place or could take place in the future. But he does not and cannot foreknow (infallibly foresee) the outcome of each individual free deliberation. Again, this "limitation" to God's knowledge should not be understood as a defect, because as a logical precondition for God's foreknowing the option an agent will choose in a free or open situation, God would need to become the agent whose free choice it is. That is, God would have to become subject to the circumstances within which the free agent finds himself or herself at the moment of decision (presumably even before the agent finds himself or herself in that set of circumstances) before God could have the experiences that would enable him to foresee the choice a given individual will make in that situation.

I might summarize our resolving of the alleged paradox of

omniscience in the following way. If God grants persons freedom of choice or action—that is, if God so arranges things that alternative courses of action become available to persons as they become more sophisticated, and if God values the sort of relationships this creaturely freedom makes possible—then the outcome of future free choices of human agents cannot, on logical grounds, be known in advance of a person's freely deciding upon a particular course of action. God's predictions undoubtedly will be better informed than those of others, but they will not be infallible. God could foresee infallibly the oucome of such free deliberations in advance only if (a) he were identical with the person whose choice it is, or (b) his purported foreknowledge could be proven false by the free agent (and hence would not really be knowledge), or (c) if such choices (contrary to the hypothesis), actually were not free—that is, if they were not determined or decided by the presumed agent himself or herself. Given the theist's assumptions about God's nature and about the sort of relationship that exists between God and his human creatures, all three of these options are ruled out on logical grounds. Hence, if we accept Aquinas' description of God's knowledge, that "God has most assured knowledge of all things knowable at any time and by any mind" (Aquinas, 1967:98), we see that God's lack of foreknowledge with respect to the future free choices or actions of certain of his creatures does not detract from his omniscience. He can still be said to know everything that is knowable. That he does not know what, for logical reasons, is unknowable, does not demean the vast knowledge he does have.

IV

If the remarks in the preceding sections of this essay are accurate, then it appears that the supposedly rather obvious conceptual and linguistic confusions that some philosophers have seen in the traditional theological description of God do not really exist anywhere but in the minds of those philosophers. The concept of an infinitely powerful, wise and knowledgeable, good and personal being, which nonetheless is incorporeal, is not an incoherent concept. While there may well be no such being, the theist's talk about God is not based either on a misuse of language or on conceptual confusions.

All this is not to say that all is well in the house of theology. Specifically, it has become clear to a number of thinkers that in recent years theologians have not paid sufficient attention to the metaphysical assumptions that underpin much of what they say about God and the God/world relationship. As a result, theologians all too often find themselves making statements that the educated public cannot comprehend, or dealing with intellectual problems which appear to many to be of rather doubtful relevance. Two brief examples may help to illustrate why I believe that metaphysical assumptions, rather than conceptual confusions or linguistic muddles, lie at the heart of contemporary theology's difficulty as it seeks to be taken seriously by educated readers.

Much Catholic and some Protestant theology seems to be wedded to a Platonist metaphysics, which assumes that there are various grades, or levels, of being. With this assumption, it is only natural that God is piously placed at the highest level. Thus God's being and God's properties are seen as different in kind, or qualitatively different, from those of his creatures. Consequently, the question arises concerning how finite beings could ever traverse the chain of being in order to arrive at some knowledge about God. Theories of analogical predication and other clever but misguided philosophical devices are invented in the effort to bridge a gap that by definition is not bridgeable. The theologian finds himself or herself in the dilemma of seeking to know that which is not knowable and of speaking about that for which he or she has no language. Dispensing with this outmoded Platonist metaphysics would certainly ease the theologian's task and would allow language to be used in its literal, natural sense, even when the subject being discussed is the infinite being, God. For example, God's possession of infinite properties such as infinite power, goodness, and knowledge does not need to entail that these properties are qualitatively different in God. For religious purposes, it seems to be enough that a being described as infinitely good, powerful, and wise is suffiiciently good, wise, and powerful for all situations, rather than adding that these properties are qualitatively different from properties to which we assign the same term when exhibited by human beings.

Another rather common metaphysical assumption, which for want of a better scapegoat I will attribute to Aristotle, is that being comes in various modes. With this assumption, possible existence is viewed as a weak mode, and real existence is viewed as somewhat richer, while necessary existence is seen as the ultimate mode of being. This peculiar metaphysics not only has fueled discussions of the ontological argument, but also has given seeming plausibility to the arguments for contemporary process theology. But subsistentialism, as D. C. Williams has designated this metaphysics, with its notion that possible or potential existence is a real, if weaker, mode of being, does not survive careful philosophical scrutiny (Williams, 1962). Yet it has become the rarely examined foundation for many contemporary critiques of traditional theism and the basis of some popular reconstructions of the concept of God.

While I cannot pretend to have adequately pointed to where the real work of any future theology lies, I hope that these closing comments do provide some basis for believing that the problems for contemporary theology do not lie where critics such as Nielsen and Mackie say they lie. Rather, I want to suggest that the frontiers of theology lie precisely in work on its metaphysical foundations. And although I do not find their particular solutions to theology's problems very fruitful, it is in fact the process theologians who in recent decades have pointed out to us where the theologian's primary efforts should be directed.

Notes

1. Parts of this essay were first read to participants in a 1978 NEH Summer Seminar for College Teachers on "The Concept of God." I am grateful for the helpful comments made at that time by James Keller and Donald Henson and by the seminar director, William Alston.
2. Although a number of philosophers have employed these sorts of arguments in recent years, the following books have almost become sceptical classics: Antony Flew's *God and Philosophy* (1966), Wallace

Matson's *The Existence of God* (1965), and Kai Nielsen's *Contemporay Critiques of God* (1971).

3. The point I am trying to make here is that the concept of action does not as such imply bodily movement on the part of the agent or of objects external to the agent. However, when the agent is a disembodied being, the only basis on which we can *ascribe* actions to that agent is whether some change is effected in the world. It is for this reason that I rejected the fourth interpretation of Nielsen's model sentence as one the theist would have an interest in defending.

4. I base this description of Chisholm's position primarily on his remarks to a graduate seminar at Harvard University in the spring of 1969.

5. It should be noted that here I am speaking as if actions are to be understood as events caused by agents. However, as I indicated above, only certain kinds of actions traditionally ascribed to God seem to fall most naturally under that description or paradigm of actions.

6. This same point is developed in more detail in part 4 of my essay "Once More on the Free Will Defense," *Religious Studies* 10(1974):301-11.

References

Aquinas, Thomas
    1967. *Philosophical Texts*. Trans. Thomas Gilby. London: Oxford
        University Press.

Augustine of Hippo
    1958. *The City of God*. Trans. Gerald Walsh, et al. Garden City,
        N.Y.: Image Books, Doubleday.

Hartshorne, Charles
    1941. *Man's Vision of God and the Logic of Theism*. New York:
        Harper & Brothers.

Mackie, J. L.
    1962. "Omnipotence." *Sophia* vol I.
    1964. "Evil and Omnipotence." *God and Evil*. Ed. Nelson Pike.
        Englewood Cliffs, N.J.: Prentice-Hall.

Nielsen, Kai
    1971. *Contemporary Critiques of Religion*. New York: Herder &
        Herder.

Shaffer, Jerome
    1968. *Philosophy of Mind*. Englewood Cliffs, N.J.: Prentice-Hall.

Strawson, Peter
    1963. *Individuals*. Garden City, N.Y.: Anchor Books, Double-
        day.

Williams, Donald
    1962. "Dispensing With Existence." *Journal of Philosophy*
        59(December): 748-64.

About Gordon D. Kaufman's Essay

More than most American theologians, Gordon
Kaufman has consistently focused on the doctrine of God
in his theological work. In his *Systematic Theology*
(1968), in *God The Problem* (1972), and again in *An
Essay on Theological Method* (1975) the concept of God
has contributed significantly to the shape of his theology.
However, his thought has continued to change in
important ways, and the present essay represents a new
stage of development.

Although his own theological perspective is rooted in
large part in the nineteenth-century German philosophical
tradition (Kant, Hegel, Feuerbach), Kaufman's ongoing
dialogue with diverse philosophical positions such as
existentialism, process thought, logical empiricism, and
language analysis is evident in the present essay,
"Constructing the Concept of God." Indeed, it might be
read profitably as a reaction to, and to some extent a
synthesis of, these assorted perspectives.

It is significant that Kaufman despairs neither of the
concept of God nor of the future of theology. As long as
men and women require a *framework* for interpreting life
and experience, theology will have the task of
constructing, evaluating, and symbolizing those
conceptual frames or world-pictures; and as long as we
recognize that the concept or image of God is an
imaginative construct, a product of the human mind that
serves as a focal point or center for those conceptual
frames, Kaufman believes that the concept of God
provides an important and perhaps necessary function in

the orientation of human life and thought. Thus talk
about God cannot be talk about some independently
existing or objective being, and it is a mistake to "do
theology" in ways that reify God—that is, in ways that do
not acknowledge that it is we who must construct and
reconstruct the concept of God. However, this
construction must be self-conscious and critical so that it
will meet the peculiarly human need for an "appropriate
object for ultimate human devotion and service." As long
as this task remains, theology has a vital role to play.

It should be noted that in this essay Kaufman intends
to be primarily descriptive. That is, he intends to point
out that (a) *in actual practice* the concept of God
"functions as the principal focal point of an overall
world-picture"; and (b) (as most intellectual disciplines,
apart from theology, have already recognized) "all thought
and experience are decisively shaped by the overall
world-picture or conceptual frame within which they
occur." If one grants Kaufman these two claims, then
much of the rest of what he says in his essay would seem
to follow. Thus, for example, the central place in human
life of the concept of God as a symbol that can focus and
direct human energy and feeling toward certain goals
seems to be guaranteed if the first claim is true. The
truth of the second claim would preclude, Kaufman
maintains, both any "direct" experience of God and any
finding that "God" refers to an objective being; it also
suggests the futility of any theology that sees itself as
trying to arrive at a final or objective description of God's
nature or will. Indeed, only a recognition of the fact that
the concept of God is a construct of the human
imagination will allow us to see why it has functioned so
successfully in the past as an object of human devotion
and service, and to discover ways our concept can be
adapted to meet changes in the human perspective on
the world. Those readers who desire a God less
dependent on human imagination and who view theology
as a more objective enterprise than Kaufman allows for,

would be concerned to challenge the validity of
Kaufman's descriptive claims and to argue that only a
more objective concept of God can do justice to the
reality Christians encounter. But for Kaufman, the
question, Is God GOD? can hardly make sense as it
stands!

5. Constructing the Concept of God

Gordon D. Kaufman

Whether in prayer or sermon, in biblical exposition or theological analysis, use of the word "God" involves important imaginative and constructive activity that is often not recognized. God is not a reality immediately available in our experience for observation, inspection, and description, and speech about or to God, therefore, is never directly referential. Thus we are unable to check our concepts and images of God for accuracy and adequacy through direct confrontation with the reality *God*, as we can with most ordinary objects of perception and experience; instead, our awareness and understanding here is gained entirely in and through the images and concepts themselves, constructed and focused by the mind into a center for the self's devotion and service. God is said to be Father of us all, Creator of all things both visible and invisible, Lord of history, Judge of all the earth. These images, each drawn from ordinary political, social, or cultural experience and suitably qualified to suggest (a) being transcending everything finite and particular in glory, majesty, and power, then become the constituent elements out of which the image of God is put together by the mind. Again, God is said to be eternal and transcendent and absolute, one who alone has aseity and upon whom all other beings depend for their existence. Concepts such as these are taken to characterize, in religiously and metaphysically distinctive ways, who or what God is, and thus they also become constitutive of this focus for devotion, life, and meaning. The mind's ability to create images and characterizations, and to weld them imaginatively together into a unified focus for attention, contemplation, devotion, or

111

address, is at work in the humblest believer's prayers as well
as in the most sophisticated philosopher's speculations.[1] In
this respect, all speech to and about God and all "experience of
God" is made possible by and is a function of the constructive
powers of the imagination.

The idea of God gains its own distinctive and unique
meaning for us through contrast with all the particulars of
experience, and also through contrast with that structured
whole within which all experience falls, and which we call the
world—even while being built up and put together out of
images and analogies drawn from this very experience. This
idea is in many ways the mind's supreme imaginative
construct, related to all other dimensions, realities, and
qualities of experience and the world, and yet seen as distinct
from and grounding them all. Little wonder that, as the
tradition has always recognized, God is not an object of
ordinary perception, directly accessible to us, but is believed
to be transcendent and mysterious, hidden from our sight,
even unknowable.

> Lo, he passes by me, and I see him not;
>   he moves on, but I do not perceive him. . . .
> Behold, I go forward, but he is not there;
>   and backward, but I cannot perceive him;
> on the left hand I seek him, but I cannot behold him;
>   I turn to the right hand, but I cannot see him.
> *Job 9:11; 23:8-9 RSV*

Of course, no individual human mind constructs the idea of
God from scratch. All thinking about God and all devotion to
God take place within a cultural and linguistic context in
which the notion of God already has been highly developed
through the imaginative work of many preceding generations.
So the idea of God with which any particular individual works
is always a qualification and development of notions inherited
from earlier worshipers and prophets, poets and thinkers. For
much of Western history, the Bible has been the principal
resource collection of earlier stages of reflection on and
construction of the concept of God, and biblical attitudes

toward God have been built in at deep levels of Western consciousness of life, humanness, and reality.

But the Bible's significance for Western thinking about God has gone far beyond mere informal influence of this sort. The Bible was long regarded as the locus of God's revelation to humanity (the "Word of God"); it therefore carried an authority powerful enough to override ordinary human experience and rational argument. Although the "creator of the heavens and the earth" was not an object available for direct confrontation and observation, and knowledge about God could not be gained in any ordinary way, this lack, in God's graciousness and mercy, had been divinely supplied in and through the Bible. The presence of this authoritative resource for normative images and concepts of God meant that God's being and activity could be regarded as completely objective and "real"—indeed, even more real than the objects and qualities of ordinary experience. For the Bible presented the story, or history, of all the world and of humanity—a story of which we humans also are a significant and living part. And in that story God is the supreme active character—the creator of the world, the lord and principal mover of history, the one in relation to whom human life finds fulfillment and meaning, and in turning from whom, it withers away and dies. For those who lived out their lives with this story as the fundamental context within which events and experiences were understood, every occurrence had a divine significance. It was God with whom one actually was dealing in every moment and relationship in life, and there was little question of God's reality, power, or significance.

The authority of the Bible and the reality and power of God within the biblical story assured that questions about the mode of God's presence to the mind—through the mind's own activity of imaginative construction—would not quickly arise. This was so even though God's reality in the Bible was that of a character in a story and even though this reality was apprehended by believers in much the same way they grasped other story characters—through powerful acts of imaginative reconstruction carried out in and by their own minds as they read or heard the text.[2] However, after two centuries of

modern historical scholarship, it is possible to see that the
image/concept of God in the Bible is a product of imaginative
construction and also to see something of the various historical
stages through which that construction developed. Thus we
can gain some understanding of why and how the notion of
God came to have the particular shape and content that has
been so authoritative in the West. This in turn puts us into a
position to ask whether and to what extent we should continue
to use biblical motifs and images in our own contemporary
attempts to construct an adequate concept of God.

I

According to modern critical historical scholarship, the
fundamental biblical picture of human life is rooted in very
ancient Near Eastern mythological traditions. Out of these
remote mists, Yahweh appears in the Mosaic period, as a
distinct character. He rescues a group of slaves from Egypt,
makes a covenant with them in the desert, and goes before
them to destroy their enemies and to bestow upon them the
land of Israel.[3] At first Yahweh seems to be essentially a
"mighty warrior" who fights—and wins—his people's battles
for them, as long as they remain faithful to him. Soon,
however, that simple picture proves insufficient. With the
settling of the land, the rude desert nomads who were
Yahweh's devotees become farmers and city dwellers, and
Yahweh must expand his capacities to deal with new problems
that arise in these new situations. So in prophets such as
Hosea and Jeremiah, we can see Yahweh increasingly
envisioned as one who gives rainfall and fertility to the crops,
heals diseases, and performs other activities which earlier had
been ascribed to other gods and to goddesses. Moreover, with
the rise of civilization among the Hebrews and with increasing
economic stratification and centralized political power, new
social problems appear in the cities; and so Yahweh, through
the mouths of such prophets as Elijah and Amos, becomes a
strong advocate of social justice. Above all, with the crises of
political defeat and renewed enslavement, first by Assyria and

then by Babylon, it becomes necessary to reconceive Yahweh thoroughly, from one whose being and activities are essentially an extension of the wishes and needs of his people, to one who is totally independent of them and their desires. Yahweh becomes understood as the creator and lord of all the world, who directs the movemets and activities of all nations and peoples according to his own inscrutable purposes, and who is free and able to allow Israel simply to die or to be destroyed if the people do not keep the (now somewhat expanded) covenant made with him. The eighth-century prophets (with the help of the preceding Yahwist historical writer[s]), and above all Second Isaiah, are the first to come to this exalted vision of the one God, "high and lifted up" above all things earthly and human, the creator of all the world and its sole lord.

All this, of course, could be sketched in much greater detail, and this historical development of the conception of Yahweh could be followed much farther into the Christian era and into the subsequent mixing of Hebraic and Hellenic cultural and religious traditions. But it is not necessary to do so here. The point I wish to emphasize is that this Hebraic world-view focused in its lordly creator-god, like other great religious frameworks, gradually developed as the seers, poets, and prophets of the community found it necessary to come to terms with new situations and new experiences. The mythic imagination was able to shape and reshape the early Near Eastern stories of a hierarchy of warring gods into what became ultimately a picture of a unified world ruled over by the one God, Yahweh, its creator and lord, who was working in that world to accomplish his own purposes. The whole of human history thus was caught up in a movement toward the goal which Yahweh had posited for it from the beginning, and to which he would ultimately bring it. Within the overall sweep of this cosmic historical movement, the Christian acclamation of Jesus as Yahweh's Messiah came as a climax and principal turning point.

It is important for us to observe here that the notion of God which was gradually emerging in the biblical history, and the interpretation of human life as God's gift and of human existence as being "under God," are parts of, and essentially functions of, an overall world-picture that was gradually developing. Political and personal metaphors were utilized as the fundamental building blocks in these conceptions. The world that God had created is like a kingdom. It is ordered by God's sovereign will, ruling through earthly intermediaries (kings and/or prophets and priests) who know what God wants done and seek to carry it out. This High King, however, was not to remain simply an arbitrary imperial potentate or a rigid legalistic judge and protector of law and order; in course of time he became understood as a heavenly "father"—one who loves and cares for his children, one who continually seeks to extricate them from difficulties into which they have fallen. Within this picture, human life was to be lived out in response to and under the love and care of this just, merciful, and almighty God, who is the fundamental Reality behind all other reality, and relationship to whom gives life its only proper orientation and meaning.

Every feature of experience and life is interpretable within this framework. Even events of suffering and apparent meaninglessness or absurdity are given significance here, because they also come (though we cannot understand how) from the hand of the absolutely trustworthy God: "Though he slay me, yet will I trust in him" (Job 13:15). Since God is the ultimate point of reference in terms of which all else is understood, and apart from which nothing can be rightly grasped or known, God's own reality or existence is absolutely certain. In later formulations, this was put very strongly: God is the ultimate reality, the only being with absolute aseity, the one whose very essence is to exist, that than which nothing greater can be conceived.

An overall framework of interpretation of this sort, which gives meaning to existence, is indispensable to humans. We cannot gain orientation in life and cannot act without some conception or vision of the context within which we are living and moving, and without some understanding of our own place and role within that context. Such a framework of interpretation, however, is like the air we breathe: It does not easily or quickly become an object directly perceived or

noticed. In consequence, it is seldom realized that the terms,
or foci, which structure the framework and provide its
peculiar pattern of meaning, in fact function only within and as
a part of the framework itself. This can be seen most readily,
perhaps, when we consider world-views to which we are not
closely attached. Terms like "Brahman," "karma," "Nirvana,"
"yin/yang," "mana," all gain their meaning not through the
particular beings or experiences they name, but rather as
essential constituent elements within the framework of
interpretation of the whole of life to which they belong. The
same can be said for such more contemporary terms as
"evolution," "class struggle," "creativity," and "universe."
When these notions are used in setting out, or explicating, an
overall view of life and reality, they articulate the human
imagination's attempt to grasp and understand and interpret
the *whole* within which human life falls; their creation and use
is thus a function of the imagination's power to unify and
organize and synthesize into one grand vision that which
comes to us only episodically and in fragments. It should not
surprise us to discover that in the various separated
geographical settings in which humans gradually created
great civilizations, there developed quite diverse conceptions
of the world and of the human place within the world, as the
imagination generated and followed increasingly different
perspectives in the several great cultural and religious
traditions. Since the terms and images that articulate these
world-conceptions, or world-pictures, never are simply
representations gained in direct perception, they should not
be understood as directly descriptive of objects (of experience). As products of and constitutive of a poetic or
imaginative vision, they are properly understood essentially
as elements within and functions of that overarching vision or
conception.

In a radically unified world-view such as a monotheism, the
central focus of meaning, "God," easily becomes reified into
an independently existing being. But the constituting
elements of frameworks of interpretation are not distinctly
locatable objects of this sort at all (and it is significant in this
respect that the tradition was well aware that God could not be

directly "seen"). It is a mistake, therefore, to regard qualities attributed to God (e.g., aseity, holiness, omnipotence, omniscience, providence, love, self-revelation) as though they were features or activities of such a particular being. In the mind's construction of the image/concept of God, the ordinary relation of subject and predicate is reversed. Rather than the subject (God) being a *given* to which the various predicate adjectives are then assigned, here the descriptive terms themselves are the building blocks the imagination uses to put together its conception. As the principal character in a great dramatic story, God is conceived as absolute, all-powerful, all-knowing, holy, and the like—or in the more mythic and holistic mode in which the imagination first did its work, as a "mighty warrior," a "stern judge," "king of kings and lord of lords," "maker of heaven and earth," "heavenly father." This character, then, often lifted out of the original story context which gave it life and meaning, becomes the core of the notion of God; and all of life and the world are grasped as ultimately grounded upon and centered in this God.

God thus is the ultimate point of reference, in terms of which all else is understood, and the ultimate focus of life and of human devotion. The technical theological vocabulary—including concepts such as aseity, sin, creation, salvation, trinity, providence, miracle, revelation, incarnation—was developed over the centuries as an articulated schema for expressing and interpreting this claim, and it remains a principal resource and tool for theological work today. However, contemporary theological construction must recognize that these terms and concepts do not refer directly to "objects" or "realities" or their qualities and relations, but function instead as the building blocks, or reference points, which articulate the theistic world-picture or vision of life. For this reason it is a mistake to take over traditional vocabulary and methods uncritically, since these were worked out largely on the assumption that God-language was directly objectivist or referential and thus are usually cast in a reifying mode.

Theology has always been constructive in character. In its original mythopoeic form, theological images and concepts were utilized to create a world-picture in which all of life was seen to be derived from and ordered to God; and this vision was gradually developed and shaped—constructed and reconstructed—under the impact of centuries of prophetic criticism and insight. When Greek culture was encountered, theology became philosophically self-conscious and critical and thus attended more directly to problems of conceptual analysis and systematic conceptual construction, but it remained wedded to the reifying referential mode in which its mythic origins had cast it, and it understood itself to be attempting to express in human words and concepts what was objectively and authoritatively given in divine revelation; the thoroughly constructive character of theology was not clearly recognized. With the contemporary theory of world-views and conceptual frameworks, however, more adequate understanding of the human function and of the logical standing of religious and theological language is made possible, and this deficiency is overcome. Theological work, therefore, now can be carried on as a fully critical and self-conscious constructive activity, in a way that never before has been possible.[4]

II

If we can no longer presume that theology is working directly from an authoritative divine revelation, how are we to proceed? What are we to construct here, and in what way? It is clear that we cannot simply fabricate a concept of God out of whole cloth. Of what elements is it to be composed, and how should they be put together? Is it really possible to set out a meaningful concept of God once the radically constructive character of theology is acknowledged?

A framework of interpretation for life and experience cannot be built up artificially from scratch and then simply "adopted" by persons who find it attractive and plausible. Since all experiencing, thinking, and acting presuppose a world-view or perspective which shapes the questions being formulated and provides the categories by means of which life will be grasped and interpreted, we are never able to get to a presuppositionless point from which we can choose our framework of interpretation freely and without bias. We are always already living in and operating out of one (or more) world-picture(s). The most we can hope, therefore, is to become sufficiently conscious of the stance within which we are living and acting as to become critical of it to some degree and thus to be in a position to reconstruct it significantly.

It is in response to meaning already abroad in the culture and language—meaning given in and through the symbol "God"—that theological criticism and construction arise. (In this sense theology always begins in "faith" and in response to "revelation" and always is in the service of faith.) When a theologian becomes conscious that the images and forms mediating this meaning are not adequate to convey it precisely or effectively, but that the meaning comes through stunted or distorted and subject to misunderstanding, criticism and reconstruction are undertaken in the attempt to enable the symbol to become a more valid and effective center of orientation for modern life. Earlier in this paper we have already begun this task of theological reconstruction. I have been arguing that God is to be understood not primarily as a "free-standing" separate or distinct "object" or being (a mistake into which we are often led by our imagery), but as an important constituent of and simultaneously a function of an overarching world-view. We must now attempt to work out what God can mean positively and significantly, when the logical standing of God-talk is reconceived in this way.

To begin, let us ask, What sort of function does the symbol "God" have for those to whom it is still significant? We may give a summary answer to this question by saying that the image/concept of God serves as a focus, or center, for devotion and orientation.[5] Value-claims of many sorts attract our commitment and loyalty: family, nation, truth, pleasure, power, work, political causes, beauty, health, charismatic leaders, sex, sports, ideologies, physical discipline or indulgence, and many more. Particular moments—or major segments—of life may be oriented in terms of one or more in this immense variety of fascinating objects which come to our attention. On occasion, the attraction in diverse directions of incompatible values may threaten to pull us to pieces; intemperate subservience to particular values may enslave and ultimately destroy us. In contrast with all such "idolatrous" attachments, however, the symbol of God claims to represent for us a focus for orientation which will bring true fulfillment and meaning to human life. It sums up, unifies, and represents, in a personification, the human ideals and values that are assumed to be the highest and most indispensable, making them a visible standard for measuring human realization and simultaneously enabling them to attract the loyalty and devotion that can order and continuously transform individuals and societies toward fulfillment (*i.e.*, bring "salvation").[6]

The metaphysical claim that God is "ultimate reality" or "being itself " or "the source and ground of all that is," is made to undergird and make plausible the religious claim that God is the single appropriate object for ultimate human devotion and service. But it is the performance of this latter religious function that identifies God as GOD. An abstract metaphysical conception of the "ultimately real" in and of itself does not warrant and can hardly attract full human devotion; that high place is given instead to those metaphysical conceptions that explicate and secure the significance and standing of that which already provides a meaningful focus for affection and orientation.

Every conceptual frame or world-picture can demonstrate some grounding for that which it holds ultimately significant, but since it is never possible to step entirely outside the frame of orientation being examined onto "neutral" ground, to see whether and how well it "corresponds" with "what is really the case," the metaphysical "truth" of an all-inclusive conceptual framework of this sort can never be ascertained directly and easily. (The notions of "correspondence" and "what is really the case," it should be noted, are themselves concepts of ours, given meaning by their place in the frame of orientation which philosophically trained Western minds have come to take for . granted.) The best way to assess the appropriateness or adequacy of a particular frame of orientation is through comparison with alternatives. One can attempt to observe and evaluate the different styles and modes of human existence and community and the forms of human realization made

122   Is God GOD?

possible by the various world-pictures and conceptual frames
employed by the several great human civilizations. This is an
exceedingly difficult task, one for which we are barely
beginning to acquire the necessary tools, and which, in any
case, cannot be undertaken in this paper. It looms as
important work for future theologies and philosophies of
religion. The most that can be attempted here is to sketch the
outline of a critical modern theistic position and to include
some suggestions about its metaphysical grounding. At some
later time, perhaps, this could be laid alongside other critical
modern world-views—for example, Buddhist, Marxist, secular evolutionary-humanist—for comparative evaluation and
for the metaphysical assessment such comparison would make
possible.

I will turn now to an analysis of those characteristics in the
monotheistic notion of God received from the tradition which
make God a suitable and appropriate object of human service
and devotion.[7]

III

The concept of God as the sole proper object of unqualified
human devotion and service appears to be structured by a
unique and powerful internal dialectic. On the one hand (as
we have already noted), God is conceived as a humanizing
center of orientation, one who brings about human salvation
and who is conceived (usually) in quasi-human or anthropomorphic images. On the other hand, however, God is
envisioned as mysterious and beyond all human knowing, the
all-powerful creator of the heavens and the earth and the
determiner of destiny, one who "builds" and "plants," but
who also "plucks up" and "breaks down," "destroys" and
"overthrows" (Jer. 1:10), the relativizer of everything human
and finite. God thus is conceived to be radically independent
of all human striving and desiring—certainly no product of our
fantasies and wishes—while at the same time it is only in
relation to God that genuine human fulfillment is to be found.
God transcends all things human—indeed all things finite—
even while being that which creates, sustains, and nourishes

the entire finite order. I want to argue that either of these dimensions without the other would undermine and ultimately destroy the function and significance of God as the proper object of human devotion and service; but they need very careful formulation if we are to avoid the reification so characteristic of the tradition.

Let us consider first the motif of God's radical transcendence and otherness. This theme is developed particularly in the image of God as creator of the heavens and the earth, lord of history, and judge of the world. It is also expressed in the notions of God's eternity, transcendence, aseity, and absoluteness. In all these conceptions, God's otherness from and radical independence of the human and all else finite is underlined. God is not to be understood as our tool or device, to be used for our advantage or as we please. We are *God's* servants, not God ours. We must subject ourselves to the order God imposes; God is not subject to our arranging and ordering.

What seems to be at stake here is a claim that human individuals and communities need a center of orientation and devotion outside themselves and their perceived desires and needs, if they are to find genuine fulfillment. As finite beings seeking security and satisfaction, we much too easily make ourselves the center of life, rearranging all else so that it conforms with our wishes. Our relations within the finite order are all characterized by reciprocity and mutual interdependence, and this makes it possible for us to employ them in ways directed toward the fulfillment of our own desires, to utilize the finite realities to which we are related as "means only," rather than treating them as "ends in themselves" (Kant). Our narcissism as individuals seems inevitably to lead to corruption of these relationships, and our similar ethnocentrism as communities and anthropocentrism as a species leads to warfare among peoples and to the exploitation of the resources in our environment. To break through this curved-in character of human existence, we need a center and focus of meaning which can evoke from us devotion and service, drawing us out of our preoccupation with ourselves and our own wishes. The image/concept of a

God radically objective to us, entirely independent of all our desires and not susceptible to any remaking or reshaping in accord with our wishes, one which we can in no way control, has traditionally performed this function. God has been a center of devotion and service, drawing persons and communities out of themselves; overcoming the warfare of a thousand centers, each attempting to order everything in its own terms; opening up human life to structures of order and meaning otherwise outside its reach.

It was the employment of objectivistic images such as creator, lord, and judge, emphasizing God's radical transcendence and over-againstness while simultaneously suggesting God's absolute authority and power over human existence, which gave the symbol of God its great power to evoke this kind of human self-transcendence. These same images, of course, have been the basis for the understanding of God as (an) existent being, as the ultimate reality on which all other reality depends; and it may seem that belief in God's existing over against us is essential to God's functioning as a center of orientation and devotion which can draw us out of ourselves. I do not, however, think that this is necessarily the case. For it was not so much God's objectivity and existence in the present that gave the traditional images their great power of evocation, as memories of what God had done in the past and hopes for what God would do in the future.[8] To live "under God" was to live remembering God's "mighty deeds" already performed and expecting that future which God was about to bring. This would be a "kingdom" in which all evil, unrighteousness, and falsehood were overthrown, and truth, peace, and love were ushered in—whether this was understood in terms of individual guilt and sin and the hoped for release of forgiveness and salvation, or in terms of the transformation of the whole sociocultural order in a great consummation of history. "God" and the "kingdom of God" thus signified a movement through history, from a past of sin and bondage to a future of judgment and salvation, and it was in terms of that great historical movement that the image/concept of God actually exercised its power, both through the terror it evoked and the love it inspired. The

fulfillment of human life, both individual and social—or its
absolute destruction—was in God's hands: It was this
awareness that was the real ground of God's power to draw
human existence outside itself.[9]

These observations reinforce a point made earlier in this
paper: In actual practice, the image/concept of God does not
function simply as referring to some being which is grasped
and understood simply in terms of itself; on the contrary, it
functions as the principal focal point of an overall world-
picture, and it is in terms of that interpretive frame that it
must be understood. The world-picture within which the
biblical God functions is historicist in character. All of life and
reality are seen as a vast historical movement, from creation to
eschaton, and God is the principal actor in that movement. It
is within this context that human life is to be understood and is
to find its proper place and fulfillment. So it is as true to say
that the meaning of human life is found within the ongoing
movement of (God's) history as to say that it is found in relation
to God—for the two expressions come down to the same
thing. Living within a world-view with God as its focus is no
different from living in significant relation to that God who is
the focal center for this world-view. In either mode of
expression, human existence is understood in terms of its
relation to and dependence upon a reality other than itself—a
reality which calls it into being, sustains it in existence, and
gives it a ground for hope of fulfillment (salvation). In the one
case, this Other is seen as a particular being, God, who is
working in and through history; in the other case, it is seen as
the cosmic historical movement ordered by God's purposes.

Since (as we have seen) it is an error to reify God into an
independent being, the two forms of expression are actually
equivalent. But from the point of view of contemporary
theological reconstruction, the understanding in terms of
world historical movement is distinctly preferable. For it
provides a way to speak of an independence and otherness,
and even aseity, over against the human—the requisite
condition for breaking our narcissism and anthropocentrism
and drawing us out of ourselves—without positing a particular
existing being (named "God") as that in which this otherness is

lodged. The historical movement as a whole, and in particular its forward movement toward future possibilities which we cannot envision at this moment, but for which we must become open, can now be seen as that independent Reality in relation to which our existence and activity must be oriented. Since the characteristically modern interpretations of the overall context of human existence and experience—the "world" within which our lives fall—are evolutionary-historical in pattern, the shift in emphasis I am advocating here enables our theological reconstruction to establish effective contact with major presuppositions and perspectives of modern intellectual and cultural life.

For the moment, I do not wish to elaborate further upon the way the motif of God's otherness or transcendence—that dimenson of the concept of God which relativizes and calls into question all human wishes and concerns, ideas, and ideals—would be developed in the theological reconstruction I am proposing here. Let us turn, rather, to the other equally important motif in the concept of God—what I would like to call God's "humaneness": God's concern for and active promotion of human well-being and fulfillment. Some traditions have believed their gods to be indifferent to human needs and suffering, or even malevolent; in the traditions growing out of Hebraic culture, however, God came increasingly to be depicted as representing the epitome of humane virtues and as being thoroughly devoted to the welfare of humans and other creatures. Thus God was thought of as *good*, not only powerful—as just, merciful, caring, loving, and forgiving. In the Christian version of the divine activity, God is represented as sacrificing self without reservation—as sending "his only son" to rescue humanity from the mass of sin and perdition into which it had fallen. The use of such anthropomorphic imagery contributed to the overall impression that God was thoroughly "trustworthy"; thus one could give oneself without reservation in service and devotion to God. God was like a thoroughly humane, just, and loving father, and we are the children for whom God has unlimited care, for whom God's only desire is that we reach maturity and fulfillment. But this is no mere "wish" of God's:

God is also pictured as a powerful will, the very King of the Universe, who is working effectively to accomplish the humane objectives set since creation. In the "end," a humane communal order of justice, mercy, and love—the "kingdom of God"—will be fully established and we human children and loyal subjects of God will reach our destined salvation. However much it is necesssary to curb our superficial wishes and desires in order to worship and serve God, ultimately our own deepest interests and needs will be realized, for God's will and work for us is unqualifiedly humane.

This emphasis on God's humaneness in the traditional theistic world-view meant that the events and processes of the natural order within which human life fell were not to be understood in wholly impersonal terms: They were themselves in some sense the expression of (the humane) God's purposive activity, and in and through them God was working to create and sustain human life and bring it to its proper fulfillment. We can put this point in more contemporary terms and say that there have been tendencies and forces working in and through the evolution of life which eventuated in the appearance of human beings; and in the history of the humanity that subsequently unfolded, interest in, attraction toward, and commitment to "humane" values, attitudes, ideologies, and institutions appeared, and in some historical strands, began effectively to transform and shape personal and social life. One could speak, then, of a movement of cosmic history that eventuated in the production of the human and the humane, and one might hope for a further development of that historical tendency toward a more genuinely humane society—what in the traditional mythology was expected as the "kingdom of God."

Within such an evolutionary-historical understanding of the world, and of the appearance of humanity within the world, the image/concept of God would continue to have a significant place and function. As finite but self-conscious beings within the ongoing evolutionary-historical process—beings capable of shaping and directing our own development in certain respects—it is important that we be able to focus our attention on those features of the overarching cosmic process

that create and sustain and fulfill us as specifically *human*.
That is, we need to be able to focus our devotion, our
reflection, and our activity on that which grounds and fulfills
our humanity, can enable it to come to its highest and most
mature expression, and therefore can open us to that fuller
realization of humanity toward which (we may dare to hope)
history is moving. *God* is the symbol that holds all this
together in a unified personifying image/concept suitable for
devotion, meditation, and the orientation of life. As such, God
symbolizes that which, in the ongoing evolutionary-historical
process, grounds our being as distinctively human and draws
(or drives) us on toward authentic human fulfillment
(salvation). In this interpretation, God would continue to
symbolize that which is outside and other than the human,
that which effectively relativizes present human existence and
consciousness, that which draws the human out of itself,
opening it to new possibilities in the future.[10] And ritualized
devotion to God in religious cult, as well as in the private
disciplines of prayer and meditation, would still have an
important function to play in life.

IV

There are, of course, wide differences in understanding of
the human among individuals and among societies. The
anthropomorphic elements in the image/concept of God,
especially those elements which define what I have called
God's humaneness, naturally reflect these differing views of
human nature and human fulfillment—and this accounts in
part for the diverse conceptions of God. A fully argued
reconstruction of the concept of God would require a
thorough consideration of these matters, but that cannot be
undertaken here. However, I would like to suggest that it is at
this point that specifically *Christian* theology becomes
interesting and important, because of the special constraints
laid upon it.

For Christian faith, Jesus Christ has had a double normative
significance (Chalcedon): He provided a basis for understanding what the human truly is, and how it is to comport

itself, and also for understanding who God is and how God acts
to and for humans. Thus for Christian theology, the
humaneness of God is not to be understood simply or
primarily in terms of our own ideas and experience of the
human: *Jesus* provides the model on the basis of which our
notions of humaneness (whether God's or ours) are to be
developed. There are of course wide differences in view
among Christian theologians about who Jesus was and what he
did and about the way his character, actions, and fate help to
define and determine how God is to be conceived. I cannot
address these matters in detail here, but I would like to point
out certain radical implications that can follow from taking
Jesus as the paradigm for understanding humaneness. When
one proceeds in this way, such qualities as love, mercy, and
forgiveness—even "nonresistance" (Matt. 5:39) or "weakness" in the face of aggression (I Cor. 1:25)—will be given
prominence in the conception of the truly human and in the
understanding of God.[11] Since these qualities all tend toward a
universalistic and humane ethic, rather than ethnocentric or
politically and socially chauvinistic positions, emphasis on
their importance presses the anthropomorphic or "humane"
side of the conception of God to break through from its
henotheistic tendencies to the full universalism of "radical
monotheism."[12]

When developed in this way, the motifs of humaneness and
absoluteness in the concept of God, though remaining in a
certain tension, reinforce each other instead of undercutting
and threatening to destroy each other. It now becomes clear
that the absoluteness of God (and of history) cannot be
identified with that tyrannical power which destroys its
enemies mercilessly, nor is it to be understood as some
inscrutable mystery that ultimately fades into the complete
emptiness of an unknowable X; it is, rather, that which
creates, sustains, and continues to nurture humans even in
the face of hostility and rejection, so as to effect their
transformation and ultimate fulfillment. And the humaneness
of God (and of history) is not some simple realization of our
wishes or desires, but rather the insistence, which we in our
self-centeredness always resist, that we become transformed

into beings who love and serve one another; that we become a "new humanity" characterized preeminently by such virtues as love, freedom, reconciling forgiveness and openness, and creativity.

The import and meaning for human life supplied by an image/concept of God constructed in this way should be obvious. Though such a focus for devotion and service would not solve all, or even any of our immensely difficult concrete problems, it would help to mobilize our energies and intelligence to attack those problems by combating the ego-, ethno-, and anthropocentric tendencies in our lives, opening us up for that universalistic "benevolence toward being in general" (Edwards), without which a truly orderly and at the same time genuinely humane world can scarcely be conceived.

V

I have attempted here to sketch *desiderata* for the image/concept of God that are rooted in the Christian tradition. In the present argument, however, the significance of these *desiderata* is not grounded on the supposed authority of "revelation," but upon the claim that it is both appropriate and humanly desirable that our devotion and service be focused on a symbol defined in this way. It is clear that much fuller discussion would be required to show that a center of orientation of this sort would indeed promote genuine human fulfillment (salvation), but I think perhaps enough has been said to suggest the lines along which such further elaboration might be undertaken. I will turn now to a summary assessment of this whole approach to theology by considering briefly the question of God's "existence."

We must not be misled here into repeating the common error of searching for some particular being or reality to which the name "God" can be applied. As we have seen, "God" is the focal term of an overarching conceptual framework (in terms of which all experience is grasped, understood, and interpreted) and is not the name of an object perceived or experienced independently of that frame. The question, therefore, to which we must attend—often improperly posed as "asking about the existence of God"—is actually concerned with the viability and appropriateness of this whole frame of orientation.

Human ideals and values, foci for devotion and loyalty and the standards by which humans judge themselves, do not and could not exist independently of and without regard for "the way things are." If they had no significant connection with or relationship to "the real world," it is inconceivable that they would provide useful guidance and orientation for beings living and acting within that world. In this respect all the mythologies or world-views that the human imagination has conceived—even those that seem grotesque, superstitious, and completely unbelievable to us today—must in their own way bear some significant relation to the reality in which their devotees live. What can be said now about a frame of orientation centered on and symbolized by God—or more specifically, by a God constructed according to Christian criteria? Does or can devotion to this God in fact provide us with significant and valid orientation in the "real world"? If it does, then this frame of orientation must in some significant sense correspond to "the way things are," and talk about God, the symbolic focus of this perspective, must represent something "real." I have argued that terms articulating a frame of orientation cannot be expected to correspond directly to "existent realities." But it would be hard to conceive how the ruling focus of a highly centered frame of orientation could be completely out of touch with that which is metaphysically real. I am not preparing to develop here an "argument for the existence of God"—I am claiming that the symbol of God must in some way correspond to or represent something metaphysically real, if it is in fact true that devotion to that symbol provides proper orientation for human life. What, in "reality," then, might one contend that this symbol stands for?

The Christian image/concept of God, as I have presented it here, is an imaginative construct which orients selves and communities so as to facilitate development toward loving and caring selfhood and communities of openness, love, and freedom. Other ways of understanding God or other foci of devotion—other value schemes or frames of orientation—

presumably would lead human development and realization in other directions. Clearly there are many different ways in which individuals and communities can grow; there are many different ways of being human. And the models and images that humans accept as their own have much to do with the style of life that will ultimately become theirs. Here we must ask, Are there some styles of life in which human possibilities come to fuller realization? Though it is exceedingly difficult to define criteria that will enable different forms of existence to be ranked according to the degree in which human potential is realized, few, I suppose, would hold that every form which human life has taken historically is equivalent to every other. Some are exceedingly frustrating and ultimately prove abortive; others open up human life to a wide range of values and meanings.

The question about the validity or truth of a theistic frame of orientation concerns the degree to which it reflects the actual situation of human existence and thus opens up the possibility for persons and communities to come to full(er) realization (i.e., "salvation"). To speak of God's "reality" or "existence"—to speak of the validity or truth of the theistic perspective—is to maintain that the modes of life made possible when existence is oriented according to this perspective are full and genuine realizations of the actual potentialities of human nature—are in accord, that is, with "the way things are." In other words, life that comes to expression in love for and concern for other persons and in the creation of communities of justice and freedom, is grounded not merely in fantasy, but in *actuality*. Doubtless it is difficult or even impossible to establish scientifically the existence of vital cosmic forces which undergird and even in some sense "work toward" the establishment of human existence conceived in this way. Nonetheless, in the long course of the evolution of life on this planet, human forms eventually emerged; and in the course of human history, full self-consciousness, love, and freedom gradually came into view as possibilities for human life. To see these possibilities as ultimately normative for human existence is to hold them to be grounded in and expressive of "reality" in a way not true of

other radically different modes of life. To say that the
Christian God is "real" or "existent" symbolically expresses
this conviction that free and loving "persons in community"
have a substantial metaphysical foundation and that there are,
therefore, cosmic forces working toward this sort of
humanization. To the extent that there has been in fact a
genuine evolutionary movement through cosmic history
toward the production of our humanity, the ancient mythic
notions—that the will and purposes of God are working
through time toward the realization of humane ends—begin
to become intelligible in modern terms.

Here we are at one of the great divides that separate theistic
faith from unbelief. Faith lives from a belief, a confidence, that
there is indeed a cosmic and vital movement—grounded in
what is ultimately real—toward humaneness, that our being
conscious and purposive and thirsting for love and freedom is
no mere accident but is undergirded somehow in the very
nature of things. This is a momentous claim. For those
subscribing to it, our efforts toward the building of a more
humane world are not merely our own, but are themselves the
expression of deeper hidden forces working in nature and in
life. In striving for such a world, we are supported and
sustained and inspired by a dynamism in the foundations of
the universe. Such a faith can give a grounding and a
confidence in our struggles for a more just and humane world,
which may be the only antidote in these desperate times for an
ultimate and enervating despair.

It is this attention to and reliance on the ultimate cosmic
grounding of our humanity that is focused and concentrated in
belief in God. "God" is the personifying symbol of that cosmic
activity which has created our humanity and which continues
to press for its full realization. Such a personification has a
considerable advantage, for some purposes, over abstract
concepts—for example, "cosmic forces" or "foundation for our
humanity in the ultimate nature of things": The symbol "God"
is concrete and definite, a sharply focused image, and as such
it can readily become the central focus for devotion and
service. Sympathy and love and care and trust and loyalty are
evoked from us by other personal selves; it is to other persons

with whom we are in active interrelation that we can most fully
and unreservedly give ourselves. The image, then, of a divine
Person who has created us, who sustains us, who loves and
cares for us, and who is seeking our full realization (our
salvation), vividly and meaningfully presents to human
consciousness that to which we should be devoted if the
further realization of our human potential is to be achieved.
"God" is a symbol that gathers up into itself and focuses for us
all those cosmic forces that are working toward the fully
humane existence for which we long.

Human existence, conceived as defined essentially by love,
freedom, and creativity, would hardly have gained the
important foothold it has in consciousness and history, apart
from the mode of life and the confidence and insight
engendered by devotion to the God who loves and cares, who
is free and creative. This humanizing image has disciplined
and shaped the consciousness of those who held it before
themselves in devotion and adoration, helping to generate
norms for authentic human selfhood and community. The
concept of God—properly demythologized and rightly
constructed and defined—still has much to contribute toward
the proper focusing of our energies and affections upon the
realization of a more humane society. Some may find
sustenance and support for living and acting humanely and
effectively in the abstract concept of a "cosmic movement"
toward our fuller humanization; but for the larger part of
humanity, the symbol of a loving God will surely remain the
principal focus of devotion and affection and service, which
has truly humanizing effects. For this symbol represents with
great vividness and power the fact that we are created,
sustained, and fulfilled as human and humane, not by our
efforts alone, but from beyond ourselves, from resources in
the ultimate nature of things.

VI

The concept of God which I have been sketching out in this
essay requires and enables us to employ varying sorts of
representations, falling on a continuum that runs from highly

mythical and symbolical images—God as a personal being
who loves and cares—to the more abstract notion of the
cosmic ground of our humanity. Its strength resides precisely
in the contention that images and concepts along this entire
continuum must be used in constructing an adequate
contemporary concept of God; to concentrate on one
extremity at the expense of the other can result only in
misunderstanding and failure. If one emphasizes only the
mythic and anthropomorphic characterizations that make
God religiously attractive, one increasingly moves away from
plausible metaphysical talk about God as suggested by the
actual cosmic and evolutionary foundations of our humanity,
and the concept becomes empty; but conversely, if one
emphasizes abstract metaphysical concepts about a "cosmic
movement" toward, or "cosmic ground" of our humanity, to
the exclusion of more anthropomorphic and personalistic
imagery, the concept loses its religious power and its
attractiveness as a focus for devotion and orientation.
However difficult it may be to do so, the mythic and the
metaphysical dimensions of the image/concept of God must be
held together in order for that notion to function properly.

Contemporary efforts to construct an adequate conception
of God have met with great difficulty at this point, partly,
perhaps, because it has seemed important to interpret the
meaning of "God" in purely (or largely) immanent or
intramundane terms. This move brings the referent for our
God-talk very "close" to our experience and observation, so to
speak, thus clearly exposing the tension—almost the incoherence—generated in the idea by the juxtaposition of the mythic
and the metaphysical. This tension was not felt so strongly in
more traditional constructions of the concept of God, because
God as "creator" or "ground" of the world was posited as
utterly "transcendent" of it. God's "essence" or "nature" thus,
in principle, was inaccessible to human experience and
reflection, and the incoherence or lack of "fit" between the
more anthropomorphic language and the abstract characterizations could be regarded as somehow resolved in the
ultimate mystery of God's being. As long as it was believed
that divine "revelation" certified God to be both truly absolute

and truly humane—simultaneously metaphysically ultimate and our savior—this traditional solution did not raise unmanageable problems. God could function as the focus for worship and for the orientation of human life, and also as the ultimate point of reference in terms of which all else was understood and which relativizes all.

Constructing the idea of God with this emphasis on God's transcendence of and distinctness from the world has the undeniable strength of highlighting the respect in which human existence is ensconced in impenetrable Mystery and thus underlines in a valuable way the relativity and incompleteness and potential error of all our experience and knowledge. But it gains these advantages at the expense of positing an ultimate dualism between the world and God—between the context of our lives and (a) "being" which "exists" somehow "beyond" or "outside" that context.[13] Once it is recognized that all speech and ideas about such (a) being are grounded in our own imaginative powers and in our need to construct world-views—and that even claims about "God's revelation" from this "beyond" are thus our own construction—this method of interpreting the meaning of God-talk tends to lose plausibility. In earlier sections of this essay I have attempted to show why this is the case.

If one gives up the cosmological dualism that underlies and is implied by the notion of God's existence as (a) transcendent being, several alternative ways of dealing with the tension between the mythic and the metaphysical dimensions in the concept of God seem to be open. The first and simplest, of course, is to give up one or the other side of the concept. One may, for example, develop a largely mythic notion and make no real attempt to explain how this relates to the rest of our experience and knowledge, as was characteristic of much neo-orthodox theology. Or one may confine oneself to conceptions which are metaphysically plausible but have little or no religious power.

A second move appears to acknowledge that it is necessary to attend to both the mythic and the metaphysical dimensions of the concept of God but does not work through their interrelations and interdependence conceptually. Thus one may hold "God" to be simply the religious name for "what is," "the structure in things," "being-itself."[14] When one goes this route, there is no question about God's metaphysical absoluteness and reality, but there are many questions about whether God can or should be worshiped, whether God is "good," whether God can in any sense be said to "love" humankind or to be "working toward our salvation." Despite all the evil in human affairs and in the world and despite the evidently impersonal and uncaring character of the cosmic process, this view declares that "whatever is, is good," that the foundation of the world is loving and caring, and that it is steadily gifting its salvation to us. Here an overwhelming tension develops between the motifs of humaneness and absoluteness in the concept of God. Moreover, there seems to be no way to relieve this tension; it must be simply ignored—or it may be obliterated in a rhetorical *tour de force*.

In this paper I have attempted to hold together the mythic and the metaphysical dimensions in the concept of God and to show how they are related to each other. By identifying God with the mundane cosmic, vital, and historical powers which have given rise to our humanity and which undergird all our efforts to achieve a fully humane society, I have attempted to provide a metaphysically plausible referent for a religiously significant symbol. With this move the tension between the mythic and the metaphysical is partially reduced by qualifying God's "absoluteness": The referent of "God" is identified with those specific cosmic forces that undergird our distinctively human forms of being. The tension becomes further reduced by a significant qualification of God's "humaneness": God is interpreted as a symbol for vital and humanizing powers, rather than as "a personal being." By compromising each of these two motifs a bit, they are pulled together into a symbol/concept which can claim both metaphysical plausibility and some religious power.

Some may object that this conception results in a "finite God" and thus gives up any credibility as a monotheistic position. That is certainly one possible interpretation, though not the only one. With an evolutionary-historical cosmology, it is possible (though certainly not necessary) to hold that the

temporal movement—from a material order, through the
various stages of life, to the appearance of humanity and
historical forms of order—expresses the basic character of
Reality and is not simply one among many cosmic developments. With this view, speaking of God would signify not only
the fact that our humanity is cosmically grounded and
sustained, but God would symbolize a fundamental *telos* in
the universe toward the humane. The creation, sustenance,
and enhancement of our humanity, then, would be in some
significant sense an expression of the whole cosmic order and
not simply of one complex of cosmic powers among many. A
choice between such a monotheistic interpretation and a
finitistic one would depend, on the one hand, on the relative
plausibility of this conception of cosmic teleology, and on the
other, on the relative weight given to the religious need for a
single unified ultimate center of orientation and devotion for
human life.

It is, of course, not necessary in every situation in which
theological language is used to attempt to resolve the question
of the relationship between the mythic and the metaphysical
dimensions in the concept of God. In liturgical or homiletical
situations or in the performance of pastoral activities
intended, for example, to strengthen the church as a cultic
community devoted to Christ, it would hardly be appropriate
to raise such issues; and theological writing directed to such
uses could well skirt them also. Instead, using the mythic
mode which makes both the humaneness and the absoluteness of God so vivid and appealing, one might speak simply of
"God's self-revelation," "God's 'mighty acts' in history,"
"God's direct responses to personal prayers," "God's sending
forth 'his only begotten Son.' " Such language, however,
should be used with great care and discrimination, and if it is
to retain its meaning, one must be prepared to back it up with
a fuller theological interpretation. Sophisticated lay people
increasingly find such mythic modes of expression unintelligible or incredible, and this way of speaking has become a
serious stumbling block for many who otherwise desire to be
sincere and committed believers.

Mythic language is so commonplace in the life of the church

and in the work of leading theologians that it is often regarded
as the only appropriate language for theology; and it is
sometimes assumed that piety, if it is to be genuine, must take
this language in a literalistic reifying way. For any who hold
this position, the carefully qualified interpretation of the
concept of God which I have given in this essay may seem
unacceptable. To them it will appear that God's reality must
be much "harder" and "firmer" than is allowed by talk about a
"focus" for orientation and devotion provided by a world-view
or conceptual frame. I do not believe, however, that careful
examination of the work of leading theologians of the
twentieth century will uncover any who in fact take such a
"stronger" position. It is true that one may discover many loud
and confident *assertions* in the rhetoric of piety about God's
existence, nature, and activity, but when one examines the
grounds on which these are made, they inevitably turn out to
be subjective feelings of confidence and conviction ("faith"), in
combination with biblical and other traditional authorities—
that is, the appeal is precisely to what I have described here as
the Christian or theistic world-view or conceptual frame.
(Some might wish to take exception to this claim in behalf of
certain Whiteheadian theologians who do not seem so fully
bound to traditional theistic conceptual schemes, but I do not
think this exception really holds: In this case, the authoritative
conceptual framework is simply drawn largely from Whitehead instead.) What this paper represents is an attempt to
analyze more fully—and perhaps more candidly—just what
this grounding of theological work in a world-picture or
conceptual frame actually means, and to propose that theology
now should be done with much more direct and full
consciousness of this meaning.

The moves advocated in this paper should strengthen
theology and its credibility as an intellectual discipline. The
understanding that all thought and experience are decisively
shaped by the overall world-picture or conceptual frame
within which they occur is strongly confirmed on many sides
today. Epistemological studies, psychological studies of
perception and belief, studies in comparative religion and in
comparative linguistics, in the sociology of knowledge and in

the sociology of religions, and in the history of science—all
bear witness to this newer understanding, and theologians
must take its implications for their work seriously, if theology
is to remain a significant intellectual enterprise.

Notes

I wish to express my appreciation to Sheila Davaney for criticism that proved
very helpful in sharpening up certain issues in this paper.

1. Even in perception of ordinary objects the mind always employs
   "subsidiary" clues, feelings, and impulses in order to achieve "focal"
   awareness of the object or meaning with which it is concerned; such
   constructive activity is indispensable to the grasping of any meanings by
   the mind (see Michael Polanyi and Harry Prosch, *Meaning* [1975], esp.
   chs. 2, 4). With a reality or meaning, such as "God," which is not and
   cannot be directly perceived, the mind's construction of the image or
   concept out of subsidiary concepts and images—which it uses, but to
   which its attention is not at the moment directed—is (as I will argue
   hereafter) completely constitutive.

2. For detailed discussion of the significance of the narrative form of the
   Bible and the way in which this form itself contributed importantly to the
   notion of God and the kind of meaning that notion has had in much of
   Western history, together with an interpretation of the historical
   breakdown of that notion in modern times, see Hans Frei, *The Eclipse of
   Biblical Narrative* (1974).

3. In summarizing biblical and other traditional material, I use the male
   linguistic forms found there in reference to God. When representing my
   own position, I shall avoid sexist expressions.

4. For a fuller statement of the view that all theology is and always has been
   essentially imaginative construction, see my *Essay on Theological
   Method* (1975, rev. ed. 1979). All references are to the rev. ed.

5. The provisional or preliminary conception of "God" with which one
   begins an attempt at theological reconstruction may have very
   far-reaching consequences. In the present paper, I am following an
   "existential" approach to the analysis of God-talk rather than a
   "cosmological" approach (see my *Essay*, p. 69, n.8; pp. 70-71, n.18). That
   is, I am attempting to get at the meaning of the concept of God by
   exploring its use in concrete personal and communal life, rather than
   emphasizing (initially) its claims to universality and ultimacy. Beginning
   in this way, with the "subjective" rather than the "objective" pole of the
   concept, facilitates the interpretation of God's transcendence or
   absoluteness in a more immanental or this-worldly way—and thus,
   perhaps, in a way more plausible to modern consciousness than I was able
   to achieve in the *Essay*. But it does so at the cost of sacrificing something
   of God's absoluteness and universality, characteristics which in that essay
   were taken to be the marks that distinguish God from everything else in
   the world and even from the world itself (see esp. pp. 49-68).

6. H. R. Niebuhr's analysis of God as a "center of value" is the most suggestive I know in developing these themes. See *Radical Monotheism and Western Culture* (1960), esp. chs. 1, 2 and Suppl. Essays 2, 3.

7. If we were to define and characterize adequately that center, devotion to which and service of which will bring about human fulfillment and meaning, we would need answers to two major questions. (1) What is human "fulfillment," and how is that to be determined? Obviously there are many and various views on this issue, and procedures for deciding among them would have to be worked out. (2) Which among the many possible "objects of devotion" most fully contributes to, or facilitates, such fulfillment? This second would seem to be an empirical issue which cannot be given a precise answer apart from appropriate psychological, sociological, and other studies. In a fully articulated contemporary constructive theology, it would be necessary to devote considerable attention to each of these questions; but here I shall have to pass by most of the issues they raise.

8. See Dietrich Ritschl, *Memory and Hope* (1967).

9. It might be noted in passing that here I am setting myself firmly against Schleiermacher's view that the notion of God is grounded fundamentally and directly in a "feeling of absolute dependence." (Cf. *The Christian Faith* [1928], section 4.)

10. In any functional approach to the understanding of religion (such as the present one), it is especially important that this motif of God's otherness be emphasized. For it is a short step from uncovering the "function" that human practices, ideas, or institutions perform, to supposing that they can be understood exhaustively as simply the means or instruments for meeting certain human needs, achieving certain human objectives, fulfilling certain human wishes (cf. Marx, Nietzsche, Freud); and thus the trap of anthropocentrism remains unbroken. The "function," however, which the motif of God's radical transcendence and independence performs, is precisely to spring that trap, to provide a center for human endeavor and affection which is not simply a direct projection of human wishes and needs, to give us a center outside of and beyond ourselves. Orientation on such a center, which gives a kind of critical leverage in terms of which all that we are and do can be "independently" appraised and thus creatively transformed, may, of course, also be understood to be a human "need"—especially in view of the difficulties and even chaos into which our proclivities toward egocentrism and anthropocentrism inevitably draw us. But it is a need of quite a different order from ordinary human wishes and desires, for it is the "need" to break loose from enslavement to our wishes and desires, to break out of the tight little circle that is centered on us (and our "needs"), becoming open and significantly related to that which is beyond us. In this respect, the idea of God's transcendence has the highly dialectical function of reordering human life and insight so they will not be simply "functions of human needs" but will be open to all that lies beyond the human. It can give a vantage point from which our consciousness can be broken loose from the ideologies and rationalizations that always entrap us into pursuit of our own interests and into defence of our own values, ideals, and ideas—even when we are trying to be "scientific" and open to "how things are"—thus helping to provide us with a true disinterestedness in our search for truth

and with a critical leverage against even that which we now hold most dear. ("Whoever would save his life will lose it; and whoever loses his life for my sake and the gospel's will save it" [Mark 8:35].) It is highly desirable that contemporary reconstruction of the concept of God retain, in some significant and effective form, the motif of God's radical otherness or transcendence; without this, "God" would be little more than a projected fulfillment of our own wishes. (For a contemporary sociological discussion of the importance of the motif of transcendence or otherness if God-talk is to be truly effective in undergirding human identity and in performing other essential religious functions in modern society, see Hans Mol, *Identity and the Sacred* [1976], esp. ch. 6.)

11. For presentation of a conception of God which attempts to utilize Jesus as a "model" and which highlights points such as these, see my *Systematic Theology: A Historicist Perspective* (1968, rev. ed. 1978), pt. 1, esp. chs. 11–14. As the new preface to that work indicates, although I now regard its methodological foundations as quite unsatisfactory, the material development there of the concept of God (though it remains largely in the mythic mode) and of the human, still seems to me to be substantially correct.

12. Niebuhr's term. For his illuminating and powerful discussion contrasting radical monotheism with henotheism and polytheism, see *Monotheism*.

13. In my *Essay*, in which I followed the "cosmological" approach to the analysis of the concept of God (see n.5 above), a defining significance was given to the dualistic metaphor of creator/creation. The more or less traditional interpretation of God's transcendence or otherness that this metaphor fosters, helped to conceal, in that work, the tension between the mythic and metaphysical dimensions in the concept of God.

14. Cf., among others, Niebuhr, *Monotheism*, pp. 31-44, 122-26.

References

Frei, Hans
   1975. *The Eclipse of Biblical Narrative*. New Haven: Yale University Press.

Kaufman, Gordon D.
   (1968) 1978. *Systematic Theology: A Historicist Perspective*. Rev. ed. New York: Charles Scribner's Sons.

   (1975) 1979. *Essay On Theological Method*. Rev. ed. Missoula, Mont.: Scholars Press.

Mol, Hans
   1976. *Identity and the Sacred*. New York: Free Press.

Niebuhr, H. R.
   1960. *Radical Monotheism and Western Culture*. New York: Harper & Row.

Polanyi, Michael and Prosch, Harry
  1975. *Meaning*. Chicago: University of Chicago Press.
Ritschl, Dietrich
  1967. *Memory and Hope*. New York: Macmillan & Co.
Schleiermacher, Friedrich
  1928. *The Christian Faith*. Edinburgh: T. & T. Clark.

About William P. Alston's Essay

Analytical philosophy has been widely regarded (or disregarded) by believers as inherently atheistic. There is some reason for this suspicious view. Recently two conclusions—that talk about God is incoherent and that theology is therefore an impossible enterprise—have found acceptance among a number of such philosophers and even among some theologians. All that is left, on that view, is to regard the word "God" as an emotional expression, or as a symbol (of something other than God, of course), or as a mistaken attempt to refer to a nonreferent. In this essay, William Alston reexamines both the ancient problem of how we can talk about God and this modern philosophical conclusion that such talk is impossible. He does so, however, not from a standpoint suspicious of analytical philosophy, but from its own standpoint and exclusively by use of its methods. And he reaches an answer different from that of some other analysts.

This is even more interesting since Alston has made his reputation as a philosopher of language. His distinguished contributions to this field are widely respected; indeed, it is not generally known that his earliest contributions were to the philosophy of religion. As he returns to this field, Alston uses analytic and linguistic methods. Careful attention to the way terms function in actual use in a language yields insights into what had seemed to be intractable philosophical dilemmas. The analyses of key psychological concepts and terms become models here for meaningful literal talk about God. This makes the present

essay a stumbling block for theologians who have
assumed that literal talk of God must be, in the nature of
the case, impossible. (See, for example, Gordon
Kaufman's preceding contribution.)

Alston introduces his essay with a careful statement of
the issues he proposes to address and with definitions of
some of the terms he plans to employ. He then turns to
a more extensive analysis of the term "literal," to discuss
what we must mean when we say that a predicate term
applies literally to a subject.

The heart of the essay consists of an examination of
various philosophical theories as to the way we go about
ascribing personal predicates to a subject, and asks
whether the incorporeality of a proposed subject (God)
would bar such ascriptions. Alston argues that there are
no conceptual bars to the literal application of both action
predicates and mental predicates to God. The various
objections to ascribing such predicates to God are found,
upon careful examination, to be unconvincing. Thus, in
light of the most plausible theories of the way personal
predicates are ascribed to subjects, Alston finds that
literal speech about God cannot be ruled out on logical
or conceptual grounds. The reader will want to compare
this essay with Paul van Buren's, where it is radically
asserted that God must have a body.

Here Alston does not intend to show either that there
is a God or that such a God would be accurately
described in terms of the personal (i.e., action and
mental) predicates traditionally employed by theologians.
His goal is a much more limited conceptual exploration of
the logical status of talk about God. Nonetheless, if the
theologian's talk about an incorporeal, personal God is
not incoherent, the much proclaimed 'end of theology'
does not rest on as solid philosophical ground as is often
supposed. In fact, that proclamation will be found to have
rested on conceptual confusions.

6. Can We Speak Literally of God?

William P. Alston

I

In this essay we shall be concerned with only one stretch of talk about God, but a particularly central stretch—subject-predicate statements in which the subject-term is used to refer to God. I mean this to be limited to *statements* in a strict sense, utterances that are put forward with a "truth-claim." This is a crucial stretch of the territory, because any other talk that involves reference to God presupposes the truth of one or more *statements* about God. For example, if I ask God to give me courage, I am presupposing that God is the sort of being to whom requests can be sensibly addressed. Thus our more specific topic concerns whether terms can be literally predicated of God.

According to contemporary Protestant theologians of a liberal cast, it is almost an article of faith that this is impossible. Let us be somewhat more explicit than people like that generally are, as to just what is being denied. When someone says that we cannot speak literally of God, that person does not mean to deny us the capacity to form a subject-predicate sentence that contains a subject-term used to refer to God, making a literal use of the predicate term and uttering the sentence with the claim that the predicate is true of the subject. I could easily refute that denial here and now—"God has commanded us to love one another." I have just done it. But presumably it is not that sort of ability that is in question. It is rather a question as to whether any such truth-claim can succeed. What is being denied is that any predicate term, used literally, can be *truly applied* to God, or as we might say, that any predicate is *literally true* of God.

146

But even this is stronger than a charitable interpretation would require. Presumably, no one who thinks it possible to refer to God would deny that some negative predicates are literally true of God—for instance, incorporeal, immutable, or not-identical-with-Richard-Nixon. Nor would all extrinsic predicates be ruled out; it would be difficult to deny that 'thought of now by me' could be literally true of God. Now it is notoriously difficult to draw an exact line between positive and negative predicates; and the class of predicates I am calling "extrinsic" is hardly easier to demarcate. It is either very difficult or impossible to give a precise characterization of the class of predicates to which the deniers of literal talk should be addressing themselves. Here I shall confine myself to the following brief statement. The reason various predicates are obvious examples of "negative" or "extrinsic" predicates is that they do not "tell us anything" about the subject—about the nature or operations of the subject. Let us call predicates that do "tell us something" about such matters "intrinsic" predicates. We may then take it that an intelligent opponent of literal theological talk would be denying that any *intrinsic* predicate can be literally true of God. It will be noted that "intrinsic" predicates, as we have explained the term, include various *relational* predicates, such as "made the heavens and the earth" and "spoke to Moses."

Various reasons have been given for the impossibility of literal predication in theology. Among the most prominent have been the following.

1. Since God is an absolutely undifferentiated unity, and since all positive predications impute complexity to their subject, no such predications can be true of God. This line of thought is most characteristic of the mystical tradition, but something like it can be found in other philosophical theologies as well.
2. God is so "transcendent," so "wholly other," that no concepts we can form would apply to him.
3. The attempt to apply predicates literally to God inevitably leads to paradoxes.

It is the second reason that bulks largest in twentieth-century Protestant theology. It has taken several forms, one of the more fashionable being the position of Paul Tillich that (a) God is not *a* being but Being-Itself, since anything that is *a* being would not be an appropriate object of "ultimate concern"; and (b) only what is *a* being can be literally characterized.

In my opinion, all these arguments are radically insufficient to support the sweeping denial that *any* intrinsic predicate can be literally true of God. But this is not the place to go into that. Nor will I take up the cudgel for the other side on this issue, to argue that it must be possible for *some* intrinsic predicates or other to be literally true of God. Instead I will focus on a particularly important class of predicates—those I shall call "personalistic" (or, following Strawson, 'P-predicates')—and consider the more specific question, whether any P-predicates can be literally true of God. Or rather, as I shall make explicit shortly, I will consider one small part of this very large question. By "personalistic" predicates, I mean those that, as a group, apply to a being only if that being is a "personal agent"—an agent that carries out intentions, plans, or purposes in its actions, that acts in the light of knowledge or belief; a being whose actions express attitudes and are guided by standards and principles; a being capable of communicating with other such agents and entering into other forms of personal relations with them. It is hardly worth mentioning that the conception of God as a personal agent is deeply embedded in Christianity and in other theistic religions. Communication between God and man, verbal and otherwise, is at the heart of the Judaeo-Christian tradition. Equally fundamental is the thought of God as a being who lays down commands, injunctions, rules and regulations, and who monitors compliance or noncompliance; who created the world and directs it to the attainment of certain ends; who enters into convenants; who rewards and punishes; who loves and forgives; who acts in history and in the lives of men to carry out his purposes. The last few sentences indicate some of the kinds of P-predicates that have traditionally been applied to God.

II

Before coming to grips with this problem, we must provide some clarification of the central term 'literal.' To begin on a negative note, despite the frequent occurrence of phrases such as 'literal *meaning*' and 'literal *sense*,' I believe that such phrases constitute a confused, or at least a loose way of thinking about the subject. To get straight about the matter, we need to keep a firm hold on the distinction between *language* and *speech*. A (natural) language is an abstract system, a system of sound types or, in principle, types of other sorts of perceptible items. The systematicity involved is both "internal" and "external." The phonology, morphology, and syntax of a language reveal its internal system—the ways its elements can be combined to form larger units. The external system is revealed by the semantics of the language—the way units of language have the function of "representing" things in the world and features of the world.[1] A language serves as a means of communication; in fact, it is plausible to look on the entire complex structure as "being there" in order to make a language an effective device for communication. Speech, on the other hand, is the *use* of language in communication (using 'speech' in an extended sense, to cover written as well as oral communication). It is what we *do* in the course of exploiting a linguistic system for purposes of communication.

Now the fact that a given word or phrase has the meaning(s) or sense(s) that it has is a fact about the language; it is part of the semantic constitution of the language.[2] Thus it is a semantic fact about English that 'player' has among its meanings:

1. an idler;
2. one who plays some (specified) game;
3. a gambler;
4. an actor.[3]

It is partly the fact that a word *has* a certain meaning in a language that gives the word its usability for communication; this fact constitutes one of the linguistic resources we draw upon in saying what we have to say.

The term 'literal,' on the other hand, stands for a certain way of *using* words, phrases, and so on; it stands for a mode of *speech* rather than for a type of meaning or any other feature of *language*. As such, it stands in contrast with a family of *fiigurative* uses of terms—"figures of speech," as they are appropriately termed in the tradition—the most familiar of which is metaphor. Let us make explicit the difference between literal and metaphorical uses, restricting ourselves to uses of predicates in subject-predicate statements.

We may think of each meaning of a predicate term as "correlating" the term with some, possibly very complex, property.[4] Different theories of meaning provide differing accounts of the nature of this correlation. Thus the "ideational" theory of meaning, found for example in Locke's *Essay,* holds that a meaning of a predicate term correlates it with a certain property—P—*iff* (if and only if) the term functions as a sign of the *idea* of P in communication. Other theories provide other accounts. It will be convenient to speak of the predicate term as "signifying" or "standing for" the correlated property.

Now when I make a *literal* use of a predicate term (in one of its meanings) in a subject-predicate statement, I utter the sentence with the claim that the property signified by the predicate term is possessed by the subject (i.e., the referent of the subject term), or holds between the subjects, if the predicate is a relational one. Thus, if I make a literal use of 'player' in saying, "He's one of the players," I am claiming, let us say, that the person referred to has the property specified in the fourth definition listed above. And if my statement is true, if the person referred to really does have that property, we may say that 'player' is *literally true* of him in that sense—does *literally apply* to him in that sense.

But suppose I say, as Shakespeare has Macbeth say, "Life's . . . a poor player that struts and frets his hour upon the stage and then is heard no more." It is clear that life is not really an actor; nor, if we surveyed the other established meanings of 'player,' would we find any properties signified that are exemplified by life. Hence in uttering Macbeth's sentence, I will, if I am sensible, be using the term 'player' metaphorically rather than literally. Since figurative uses appear in this paper only as a foil for literal uses, I will not be able to embark on the complex task of characterizing the figures of speech. Suffice it to say that when I use a term metaphorically, I exploit some meaning the term has in the language, but not in the straightforward way that is involved in literal usage. Rather than claiming that the property signified by the predicate does apply to the subject(s), I do something more complex, more indirect. I first, so to speak, "present" the hearer with the sort of thing to which the term literally applies (call it an exemplar) and then suggest that the exemplar can be taken as a "model" of the subject(s); I suggest that by considering the exemplar, one will thereby be put in mind of certain features of the subject(s). In the example just given, the exemplar is an (insignificant) actor who plays his part in a stage production and then disappears from the view of the audience; the suggestion is that a human life is like that in some significant respect(s).[5]

The term 'literal' has picked up a number of adventitious associations in recent times. I think particularly of 'precise,' 'univocal,' 'specific,' 'empirical,' and 'ordinary.' However common the conflation, it is simply a confusion to suppose that 'literal,' in the historically distinctive sense just set out, implies any of the features just mentioned. Meanings that words have in a language can be more or less vague, open-textured, unspecific, and otherwise indeterminate. Hence I can be using words literally and still be speaking vaguely, ambiguously, or unspecifically. Again, I can be using my words just as literally when asking questions, cursing fate, or expressing rage, as when I am soberly asserting that the cat is on the mat. The conflation of 'literal' with 'empirical,' however, is more than a vulgar error; it reflects a conviction as to the conditions under which a word can acquire a meaning in the language. If this requires contact with "experience" in one or another of the ways spelled out in empiricist theories of meaning, then only terms with empirical meanings can be used literally, for only such terms *have* established senses. But that does not follow merely from the meaning of 'literal'; it also requires an empiricist theory of meaning, and it is by no means clear that any such theory is acceptable.

It might be thought that after the term 'literal' has been stripped of all these interesting connotations, the question as to whether we can speak literally of God has lost its importance. Not so. To demonstrate its importance, we merely need appeal to some highly plausible principles which connect meanings and concepts. It seems clear that I can attach a certain meaning to a predicate term only if I have a concept of the property signified by the term when used with that meaning; otherwise, how can I "get at" the property so as to signify it by that term? And on the other hand, if I do have a concept of that property, it could not be impossible for me to use a term to signify that property. And if a sufficient number of members of my linguistic community share that concept, it could not be, in principle, impossible for a term to signify that property in the language. Thus it is possible for a term in a certain language to signify a certain property, *iff* speakers of that language have or can have a concept of that property. Hence our language can contain terms that stand for intrinsic properties of God, *iff* we can form concepts of intrinsic properties of God. And since we can make true literal predications of God, *iff* our language contains terms that stand for properties exemplified by God, we may say, finally, that we can speak literally of God (in the relevant sense of true literal predication), *iff* we can form concepts of intrinsic divine properties. And whether this last is true is *obviously* an important issue—one that has been at the very center of metatheology from the beginning.

The question whether certain terms can be literally applied to God is often identified with the question whether those terms are literally true of God in senses they bear outside theology. Thus with respect to P-predicates, it is often supposed that God can be spoken of as literally having knowledge and intentions, as creating, commanding, and forgiving, only if those terms are literally true of God in the same senses as those in which they are literally true of human beings. The reason usually given for this supposition is that we first come to attach meaning to these terms by learning what it is for human beings to command, forgive, and so on, and that there is no other way we can proceed. We cannot begin by learning what it is for God to know, command, or forgive. Now, I do not want to contest this claim about the necessary order of language learning, though there is much to be said on both sides. I will confine myself to pointing out that even if this claim is granted, it does *not* follow that terms can be literally applied to God only in senses in which they also are true of human beings and other creatures. For the fact that we must begin with creatures is quite compatible with the supposition that at some later stage, terms take on special technical senses in theology. After all, that is what happens in science. There, too, it can be plausibly argued that we can learn theoretical terms in science only if we have already learned commonsense meanings of these and other terms—senses in which the terms are true of ordinary middle-sized objects. But even if that is true, it does not prevent such terms as 'force' and 'energy' from taking on new technical senses in the development of sophisticated theories. Why should not the same be true of theology?

Many will claim that the same cannot be true of theology, because the conditions that permit technical senses to emerge in science do not obtain in theology. For example, it may be claimed that theological systems do not have the kind of explanatory efficacy possessed by scientific theories. These are important questions, but they will have to be taken up in another paper. I can sidestep them for now, because I will restrict myself here to whether (some) P-predicates can be true of God in (some of) the senses in which they are true of human beings. The only qualification I make on that is that I shall consider a simple transformation of certain human action-predicates—"simple," in that the change does not involve any radical conceptual innovation: The revised action-predicates are fundamentally of the same sort as human action-predicates, though different in some details.

Whether certain predicates are literally true of God depends upon both parties to the transaction; it depends both upon what God is like and upon the content of the predicates. To carry out a proper discussion of the present issue, I would need to (a) present and defend an account of the nature of God, and (b) present and defend an analysis of such P-predicates as will be considered. That would put us in a position to make some well-grounded judgments as to whether such predicates could be literally true of God. Needless to say, I will not have time for all that; I would not have had time, even if I had cut the preliminary cackle and buckled down to the job straight away. Hence I must scale down my aspirations. Instead of trying to"tell it like it is" with God, I shall simply pick one commonly recognized attribute of God—incorporeality— which has been widely thought to rule out personal agency, and I shall consider whether it does so. My main reasons for focusing on incorporeality, rather than on simplicity, infinity, timelessness, or immutability, are that it, much more than the others, is widely accepted today as a divine attribute and that it has bulked large in some recent arguments against the literal applicability of P-predicates (Nielsen, 1971: ch. 6; Edwards, 1968). On the side of the predicates, I shall consider those types of analyses that are, in my judgment, the strongest contenders and ask what each of them implies as to literal applicability to an incorporeal being.[6]

Needless to say, this investigation is only a fragment of the total job. It is radically incomplete from both sides, and especially from the side of the divine nature. Even if we satisfy ourselves that personalistic terms can be literally true of an incorporeal being, that will by no means suffice to show that they are literally true of God. God is not just any old incorporeal being. There may well be other divine attributes that inhibit us from thinking literally of God as a personal agent—simplicity, infinity, immutability, and timelessness. But sufficient unto the day is the problem thereof.

III

P-predicates may be conveniently divided into mental or psychological predicates (M-predicates) and action predicates (A-predicates). M-predicates have to do with cognitions, feelings, emotions, attitudes, wants, thoughts, fantasies, and other internal psychological states, events, and processes.

A-predicates have to do with what, in a broad sense, an agent *does*. For reasons that will emerge in the course of the discussion, it will be best to begin with theories of M-predicates. I shall oscillate freely between speaking of the *meanings* of predicates and the *concepts* those predicates express by virtue of having those meanings.

The main divide in theories of M-predicates concerns whether they are properly defined in terms of their behavioral manifestations.[7] On the negative side of that issue is the view that was dominant from the seventeenth through the nineteenth centuries—what we may call the Private Paradigm (PP) view. According to this position, the meaning of an M-predicate—for example, 'feels depressed'—is given, for each person, by certain paradigms of feelings of depression within his own experience. By 'feels depressed,' I mean a state such as x, y, z, . . . , where these are clear cases of feeling depressed that I can remember having experienced. We might say that on this model an M-predicate acquires meaning through "inner ostension"; I attach meaning to the term by "associating" it with samples of the state it signifies. On the PP view, an M-predicate is not properly defined in terms of its invariable, normal, or typical behavioral manifestations. Even if it is in fact true that feelings of depression are typically manifested by droopy appearance, slowness of response, and lack of vigor, it is no part of the *meaning* of the term that these are the typical manifestations. Our *concept* of feeling depressed is such that it makes sense to think of a world in which feelings of depression typically manifest themselves in alert posture and vigorous reactions. Since the term simply designates certain feeling qualities, it is just a matter of fact that feelings of depression manifest themselves in the way they do.[8]

There are solid reasons for the PP view, especially for feeling and sensation terms. (1) If I have never felt depressed, then in an important sense, I do not understand the term, for I do not know *what it is like* to feel depressed; I simply do not have the concept of that sort of feeling. (2) My knowledge of my own feelings is quite independent of my knowledge of my behavior or demeanor; I do not have to watch myself in a mirror to know how I feel. Hence it seems that what I know when I know how I feel cannot consist in any behavioral manifestations or tendencies thereto. (3) It does seem an *intelligible* supposition that the kind of feeling we call a feeling of depression should be manifested in ways that are radically different from those that do in fact obtain. And the PP account allows for this.

However, the PP account has been under attack throughout this century. There are four main motives for this dissatisfaction. (1) If feeling depressed is not, by definition, typically manifested in certain ways, then how can I tell what other people are feeling, on the basis of their behavior and demeanor? For I can discover a correlation between a certain kind of feeling and certain kinds of behavior only in my own case; and how can I generalize from one case? Thus the PP view has been felt to rule out knowledge of the mental states of others. (2) How can you and I have any reason to suppose that we attach the same meaning to any M-predicate, if each of us learns the meaning from nonshareable paradigms? How can I tell whether my paradigms of feeling depressed are like your paradigms? Thus the PP view has been thought to sap our conviction that we share a public language for talking about the mind. (3) On the widely influential Verifiability Theory of Meaning, the meaning of a term is given by specifying the ways in which we can tell that it applies. Since we can tell whether M-predicates apply to others by observing their demeanor and behavior, the latter must enter into the meaning of the term. (4) Wittgenstein (1953: § 258-70) mounted a very influential attack on the possibility of attaching meaning to terms by private ostension.[9]

These arguments against PP support the idea that mental states are identified in terms of their typical manifestations in overt behavior and demeanor. We may use the term Logical Connectionism (LC) as a general term for views of this sort, on the ground that these views hold that there is a logical (conceptual) connection between a mental state and its manifestations.

The general concept of LC allows plenty of room for variation. The simplest form that is not wildly implausible is Logical Behaviorism (LB). LB may be formulated as the view

that an M-predicate signifies a set of behavioral dispositions—dispositions to behave in a certain way, given certain
conditions. [10] Thus a logical behaviorist would explain "S feels
depressed" in some such way as this: If someone makes a
suggestion to S, S will respond slowly and without
enthusiasm; if S is presented with something S usually likes, S
will not smile as S normally does in such situations, and so
on. [11] LB is not nearly as prominent now as a decade or so ago,
and in my opinion, there are excellent reasons for this. The
fatal difficulty is this. The response tendencies associated with
a particular case of a mental state will depend upon the total
psychological field of the moment—that is, the other mental
states present at the time. For example, whether a person who
feels depressed will react in a characteristically depressed way
depends upon whether he is sufficiently motivated to conceal
his condition. If he is, the typical manifestation may well not
be forthcoming. Thus any particular behavioral reaction
emerges from the total contemporary psychological field and
is not wholly determined by any one component thereof. This
consideration should inhibit us from attempting to identify
any particular M-concept with the concept of any particular
set of behavioral dispositions.

Under the impact of these considerations, more subtle
forms of LC have developed, for which we may use the
generic term, Functionalism. The general idea of Functionalism is that each M-concept is a concept of a certain
functional role in the psychological economy, in the
operation of the psyche. A major emphasis in this position
has been the functional character of M-concepts. In
attributing a certain belief, attitude, or feeling to S, we are
committing ourselves to the position that a certain function
is being carried out in S's psyche, or at least that S is
prepared to carry it out if the need arises. We are not
committing ourselves as to the physical (or spiritual)
structure or composition of whatever is performing this
function; our concept is neutral as to that. M-concepts, on
this position, are functional in essentially the same way as
the concept of a mousetrap. A mousetrap, by definition, is a
device for catching mice; the definition is neutral as to the

composition and structure of devices that perform this function. That is why it is possible to build a better mousetrap.[12]

To exploit this initial insight, the functionalist will have to find a way of specifying functional roles in the psyche. It is now generally assumed by functionalists that the basic function of the psyche as a whole is the production of overt behavior. That is why Functionalism counts as a form of LC. To understand the concept of belief is, at least in part, to understand the role of beliefs in the production of behavior. But "at least in part" is crucial; it is what enables Functionalism to escape the above objections to LB. Functionalism is thoroughly systemic. The vicissitudes of LB have taught it to avoid the supposition that each distinguishable mental state is related separately to overt behavior. It has thoroughly internalized the point that a given belief, attitude, or feeling gives rise to a certain distinctive mode of behavior only in conjunction with the rest of the contemporary psychological field. Therefore in specifying the function of an enthusiasm for Mozart, for example, in the production of behavior, we must specify the way that enthusiasm combines with each of various other combinations of factors to affect behavioral output. It also recognizes that intrapsychic functions enter into M-concepts. Our concept of the *belief that it is raining now* includes (a) the way this belief will combine with others to inferentially generate other beliefs, and (b) the way it will combine with an aversion to rainy weather, to produce dismay, as well as (c) the way it will combine with an aversion to getting wet, to produce the behavior of getting out one's umbrella. Clearly, a full functionalist specification of an M-concept would be an enormously complicated affair.[13]

With an eye to putting some flesh on this skeleton, consider this attempt by R.B. Brandt and Jaegwon Kim (1963) to formulate a functionalist analysis of the ordinary concept of *want*, conceived in a broad sense as any state in which the object of the "want" has what Lewin called positive valence for the subject.[14]

"X wants p" has the meaning it does for us because we believe roughly the following statements.

1. If, given that x had not been expecting p but now suddenly judged that p would be the case, x would feel joy, then x wants p.
2. If, given that x had been expecting p but then suddenly judged that p would not be the case, x would feel disappointment, then s wants p.
3. If daydreaming about p is pleasant to x, then x wants p.
4. If x wants p, then, under favorable conditions, if x judges that doing A will probably lead to p and that not doing A will probably lead to not p, x will feel some impulse to do A.
5. If x wants p, then, under favorable conditions, if x thinks some means M is a way of bringing p about, x will be more likely to notice an M than he would otherwise have been.
6. If x wants p, then, under favorable conditions, if p occurs, without the simultaneous occurrence of events x does not want, x will be pleased.

In terms of our general characterization of Functionalism, we can think of each of these lawlike generalizations as specifying a *function* performed by wants. Thus a "want" is the sort of state that (a) together with unexpected fulfillment, gives rise to feelings of joy; (b) renders daydreaming about its object pleasant; (c) is the crucial connection with behavior, though in this formulation it is quite indirect, coming through a connection with an "impulse" to perform a certain action.[15] This is in contrast to PP, which would view a want for p as a certain kind of introspectable state, event, or process with a distinctive "feel"—for instance, a sense of the attractiveness of p, or a felt urge to realize p.[16]

Now let us turn to the way these views bear upon the applicability of M-predicates to an incorporeal being. I believe it would be generally supposed that our two views have opposite consequences: that on a PP view, M-predicates could be applied to an incorporeal being, but not on an LC view. However, I will contest this received position to the extent of arguing that neither position presents any conceptual bar to the literal application of M-predicates.

First, a brief word about the bearing of the PP view before turning to the debate over LC, which is my main concern in this section. Presumably, an incorporeal subject, if there can be such a thing, could have states of consciousness with distinctive phenomenological qualities, just as well as we could. Hence terms that signify such states of consciousness would not be inapplicable in principle to such a being. But though I believe this is correct, I do not feel that it is of much significance for theology, and this for two reasons.

First, the PP account is most plausible with respect to feelings, sensations, and other M-states which clearly have a distinctive "feel." It is much less plausible with respect to "colorless" mental states such as beliefs, attitudes, thoughts, and intentions. We cannot hold an intention or a belief "before the mind" as we can a feeling of dismay, and thereby form a conception of "what it is like." But it is M-predicates of the colorless sort that are of most interest to theology. In thinking of God as a personal agent, we think of God as possessing (and using) knowledge, purpose, intention, and the like. Feelings and sensations either are not applicable to God at all, or they are of secondary importance. Theology quite properly avoids trying to figure out what it *feels* like to be God.

Second, suppose that one defends the applicability of M-predicates on a PP basis because he considers them inapplicable on an LC construal. This latter conviction would presumably be based on an argument similar to the one to be given shortly, to the effect that M-predicates, as analyzed in LC, are inapplicable to God because, as an incorporeal being, God is incapable of overt behavior. In that case, even if our theorist succeeds in showing that PP predicates can apply, he has won, at most, a Pyrrhic victory. To secure application of M-predicates at the price of abandoning the idea that God acts on or in the world is to doom the enterprise to irrelevance. Whatever may be the case with the gods of Aristotle and the Epicureans, the God of the Judaeo-Christian tradition is preeminently a God who *acts*, in history and in the lives of individuals, not to mention his creation and preservation of the world. Hence even if, on the PP view, M-predicates are applicable to an incorporeal being incapable of overt action, that does nothing to show that M-predicates are applicable to the Judaeo-Christian God.

Turning now to LC, let us look at a typical statement by one who is arguing from an LC position.

> What would it be like for an x to be just loving without doing anything or being capable of doing anything? . . . Surely 'to do something', 'to behave in a certain way', is to make—though this is not all that it is—certain bodily movement. . . . For it to make sense to speak of x's acting or failing to act, x must have a body. Thus if 'love' is to continue to mean anything at all near to what it normally means, it is meaningless to say that God loves mankind. Similar considerations apply to the other psychological predicates tied to the concept of God. (Nielsen, 1971:117; see also Edwards, 1968:45 ff.)

It will help us in evaluating this argument to set it out more carefully.

1. On LC, an M-concept is, at least in part, a concept of dispositions to overt behavior (perhaps through the mediation of other mental states).[17]
2. Overt behavior requires bodily movements of the agent.
3. An incorporeal being, lacking a body, cannot move its body.
4. An incorporeal being cannot engage in overt behavior.
5. A being that is, in principle, incapable of overt behavior, cannot have dispositions to overt behavior.
6. M-concepts are, in principle, inapplicable to an incorporeal being.

This argument is certainly on sound ground in claiming that, on LC, an M-predicate is applicable to S only if A-predicates are so applicable. Its Achilles' heel, I will claim, is statement number two, the thesis that overt behavior requires bodily movements of the agent. My attack on that thesis will occupy the next section. Let us take the upshot of this section to be that, on the most plausible account of the M-predicates that are of most interest to theology, God can literally know, purpose, and will, only if God can literally perform overt actions. This result nicely mirrors the fundamental place of divine agency in Judaeo-Christian theology.

Before embarking on the discussion of A-predicates, I want to make two points.

First, there are forms of LC that do rule out the application of M-predicates to an incorporeal being. I am thinking of those views that put certain kinds of restrictions on the input, or output, of the psyche. Some forms of LB, for example, require that the behavioral output be specified in terms of bodily movements of the agent, and the input in terms of stimulations of the agent's sense-receptors. Functionalist theories may also be so restricted. Clearly, M-predicates analyzed in this way are applicable only to beings capable of such inputs and outputs. But our concern in this paper is to determine whether any version of LC would allow the application of M-predicates to an incorporeal being.

Second, we should not suppose that the question of the applicability of A-predicates to an incorporeal being is prejudged by the fact that all cases of overt action with which we are most familiar involve bodily movements of the agent. A feature that is common to the familiar *denotata* of a term may not be reflected in the meaning of that term, even if this class of *denotata* is the one from which we learn the meaning of the term, and even if it contains the only *denotata* with which we are acquainted. It is doing small honor to human powers of conception to suppose that one must form one's concept of P in such a way as to be limited to the class of Ps from which the concept was learned. Surely we can think more abstractly and generically than that. Even though our concept of *animal* was formed solely from experience of land creatures, that concept might still be such that it contains only features that are equally applicable to fish. And even if that were not the case—even if the capacity to walk on legs is part of our concept of an animal—it may be that it can be easily extended to fish, merely by dropping out the feature just mentioned. The moral of the story is obvious. We cannot assume in advance that our concept of making, commending, or forgiving includes the concept of bodily movements of the maker, commander, or forgiver. And even if it does, this may be a relatively peripheral component which can be sheared off, leaving intact a distinctive conceptual core.

IV

Let us consider, then, whether it is conceptually possible for an incorporeal being to perform overt actions. Our entrée to that discussion will be a consideration of the vulnerable premise in the argument, the thesis that overt behavior requires bodily movements.

To understand the grounds for this thesis, we must introduce the notion of a *basic action*. Roughly speaking, a basic action is one that is performed *not* by or in (simultaneously) performing some other action. Thus if I sign my name, *that* is done by moving my hand in a certain way, so the action is not basic; but if moving my hand is *not* done *by* doing something else, it will count as a basic action. Just where to locate basic human actions is philosophically controversial. If contracting muscles in my hand is something I *do* (in the intended sense of "do") then it seems that I move my hand *by* contracting my muscles, and moving my hand will not count as a basic action. Again, if sending neural impulses to the muscles is something I *do*, then it seems that I contract the muscles *by* sending neural impulses to them, and so the contraction of muscles will not count as a basic action. Since I do not have time to go into this issue, I shall simply follow a widespread practice and assume that all overt human basic actions consist in the movements of certain parts of the body which ordinarily would be thought to be under "voluntary control," such as the hand.

It follows from our explanation of the term "basic action" that every nonbasic action is done *by* performing a basic action. If we are further correct in ruling that every human basic action consists in moving some part of one's body, then it follows that every human nonbasic action is built on, or presupposes, some bodily movement of the agent. The relationship differs in different cases: Sometimes the nonbasic action involves an effect of some bodily movement(s), as in the action of knocking over a vase; sometimes it involves the bodily movement's falling under a rule or convention of some kind, as in signaling a turn. But whatever the details, it follows from what has been laid down thus far that a human being cannot do anything overt without moving some part of the body. Either the action is basic, in which case it merely *consists* in moving some part of one's body; or it is not, in which case it is done *by* moving some part of one's body.

But granted that this is the way it is with human action, what does this have to do with A-*concepts?* As noted earlier, our concept of a Ø never includes all the characteristics that are in fact common to Øs we have experienced. So why should we suppose that our concepts of various human actions—making or commanding, for example—contain any reference to bodily movement?

Again it will be most useful to divide this question in accordance with the basic-nonbasic distinction. Our concepts of particular types of human basic actions certainly do involve specifications of bodily movements. This is because that is what such actions *are*. Their whole content is a certain kind of movement of a certain part of the body. That is what distinguishes one type of human basic action from another. Hence we cannot say what kind of basic action we are talking about without mentioning some bodily movement. Here we have no choice but to conceptualize each type of action in terms of some bodily movement—stretching, kicking, raising the arm, or whatever. Clearly, A-predicates such as these are not literally applicable to an incorporeal being. But this will be no loss to theology. I take it that none of us is tempted to think that it could be literally true that God stretches out his arm or activates his vocal organs.

The more relevant question concerns the status of such human nonbasic A-predicates as 'makes,' 'speaks,' 'commands,' 'forgives,' 'comforts,' and 'guides.' In saying of S that he commanded me to love my neighbor, am I thereby committing myself to the proposition that S moved some part of his body? Is bodily movement of the agent part of what is *meant* by commanding?

One point at least is clear. Nonbasic human A-concepts do

not, in general, carry any reference to particular types of
bodily movements. There is indeed wide variation in this
regard. At the specific end of the continuum, we have a
predicate such as 'kicks open the door,' which clearly requires
a certain kind of motion of a leg. But 'make a soufflé' and
'command' are more typical, in that the concept is clearly not
tied to any particular *kind* of underlying bodily movement. I
can issue a command orally or in writing. Indeed, in view of
the fact that no limit can be placed on what can be used as a
system of communication, any bodily movements whatever
could, with the appropriate background, subserve the issuing
of a command. In like manner, although there are normal or
typical ways of moving the body for making a soufflé, we
cannot suppose that these exhaust the possibilities. In this age
of electronic marvels, one could presumably make a soufflé by
pushing some buttons on a machine with one's toes.

Thus if any reference to bodily movement is included in
such A-concepts as making and commanding, it will have to be
quite unspecific. The most we could have would be along
these lines:

Making a soufflé—causing a soufflé to come into being by
  some movements of one's body.
Commanding—producing a command by some movements
  of one's body.[18]

But can we have even this much? Is it any part of the meaning
of these terms, in the sense in which they are applied to
human beings, that the external effects in question are
produced by movements of the agent's body? No doubt it is
completely obvious to all of us that human beings cannot bring
about such consequences except by moving their bodies. But
to repeat the point once more, it does not follow that this fact is
built into human A-concepts. Perhaps our *concept* of making a
soufflé is simply that of *bringing a soufflé into existence*, the
concept being neutral as to how this is done.

What we have here is one of the numerous difficulties in
distinguishing between what we mean by a term and what we
firmly believe to be true of the things to which the term

applies—in other words, distinguishing between analytic and synthetic truths. These persistent difficulties have been among the factors leading to widespread scepticism about the viability of such distinctions. But for our purpose we need not decide the issue. Let us yield to our opponent. If we can make our case even on the position most favorable to our opponent, we can ignore the outcome of this skirmish.

Let us suppose, then, that all human A-concepts do contain a bodily movement requirement. It clearly follows that no *human* A-concepts are applicable to an incorporeal being. But that by no means shows that *no* A-concepts are applicable. Why should we suppose that the A-concepts we apply to human beings exhaust the field? We must at least explore the possibility that we can form A-concepts that are (a) distinctively and recognizably *action* concepts and (b) do not require any bodily movements of the agent.

In order to do this we must bring out the distinctive features of A-concepts that make them concepts of *actions*. Thus far in discussing human A-concepts, we have only gone as far as the thesis that every human A-concept involves some reference to bodily movement. But that by no means suffices to make them concepts of *actions*. The concept of a heart beat or of a facial tic involves reference to bodily movements, but it is not a concept of an action. What else is required?

I will continue to use human A-concepts as my point of departure for the exploration of the general field, since that is where we get our general concept of action. And I will continue to concentrate on concepts of *basic* actions; since they are relatively simple, the crucial features of A-concepts stand out more clearly there.[19] To further focus the discussion, I shall restrict attention to *intentional* actions—those the agent "meant" to perform.[20]

Now, as intimated above, although every human basic action consists in moving some part of the body, not just any bodily movement constitutes a basic *action*. It is possible for my arm to move without my having *moved* it, as in automatic twitches and jerks. In order for it to be the case that I performed the basic action of raising my arm, some further condition must hold, over and above the fact that my arm rose.

Thus we can pose the crucial question about the constitution of human basic actions in the classic Wittgensteinian form: "What is left over if I subtract the fact that my arm goes up from the fact that I raise my arm?" (Wittgenstein, 1953: § 621). Or, putting it the other way round, what must be added to the fact that my arm goes up, to make it the case that I raise my arm?

The recent literature contains many attempts to answer this question, and I shall not have time for a survey. Leaving aside views that, in my opinion, do not survive critical scrutiny (such as the "ascriptive" view, according to which it is an action because we hold the agent responsible for it [Hart, 1949], and the view that "it all depends on context" [Melden, 1956, 1961]), we have two serious contenders.

1. *Psychological causation (explanation) view*. What distinguishes the action from the "mere" movement is the psychological background of the movement, what gives rise to it, or issues in it (Goldman, 1970:chs. 1–3; C. Taylor, 1964:chs. 2, 3; Shwayder, 1965: pt. 2; Alston, 1974:pt. 2).

2. *Agent causation view*. A bodily movement is an action *iff* it is caused in a certain special way—not by some other event or state, but by the agent itself (Chisholm, 1964*a*, 1964*b*, 1966; R. Taylor, 1963:ch. 4, 1966:chs. 1–9).

The psychological causation view exists in many forms, depending on just what pychological factors are specified and just what relation to the bodily movement is required. As for the former, popular candidates have been the will, volitions, intentions, and wants-and-beliefs. On the second score, it is generally required that the movement occur "because of" the psychological factor in question, but there has been considerable controversy over whether to regard the relation as "causal." So as to have a simple form of the view to work with, let us focus on the position that what makes a case of my arm's rising into a case of my raising my arm, is that my arm rose because it was in accordance with my dominant *intentions* at the moment that it should rise.

168

Is God GOD?

So the model of a basic action that we get from the human case is:

1. bodily movement
2. caused by _____.

To construct an analogous model for incorporeal action that will be an unmistakable model for *action*, we must (a) find a suitable replacement for bodily movements and (b) show that incorporeality is no bar to the satisfaction of a causal condition that will make the whole package into an *action*. It will prove best to begin with the second task.

The second (causal) condition for a human basic action is the controversial one. I shall proceed as I did with M-concepts—by considering, with respect to each of our contenders, whether that condition could be satisfied by an incorporeal being.

As for the agent causation view, the concept of agent causation may well be obscure, and it certainly runs violently counter to some deeply rooted contemporary prejudices, but at least it is clear that it does not carry a restriction to *corporeal* substances. The theory avoids, on principle, any specification of the internal machinery by which an agent exercises its causal efficacy—"on principle," since the whole thrust of the position is that when I bring about a bodily movement in performing a basic action, I am not bringing about that movement by initiating certain other events which, in turn, bring about the movement by "event causation." Rather, I directly bring about the bodily movement simply by exploiting my basic capacity to do so. Hence the agent causality interpretation is not restricted to substances possessing one kind of internal structure or equipment rather than another.

On the psychological explanation view, things are a bit more complicated. Let us recall that the "causal condition" on this view is that the bodily movement results from an intention, or the like. So our question divides into two parts. (1) Can an incorporeal being have intentions, or whatever kind of psychological cause is required by the particular version of the theory under discussion? (2) Can an intention cause whatever substitutes for bodily movement in incorporeal basic action? As for (2), it is difficult to discuss this without deciding what does play the role of bodily movement in incorporeal basic actions. Hence we will postpone this question until we specify that substitute.

That leaves us with the question as to whether an incorporeal being can have intentions and the like. And now we find ourselves in a curious position. For that is exactly the question we were asking in the previous section on M-concepts. The conclusion we reached there, on an LC position, was that these concepts are applicable to a subject only if A-concepts are applicable. And now we see that, on the psychological explanation view, A-concepts are applicable to S only if M-concepts are applicable. Where does that leave us? We obviously are in some kind of circle. But is it the vicious circle of chasing our own tail, or a virtuous circle of the sort in which the heavenly bodies were once deemed to move?

Here it is crucial to remember the task we set out to accomplish. If we were trying to *prove* that M and A-concepts *are* applicable to an incorporeal being, we would have reached an impasse. For since each application depends on the other as a necessary condition, we would not have established either, unless we had some independent argument for the applicability of one or the other. But in fact, we set ourselves a more modest goal—to determine whether the incorporeality of a being is sufficient ground for *denying* the applicability of such concepts. We are considering whether incorporeality renders their applicability impossible. And from that standpoint, the circle is virtuous. The reciprocity we have uncovered provides no reason for *denying* the applicability of either sort of concept. Psychological concepts are applicable only if action concepts are applicable, and vice versa. As far as that consideration goes, it is quite possible that both kinds are applicable. This circle leaves standing the *possibility* that an incorporeal being is such that actions and intentions fit smoothly into the economy of its operations.

Let us now return to the first condition of human basic action concepts, to the problem of finding something that could play the same role for incorporeal basic actions that bodily movements play for corporeal basic actions. I believe that the entrée to this question is an appreciation of the difference between the general concept of a basic action and specific concepts of particular human basic actions. Although concepts of the latter sort contain concepts of particular types of bodily movements, this is not because it is required by the general concept of a basic action. That general concept, as we set it out initially, is simply the concept of an action that is not performed *by* or *in* (simultaneously) performing some other action. This general concept is quite neutral as to what kinds of actions have that status for one or another type of agent. It is just a fact about human beings (*not* a general constraint on action or basic action) that only movements of certain parts of their bodies are under their direct voluntary control and that anything else they bring off, they must accomplish *by* moving their bodies in certain ways. If *I* am to knock over a vase or make a soufflé or communicate with someone, I must do so by moving my hands, legs, vocal organs, or whatever. But that is only because of my limitations. We can conceive of agents, corporeal or otherwise, such that things other than their bodies (if any) are under their direct voluntary control. Some agents might be such that they could knock over a vase or bring a soufflé into being without doing something else in order to do so.[21]

What these consideratons suggest is that it is conceptually possible for any change whatsoever to be the core of a basic action. Movements of an agent's body are only what we happen to be restricted to in the human case. Just what changes are within the basic-action repertoire of a given incorporeal agent would depend upon the nature of that agent. But the main point is that since such changes are not necessarily restricted to bodily movements of the agent, a subject's bodilessness is no conceptual bar to the performance of basic actions by that subject.

I believe that the case in which we are particularly interested, divine action, can be thought of along the lines of the preceding discussion. Of course, one can think of God as creating light by saying to himself, "Let there be light," or as parting the sea of reeds by saying to himself, "Let the sea of reeds be parted." In that case the basic actions would be mental actions. But what the above discussion indicates is that we are not conceptually required to postulate this mental machinery. We could think just as well of the coming into being of light or of the parting of the sea of reeds as directly under God's voluntary control.

This further suggests that all God's actions might be basic actions. If any change whatsoever could conceivably be the core of a basic action, and if God is omnipotent, then clearly, God *could* exercise direct voluntary control over every change in the world which he influences by his activity. However I do not claim to have done more than exhibit this as a possibility. It is equally possible that God chooses to influence some situations *indirectly*. He might choose to lead or inspire Cyrus to free the Israelites, thus using Cyrus as an instrument to bring about that result. In that case, freeing the Israelites would be a nonbasic action. I am quite willing to leave the decision on this one up to God.[22]

Now let us just glance at the question I postponed— whether it is possible for intentions, and the like, to give rise directly to changes outside the agent's body (if any). I do not have much to say about this—it obviously is something outside our ordinary experience. But I can see nothing in our present understanding of the psyche and of causality that would show it to be impossible in principle. So, pending further insights into those matters, I am inclined to take a quasi-Humean line and say that what can cause what is "up for grabs." And of course, if it is an omnipotent deity that is in question, I suppose he could ordain that intentions can directly cause a parting of waters, provided this is a logical possibility.

Let me sum up these last two sections. Action concepts applicable to an incorporeal being can be constructed that would differ from human action-concepts (on the most plausible accounts of the latter) only by the substitution of other changes for bodily movements of the agent in basic action concepts. Hence there is no conceptual bar to the performance of *overt* actions by incorporeal agents and hence no conceptual bar, even on an LC position, to the application of M-predicates to incorporeal beings.

As indicated earlier, this paper constitutes but a fragment of a thoroughgoing discussion of the title question. Other fragments would go into the question as to whether timelessness, immutability, and other traditional attributes constitute a bar to the literal predication of one or another kind of predicate. And of course we would have to discuss whether God *is* timeless, immutable, and so on. Moreover, we would have to scrutinize the classical arguments for the denial that *any* intrinsic predicates can be literally predicated of God. But perhaps even this fragment has sufficed to show that the prospects for speaking literally about God are not as dim as is often supposed by contemporary thinkers.

Notes

1. This is a very crude way to characterize semantics, but it will have to do for now. There is no general agreement on what an adequate semantics would look like.
2. We shall not distinguish between *meaning* and *sense*.
3. *Webster's New Collegiate Dictionary*, s.v. I am far from claiming that this is the best or most adequate way to specify these meanings. Indeed, in the present state of the art, the most adequate way to specify meanings is far from clear. But it does seem clear that 'player' does have the four meanings thus specified, however lamely and haltingly, and that its having these four meanings is (a small) part of what makes the English language what it is at this stage of its history.
4. I would want this supposition to be compatible with the fact that most or all predicate terms have meanings that are vague, have "open texture," or suffer from indeterminacy in other ways. This means that an adequate formulation would have to be considerably more complicated than the one given here.
5. "Metaphor" is a topic of infinite subtlety and complexity; the above formulation barely scratches the surface, and besides, is highly controversial. But it will have to suffice for present purposes.
6. The question as to whether P-predicates could be applied to an incorporeal being presupposes that we can form a coherent notion of an incorporeal substance or concrete subject of attributes. This presupposition has often been denied on the grounds that it is, in principle, impossible to identify, reidentify (through time), or individuate such a being (Penelhum, 1970:ch. 6; Flew, 1966:ch. 2; Shoemaker, 1963:chs. 4, 5). If arguments like this were successful, as I believe they are not, our

problem would not arise. Unfortunately, I will not have time to go into the issue.

7. Note that the issue here is the content (character, correct analysis) of psychological *predicates* or *concepts*, not the *nature* of the human psyche or the *nature* of human thought, intention, perception, or emotion. Obviously, the divine psyche, if there be such, is radically different in nature from the human psyche. The only question is whether any psychological *concepts* apply to both. Hence our specific interest is in what we are *saying* about a human being when we say of that person that he or she is thinking or perceiving, having certian intentions, attitudes, or whatever. Therefore the classification to follow is *not* a classification of theories of the nature of the human mind—dualism, materialism, epiphenomenalism, etc.

8. The PP view was presupposed by the great seventeenth- and eighteenth-century philosophers, Descartes, Spinoza, Locke, Leibniz, Berkeley, Hume, and Reid. It frequently surfaces as an explicit dogma in book 2 of Locke's *Essay Concerning Human Understanding,* throughout Hume's *Treatise of Human Nature,* and in essay 1 of Reid's *Essays on the Intellectual Powers of Man.*

9. In briefly indicating the main arguments for and against the PP view, I am merely trying to convey some sense of why different positions have seemed plausible. No endorsement of any particular argument is intended.

10. For an important statement of LB, see Carnap (1931). Ryle(1949) is an influential work that is often regarded as a form of LB.

11. In this quick survey, I am ignoring many complexities. For example, the most plausible LB account of feeling depressed would involve some "categorical" overt manifestations, such as "looking droopy," as well as response tendencies like those cited in the text.

    I also am forced to omit any consideration of the relation of LB to behaviorism in psychology. It is a complicated story. Behaviorism in psychology is characterized most generally by the intention of "doing psychology" in terms of publicly observable variables like overt behavior and physical stimulation of the organism. The analysis of mental terms into stimulus-response dispositions would be one way of accomplishing this; and some behaviorists such as E. C. Tolman have explicitly adopted LB(Tolman, 1936). Other behaviorists, most notably B.F. Skinner, have disavowed any interest in traditional M-predicates and so have no interest in LB(Skinner, 1958).

12. I am indebted to Jerry Fodor (1968:115-16) for this felicitous analogy.

13. The functionalist is not committed to holding that all functional relations in which a given mental state in fact stands will enter into our ordinary concept of that state. Picking out those that do, admittedly is a tricky job; but that kind of difficulty is by no means restricted to Functionalism.

14. I am following Brandt and Kim in taking Functionalism, as well as the other views canvased, to be an account of the ordinary meanings of M-predicates. Some theorists present it as a proposal for developing psychological concepts for scientific purposes, or as an account of the *nature* of mental states.

15. Various forms of Functionalism display special features not mentioned in

this brief survey. Cybernetic analogies are prominent in many versions (Putnam, 1975, vol. 2, essays 18-21; Dennett, 1969). Psychological functions are thought of on the model of the machine table of a computer. Others, like the Brandt and Kim account of wants, start from the way in which theoretical terms get their meaning from the ways in which they figure in the lawlike generalizations of a theory (Armstrong, 1968; Harman, 1973:chs. 3, 4).

16. It may be doubted that the term 'want' is a serious candidate for theological predication. Indeed it would not be, if the term were being used in a narrow sense that implied felt craving or lack or need. But I, along with many philosophers, mean to be using it in the broad sense just indicated. (Perhaps this is broader than any ordinary sense, but at least it is a broadening along the lines we find in ordinary senses.) To indicate how the term so conceived might be applied to God, Aquinas uses the term 'appetition' more or less in the way Brandt and Kim explain 'want'; *will* for Aquinas is "intellectual appetition," and he applies the term 'will' to God.

17. Let us define "overt" behavior as action that essentially involves some occurrence outside the present consciousness of the agent. This will exclude, e.g., "mental" actions such as focusing one's attention on something or resolving to get out of bed. The kinds of actions that are crucial to the Judaeo-Christian concept of God—creating the world, issuing commands, and guiding and comforting individuals—count as overt actions on this definition.

18. These formulations raise numerous questions that are not directly relevant to our concerns in this paper, e.g., in what way we are thinking of "a command" so that it might be "produced" by an agent. I should note, however, that the causation involved is not restricted to direct causation; intermediaries are allowed.

19. There is another reason for this procedure. Since nonbasic actions presuppose basic actions, and not vice versa, there could conceivably be only basic actions, but it is not possible that there should be only nonbasic actions. We shall see that it is a live possibility that all God's actions are basic.

20. Again, the basic (not as obvious) point is that intentional actions are conceptually more basic. Although I cannot defend this position here, it seems that the analysis of action concepts is best set out by beginning with intentional actions and then defining unintentional actions as a certain derivation from that, rather than beginning by analyzing a neutral concept and then explaining *intentional* and *unintentional* as different modifications of that. On this preferred approach it turns out that all basic actions are intentional (See Goldman, 1970:ch. 3).

21. Be careful to envisage this situation just as I have described it. The agent knocks over the vase not by doing anything else—even anything mental. Telekinesis often is thought of as an agent saying to himself something like "Let the vase be knocked over," and *this* causes the vase to fall over. But this does not make knocking over the vase a basic action. It is still knocking over the vase *by* doing something else—albeit something mental rather than physical. In order for knocking over a vase to be a basic action, it would have to be just as immediate as is my raising my arm

in the normal case, where I do this not by saying to myself "Let the arm rise," whereupon it rises, but where I just raise the arm intentionally.

22. It might be contended that if the physical universe, or any part thereof, is under God's direct voluntary control, this implies that the world is the body of God, which in turn implies that God is not an incorporeal being; so that our case for incorporeal basic action fails. That is, the claim would be that in order to ascribe basic actions to S, we have to pay the price of construing the changes in question as movements of S's body. This claim could be supported by arguing that a sufficient condition for something to be part of my body is that it be under my direct voluntary control. (Obviously this is not a necessary condition; that would exclude, e.g., the liver.) So if the physical universe is under God's direct voluntary control, it is his body. Against this, I would argue that we have many different ways of picking out the body of a human being. In addition to the one mentioned, my body is distinctive in that it is the perspective from which I perceive the world; it provides the immediate causal conditions of my consciousness; and it constitutes the phenomenological locus of my "bodily sensations." Since we have multiple criteria, we have room to maneuver. Hence, holding the other criteria constant, we can envisage a state of affairs in which something *other than my body*, e.g., my wristwatch, is under my direct voluntary control. Thus I would deny that my position requires God to have a body.

References

Alston, William P.
1974. "Conceptual Prolegomena to a Psychological Theory of Intentional Action." *Philosophy of Psychology*. Ed. S. C. Brown. London: Macmillan.

Armstrong, D. M.
1968. *A Materialist Theory of the Mind*. New York: Humanities Press.

Brandt, R. B. and Kim, J.
1963. "Wants as Explanations of Actions." *Journal of Philosophy* 60:425-35.

Carnap, R.
(1932) 1959. ("Psychologie in physikalischer Sprache." *Erkenntnis*. Vol. 3) *Logical Positivism*. Trans. George Schick. Ed. A. J. Ayer. New York: Free Press.

Chisholm, R. M.
1964a. *Human Freedom and the Self*. Lawrence, Kan.: University of Kansas Press.
1964b. "The Descriptive Element in the Concept of 'Action.'" *Journal of Philosophy* 61:613-24.

1969. "Freedom and Action." *Freedom and Determinism*. Ed. K. Lehrer. New York: Random House.

Dennett, D. C.
1969. *Content and Consciousness*. New York: Humanities Press.

Edwards, Paul.
1968. "Difficulties in the Idea of God." *The Idea of God*. Ed. E. H. Madden, R. Handy, and M. Farber. Springfield, Ill.: Charles Thomas.

Flew, Antony
1966. *God and Philosophy*. London: Hutchinson.

Fodor, J. A.
1968. *Psychological Explanation*. New York: Random House.

Goldman, A. I.
1970. *A Theory of Human Action*. Englewood Cliffs, N.J.: Prentice-Hall.

Harman, Gilbert.
1973. *Thought*. Princeton, N.J.: Princeton University Press.

Hart, H.L.A.
1949. "The Ascription of Responsibility and Rights." *Proceedings of the Aristotlean Society* 69:171-94.

Melden, A. I.
1956. "Action." *Philosophical Review* 61:529-41.
1961. *Free Action*. New York: Humanities Press.

Nielsen, Kai.
1971. *Contemporary Critiques of Religion*. London: Macmillan.

Penelhum, Terence.
1970. *Survival and Disembodied Existence*. New York: Humanities Press.

Putnam, Hilary.
1975. *Mind, Language and Reality*. Cambridge, Mass.: Cambridge University Press.

Ryle, Gilbert.
1949. *The Concept of Mind*. London: Hutchinson.

Shoemaker, Sydney.
1963. *Self-Knowledge and Self-Identity*. Ithaca, N.Y.: Cornell University Press.

Shwayder, D. S.
1965. *The Stratification of Behavior*. New York: Humanities Press.

Skinner, B. F.
  1953. *Science and Human Behavior*. New York: Macmillan & Co.
Taylor, Charles
  1964. *The Explanation of Behavior*. New York: Humanities Press.
Taylor, Richard
  1963. *Metaphysics*. Englewood Cliffs, N.J.: Prentice-Hall.
  1966. *Action and Purpose*. Englewood Cliffs, N.J.: Prentice-Hall.
Tolman, E. C.
  1936. "Operational Behaviorism and Current Trends in Psychology." *Proceedings of the 25th Anniversary Celebration of the Inauguration of Graduate Studies*. Los Angeles: University of Southern California Press.
Wittgenstein, Ludwig
  1953. *Philosophical Investigations*. Trans. G.E.M. Anscombe. Oxford: Basil Blackwell.

III. GOD AND THE STORY

About
James Wm. McClendon, Jr.'s
Essay

James McClendon's essay sets itself the task of comparing and contrasting the God of the post-Enlightenment theologians with the concept of God as understood by the early Christian community (or in his words, "with the God of Jesus Christ"). McClendon takes this historical and comparative approach in an effort to remind us that meaningful theology arises only from within the context of a religious tradition that can serve as the theologian's starting point and ultimate judge.

The judgment on most contemporary theologians is harsh. Cut off from its foundations in the living Christian tradition by the Enlightenment and its presuppositions, contemporary theology too often tries to reconstruct the concept of God with woefully inadequate conceptual and spiritual materials and, not surprisingly, continues to rehash a sterile notion of God that is incapable of expressing the complexity and richness of the God that Jesus, Pascal, and undoubtedly many other Christians have encountered in lives of devotion and prayer.

The elegance with which McClendon writes should not lead the reader to overlook the tightly knit argument he presents for doing theology in a new key. Well aware that employing the primitive Christian concept of God (the God of Jesus Christ) as a standard for judging the work of post-Enlightenment theologians raises some thorny historical issues, McClendon directs a major part of his essay to the attempt to show that the picture of God held by the early church is not as 'unavailable' as some writers have supposed. Specifically, the biblical

witness, with its histories or stories of Israel, Jesus, Paul,
and the church, provides good testimony that the
primitive Christian understanding of God has a richness
and intricacy not reflected in contemporary versions of
Christian theology. Thus, employing the theme
"biography as theology," which served as the title for an
earlier book, McClendon argues that we can gain a fairly
sophisticated insight into the theological ideas of the early
Christian community by reading and reflecting upon the
stories it found particularly valuable and which it
preserved in the Bible.

One discovers, through this sort of attention to the
biblical and even extrabiblical testimonies of the early
church, that three different, yet always interconnected
strands can be discerned in the understanding of God in
which that community shared. Since most post-
Enlightenment theology (including presumably some of
the examples found in this volume) is not complex
enough to take account of those various strands, such
theology is bound to be inadequate.

Although in part McClendon is echoing Pascal's
warnings about the dangers of divorcing reflections about
God from their religious roots, this essay seems especially
timely in an era such as ours, when the puzzling
phenomenon of the "alienated theologian" has become
the subject of a growing body of literature. Nonetheless,
the reader may wish to ask some of these questions.
(1) Given the acknowledged tensions between the three
strands that McClendon has discovered in the early
church's understanding of God, is there really convincing
evidence that any one person (e.g., Jesus or Paul) held
all of them simultaneously? If not, to whom does the
contemporary theologian owe the duty to represent all
these strands in the doctrine of God? (2) Why is the early
church's understanding of God *the* test of good Christian
theology? Is there a danger here of committing the
genetic fallacy (holding that the origin determines the
worth)? (3) Why is the deistic God described as personal?
Deism has often been criticized for its impersonal picture

of God. (4) After seemingly granting that the religion *of* Jesus (Jesus' mind) is not accessible to us, is McClendon justified in claiming that the religion *about* Jesus (primitive Christianity) can give us insights into the God of Jesus Christ? Yet even in asking these questions, we are reminded that to qualify as *Christian* theology, contemporary reconstructions of the concept of God need to place themselves within the ongoing religious tradition for which they propose to speak.

7. The God of the Theologians and the God of Jesus Christ

James Wm. McClendon, Jr.

God of Abraham, God of Isaac, God of Jacob,
not of the philosophers and scholars.
Certitude. Certitude. Feeling. Joy. Peace.
God of Jesus Christ.
— Blaise Pascal

Sometimes in the course of the human adventure it happens that a fundamental fork in the road is unforgettably marked by a single phrase. Such a phrase may be uttered at the end of the journey—a backward look that recalls the ways we saw and the way we went, says what was lost and gained. Or at the outset, so that we appreciate its aptness more now than we did at the time it was uttered. Our lines from Pascal's "Memorial" (1654) are of the latter sort. The gap between the God of Jesus Christ and the God of the philosophers that Pascal in his century saw opening, has widened into a silent, uncrossed ocean, a sterile sea separating continents no longer joined. Philosophy in the period now ending has signaled the drift of culture by maintaining massive indifference to God. Attempts to pluck some remaining lines of connection from this indifference, however pious the intent, are at best pathetic. There has been in our time no "God of the philosophers."

So the tepid task of investigating the concept of God in the light of philosophy has gone by default to the theologians. And so has the accusation fallen upon theologians that they are investigating the irrelevant—raising questions remote from the passion of the God of Jesus Christ. This shift in target, if ironic, undoubtedly is exhilarating. Not only has it afforded each successive generation of theologians opportunity, when moved by an awareness of God not found in the theology of their elders, to quote the psalmist: "I know more than all my teachers"; it also has opened once again the hope that if old theology had nothing helpful to say about God, perhaps God himself was about to speak. Pascal, who was also a philosopher, said that the God who laid hold on him was not the God of the philosophers. Was that not after all a hopeful word?

Still, we had best not be cocky. Not every king who rides past naïve children is in fact naked. Perhaps the abstruse questions of the theologians (questions investigated, by the way, in other essays in this volume)—Is God a person? Can God be named? Has God a body? Is God the subject or object of experience? and the like—have a point, even if that point sometimes be lost in the dry fury of theological debate. Our resolve should be not to foretell the outcome of our questioning, but to look and see.

One more clue from Blaise Pascal may prove valuable. Those who gathered up his possessions after his untimely death found not one but two unknown 'documents' of immense importance. One was the memorandum we call the "Memorial"— it seems to be a brief description of a single evening in Pascal's life, with the precise date and hours being noted. There follows, on a separate line, the word FIRE, with a corona penned around it. The next words seem to be the record of an intense mystical experience. While the paper was found sewn into Pascal's coat lining, so that, as my teacher Emile Cailliet used to say, Pascal could have felt it rustling there and so been tangibly reminded of his great night, there is no evidence that he intended to share it with anyone else.

The other 'document' was a heap of notes on assorted bits of paper, piled into a drawer. There is considerable evidence that Pascal intended to use these notes to compose, according to a structure he already had in mind, what would have become a great new apology or defense of the Christian religion. These notes were published posthumously as "thoughts"—the *Pensées* (1662)—but that aphoristic form certainly was not all that Pascal had intended for them.

For us the interesting fact is this: In the public document,

the appeal to evidences for Christian belief is not an appeal to
inner experience at all. The "apology" (*Pensées*) does not draw
on the "Memorial" and its "certitude" of feeling. It is as if
Pascal the scientist, richly equipped with inner experience,
did not regard that as a *public* experiential ground of belief at
all. Instead, his argument for belief in the "God of Abraham" is
finally an appeal to history: Consider the Jews.

> But, in thus considering this changeable and singular variety of
> morals and beliefs at different times, I find in one corner of the
> world a peculiar people, separated from all other peoples on
> earth, the most ancient of all, and whose histories are earlier
> by many generations than the most ancient which we
> possess. . . .
> I first see that they are a people wholly composed of
> brethren, and whereas all others are formed by the assemblage
> of an infinity of families, this, though so wonderfully fruitful,
> has all sprung from one man alone, and, being thus all one
> flesh, and members one of another, they constitute a powerful
> state of one family. This is unique.
> This family, or people, is the most ancient within human
> knowledge, a fact which seems to me to inspire a peculiar
> veneration for it, especially in view of our present inquiry;
> since if God had from all time revealed Himself to men, it is to
> these we must turn for knowledge of the tradition.
> This people are not eminent solely by their antiquity, but
> are also singular by their duration, which has always continued
> from their origin till now. For whereas the nations of Greece
> and of Italy, of Lacedaemon, of Athens and of Rome, and
> others who came long after, have long since perished, these
> ever remain, and in spite of the endeavours of many powerful
> kings who have a hundred times tried to destroy them, as their
> historians testify, and as it is easy to conjecture from the
> natural order of things during so long a space of years, they
> have nevertheless been preserved (and this preservation has
> been foretold); and extending from the earliest times to the
> latest, their history comprehends in its duration all our
> histories which it preceded by a long time. (Pascal,
> 1662a:618-19)

The present survival of the Jewish people was not, for Pascal,
an embarrassment to be tolerated (as it has been for many

Christians). Even though in some ways he shared the anti-Jewishness of 'Christian' Europe, he yet saw Jewish survival as evidence, not to be gainsaid, of the faithfulness of God, evidence of God himself.

Pascal's intuition of the strategy of evangelism and apologetics in the modern world was indeed farsighted: Christian faith in God cannot be Christian; faith in God cannot be Christian faith; God cannot be the God Christians dread, delight in, and serve, unless that God, unless that faith, unless that service be rooted and grounded in a true story—unless it be historical. The kind of 'experience' to which, in the nature of the case, Christians *must* appeal, then, is not merely that inner experience illustrated by Pascal's "Memorial," but the outer, historical experience (*Erfahrung,* not *Erlebnis*) which is essentially public. This sort of experience may serve to tell us whether the God of the theologians is, or is other than the God of Jesus Christ; particularly so if the historic narrative to which we attend is that vital slice of Jewish history—the history, the story, of Jesus of Nazareth.

To speak of the history of Jesus of Nazareth, however, is to enter a briar patch of difficulties. Many of these difficulties are perfectly evident to the plain Christian who lives in the present: Can we have any sure knowledge of Jesus? Did he live? Was he at all like the one presented in the Gospels? Does not actual history tend to disconfirm the Christian picture of the Christ? If so, is not faith in that one dishonest (Harvey)? Or if not, does not faith at least hang precariously separate from whatever one could know or fairly believe about Jesus (Bultman)? Perhaps, given the difficulties, the theologians do well to lead us up into the thin, dry air of philosophic inquiry about God, rather than allow us to linger, breathing the miasmic atmosphere of Jesus-of-history research?

Perhaps. Still, as Pascal sensed, there are powerful theological motives within Christianity for entering these tangled jungles where our historic beginnings lie. These are the cautions one had best adopt, however. We will not expect to approach this history (or any history) without presuppositions. "Presuppositionless investigation" is by now a myth pretty well laid to rest, and the old quest for the Jesus of history was one of its particular casualties. Catholic Modernist George Tyrrell's sally, "The Christ that Harnack sees, looking back through nineteen centuries of Catholic darkness, is only the reflection of a Liberal Protestant face, seen at the bottom of a deep well" (Tyrrell, 1909: 49), nicely epitomizes the larger truth: We seldom find more than we know to seek. To be concrete, one Christian presupposition I would not discard is that the quest for Jesus is worthwhile; what we seek in Jesus Christ is preeminently valuable. Another presupposition I retain is the role of Scripture: In seeking through the text to find the Jesus who is not identical with the text—that is, in using the text to find the historical truth—as Christians, we may not ever just discard the text, kicking it aside once its ladder-work has been done. Yet these need not be corruptive presuppositions if we recall that the text is the context of the life we seek, its historical afterglow and beacon urging us on beyond itself to that preemptive life—to Jesus himself. And both these presuppositions are guarded by another: Our presuppositions themselves—though we *must* have *some*—may change; no one of them is timeless or incorrigible. They may challenge one another, may be challenged by 'the facts' and by rival presuppositions, may be reinterpreted, revised, even rejected in favor of better ones (McClendon and Smith, 1975:ch. 6).

The previous cautions were based upon very general, even philosophical considerations, drawn from the concepts of history and of human convictions themselves; the next is drawn from experience with the particular subject matter at hand. Christians (and perhaps others as well) are likely to be made uncomfortable by the authentic Jesus, insofar as we find him. In the late nineteenth century, this discomfort was indeed felt by virtue of a research more penetrating than that of Harnack: The picture of Jesus which then arose was not that of a liberal face; rather, the face found by Johannes Weiss and Albert Schweitzer, and acknowledged by Alfred Loisy and George Tyrrell, was of Jesus the eschatological freak, a God-obsessed figure who could by no means be allowed to preside over the fortunes of comfortably 'Christian' Europe. In other times, the discomfort has arisen in other ways, but the general experience has been that the Christian search for the one called Christ has not been comforting. Van Harvey, in *The Historian and the Believer* (1966:102-3), relates the story of a young theologian, forced by his inquiries about the Jesus of history to give up his faith. Harvey treats this as an illustration of the pathos of Christian faith, driven by its tendency to truthfulness to deny itself because of the contradictions it might encounter in history. This is not unfair, I suppose, but the story also illustrates a broader point: From the vision of the seer of Patmos to the most recent attempts to see Jesus as a Zealot revolutionary, what has been seen, however partially, has tended to upset, to dismay, to offend the seekers. In the words of Eduard Schweizer (1971), Jesus is always found to be "the man who fits no formula."

This brings up still another caution: To find out about Jesus, called Christ, is to be drawn into response to that which is found. As with a very few other persons in human history, the quest for Jesus is self-involving. I take this to be the central point of the so-called New Quest (Robinson, 1959). The involvement, to be sure, need not be faith; instead it may mean actually relinquishing the faith one supposed one had, having discovered that *that* faith, after all, is not worth living by. According to Mark's story, a young man called by Jesus to "come and follow me" went away with "gloom spread over his face, because he was very rich" (Mark 10:22 TEV). Today's theological reader may find that one of his or her "riches" is that very theological doctrine of God, so proudly attained, which is the subject of these essays. The abandonment of these treasures may be the real cost of encountering the actual Jesus. A happier outcome (though not *a priori* a likelier one) might be the transformation of our lives by the encounter; the Gospels include paradigm stories of such transformations as well as the sad story just told. One result of such a transformation might be a significant shift in the concept of God held by the inquirer—riches lost, but riches gained (cf. Mark 10:29-30).

What is the character of Jesus Christ that can govern Christian understanding of God? This is the present question, and (a final caution) we thereby see that our inquiry cannot be *merely*, What did Jesus teach about God? and far less, How did Jesus picture God to himself? It cannot be the latter, for

Jesus' mental pictures and inner thought processes are indeed inaccessible to us save as they issue in his known actions; nor can it be the former, for his teaching is distorted beyond recognition when it is separated from the course of his public mission. So, whatever it meant to Pascal, for us "the God of Jesus Christ" must mean God as he can be understood in light of that entire complex of first- and early second-century events which constituted the birth of Christianity: the ferment in first-century Judaism, with its sects and parties, its Zealots and its Baptist prophet; the appearance of the Master, his life mission and its denouement in Jerusalem, his resurrection and the expectations thereby created; but also the formation of the primitive Christian movement, its Way and its spreading power, its apostle Paul and his gospel, its shared life and its historic literature, gospel and epistle, acts and apocalypse—all seen, as Pascal understood, engrafted into a live and momentous Judaic stem.

Described in this way, the present problem becomes one of synopsis and condensation: To what characteristic features of the Christ movement must today's Christian doctrine of God necessarily attend? From a longer list, I select three such features (McClendon, 1978) centrally present in the historic person Jesus and amplified in the movement as disclosed in the New Testament: (a) *the appearance of eschatological transformation*—the centrality of the resurrection; (b) *the formation of a Way of life which, by its own nature, confronts a cross*—a shaping of community in this mode; (c) *the renewal of organic life in connection with these events*—the role of nature in primitive Christianity. From each of these and from all together grows a concept of God that demands its rights from the God of the theologians. In the next section I will further identify these three features.

II

1. A vast divide separates our present Western consciousness from the eschatological outlook of early Christians. This is not a function of modern science—the divide had already been crossed by the time of Augustine of Hippo (baptized

387). Augustine is near enough to the primitive Christian view
to retain many of its concepts and even more of its language:
With his Church he prays the Our Father, with its call for the
coming Kingdom and its dread of the imminent testing-time;
he still believes in a future general resurrection, the rewards
of heaven and the punishments of hell; he also sees the
incarnation of Christ as the decisive event in holy history. Yet
for him, the promised thousand-year reign of Christ has
become only the symbolic total duration of the church on
earth. His view of this duration and its spiritual significance,
unfolded in *City of God,* has abandoned the primitive idea of
the Kingdom in favor of a 'philosophy of history,' or as it might
better be called, a theology of history. Undismayed by the
barbarians' threat to the Roman Empire, Augustine maintains
a massive calm as he surveys the past and future glories of
God's purpose discernible in these events.

Yet to press just behind the age of Augustine is to enter a
different world. The fiery evidence is nicely summarized in as
dull a volume as J. N. D. Kelly's *Early Christian Doctrines*
(1958:ch. 17). Even through Kelly's monotone, we hear the
startling voice of early Christian eschatology with its pageant
of resurrections, second comings, millenia, judgments,
powers, demons. The spirit struggles against the letter.
Apologists strive manfully to impose their 'reason' on this rich
ferment—and often they fail. Origen 'spiritualizes,' Metho-
dius of Olympus (†311) argues about personal identity after
resurrection, Jerome switches radically in the year 394, from
his earlier Hellenism to a "crudely literalistic" view of the
resurrection of believers. One senses intellectual tragedy in
the ancient Christian eschatology. The attempt to force the
new wine of primitive Christianity into the thought-forms of
hellenistic paganism finally fails. For us, what matters is not
the inevitable failure, but the witness it provides to the
persistent survival of an earlier Christian mind-set.

And so we come retrospectively to the age of the New
Testament, to Didache and to the early-catholic General
Epistles, which sought in more communitarian, less intellectual ways to bottle the wine of the inrushing future: Prophets
are to be tested; the Hope is to be expressed in quiet

communal obedience. A little earlier we find the Gospels, displaying an eschatology fully embraced, if not fully understood. Remembered words of Jesus are turned over, reconsidered, sometimes reshaped in the interest of present application. 'Realized' hope strains against 'futurist' hope in a contest not fully resolved in any of our Gospels—so both these elements were recognized aspects of canonical Christianty. Most important of all, each Gospel attempts to contain the eschatological, not by linking it to hellenistic 'reason' or to a 'philosophy of history,' but by grounding it in a narrative—the true story of Israel, of Jesus, and of the church. So the new wine is poured into the elastic wineskin of that ongoing story.

Our retrospect reaches Paul, the apostle born, as he said, out of due time. Even if the thesis of Johannes Munck (1959) and Krister Stendahl (1976:vi) is somewhat one-sided, there remains the solid evidence they present: The figure of Paul, like that of Jesus, makes more historical sense when gathered around its eschatological motifs. The mission of Paul to the nations is not mere Christian expansionism; Paul is not the Alexander the Great of world religion. He sees himself rather as called to a role in salvation history. This unpleasing little Jew (so he saw himself) must witness to all nations of Gentiles; then and only then will the Kingdom come and all Israel be saved. His 'monomania' is (from our vantage point in time) ridiculous; but the motif, eschatology impinging upon the alien order of this present age, is at the very center of Christianity.

Whence come these ideas? Given all we now know of the rest of early Christianity, had there been no eschatological Jesus we should have had to invent him, but in fact, the historical evidence essentially supports the Weiss-Schweitzer thesis already mentioned. Almost a century of the most urgent and ambitious scholarship has not overturned the conclusion that behind the eschatological drive of early Christianity stands one unwavering figure of vast authority, carrying these eschatological convictions into life, even for followers not disposed to believe them or able to comprehend them. That figure can be only Jesus of Nazareth. Jesus breathed and lived eschatology; he *was* the eschaton; it was recognizing this in the

power of the resurrection that made Christians Christians
(I Cor. 15:1-11). But even here the retrospective is not ended,
for behind Jesus the Jew stand the still-elusive Jewish
apocalyptists, and behind them, the Hebrew prophets
themselves.

Now we ask, for theology's sake, What is to be made of these
facts, so central and yet so exotic? How shall our concept of
God accommodate thoroughgoing eschatology? Is there not a
real tension between the God of contemporary theology (what
Pascal calls the God of the *philosophers*) and any God who can
be the God of eschatological religion? To make the matter
concrete: Could the God of Paul Tillich be the God of
first-century Jehovah's witnesses? Dismiss that as caricature;
acknowledge that Jesus' eschatology (both the eschatology he
taught and the eschatology he lived out) is highly elusive—still
our question remains: How adequate is our sense of "God" to
this given foundation?

For the eschatology of Jesus Christ calls into question
fundamental assumptions of our Enlightenment minds. The
Enlightenment assumes that the future will be like the past,
though it sometimes puzzles over how it knows this (cf.
Hume); primitive Christianity knows the future *is no longer*
like the past, and it puzzles only over how to say what it knows.
The Enlightenment banishes God to a decent deistic distance
from humankind's earth; primitive Christianity awaits earth's
renewal (and heaven's renewal!) by the power of the Spirit
(Rom. 8:21; Rev. 21). How can one even coordinate a dispute
between the God of Enlightened theologians (and are they not
ourselves?) and *this* God?

Two features seem to me to demand treatment if our
theology in this regard is to be recast. First, the God of
Christian eschatology must be the Ground—not of being, but
. . . of adventure. The future will not be like the past. In their
way, process theologians seem to touch this point, but their
"adventures" (of ideas, mostly) seem too tame to fill the bill.
Yet at whatever level one grips it, the resurrection demands
and provides adventure: It demands adventurous metaphysics; it evokes venturesome theology; it invites a religion of
hope for what is about to be but is not yet; it provides an ethic

of novelty and heroism—much to lose, much to gain; it requires a politics of the unforeseen in human affairs—all these grounded in a God who is not confined by the past, but whose adventure joyfully opens toward our own.

And second, God in this light must be seen as the power of *transformation*. Transformation is not creation, at least not creation out of nothing; that aspect of divinity will be treated shortly in the third feature. Transformation is rather the re-creation of the created; it is that power by which, contrary to all expectation, what *is to be* appears out of that which is. The eschatological hope of primitive Christianity was a hope of transformation (Rom. 8:11 ff.); and so was the prophetic hope that dreamed of a new Israel and finally of a new earth (Isa. 40-66). But the foundation of such hopes, in the earth, in a people, in one's own life story, did not lie in observation and experience; this was no extrapolation from recurrent spring-time, no analogy drawn from seedtime and harvest. Rather, hope is grounded in the transformative character of God. At the burning bush when Moses demands the "name," the declared character of the deity that confronts him there, the answer comes, *"Ehyeh asher ehyeh"* (Exod. 3:14). The Platonizing West has translated this as, Ἐγώ εἰμι ὁ ὤν (70), "I am that I am"—God is timeless, intact, he who is. But Hebraists, noting the form of *ehyeh* to be imperfect and causative, suggest the translation, "I will be what I will be" (RSV margin), or more freely, "I will always be ahead of you; find Me as you follow the journey."

Our theological tradition, to be sure, has sensed this element of rebirth at Christianity's center, but it has tied it not to the nature of God, but to contingent human nature. We are sinners; therefore God must transform us. Schleiermacher more boldly defines Christianity as a religion of redemption (*Alles in derselben bezogen wird auf die durch Jesum von Nazareth vollbrachte Erlösung*[1835: § 11]); he then links this definition, following a sound instinct, to God's nature. But for Schleiermacher, the price is that God becomes the author of sin: God wills sin so that he can redeem us—*felix culpa* indeed! My alternative claim here is that transformation does not depend upon our prior sin; sin is more fitly relegated to the realm of contingency. Our hope is grounded rather in the Ground of adventure and transformation, the "I will be what I will be," whose nature is truly declared in the resurrection, and whose anastatic gift is life in the Spirit. As a contingent and for us inescapable fact, we have sinned, and so our knowledge of God's transformative gift must be redemptive, overcoming our sin in order to introduce us to the divine Adventure; but we have reason to believe that in a sin-free world, transformation and adventure still would be God's typical gifts.

2. Because it has been so neglected, I have devoted more space to the anastatic nature of God; I can speak now more briefly of two more familiar divine qualities. In exploring God's anastatic nature it has been appropriate to allude to God's involvement in narrative: He is not a timeless but a timely God. For us, God *is* history; this is epitomized in the Incarnate One, but it is present wherever God is seen as the Companion on Israel's long journey.

Again, it has already been appropriate to refer to God's social dimension. By his transformative power he takes up and maintains relations with his creature. Where the creature is simply nature, this relation is best discussed under the next heading, but where it is a human world, our Companion appears in personal, that is, social modes, reigning as our King, guiding as our Lawgiver, leading as our Father, nurturing as our Mother, conversing as our Friend. Where (as in fact) we the creature have rebelled, God's concern as Reconciler will dominate the face he turns to us; in our world, for us, the Incarnate One can be only the Crucified.

The Journey and the Companion: Once more we may need to be reminded that these are Jewish themes before they are Christian. There is nothing deeper in God than his purpose to draw his people into (redemptive) community with one another and with him. This is expressed by Karl Barth in the thesis that the covenant is the internal basis of creation (1958:§41), and it is expressed by my teacher Walter Thomas Conner (1877–1952) in the thesis that "creation is laid out on redemption lines."

So the biblical God (however it may be with the God of the

theologians) is a social God—One who participates in the practices of a society, promising and keeping promises, negotiating and conciliating, rewarding and punishing, electing in love (*ahavah*) and keeping the loving troth (*chesed*) with his elect people. But to share in community is to condescend (in that old word's old sense); ours is a God of weakness, of imperfection, of time's changes and history's vagaries; he enters fully into the life of *this* world (though selectively, not distributively) and thereby makes himself hostage to the world's worldliness. The career of Jesus of Nazareth is in Christian eyes the full and sufficient exemplar of these personal qualities; that Jesus Christ is God entails for us that God, the only God, is Christ Jesus.

3. There was yet another dimension of the experience of the first followers of Christ. They saw themselves involved with the cosmos, with what we would call the world of nature, and that involvement also reflected their sense of God confronting them.

It is a truism that Hebrew religion had come into its own only as the tribal Lord was acknowledged to be Lord of the land—the land of Israel, but also of all land. God was the Creator: Second Isaiah and Genesis 1–3 were theological achievements of immense significance. The meaning of this is not so generally recognized by recent theology: that God was a God of place as well as of time; of the earth in its earthiness as well as of history in its timeliness. This inference is resisted by those mid-century theologians who saw Jahweh only as *competitor* to the numina of springs and brooks and high places. But even competitors cannot be utterly unlike one another. And if the God of Israel finally is God of all the places—Numen, so to speak, of all the earth—that still is to be a God of place. To forget that this is so is to cultivate a sort of 'historicist' Kantian gnosticism.

Our great difficulty, however frankly we face those facts, will be in seeing that a God who presides over nature need not confront that nature only in the categories of a God who rules over (or fathers, or otherwise participates as a person with) a people. Creator does not *mean* Lord; the maker need not be the ruler. But the distinction, though real, is obscured, because so often the biblical writers did use the language of community in order to express their doctrine of creation—metaphors of society proclaiming the God of the land.

Often, but not always. Thus according to Acts, Paul, when he confronts Hellenic listeners (in ways that were suited to their capacities) with the claim of the God of Jesus Christ, allows himself to quote not only "we too are his children," but also "in him we live and move and exist" (17:28 TEV). And in Romans 1:19-20, he presents a 'natural theology' that would do credit to the eighteenth century. Is Paul merely accommodating, or are there deeper motives in Christianity and in Paul's Jewishness to authorize such utterance?

We might do well, in answer, to consult the wisdom literature within Paul's Bible—not only the traditional books of Job, Proverbs, Ecclesiastes, and perhaps Ruth, but also wisdom passages in the psalms, the prophets, and the Pentateuch. Here again the evidence is not unambiguous; a strong strain in these writings is based on community categories and sees God in interpersonal terms as the people's Ruler. Yet there is the other: a nature desacralized, a created order that is just *there*, and a 'wisdom' that is other than the wisdom of persons, with their hates and loves and social practices. "What has been is what will be, and what has been done is what will be done; and there is nothing new under the sun" (Eccl. 1:9). Yet these two realms—nature's wisdom and the good man's wisdom—are not antithetical; they fit well together (e.g., see Prov. 4:18-19).

Do not these considerations also give a clue to the theology of nature in Jesus' parables? In the parables, things just are what they are: Seed grows, rain falls, weak foundations crumble. There is a concern for theodicy here that is far different from the theodicy that invokes "what God is doing in history." In this theodicy in the world of the parables, things work out with the inexorable givenness of a Robinson Jeffers poem. God is there, not merely as the Power of tomorrow or as the sovereign Father, but as the wisdom of what is, the numen of the cosmos, the Creator of a world that in and of itself is good.

III

Where are we being led by these considerations? Our task was to compare or contrast the God of the theologians (that being by and large the concept of God also entertained in the churches) with the God of Jesus Christ—that is, the concept of God grasped in primitive Christianity and witnessed in Scripture. Some might object that, brief as our survey of the biblical God has been, the God of the theologians has received even shorter shrift. That is true, and we must make some amends in the present section; but by way of preparation let us summarize the results of the preceding one. Simply put, God, the object of worship, trust, and service of the early Christians and of Israel, is a God of great complexity. Here the complexity has been simplified, not elaborated, by the (apparently arbitrary) introduction of three strands of biblical thought—*the eschatological, the communal, the natural*—with corresponding facets of divinity observed in each strand. This is simplified, for within each strand, we have seen elements which strained against each other—future adventure against present transformation in the anastatic strand, for example, or law against gospel in the corporate-communal strand. And that tension may seem mild, compared to the tension between the strands. Can the anastatic God really be the Lord of corporate history? Can the Lord of somatic social structure be the Numen of nature and creation? And to complete the circle, can the Numen of nature and creation be the Ground of transformation and adventure? To some extent, these are historical questions about the beliefs and intentions of a historical, worshiping church; to some extent, though, they are conceptual questions which philosophical theology can address. In a word, here the God of the theologians ought to be produced.

No contemporary theologian has grasped these issues more clearly than has Jürgen Moltmann. Because of the intricacy with which the business of German academic theology is conducted, the details of Moltmann's work, even in translation, must seem somewhat obscure to American readers. However, the main outlines are clear. In *Theologie der Hoffung* (1965; English trans. 1967), Moltmann took up the eschatological character of the Christian message, presenting its import for a post-Marxian European Christian self-understanding. What must the church of the resurrection be and do in today's world? Commentators on this side of the Atlantic, who assumed that Moltmann's total focus was now to be eschatology, wrote of the "theology of hope," and it gained the status of a fad. Then in 1973 there appeared *Der gekreuzigte Gott*, translated as *The Crucified God* (1974). In the second book, Moltmann shows what he always intended (1974:5), bringing resurrection and cross, eschatology and communal history into constructive relation with one another. The resurrection is the resurrection of the crucified.

Seeing at least these two of our three strands, and seeing that in the end they *must* be considered together, Moltmann seems in good position to provide the help we need—to show us how, from the complexity of a biblical awareness of eschatology *and* of the crucified One, a concept of God at once complex and indivisible, a unity that is expressed in exactly this complexity, must appear. Regretfully, this hope is not fulfilled in *The Crucified God*. Moltmann instead believes that monotheism is the enemy of authentic Christianity (1974:215): Monotheism leads to imperial Islam; it leads to atheism (since it provides a 'God' who can be rejected); it is false to the New Testament. The only 'God' validated by the New Testament is an *event*, "the event of Golgotha, the event of the love of the Son and the grief of the Father from which the Spirit who opens up the future and creates life in fact derives" (1974:247).

Now we ought not be the prisoners of our own terminology; it may be that in Moltmann's terms, contrary though they are to our usage here (and to the trinitarianism of H. R. Niebuhr [1960]), there lie helpful suggestions above and beyond the 'Christian atheism' which Moltmann appears to espouse. But these hints are not developed. The hard question for Moltmann is, therefore, our own: How can the God of a theology of hope be also the crucified God—one God?

In considering this question, Scripture must be our touchstone, since it is in Scripture that the complexity itself is grounded. But the constant drive of the scriptural witness to God, in spite of all difficulties, is to retain the ancient Semitic vision of the divine unity. In our present Bible we first meet God as the creator. It is vital to remember that this was *not* the historic order of awareness. Israel's God 'began' as a communal deity, barely more than the god of a tribe. Therefore the theological reconstruction which saw this very God as also the beckoning Ground of the future (whose name is "I will be what I will be") and as Maker of heaven and earth (thereby displacing Babylonian mythic deities in the creation stories) was more than evolution and synthesis. This was revelation. The God of Abraham is the Creator is the Coming One. In terms of the present essay, the Holy Lord is the Cosmic Source is the Ground of Adventure. Or in terms of Christian trinitarianism, the Father, the Son, the Holy Spirit constitute one God.

To add that last line suggests that here we are addressing the same question that was addressed by the ancients in formulating trinitarian doctrine. But is this so? Our answer must be both yes and no. If we meant to ask, Did the problem of the divine unity and complexity arise for the ancient trinitarians as it does here for us? we must admit that it did not. In fact, there is no concise way to select any one problem that the trinitarian formulae, embracing as they do centuries of doctrinal struggle across the Mediterranean world, were meant to resolve. The beauty of the formulae, once evolved, was exactly their capacity to encompass social, political, metaphysical, and religious issues of great diversity, ensuring the catholicity of the Catholic faith.

But there is a parallel between what they achieved and what we must. Their task was to maintain the hard-won unity of the Christian godhead while simultaneously encountering and subsuming Hellenic and Roman thought. In short, the one God of Jesus Christ must remain the God of Christian experience in all its complexity, even as Christianity met and incorporated the language of Greek speculation. And that is not so different from our present task of theological reconstruction vis-à-vis the theology we have inherited (more from Pascal's "philosophers" than from Pascal or from our primitive biblical wellsprings).

I think, in other words, that it will not help much to identify, say, the Ground of transformation with the ancients' "Spirit," or nature's Numen with their "Father." The categories cross one another too much for that. At least we might note a couple of procedural principles which arose from their difficulties and apply them to our own. One, that the doctrine of the Trinity is "not about three of anything." It was not meant to correlate three entities, but to hold on to the complexity involved in the one God of Jesus Christ, "neither confounding the Persons nor dividing the Substance," as the medieval Quicunque Vult puts it. The other principle is that the complexity, though maintained, must not lead to compartmentalization in the understanding of God's operations. Here their motto was *Opera trinitatis ad extra indivisa sunt*—the works of the triune God toward what is outside God are indivisible. So they were not merely to say, "The Father creates, but the Son saves, whereas the Spirit guides." Rather, creation is the work of one God who is Father and Son and Spirit; the Father creates, but so does the Son, and the Spirit is *Creator Spiritus*. For us that must mean that there is but one God of Jesus Christ, whether we contemplate eschatology, or community, or the natural sphere—a point already expounded by Paul in Romans 8.

Yet when it involves not works *ad extra*, but God's own nature, we must follow the ancient trinitarians in attending to distinctions in order not to suppress actual complexity in God. A single illustration must suffice here: It is often asked in today's theology whether God is a person. (It is important to note well that today's sense of "person" is quite other than the ancient Latin *personae* of the Trinity.) Much is assumed to hang on that question: To the disputants on one side, personality in God seems to permit the unwarranted predication of human attributes to God; to those on the other, personality seems to be required by the very concept of God. A personal God can act, can will, can care; an impersonal one, on the other hand, frees theology from such difficult problems as the imputation of evil to God (for nonpersons cannot be blamed for evil deeds). Now what if we address the question, Is God a person? to the concept of the God of Jesus Christ which our inquiry here has yielded? But *now* the question itself seems partly misplaced. As God appears in the communal or somatic strand, he is indeed a divine person: Judge, Lawgiver, Kinsman-redeemer, Friend. Inasmuch as we have to do with God in social ways, God is God for us by making those ways his own. The incarnation is only the clearest fulfillment of a theme that appears throughout the biblical narratives.

But insofar as there are other categories of our life under God, namely our participation in the natural order and our existence under a destiny not of our own construction—insofar as God is Creator and Destiny as well as Master—to ask, Is God a person? is to *extend that social concept beyond the strand in which it appears, thus fallaciously denying the categorical integrity of the other strands* of Christian experience.

So by drawing on ancient, and even more on primitive Christian insights, we are confronted with a subtle complexity that necessarily is present even in childlike expressions of Christian faith, and which requires a rethinking of the modern theologian's puzzling questions. Our questions still will be difficult—perhaps even more difficult—but the difficulties will be in the right places. It cannot be the role of this short essay to press on through that reconception. However, one objection can be noted and disposed of. Someone may say, "It is all very well to note the varied dimensions of God's existence in these discriminable strands of Christian discourse. But once the *personal* dimension appears, won't it supersede the others? Isn't personality a preemptive category? In other words, isn't God *really* the God of your second strand?"

In answer, one may remember the way the concept of God took shape for the fourth-century Arians. Beguiled by Greek models, they were willing in some way to grant 'divinity' to the Word. But the *real* God was for them only the Father. This made sense—in their conceptuality. But it was exactly that conceptuality that needed to be challenged, and the challenge did come from the reality of Christian life and worship, where

God was also the Word incarnate; where God was also the Spirit indwelling the Christian fellowship. On those rocks, Arianism struck and slowly sank. What corresponds to this tale today? Philosophical theologians, inheriting a deistic 'personal' God from their Enlightenment forefathers, can no more make their deistic theism encompass the rich facts of Christian life under God than could the Arians. Will they resolve the sensed difficulty by retreating, as some have, into Christian atheism— or by addressing the actual complexity of the source of our faith with a suitably complex doctrine of God?

If the theologians do not recognize the disparity between the god their hands have made (cf. Isa. 44) and the God of Jesus Christ, perhaps external criticism will do the job for them. William R. Jones, in his too-little read *Is God a White Racist?* (1973), raises the question trenchantly. Black theologians (Jones' foreground target) have argued (a) that God is in charge of human history, and (b) that God is on the side of oppressed blacks. But, Jones asks, Do not the facts of history make it appear that any God in charge of history must be, not on the side of blacks, but instead, a white racist God? Jones' book has gone quickly out of print; perhaps not many wanted such questions raised. Yet he asks an excellent question, to which the theologians (black or other) can have little answer as long as theirs is the philosophic deity inherited from the (white racist?) Enlightenment.

Jones's own reconstruction, "humanocentric theism" (1973:ch. 12), does not seem to me a solution, but another retreat: Humanocentric theism is even more deistic than the deistic theism of the Enlightened theologians. But his argument offers a powerful incentive for a concerned theology of the God of Jesus Christ. If the One with whom Jews and Christians have to do is not *merely* a God of history as Jones and his opponents the black theologians suppose, or for that matter *merely* the Ground of transformation, or *merely* the Wisdom of the given inorganic and organic world—but all of this and yet One—then the theodicy Jones demands cannot be forthcoming in the way he demands, because the God he spurns is *not* that One. Yet there may be another theodicy based on another theology, another God.

We come back to Pascal's apology, for it depends upon our making his distinction between the God of the philosophers (i.e., the philosophers of his day and, as I have suggested, the theologians of our own) and the God of Abraham, of Isaac, of Jacob, of Jesus Christ. Pascal saw that the appeal in defense of this God must be historic—must not be the appeal of a private memorial to personal experience, even though the latter was sewn into one's coat. But the historic point of departure would not be the gospel of the wealth of Christian Europe, with its armies, its empires, its religion, its successes. Rather, he appealed to this fact: Consider that despised, rejected, strangely surviving people; consider the Jews. Thus he took a clue from history, which disclosed not its gross movement or success stories, but its deeper meaning. That meaning, fully penetrated, leads back to the God of Jesus Christ, the God of Abraham. It makes sense, not of all history (for much of history is inimical to this Story), but of a history the world cannot grasp while it remains merely the world. For to grasp this history is to be grasped by that complex One who also laid hold of Pascal on his great night.

Note

I am especially grateful to the following critical readers of this paper: Frederick Borsch, Stanley Hauerwas, Massey H. Shepherd, Jr., and Robert Wilken.

References

Barth, Karl
    1958. *Church Dogmatics 3:1. The Doctrine of Creation*. Ed. G. W. Bromily and T. F. Torrance. Edinburgh: T. & T. Clark.
Harvey, Van A.
    1966. *The Historian and the Believer*. New York: Macmillan & Co.
Jones, William R.
    1973. *Is God a White Racist?* Garden City, N.Y.: Anchor Press, Doubleday & Co.

Kelly, J.N.D.
  1958. *Early Christian Doctrines*. New York: Harper & Brothers.
McClendon, James Wm., Jr., and Smith, James
  1975. *Understanding Religious Convictions*. Notre Dame, Ind.:
  University of Notre Dame Press.
  1978. "Three Strands of Christian Ethics." *Journal of Religious
  Ethics* 6/1(Spring): 54-80.
Moltmann, Jürgen
  (1965) 1967. *(Theologie der Hoffung.) Theology of Hope*. Trans.
  James W. Leitch. London: SCM Press.
  (1973) 1974. *(Der gekreuzigte Gott.) The Crucified God*. Trans.
  R.A. Wilson and John Bowden. New York: Harper & Row.
Munck, Johannes
  1959. *Paul and the Salvation of Mankind*. Trans. Frank Clark.
  Atlanta: John Knox Press.
Niebuhr, H. Richard
  1960. *Radical Monotheism and Western Culture*. New York:
  Harper & Brothers.
Pascal, Blaise
  (1662a) 1941. *Pensées*. Trans. W. F. Trotter. New York: Modern
  Library.
  (1662b) 1948. "Pascal's Memorial." *Great Shorter Works of
  Pascal*. Trans. Emile Cailliet and John C. Blankenagel.
  Philadelphia: Westminster Press.
Robinson, James M.
  1959. *A New Quest of the Historical Jesus*. London: SCM Press.
Tyrrell, George
  (1909) 1963. *Christianity at the Cross-Roads*. London: George
  Allen & Unwin.
Schweizer, Eduard.
  1971. *Jesus*. Trans. David W. Green. Richmond: John Knox
  Press.
Schleiermacher, Friedrich
  1835. *Der Christliche Glaube*. Berlin: G. Reimer.
Stendahl, Krister
  1976. *Paul Among Jews and Gentiles*. Philadelphia: Fortress
  Press.

About David B. Burrell's Essay

David B. Burrell, a highly distinguished American theologian, is a member of the Catholic religious order which founded and still serves the University of Notre Dame, where he is currently a professor. Despite these credentials (or possibly because of them?), his essay here confronts the reader with a task somewhat different from that presented by any other. In the first place, there is its very catholicity—Burrell moves easily and sometimes by mere allusion across a range of references limited to no one continent or century or creed: Jesus, Malcolm X, Augustine, Thomas Merton, Norman Mailer, Aquinas, Sebastian Moore, Kierkegaard.

Second, here there is a form of exposition that may be unfamiliar to some. In straight linear argument, I start with A, which you concede, and move point by point directly to Z, which was to be proved. Burrell's structure might be described rather as spiral: I start at any convenient point P, survey my subject matter as seen from that point, move on around to another vantage point and then another, until I regain what seems to be the starting point but actually is higher ground gained by the circuit—and so around again until the subject has been seen from its whole circumference. Here the force of the 'argument' lies not in demonstration, but in the most adequate comprehension.

Third, contained here is a testimony of shared religious experience, nonetheless genuine for being not first-person narrative (as was Augustine's *Confessions* in the fourth century or Bunyan's *Grace Abounding* in the seventeenth), but critical reflection upon the practices, the language, and the implied presuppositions of a convictional community of human beings. For Burrell, this community is the Congregation Sacrae Crucis (C.S.C.); more broadly it is the Catholic and the Christian church. The force of this essay, however, lies also in its invitation that we apply it to ourselves in our own communities, with our presupposed conviction, our 'classics,' our shared practices, and our grammar and use or disuse of the word "God."

So this essay, like an earlier book by Burrell (1974), is a condensed set of spiritual directions—instructions for participation in a community of faith-skills. In the end, we need not participate (our response may be respectfully to decline), but we cannot understand the essay without reading it as actual invitation to take part. The essay is self-involving for both writer and reader.

In a strong sense, then, here the reader is on his or her own; we offer only some clues to interpretation.

1. Burrell's philosophical grounding is Thomist and Wittgensteinian. As a Thomist, he has written an important book on analogy (1973) and another on *Aquinas: God and Action* (1979). Analogy figures again in the present essay. As a student of the work of Ludwig Wittgenstein (1889–1951), Burrell understands St. Thomas and theology generally in a distinctive way: Theology's task is to provide 'rules'—more precisely, 'grammatical rules'—for religious practice and discourse (what Wittgenstein called theology as grammar).

2. To these distinct emphases, Burrell adds a renewed and highly contemporary emphasis upon the role of narrative in theology. The life we can live in a faith community, the beliefs that matter to such a community, the doubts we can meaningfully raise there—all come to expression in the stories we tell, and these stories are not evasions of hard thinking, but provide the very grist of thought itself.

As an essay should, this one raises more questions than it means to answer. We will note a few the thoughtful reader may encounter: Does Burrell escape (as he intends to escape) the spider's web of relativism? Is the talk about God here sufficiently objective to represent (as Burrell, we believe, means to represent) a real God with whom his creatures really have to do? Has Burrell begun to rescue Catholic *spirituality* from the warm pap of sentiment and 'mystery,' restoring its ancient intellectual integrity? But there are many more.

8. Stories of God: Why We Use Them and How We Judge Them

David B. Burrell, C.S.C.

How do we come to know God and the ways of God? The same way we come to know anyone else: through the stories told about them. In the case of God, however, we *already* know enough to know that

(a) the stories told about God stretch images beyond their usual reach and deliberately exploit situations, for they purport to tell us about *divinity*; and

(b) the more we become the self that each of us is destined to become, the more discriminating we will be in discerning among contending stories.

These bits of knowledge reflect two sorts of rules that have been developed to govern our dealing with divinity:

(a') rules for the use of the term—such as those Plato elaborates early on in the *Republic* (bk. 2:379a-83b) or Aquinas, in questions 3 through 11 in the *Summa*,[1] and

(b') formative rules, which shape the primary context for discourse about divinity—rules constitutive of a community of work and worship formed by a common catechesis, and yet comprising practices as well.

The sort of knowledge we rely on here is not so much "knowing that" as "knowing how"—not so much theoretical or factual as grammatical and structural. It is grammar that structures our exchanges with one another, and our expectations as well. And if the point of our exchange is rich enough, our expectations transcendent enough, the community that shares in both will not be all work, but also will know how to play. In fact, the test of a community of work and worship will be its capacity for play; the resilience of its catechesis will be reflected in the simple enjoyment of one another.[2]

It may seem strange to speak of community and of rules in the same breath. Yet the rhythms of community life embody a structure, and a structure that freights the exchange with expectations. When those expectations match the ones we have begun to discern in ourselves, we are attracted to the life. And when the ensuing human exchange leads us toward better discerning what we really want, then we come to treasure the life. Furthermore, if the life of a community were able to do that so well that we could say it helps to reveal us to ourselves, then the rules of interaction would take on the character of revelation.

That is precisely what the formative rules of a religious community claim to be and to do. Appreciation of the discipline of the community leads us to recognize the shaping rules more as a measure of a shared humanity moving toward a shared vision, than as something imposed upon us. They become revelation for us as we recognize trustworthy guiding points, and in the process we come to realize how much the language of doctrine embodies and expresses a form of life. The consistency of that life is shown by the grammar of the language characteristically used, and the language finds its application—its verification, even—in the consistency displayed by the community's practice.

In relation to the language we use to speak to and about God, philosophical theology has always assumed the tasks of delineating the rules of the language and of teaching us how to use them. And if we are addressing ourselves to a "know-how," learning how to use them will be tantamount to establishing them. In this way, one's "doctrine of God" will be demonstrated in the way one uses the primary language—a language replete with stories and with images. So we have come to realize that the Gospels are narratives in literary structure, and each embodies a theology. That is, these narratives recount situations and utilize images in a definite way, and if someone can lay bare that structure in a rule-like manner, we will have a theological statement.

In fact, the most promising way to characterize metaphysical statements is to see them as providing rules for the proper use of our descriptive or everyday language.[3] This characterization is so promising because it affords us something of a test in metaphysics, a domain normally considered remote and arcane—and hence accessible only to a few. For rules prove themselves in use, and the way our use of images and metaphors displays those rules affords an accessible test for our metaphysics. So, for example, if we regard whatever is said about divine immutability as a set of rules to structure our preaching and our praying, then the attitudes displayed by that very preaching and praying show what sort of an 'unchangeable' God we have in mind. For John of the Cross, this "formal fact" only enhances the inward character of the intimacy one can enjoy with a loving God, whereas Aquinas' text has managed to mislead many people—*afficionados* and others—into thinking that the same formal fact entailed the impossibility of our relating *to* divinity at all![4]

The use which John of the Cross makes of this formal fact about God in the context of his final work, *The Living Flame of Love*, is telling. Near the close of the commentary on stanza 2, he speaks of the person as "interiorly and exteriorly keeping festival . . . saying within its spirit those words of Job: 'My glory shall always be renewed and as a palm tree shall I multiply my days' (29:18, 20). Which is as much as to say: God who, remaining within Himself unchangeably, makes all things new . . . will make my glory ever new" (2.36). He uses the grammar of "unchangeable" to increase the paradox even more explicitly as he tries to account for final stages of union. Commenting on the line "How gently and lovingly you awaken in my bosom," he says:

> And the manner of this movement in the soul, since God is immovable, is a wondrous thing, for, although in reality God moves not, it seems to the soul that He is indeed moving; for, as it is the soul that is renewed and moved by God to behold . . . that Divine life and the being and harmony of all creatures in it . . . it seems to the soul that it is God that is moving, and thus the cause takes the name of the effect which it produces. . . . Even as the Wise Man says: 'Wisdom is more movable

than all movable things' (Wis. 7:24) . . . what is meant here is
that wisdom is more active than all active things. (John of the
Cross, 1962: 4.6)

John knows that one can distinguish *act* from *movement*, as
also does the Zen master. Furthermore, the passages cited
show that John of the Cross has learned to exploit the formal
feature of immutability to enhance that very distinction and so
to guide us to a more accurate understanding of God's activity
in creatures, especially in those who are able to respond by
knowing and loving (Burrell, 1979:167ff.).

John is able to use the formula of immutability, then, to
illuminate us regarding divine activity and our response,
while contemporary "process theologians" find the same
formula alienating and systematically misleading. How can we
explain so great a disparity? In many ways, certainly, though
those ways most readily available to us prove to be
self-serving. That is, we are all too prone to think of a
sixteenth-century Spanish theologian as being *bound* by
tradition, while we congratulate our more *critical* posture.
There may be some truth to that caricature, but it would be
just as likely, and more modest, to suggest that the contenders
may have understood the formula differently. It is reasonably
clear that process theologians regard such statements as very
general descriptions (Ogden, 1966:94). The citations from
John of the Cross suggest that he would distinguish between
such formulae and one's experience of divinity; and more
extensive acquaintance with his work corroborates that
suggestion.

While John would not express things in the way I have
expressed them, his very use of the formulae of philosophical
theology supports my proposal that we consider such
statements as rules that structure our primary dealings with
God and with the ways of God. This view suggests another
clarification of philosophy's role in religious issues—that
metaphysics cannot stand alone, over against religious
questions, to adjudicate among them. The purpose of relevant
philosophical observations is rather to sort out the issues, so
that we can engage in the appropriate practices relatively

unencumbered. By "practices," I mean ways of relating to ourselves and to our world—those ways that are affected by the presence (or absence) of God. Metaphysics cannot rule directly for or against certain practices, but (on my characterization) metaphysical statements can always be regarded as directions for discriminating among practices by ascertaining their point and by clarifying the roles they play.

Stanley Hauerwas and I have stipulated four such rules that we may use to discriminate among stories that offer a context for human action and so tend to shape our character. They must display

1. power to release us from destructive alternatives,
2. ways of seeing through current distortions,
3. room to keep us from having to resort to violence,
4. a sense for the tragic: how meaning transcends power (Hauerwas, 1977:35).

So baldly stated, these criteria sound as though they are articulating a *position* distinct from the stories likely to have such an effect on our lives. That is not the intention, however, for it is the stories, and not our criteria, that we find normative. The criteria are simply ways to spell out the qualities that give a classic (e.g., Dante's *Divine Comedy*) its undeniable status, and to do so by describing the effects it is likely to have on anyone who takes it to heart. For it is practices we are after—not stories in isolation from the reader's life.

Practices are evoked and guided by stories whose narrative structures spell out their implications and help to forewarn us or to allay our fears.[5] To discriminate among stories, then, would be to employ criteria which display one's metaphysical commitments. Yet, however we have accustomed our students to query after *criteria*, these "cutters" are seldom accessible. And when we try to render them so, we discover that we cannot speak them straight out, as it were. We find ourselves having recourse to evocative or explicitly analogous expressions—as in the Hauerwas and Burrell illustration above, "destructive," "room," "tragic," "meaning," and "power."[6] Yet we *do* sort good stories from bad. How do we do it? What is it that we, and all literary or drama critics, are up to?

Two examples come to mind—one is more the way we plain story-readers do it; the other leans toward the sort of sophistication in which critics engage—yet each is quite accessible. The first is from the life of Malcolm X; the second from the experience of some disciples, as related by Luke. We will remember Malcolm's account of his conversion to a true Islam—that it turned upon the experience of Mecca and the way that all pilgrims, of whatever race or color, were treated and treated one another. This led him to recognize that the stories first told him were not part of the Quran, but an aberration. And the discovery was not merely a matter of finding consistency, but also a way of freeing himself to embrace a shared human destiny—hence a real transformation (1964:333-42).

In Luke 24, the two disciples had simply discarded the tale the women had told about the empty tomb and were on their way back to the place they had been before—disillusioned. But the words and the actions of the stranger who accompanied them gave those reports a plausibility and their own lives a new context. As Luke reports the recognition experience, it involved being opened to a new perspective on the Scriptures and hence on their own lives and expectations. That is what a good story succeeds in doing. Luke structures the narrative, embodying something of a critic's sophistication, to show how Jesus' words and presence effected that breakthrough.

Stories that continue to speak in this way—to individuals and to successive generations—we call *classics* (Tracy, 1979). So a large part of a critic's training lies in determining the qualities that make such works classics. In fact, one thus could fairly characterize all training in the humanities. So we not only are continually engaged in making judgments of appropriateness, but a liberal education is designed to exercise us in the skills that enable us to make those judgments in a more trustworthy and plausible manner. Such judgments become mysterious (or "subjective") only when we ask—expecting a formula answer—By what criteria do we discriminate among stories?

The entire exercise is *subjective*, to be sure, in that only subjects (persons) can carry it out. We cannot lease it out to a computer; or if we hire consultants, they can tell us only what we already know. Intelligent subjectivity remains our goal as it was Socrates'. Developing it involves learning how to articulate the grounds for our judgments in a language we share with others. For these are judgments we are making, not simple options. And if language about divinity means anything, it must both reflect and structure the judgments that shape our lives. Let us call these judgments *convictions*. If we can better articulate their structure and the ways in which we bring them up for justification, we should have a better hold on language about God—not simply the stories told, but the ways we discriminate among them to find the true ones.

I. Structure Appropriate to Religious Discourse

There is a venerable tradition which finds that the language of prayer and of theology displays semantic peculiarities. Medieval Christian thinkers—notably Aquinas—found the logical works of Aristotle helpful in locating these features. Aquinas has shown the reasons that proper (or literal) statements about divinity must employ analogous predicate terms. We can assert truthfully that God is just, provided we recognize the peculiar role that expressions such as "just" or "justice" play in our everyday discourse. For one thing, they invariably invite discussion, for they express "essentially contestable notions." One does not *describe* a situation as unjust; rather one asserts a described situation to *be* unjust. And we must be ready for vociferous disagreement with such an assessment. One thing we cannot tolerate, however, is the cool contention that appraisals of that sort are out of order: "That's just how we do things down here" (the Brazilian manager who looks after Belgian corporate interests) or "I find Mondays dull and had to do something to liven up my day" (reported remark of a teen-age sniper who killed two people in a schoolyard with her 22-caliber Christmas gift). If our flesh recoils at so calloused a statement, that only reflects our innate convictions about what being human must entail.

As it turns out, the terms we characteristically use of God are the very expressions we need for prescribing the grammar of our interaction as human beings. The variable dimensions of analogous expressions reflect the fact that "just" situations are compatible with different arrangements. There is no *the* just social order. What remains invariable, however, is the aspiration itself, which we consider part of the very structure of human interchange—and even more, we consider it constitutive of the relations we ought to maintain with the natural world.

A recently published work by Brian Wicker, *The Story-Shaped World* (1975), offers a frame to show how metaphors—when they work—function analogously. That is, they call forth our recognition of a proportioned likeness among items not customarily connected, so as to elicit a fresh understanding in us. (The difference between a job description and an arresting image tells it all: The vice president for personnel often thinks of himself as a doormat on a rainy day.) Aristotle first reminded us that an apt use of metaphors reflects a judicious sense of proportion. Wicker exhibits the relation among linguistic items by a two-dimensional matrix called (among structuralists) a meaning frame, since it allows us to compare items horizontally and vertically simultaneously.

So one might compose a parable of the personnel director's life in an animated skit involving a particular doormat. The skit must hold together as a narrative in its own right; and the more one knows about a typical day in the life of personnel directors, the better it will function as a parable. If we think of these two narratives as running parallel on a horizontal axis, the vertical relations among the narrative elements will determine the force of the parable. But it is these relations—the analogy—which cannot be expressed directly.

By using a two-dimensional matrix for their display, Wicker manages to avoid the difficulties that have accrued to Aristotle's use of a mathematical proportional scheme. Although Aristotle expressly proposed the scheme as a model for the way language works ("proportion" simply translates *analogia*), successors invariably were tricked into trying to reduce the proportion to a single fraction, or even to solve for the unknown term! Theories of analogy proposed to accomplish for linguistic expressions what mathematical operations accomplish with proportions, forgetting that models cannot simply be *applied*.

Wicker relies on artists as well as on philosophers to make his point. We can clarify his thesis by using his meaning frame to display the structure of a work by Norman Mailer—one of the novelists whom Wicker employs to illustrate his thesis. Mailer, of course, is seldom at a loss for metaphors—in fact, his use of them often is downright luxuriant. Yet his extended essay, *Armies of the Night*, whose very title announces the dominant metaphor, is admirably controlled. The novel progresses as an account of protagonist (1) *versus* protagonist (2) for the very integrity of the nation: The setting is the antiwar protest of 1969, but the theme is civil war! Wicker's frame shows how the dramatic protagonists function, one as metaphor of the other.

protagonist₁ vs. protagonist₂ for the integrity of the republic

---

(A) Mailer vs. U.S. Marshal for Pentagon turf
(B) Robert Lowell vs. Robert McNamara for intellectual probity.[7]

Lines (A) and (B) summarize the action narrated; the interaction between these distinct plots and the characters in each give the novel its depth and help us all to discover what was at stake in those contests of the 1960s. By adapting classical analogy schemes to the meaning frame, Wicker can show graphically how Mailer uses his *dramatis personae* metaphorically to display the forces at work. Very little is conveyed by my framing description of the action of *Armies of the Night*; even to read the separate accounts of Mailer and the marshal, or of Lowell and McNamara, would simply repeat a news release. Robert Lowell would be identified as a renowned poet and Robert McNamara as the automotive executive afflicted with an uncommon conscience, who was

brought in to manage the war machine. But by juxtaposing the
accounts as he has, Mailer lets each illuminate the other, so as
to convey the sense of the one conflict which pitted the
members of each pair against one another.

That is what metaphorical speech can do when it is properly
constructed to evoke the relevant analogies: It can so relate us
to a "complex" situation as to help us grasp "something simple
in the middle of it."[8] The situations articulated by religious
thinkers invariably touch upon a person's relation to that
which transcends description—to God or to the ways of God.
While these relations shape the entirety of our lives, they are
explicitly indescribable. So we must have recourse to some
other kind of speech. Wicker argues that figurative speech,
properly disciplined, *is* literal discourse in such an arena. In
fact, he contends, we have come to oppose metaphorical to
literal expressions only because we lost sight of the role that
analogy plays in legitimizing metaphors (1975:ch. 4).[9]

Once we have recovered that discovery, we are released
from a flat-footed paradigm for literal discourse and are freed
as well from making extravagant claims for metaphor.
Whereas Aquinas asked (in *Summa Theologiae* 1:13.3)
whether a certain set of expressions might "properly" be used
of God, Herbert McCabe translated *proprie* as "literally"—an
enlightened choice on his part. Aquinas devotes the entire
question to showing that analogous discourse alone literally
can signify divinity, and Wicker offers analyses of literary
works to show that the only useful descriptions of certain
situations must be metaphorical ones. This also is Mailer's
running argument in his commentary on the moonshot: *A Fire
on the Moon* (1970). The book is, in fact, its own argument, as
Mailer shows that the very methodical world of astronauts is
susceptible to mythic description.

The reason the meaning-frame device works so well, I
suspect, is that it engages the critical reader and prompts us to
formulate those structural features of *Armies of the Night*
which helped us to relate more discriminatingly to the
television reports of the protests—and even to our own
involvement in these events, for those of us who were so
affected by them. The relevant features, of course, are the

analogies displayed in the meaning frame between Mailer and
Lowell, U.S. Marshal and McNamara, Pentagon turf and
intellectual probity. Yet the bare analogies, so to speak, do
their work only when embedded in distinct yet overlapping
narratives. Similarly, "just" makes no sense when used of God
unless we have had some practice in employing it of social or
ecological arrangements. Yet that does not imply that the
features proper to any of those arrangements need be ascribed
to divinity. As we become skilled in assessing them as more or
less just (or unjust), however, the capacities we develop help
prepare us to use the expression appropriately *in divinis*.[10]
There is no doubt that we would like to use it of God; yet the
way we use it makes all the difference.

I have employed Wicker's combined literary and semantic
analysis to illustrate the structure proper to language
about God. I will follow this with another linguistic study
which shows how we might go about justifying the statements we make: *Understanding Religious Convictions* by
James McClendon and James Smith (1975).

II. Justifying Religious Convictions

McClendon and Smith are concerned with the practice of
justifying religious convictions and with the difficulties
attendant upon that task in a pluralistic culture. They
acknowledge the distinct sets of convictions which shape
diverse communities, and they set forth scenarios numerous
enough to catch anyone pretending to live or to act free of
convictions. Defining convictions as those beliefs which are
basic in shaping one's life and activity, they are forced to admit
an irreducible pluralism among convictional communities. In
fact, this feature leads them to an initially implausible rule:
One directly justifies one's convictions to oneself and to the
members of one's own convictional community, not to others.

Yet what at first seems implausible also points a way out of
simple relativism (which they call hard-perspectivism). For
one who justifies a set of convictions to oneself in this way will,
of course, be concerned to show both coherence and
correspondence—the consistency and integrity of the teach-

ing, as well as its applicability in a person's life—and in doing so, must use a language commonly shared and replete with human aspirations. So convictional communities, differing as they may in basic beliefs, nonetheless must address the same human questions in a language all will understand. And while it is normally pointless to try to justify yourself (along with your community) to someone who does not share your shaping convictions, such a one may well be struck favorably by the account you offer of yourself and your co-religionists.

Let us consider how we come to accept a religious text as a classic or how we recognize a saint as a hero. One need not imitate Augustine's move in book 8 to acknowledge the *Confessions* to be a superbly human document, nor must one accept all of Christian doctrine (along with Aquinas' synthesis thereof) to resonate with Dante's *Divine Comedy*. Similarly, one need not be Catholic (much less Italian) to be moved by a Francis of Assisi, or by a Thomas More or a Mother Teresa. Something profoundly human is struck as these individuals and these authors mine their Christian heritage. (It would make a stronger point to contend that figures like these can arise only from a cohesive convictional community, and that I would claim, though I cannot argue it here.) The present significance lies in the way the life or work of persons engaged in clarifying the sense of a convictional community for themselves (as well as for the other members of that community) can lay a yet wider claim on others who meet them or who read such works.

Furthermore, this capacity to engage a yet wider audience through its striking individuals and its literature is the way a religious community can exhibit the truthfulness of its central claims. We may try in vain to justify our convictions directly to another, yet we may find that we succeed in doing exactly that if we engage ourselves more modestly in the process of clarifying our own difficulties. On the face of it, 'clarifying' may sound like a bland procedure, yet the process of clarifying one's convictions will involve two taxing steps: (a) formulating one's beliefs, and (b) showing how these beliefs affect one's life and character. That process reminds us of Plato's strategy in the *Republic*: Unable to answer directly Thrasymachus'

challenge—Why be just anyway?—he must first (a) state
clearly what he was about in investigating justice, and then (b)
show on the blowup of a model state, how this virtue
governed interaction among the parts of a functioning polity or
an authentic person. The activity of *clarifying* convictions
clearly outstrips an exercise of defining terms, and in the
process offers us a way to assert the broader human impact and
worth of these convictions. For any clarification must do that,
even if its primary audience is "the convinced."

Thomas Merton offers a perspicuous example of this
process. No one would accuse him, at least in his later
writings, of "doing apologetics." Quite the opposite, in fact, as
he would be the first to insist. Yet his writings have proved to
be most convincing among the testimony of Catholics, to
those who would not count themselves believers, and *that* has
always been the goal of apologetics. This paradox shows (with
the help of the analysis of McClendon and Smith) that the
paradigm for apologetics generated by beleaguered religious
folk during the Enlightenment presented a travesty of
religious activity, because the paradigm was at odds with the
logic of convictions. In fact, rather than trying to prove the
validity of my religion to all comers, it makes more sense (and
proves more productive) to spend my energy clarifying it for
myself and for others who claim to believe in it. If I engage in
that task with the candor demanded by the common language
I must use to express myself, something of the veracity of that
religious tradition well may show through. In exemplifying
this latter strategy, Merton confirms the power of this analysis
of convictions, as well as offering a more adequate conception
of the activity called *apologetics*.

There is another more banal way to put the matter, by
recalling that the death-of-God movement in theology was
fueled by the startling reminder that unbelief was at home in
the believer's own household. Of a piece with descriptions of
the "crises of faith" that were attending religious folk and the
venerable dictum *ecclesia semper reformanda*, all these
observations spoke to the experience of believers by
reminding them that their faith never could be considered a
mere *given*. It is doubtful whether any of them ever

considered it so, but some of the theology which informed those preachers who cared not to examine their own faith often did so speak of it, so the reminders were needed. Merton accomplished the same end (with far less jargon) by relentlessly subjecting his own beliefs and practices to a critical scrutiny. The sign of his own faith was the bouyant manner in which he presumed that such criticism could be met—from the treasuries of tradition and from the resources of the living community.

All this so far has been an effort to show that a person who speaks out of his tradition and his living context can find himself addressing a much wider audience. Furthermore, the fact that he does so can count considerably toward establishing the truthfulness of that tradition. It is manifest that Merton was ever writing out of his tradition and his monastic way of life. What has proved startling is the way that very particular experience which informed his own critical inquiry spoke and still speaks to so many persons. In the response his writings receive, we witness the universal appeal of one who seeks to be faithful to a particular revelation and executes that task with everything in him that is human. The combination of a particular faith and a common language admits others to a shared struggle and urges their identification with the protagonist. What is going on is common to all of us; the way it is being carried out is peculiar to the community whose faith is in question. The success with which a person mines that tradition to meet the shared questions offers the best test we can propose for a particular set of religious convictions.

It is a test, furthermore, which respects the grammar of convictions in a way that many philosophers' queries of religion do not. It does not ask, for example, How might anyone believe such things as resurrection? For we are not speaking of *anyone* nor of *any* resurrection, but of this individual (you, me, or Merton) and of the resurrection of Jesus, as that very special fact has shaped the life and worship of Christian communities over the centuries. So the questions are universal because they are shared by all, not because they admit of abstract discussion. In fact, as the example of Merton and Merton's writings shows so well, whatever process of justification may be recommended for testing religious convictions, it must be one that displays the way a particular tradition allows an individual to deal with issues that press upon us all. Since one must address them in a common idiom, one's personal struggles will be accessible to others. And the force of an individual's dealings with these issues reminds readers that they cannot dodge them either—not if they would become individuals themselves.[11]

Without intending to do so, I have been constructing a rationale for the predilection that theologians have exhibited recently for biography, and especially for autobiography (Shea, 1978). James McClendon himself has authored a study of four lives, entitled *Biography as Theology* (1974), complete with an essay justifying the title. It could be considered an illustrative companion piece to *Understanding Religious Convictions*, since it forcefully reminds us that convictions must be distinguished from mere statements. For they shape the lives of the individuals who hold them, and as *religious* convictions, insert those same individuals into a community with a history—a religious tradition.

The two studies complement each other, for we realize that it is the individuals who impress us and attract us to a way of life by the way we can see it giving consistency to their lives. If they also are sufficiently conscious and skilled enough to bring that process to common expression, then we are possessed of an exemplar and a justification in the same individual. Augustine's *Confessions* provides the classical instance; I have cited Merton's later writings as a recent example.

The critical point of this reflection offers a clue to the grammar of justification in matters religious. There simply can be no question of confirming or of disconfirming religious claims unless we acknowledge them to be convictions. The key expressions involved in any such claim, then, must lay claim to us—positively or negatively. We cannot pretend to be indifferent to justice, even though our taste for it may have become increasingly dulled. "Eternal life," as John promises it, cannot represent something we are content to take or to leave; it must correspond to an aspiration coextensive with our very humanity.

Ernest Becker has offered an eloquent delineation of our needs and of our fears in this regard in his *Denial of Death* (1974). We need to be able to make a gift of our lives, yet the very fear of dying makes us hold on so tightly to what we have that we are unable to let it go—to give it away. His analysis carries us to the threshold of a result that Christians might recognize as an act of faith. In a recent extended essay, *The Crucified Jesus Is No Stranger* (1977), Sebastian Moore has shown that the death of Jesus—taken both as historic fact and as timeless symbol—can make possible that gifting of oneself that everything otherwise conspires to render impossible. His slim, yet dense volume acknowledges a debt of origin to Becker, and like Becker's analysis, makes a claim on and about the experience of each of us which amounts to virtual universality.

The key expressions will vary in meaning—in descriptive detail and in affective force—from one person to another, yet they will play similar roles in the psychology of each. That is how analogous terms function, as we have seen from the analysis of Wicker: The role they play, if you will, is the *same*; while the contexts in which they function can differ immensely. If we add the fact that the functions relevant to divine names are precisely those that we as human beings cannot avoid dealing with, we have the precise sense in which "anthropology" affords the idiom for theology. And exercises similar to Wicker's meaning frame can remind us that observations like these never are simple reductions, but rather offer clues to the way we might actually employ language in so transcendent a domain as the theological.

Once we have realized how many homegrown examples of just or unjust resolutions our daily exchange offers, we can gain some appreciation of the way God (if there be a God) might be said to be just. And as we realize that the justice dimension, if you will, of those encounters makes such inescapable claims on us, we will recognize why it is that we are claimed by a God who must be just. Claims like these need to be fleshed out from our experience, but never are simply reducible to it. In fact, they also shape that experience itself, and depending on the way they do so, we judge the

corresponding conception of divinity to be liberating and
healing, or enslaving and destructive.

III. Where Such Clarifications Lead Us

I have been offering examples of the way careful attention to
language can remind us of things we already know, criteria we
consistently employ, in finding our way in regions as
frightening as the names of God and the ways of God with
humankind. I have suggested that the issue is not belief or
unbelief, as much as discerning what is proper to believe in.
As the Hebrews saw it, the critical question was how to
distinguish the true God from the *ersatz* contenders.

Philosophical analysis can play an indispensable role in this
life-and-death drama, for confusion here can destroy individuals and communities. But this role must be played by a
masterful indirection: a series of reminders highlighting what
it is we already know, a deft analysis laying bare for us the
structure of our most trustworthy judgments. For if our
philosophy professes to do more than that—to offer, for
instance, a lofty vantage point from which to determine the
worth of religious statements—then one legitimately can ask
just what warrants assuming that position.

A skillful practitioner of linguistic analysis can, in fact, show
that a healthy faith tradition contains its own critical moments.
Furthermore, that same analysis can show the reason
"healthy" and "critical" are linked together here, by
displaying the analogous structure of religious discourse. If we
have a settled notion of justice, we possess not a virtue but an
ideology, and should we use that notion of our god, we are
entertaining an idol rather than the saving God.

Much work of this sort needs to be done to help Christians
recover a wealth of writing which has been overlooked by
theologians pretending to "scientific" rigor. I am speaking of
the genre identified as spiritual writing. It is no accident,
surely, that a generation raised on a paradigm of "critical
thinking" designed to dissolve convictions is looking nowa-
days for more instruction in "spirituality." For convictions
have a way of asserting their places in our lives. Yet

everything turns on the way we propose to study *spirituality*. I would suggest that the very abstract term can be misleading. We actually are concerned with grasping the point of a set of instructions and clarifications known as spiritual writings. To grasp their point accurately, we need to understand not only the *Sitz-im-leben* of such works—their historical context—but also the role they are intended to play.

Hence the writings of John of the Cross can be read (minimally) as a set of ethical demands, or they can be approached as a map of a journey in, and to, friendship with God. Specific instructions and key expressions will be read differently in each of these interpretations. Moreover, every generation will be prone to find a fresh perspective from which to assimilate so classical a corpus of writings. So we are not hankering after the correct interpretation, but looking for that set of critical skills which will allow us to fracture stereotypes and discover a reading conducive to finding friendship with God in our time.

Wittgenstein came to see the practice of philosophy as a form of intellectual therapy, whose primary aim was to release us from residual philosophical cramps and allow us to recognize what we really knew already. The heroic historical precedent was Socrates; a more recent example could be Kierkegaard—a philosopher whose multiple pseudonyms continued to fascinate Wittgenstein. If we were to pay attention to Kierkegaard's use of language, the way he attended to the language of the documents he comments upon—notably Plato's—we would discover not so much a protoexistentialist as a critical wit, at the service of understanding how it is one might believe. And the test of his power lies in his playfulness—however recondite the jokes and indirect the irony (Burrell, 1974:143ff.).

We have no space here, however, to consider yet another figure from the history of philosophy. I have tried to offer some indications of the philosophical tradition we have available to us. It is a tradition which offers a way to translate the ancient dictum, *fides quaerens intellectum*, into a set of skills available to each person and useful to all. And we might say justly that its application to religious issues and theological questions has barely begun. As we train these skills on the writings of the spiritual masters, as well as use them to analyze the practices of worship in which believers speak to and of their God, we will have better ways to pose the perennial questions which touch upon the verification of religious life and language (Burrell, 1974). That is the task before us, for which this paper has tried to clear a way.

Notes

1. Of these rules, Brian Wicker notes, "When we read or hear of Yahweh as a character in the story, we must already have at the back of our minds the conception of God as Creator and as the Most High" (1975:98-99).
2. When I checked my characterization of a religious community with a local pastor, Chester Soleta, C.S.C., he added the note of *play*.
3. That everyday language is not *merely* descriptive is a point that still needs to be made!
4. For a useful analysis of this notion of *formal* (or linguistic) *fact*, see Zemach (1964).
5. An excellent recent example is Richard Adams (1975) where the story of the rabbits' odyssey is punctuated by stories told to inspire the group at critical junctures in their journey. Stanley Hauerwas develops this in the first chapter in his forthcoming study of Christian social ethics, now projected as *A Community of Character*, from the University of Notre Dame Press.
6. I have developed this point at some length, notably with reference to Carnap (1973:154-55).
7. Wicker introduces the meaning-frame scheme in 1975:33. This adaptation is mine. The top line expresses what Ralph McInerny identifies as the *ratio communis* (1961:passim). Note that it says very little until we flesh out the various contenders.
8. Robert Bolt dramatizes this inescapable demand of understanding in a conversation between More and Wolsey (1960:11).
9. Alternatively, analogical usage always retains a touch of metaphor, if my thesis regarding focal meaning is correct (1973:262).
10. I have developed this argument in "Religious Belief and Rationality," in C. F. Delaney, ed. (1979).
11. The allusion is to S. Kierkegaard (1968:142)—"The Christian heroism . . . is to venture wholly to be oneself, as an individual man, this definite individual man, alone before the face of God."

References

Adams, Richard
  1975. *Watership Down*. New York: Avon Books.
Aquinas, Thomas
  1964. *Summa Theologiae*. Vol. 2 (la.2–11), *Existence and Nature
    of God*. Trans. Timothy McDermott, O.P.; Vol. 3 (la.12–13),
    Knowing and Naming God. Trans. Herbert McCabe, O.P. New
    York/London: McGraw-Hill/Eyre & Spottiswoode.
Becker, Ernest
  1974. *Denial of Death*. New York: Free Press.
Bolt, Robert
  1960. *A Man for All Seasons*. New York: Vintage Press.
Burrell, David
  1973. *Analogy and Philosophical Language*. New Haven: Yale
    University Press.
  1974. *Exercises in Religious Understanding*. Notre Dame, Ind.:
    University of Notre Dame Press.
  1979. *Aquinas: God and Action*. Notre Dame, Ind.: Univeristy of
    Notre Dame Press.
Delaney, C. F., ed.
  1979. *Rationality and Religious Belief*. Notre Dame, Ind.:
    University of Notre Dame Press.
Hauerwas, Stanley
  1977. *Truthfulness and Tragedy*. Notre Dame, Ind.: University
    of Notre Dame Press.
John of the Cross
  1962. *Living Flame of Love*. Trans. E. Allison Peers. Garden
    City, N.Y.: Doubleday & Co.
Kierkegaard, Søren
  1968. *Fear and Trembling; and The Sickness unto Death* [by
    Anti-Climacus]. Trans. Walter Lowrie. Princeton, N.J.:
    Princeton University Press.
Mailer, Norman
  1968. *Armies of the Night*. New York: New American Library.
  1970. *A Fire on the Moon*. Boston: Beacon Press, Harper & Row.
Malcolm X
  1964. *Autobiography of Malcolm X*. New York: Grove Press.
McClendon, James Wm., Jr.
  1974. *Biography as Theology*. Nashville, Tenn.: Abingdon Press.

McClendon, James Wm., Jr., and Smith, James M.
  1975. *Understanding Religious Convictions*. Notre Dame, Ind.:
  University of Notre Dame Press.

McInerny, Ralph
  1961. *Logic of Analogy*. The Hague: Nijhoff.

Moore, Sebastian
  1977. *The Crucified Jesus Is No Stranger*. New York: Seabury
  Press.

Ogden, Schubert
  1966. *Reality of God*. New York: Harper & Row.

Shea, John
  1968. *"Theology and Autobiography." Commonweal* 105:358-62.

Tracy, David
  1979. "The Particularity and Universality of Christian Revelation." *Revelation and Experience*. Ed. Edward Schillebeeck
  and Bas van Iersel. New York: Seabury Press.

Wicker, Brian
  1975. *The Story-Shaped World*. Notre Dame, Ind.: University of
  Notre Dame Press.

Zemach, Edy
  1964. "Wittgenstein's Philosophy of the Mystical." *Review of
  Metaphysics* 18:38-57.

IV. THE REALITY OF GOD

About Robert Neville's Essay

The next essay is in a style quite different from any other in the present collection. Robert Neville is unashamedly a speculative theologian, in a time which often scorns speculation. One should note carefully, however, what Neville means by "speculative." It is not at all "guesswork" or "free flights of fancy"; for Neville, speculation is as indispensable an intellectual tool as is statistical analysis for demographers, or mathematics for physicists.

On its surface, then, this is a speculative essay on the role of the Holy Spirit in a Christian theology which dares to claim the status of public truth. Interest, however, lies as much in the structure of the essay as in its subject matter. Neville has constructed four stages, or parts, with each offering a more sophisticated reflection, until in section 4, one comes to wide-ranging general remarks on language and truth in religion. So if one is suspicious of what seem too easy assumptions in section 1, it might be profitable to read the essay backward as well as forward. That is, one might begin with section 4 on public discourse, pluralism, language, and truth; proceed to section 3 on the role of speculative hypotheses in thought; then turn to section 2 on God the Creator and the Trinity; and conclude with section 1, which presents one sort of process-theological view of God the Creator at work.

Neville's process thought is not the view promulgated by the disciples of A. N. Whitehead. While that view accepts the world of things and living beings as a primary

datum of which God must make the best he can, Neville
retains the classic Christian concept of a creation out of
nothing (*creatio ex nihilo*), and shows, still using process
categories, how God (or the Holy Spirit) must be viewed
as the world's ongoing Creator. (For a more common
process theology, see the following essay by John Cobb.)

So philosophically, Neville may be closer to the historic
idealists, notably G. W. F. Hegel (1770–1831), and to
Hegel's American heir, Josiah Royce (1855–1916). Hegel's
influence has been noted more than once in the present
collection of essays; in this, we note especially Neville's
insistence that the "vague" truths of speculation are made
concrete and relevant by the particular and historic truths
of Christian doctrine. Finally, however, Neville's
American philosophical heritage issues in a pragmatic
understanding of truth based on Charles Sanders Peirce
(1839–1914) and later promoted by William James
(1842–1910) and John Dewey (1859–1952). For
pragmatists, truth is measured by its consequences; it is
that account of things which achieves what humans must
achieve for their own purposes. Theological pragmatism is
unusual, but not unattractive when linked with other
currents of thought, American and Christian, in the
imaginative ways proposed by Robert Neville.

Two sorts of questions—one doctrinal, the other
methodological—may occur to the theological reader
here. Doctrinally, do the rather surprising positions taken
up by Neville, in order to present God the Creator in
terms of his system of thought, enable us to recognize in
this description one who is worthy of worship, trust, and
service? Neville's God, for his own logical reasons, has no
determinate character at all—not love, not even
holiness—except in connection with the determinations of
the created world. In brief, is such a God GOD?
Methodologically, does Neville's procedure of progress,
from more "humble" to more "sophisticated" arguments,
honestly represent the direction of his own deepest
commitments—which we take to be commitments to
classic or historic Christianity?

9. The Holy Spirit As God

Robert Neville

The concept of the Holy Spirit can be articulated as an understanding of the presence of God as Creator. Because of the multiple layers of presuppositions involved, however, this articulation contains several levels of generality. The first section of this essay will present a relatively naïve hypothesis as to the Creator's presence, discussing briefly how this relates to certain operations traditionally associated with the Holy Spirit. This section constitutes what Peirce would have called a "humble argument," to be followed by a more sophisticated consideration of the suppositions of that argument; each succeeding section, except the last, is a humble argument with respect to the one it precedes (Peirce, 1935:311-26, 332-39). The second section presents a speculative hypothesis about God as Creator, whose presence in the world might be as depicted in section 1. The third section then discusses the nature of speculation relative to the theological problem of the Holy Spirit as God, justifying, after a fashion, the approach through speculation. The fourth section finally treats the issue of using the Christian notion of the Holy Spirit in public inquiry about God.

I. The Holy Spirit As the Creator's Presence

Within the Christian tradition, the Holy Spirit sometimes has been the concept with which to articulate any activity of God in a present moment. The activities range from the stirrings of individual hearts through the guidance of history, to the sanctification of nature by divine presence. It took many centuries to generalize the notion of the Holy Spirit in this

235

way, and perhaps the concept did not reach its greatest intellectual power until Hegel's *Phenomenology of Spirit* (1807). The concrete experiences that the notion was intended to interpret, however, were recognized in the ancient days: the experiences at Pentecost, Jesus' baptism, Elijah's still small voice, the founding activities Job learned about from the whirlwind, the voice from the burning bush, Jesus' promise to send his Spirit as a guide, the divine Spirit in prophecy.

To appreciate what is special about the Holy Spirit in a systematic concept of God, however, requires a concept of the world in and to which God as Spirit might be present, a concept that can thus articulate divine presence. If there were no such concept, there would be no cognitive way to envision how the various alleged manifestations of the Spirit would be *one*. A concept of the world, or philosophical cosmology, is thus a prerequisite for articulating divine presence.

But a philosophical cosmology cannot be constructed merely for the purpose of articulating divine presence; that would be ad hoc and lacking in force. It rather must arise from and prove itself in all the areas of inquiry relevant to basic philosophic conceptions of the world. In the twentieth century, the revolution in the scientific view of the physical universe is perhaps the most decisive contributor to philosophical cosmology; the historical recognition of evil and of human responsibility, and the development of abstraction in the arts are also decisive. The cosmological tradition of process philosophy is the most highly developed and sensitive contemporary approach to cosmological questions, and a variant of that will be sketched here in connection with the Holy Spirit as the presence of the Creator (Whitehead, 1929; Cobb, 1965; Neville, 1974). No attempt will be made here to justify the hypothesis, except insofar as it helps make sense of issues concerning the Spirit. It also should be pointed out that the cosmology presented here completely rejects the concept of God in Whitehead's process cosmology and bears little relation to process theism (Neville, 1980; Ford, 1972). In this hypothesis, the deviations from central process conceptions stem mainly from the need to amend the views of Whitehead and his followers with a quite different conception of God.[1]

Divine Presence in Existence

The most distinctive process conception is that the world consists of occasions or events. An event is a happening in which previous events, given as completed facts, are transformed and arranged in a new way, with the definiteness of an individual event. When an event has happened, it too is a completed fact. When it is happening, however, it is not an existing fact, but a fact coming into existence.

The concept of *causation* in the process view divides roughly into two components. On the one hand are the past facts which function as conditions for an event. This is the material with which things happen in an event. Limits are imposed on the event by the past events out of which it arises. But the past events do not *act*, once they have become facts. Action, on the other hand, is an expression of the present creativity within an event, whereby it brings itself into existence as a definite new fact. A present happening must take up the past events, as it were, and give them places in its own resolution.

The *character* of an event derives from two sources. Part derives from the past events that are taken up as conditions. Other elements derive from the event's internal process of integrating those diverse past conditions into a unified, definite new fact. The elements of character that derive from the past illustrate the regularities and systematic patterns of the environment of events within which the emerging event takes place. Furthermore, the elements of character that derive from the internal process must fall within the limits imposed by environmental regularities; otherwise, the event could not come to factual existence in harmony with its environment. But within those limits, and from the perspective of antecedent predictable regularities and patterns, the internal integration is spontaneous. "Spontaneity" here means "not determined according to antecedent regularities"; this may be called character-spontaneity because it refers to spontaneous elements of character (Moore, Neville, and Sullivan, 1972:392-421).

There is a larger sense of spontaneity, however, which can

be called existential spontaneity. This refers to the creative process of bringing the event into existence—the process of integration itself. Whereas the character of the integration might be determined by the very strict limits set by the environing facts out of which the event arises, the environing facts do not produce their integration in the new event. The production of the new event, however determined, is the spontaneous essential existential quality of the event itself. Existential spontaneity is the "making present" of the event; reference to existential spontaneity is made in accounting for the fact *that* the event occurs. The character of the event is *what* it is, and character-spontaneity might exist within an event, along with elements of character determined by other events; together, they comprise the event (Smith, 1961).

Existential spontaneity is *decisive* for the formation of an event; without it there would be no new event, but only the finished events that are potential conditions. If the antecedent conditions allow for alternate integrations, then some elements in the character produced by the existential spontaneity exhibit character-spontaneity. All elements in the character of an event derive either from decisions of its own character-spontaneity or from decisions that decided the past events which conditioned it. And all those past events have characters decided either by their own character-spontaneity or by that of their own antecedents, and so on, *ad indefinitum.*

The character of an event is a relative matter—relative to antecedent conditions, to future consequences, and to the products of its own character-spontaneity. Within ordinary human affairs, we attend to the actual, emerging, and potential characters of things, and we do so from relative perspectives. One may also reflect, however, on the fact *that* some event or complex of events exists, is coming to exist, or will exist. The events, of course, have characters, and to understand their characters we must trace out their relative connections. But appreciating or inquiring into the *thatness* of the events points to their absolute or ontological dimension (Neville, 1978).

Inquiring into the ontology of events, we may say that the

Holy Spirit is their existential spontaneity—God creating
each thing. The Holy Spirit, as existential spontaneity within
an event, operates within the limits set by the antecedent
conditions given to be integrated. But then each of those
antecedent conditions had its own existential spontaneity,
which operated within the limits of yet prior events, and so
forth. Therefore as existential spontaneity, the Holy Spirit is
God creating each event in both its kinds of character—that
which results from the integration of given conditions (present
existential spontaneity) and that which results from the given
conditions themselves (past existential spontaneity). From
the standpoint of each event, the Holy Spirit is actively
present in each in its own time. The Spirit thus operates at
diverse times and places. Yet because the character of any
event in large measure is a function of its connections with
conditions (and with the future things for which it will later be
a condition, a theme not developed here), the diverse times
and places of the Spirit's action exhibit a mutual relevance in
the creative activity of the Spirit (Neville, 1968).

The concept of existential spontaneity within events
articulates that most general sense of the Holy Spirit as the
creator or ground of all things. That the existential spontaneity
deserves to be described in the language of divinity derives in
part from the sense of wonder and awe we sometimes have at
the fact that things exist at all. Although *what* the world is might
not be sacred, there is something sacred about the fact *that* it is.

Another characteristic of the Holy Spirit follows immediately from the above discussion. That part of an event's
existential spontaneity which is also character-spontaneous
introduced novelty into affairs. Deriving not from antecedent
determinations of character but solely from the event's
existential spontaneity, the characters of integrations produced in that which was called character-spontaneity are the
Spirit's guidance of affairs in some measure of freedom from
antecedent commitments. The Holy Spirit thus not only
grounds and sustains but also leads. If the order of nature has
evolved from the least possible order, then the Holy Spirit has
directed the entire evolution through the introduction of each
novel component of order.

Divine Presence in Life

According to the hypothesis of process cosmology, an enduring object is a series of events, each exhibiting rather much the same character as the others and each deriving its character as a condition from antecedents within the series (this does not apply to the first member, if there is one). A *living* thing combines events in well-patterned enduring elements with events that have a significant degree of novelty, where the novelty is relevant to the enduring pattern. Most novelty, it may be presumed, is *ir*relevant to the surrounding events; it leaves no marks and conditions little if anything. But the novelty involved in a living thing affects the pattern of many elements in the series, so that novelty is organically related to antecedently fixed patterns. A novel event in a living thing requires a well-patterned environment to which it can be relevant.

The Holy Spirit can be conceived as the source of life, in the sense that the existential spontaneity in the novel event is mutually relevant with the existential spontaneity in the past, contemporary, and future environing events in the enduring living thing. The Spirit is the source of that peculiar and poignant mutual relevance of novelty and continuity in which life consists. Death either is the cessation of novelty associated with an enduring organism, or it is a radical diminishment of the relevance of the novelty to the overall organic pattern. Decay involves novelty relevant, not to the overall pattern, but to separable parts. Of course, the Holy Spirit as existential spontaneity is in those events in which death consists, including the less-than-organically relevant novelty—the Lord gives and the Lord takes away. But the Spirit makes a specially prized contribution with the mutual relevance of novelty and patterned continuity that make up the breath of life itself.

Divine Presence in Human Experience

The question of the operation of the Holy Spirit (God creating) in the more complicated structures of human life cannot be separated from questions about *what* is created. The character of the Spirit consists in what is created. This point is reflected in the traditional Christian trinitarian view that the Holy Spirit is the Spirit of the Son. The character of what is created is a matter determined empirically (Neville, 1972).

One of the most outstanding traits of human experience is the fundamental distinction between actual process and norms. The integrations of events in the past, the processes of integrating in the present, and the potentials for integration in the future are all matters of past, present, or future harmonies (Neville, 1974:ch. 3). "Harmony" is a notion connoting relative degrees, however, in principle, and it is always possible to ask whether the integration in any event or complex of events is the best harmony, the most harmonious harmony. In some spheres of experience, in fact, we imagine alternate harmonies which we recognize as more harmonious than those that actually happen. Experience is evaluative when there is some recognition of this logical character of degrees of harmony.

A religiously significant dimension of normative human activity is experiential *engagement* with the world—the transformation of mere causal relations with the environment into an experience of the environment. But our fundamental experiential images are not without norms, for they either engage us well with the world or they alienate experience, and in multifarious ways. Religions have long known that authentic life requires engaging images, and much of ritual, prayer, music, meditation, and other spiritual activity is practiced for the sake of its cultivation and disciplining of primordial imagination. From the meditative absorption in a mandala to the habitual imitation of Christ, imagination is formed so as to engage the world according to the structures that religion takes to be the most important. The Holy Spirit is God creating within the imagination that engages the world according to some image, and the successful attainment of a spiritual image can be felt as a special grace of the Holy Spirit. Destructive images often have been identified with "evil spirits," and these equally are expressions of God as Creator;

the Christian sense that the Holy Spirit stands over against evil spirits is not rendered by this concept.

Divine Presence and Human Freedom

The inference is frequently made that, if God creates everything, then there is no freedom or responsibility attributable to created persons. This inference is particularly tempting when the creating Spirit is interpreted as existential spontaneity in both present and past components of existence. Within the Christian tradition, that inference led major Reformation theologians to adopt deterministic theories of human action and to characterize God's sovereignty in terms of complete responsibility for all that happens. It also has led some contemporary Prostestant process theologians (e.g. Cobb, 1965:chs. 4–5, 1969; Ford, 1970) to assert that God is not the creator at all but an actual entity separate from the world, who grasps the world after its subjective present and guides it only with tempting lures.

But the inference need not follow. The integrity of a thing in the world, including a human being, rests in its being the character it is (Neville, 1968:ch. 4). That character is a function of the conditions of the events that make it up, plus the various processes of integrating those conditions. A thing is not a secret core which possesses its character—it *is* its character. Human freedom consists in many dimensions, but one of the most important is often alleged to be a certain indeterminacy. If a person is to be responsible for some action, and the responsibility is not to be traced back reductively to more antecedent conditions, then the future, in some features, must be indeterminate with respect to the requirements of the antecedent conditions. Furthermore, the actual decisive process within the person, starting from the antecedent conditions, must determine which of the possible outcomes will come about; otherwise, chance, not the person, would be responsible (Neville, 1974:chs. 5, 6).

There is nothing that requires, in principle, that the events of the world be completely determinate with regard to their consequences. There is a certain observed order and regularity to things, but we have not observed that there is complete regularity, as would be required for determinism. In the face of moral experience, it seems wise to assume that there is enough of the right indeterminacy so that individuals can make a moral difference.

Moreover, there is nothing, in principle, to exclude the kinds of features that on the one hand, do determine future consequences and on the other, are not determined by antecedent conditions. It is possible, in other words, for there to be character-spontaneity in events. Character-spontaneity is the coming into existence of elements in an event's character which are not determined by the antecedent events that enter as conditions. Whether there in fact is any character-spontaneity, or any of the right sort for moral experience, is an empirical matter, not one required by cosmology or by scientific assumptions necessary for finding regularities where they are. But the existence of moral experience makes a *prima facie* case for such character-spontaneity.

A person *is* the character of the events making up that person's past, present, and future life. If the person exercises freedom, that consists in certain of the decisive events that contain morally relevant character-spontaneous features. Responsibility for consequences is to be laid to the person and not to the person's antecedents on the grounds that those character-spontaneous elements made the decisive difference. Sometimes people think they are free in this sense when they are not; but this is because the decisive factors are other than the ones affected by any character-spontaneous features the people might have. We have vast experiential evidence to show that people *are* free in this sense in many situations.

With the process of integration within an event, the character-spontaneous features come into existence through existential spontaneity. In this sense, God the Creator is responsible for them and for the free responsibility to which they contribute. But since the freedom and responsibility of the person consists in being those character-spontaneous features (in harmony with all the other elements of character), the person, too, is responsible. One's free choice consists, in

part, in constituting oneself as the determiner of this
alternative, rather than that alternative. One is not free if one
is determined in one's choice completely by antecedent
reasons. Rather, free choice involves determining oneself
with an action that transforms certain antecedently entertained reasons into the decisive motives, rather than selecting
other reasons which were also potential motives. A person is
freely responsible for choices in the sense in which the person
is the choosing—where the choosing determines an otherwise
undetermined consequence. This makes logical the profound
observation that God (as Holy Spirit) is closer to me than I am
to myself.

The discussion in this section has attempted to illustrate
various ways in which the Holy Spirit can be construed as God
creating the world. The principle vehicle for this has been the
brief elucidation of a cosmology. The cosmology itself is not
strictly dependent on the need to illustrate a concept of the
Holy Spirit, but could be accepted on its own merits by people
who completely reject the Christian religious symbolism
involved in the notion of the Spirit.

What has not been discussed, however, but merely
asserted, is the claim that God is indeed creator of the cosmos.
Whether this hypothesized cosmology, or some other, is true,
can sense be made of the claim that the world is created? And
since, on at least this cosmology, the Holy Spirit can be used
with many of its traditional associations to interpret the
existential quality of affairs, how does this relate to the overall
conception of God as Creator? By what speculative hypothesis
may we conceive of God as Creator?

II. God the Creator and Trinity

Let us suppose, *ex hypothesi*, that everything determinate
is created and that we call the creator God (Neville, 1968,
1980).

Because everything determinate is created, the creator
must be indeterminate, except insofar as the creator acquires
a character from creating. The character acquired from
creating is itself a created determinate affair. Similarly, a

parent is not a parent except insofar as a child is had; but this analogy has the following limitation. Parenting is understood partly in terms of prior potentialities for parenting, and the creator cannot be said to have any potentialities "prior" to creating, since these would be determinate. Since potentialities alone prior to parenting are not sufficient to make a person a parent, however, the analogy does hold in respect to the fact that it is the act of producing offspring (transforming former potentialities) that makes a person a parent, similarly to the way the act of creating determinate things makes the creator a creator.

Because God's character, whatever it might be, derives from the creation, this is an "economic" speculative hypothesis—an economic trinitarianism, as it shall turn out (Neville, 1969). God's character is a function solely of God's creating. Apart from creating, God cannot be said to have a character, to be determinate, to be existent, one, good, true, beautiful, distinguishable from nothingness, or "God" in any sense. This claim itself is a logical implication of the hypothesized creation relation—namely, that God creates everything determinate. Perhaps appreciation of this logical implication lies behind the experience of God as the Abyss, the aboriginal fire, the ultimate Nothing from which the creation springs. But since there *is* creation—and even to deny this is to acknowledge the determinateness of intelligibility—God is *not* Nothing but the Creator of this world, with at least the characteristics of being a this-worldly creator. Since the pure divine aseity would be utterly unintelligible, we would have to say that God could *not* be Nothing. But there is no reason, in fact, to say that God *is* Nothing, since God is determinate as Creator of this determinte world.

A distinction should be clearly drawn between cosmological causation and ontological creation. Cosmological causation is any of the variety of ways determinate things within the cosmos influence one another, as one event conditions another; it is "cosmological" in that it pertains to relations between created things in the cosmos. Ontological creation, or divine creation, is the bringing into being of determinate things.[2] Cosmological causal relations are themselves ontolo-

gically created. Created things need not be completely
determinate in all respects; temporal events, for instance,
may be indeterminate with respect to the way they will later
be conditions for other things; yet insofar as they are
determinate at all, they are created, and insofar as they will
later condition other things, that conditioning is part of the
created determinate nature of those later things. Temporal
relations, with all the change and novelty involved in process,
are themselves created; the cosmological hypothesis about
process that has been sketched indicates how, on at least one
hypothesis, the creator is present, creating, in temporal
things.

To be a thing is to be determinate, or at least partially
determinate. A thing is determinate by virtue of at least two
kinds of features: (a) conditional features, by virtue of which it
is related to other things as different from them; and (b)
essential features, by virtue of which its conditional features
are not mere reflections of other things but are modifications
of those other things from the standpoint of the thing itself
(Neville, 1968:ch. 2). The essential feature would be the
thing's own nature, if it were not for the fact that a determinate
nature must be determinate *with respect to something else*;
conditional features are derived from those other things so
that the thing can be determinate with respect to them. The
conditional features would be the ways a thing is related to
other things, but this supposes that the thing has a character of
its own so that it can be related or conditioned. A thing's real
nature is a harmony, necessarily including both essential and
conditional features. In terms of the cosmology sketched in
the previous section, the antecedent conditional events would
be conditional features, and the characters arising from their
integration would be essential.

But how can the connection between essential and
conditional features be accounted for? Not by antecedent
causes, or goals, or abstract forms, or material components,
because each of those causes, at most, could account for
conditional features alone; and even then the difference made
by the essential features to the conditional ones would not be
accounted for. Therefore, the cosmological relations, causal

and otherwise, are insufficient to account for that harmony of essential and conditional features which is the being of the thing. The being of a thing must be ontologically created, and part of the meaning of this is that the *de facto* harmony of its essential and conditional features is "just made to be."

In order for a thing to have conditional features with regard to something else, both things must be in a context of mutual relevance. That is, the being of one thing must be mutually relevant to the being of the other in order for one to condition the other. The cosmological character of the conditioning itself—for instance, causal conditioning—would not be possible if there were not an ontological context of mutual relevance. This sort of context cannot be reduced to the cosmological relations of conditional features, because the being of any conditional feature requires its harmony with the essential features of the thing whose feature it is.   The ontological context of mutual relevance therefore includes the essential features of diverse things, whereas cosmologically, they are connected only conditionally. To be determinate consequently means being with other things with respect to which a thing is determinate, and this means being created in an ontological context of mutual relevance.

The creative act by which the diverse things of the world are ontologically created is unified in the sense that its product has the character of the context of mutual relevance. It is diversely located, in that each thing is created as a harmony of its own essential and conditional features. That the creative act is unified does not entail that its product is *totum simul*, but only that past-present-future things are in an ontological context of mutual relevance.

Does the created world have an integrity over against the creator? Cosmologically, this is necessary for freedom. In ascertaining what a thing (or a complex of things) is, one looks to the characters it *de facto* has. Upon analysis, some features of those characters are conditional upon other relevant things; scientific inquiry, among others, can trace out these conditional connections. Other features of those characters are intrinsic to the things themselves and can be apprehended by attaining to the perspective of the things in intuition or empathy; generally the humanities focus on understanding these essential features. Of course there is the unique harmony that makes up the thing's own real character, and such harmonies can be presented to experience imaginatively by the arts and by many other avenues of inquiry. But in no sense need one go outside the realm of created determinate things in order to understand or account for the characters they have. *What* things are is a function of their determining conditions and idiosyncratic self-realizations. The question of the ontological creation of things arises only when one wonders *that* things are. The question of the ontological existence of a thing is not the same as that which asks whether there are cosmological causes that will bring it into existence. Rather, it is whether there is an ontological context of mutual relevance in which the thing is (or was or will be) real, a context that requires the appropriate conditional causes, to be sure, but also the appropriate essential features and the harmony of both. Divine creation thus can never be cited as a reason a thing is one way rather than another, or the course of events goes one direction rather than another, except in the general and usually trivial sense that God is the creator of everything. The particular course of history, for instance, is to be understood according to historical causes of the sort historians cite. God is indeed the creator of that history; but if the historical causes had been different, and the course of history different, then God would have been the creator of that instead.

What are the implications for the character of God in this analysis of the speculative hypothesis of divine creation? As remarked above, we may not speak of God as a being apart from the creation relation with the world, for that would be indeterminate. We must speak of God rather as characterized within the creation relation. Within this relation, God has a tripartite character; no part can be understood without the other two, yet no part can be defined completely by the other parts (Neville, 1969).

First, as Creator, God is the source of all determinate being, and as Creator, God is not contingent *in the way* that determinate things are; that is to say, God is not a composite of essential and conditional features, and there is no ontological context of mutual relevance in which God is together with other things.

Second, as Creator, God cannot be separated from the product of creation and must be identified with that product. There is no determinate medium in which the realm of determinations could be separated from the creator creating them. God therefore *is* the created world, insofar as part of the divine character is the end product(s) of the creative act. To say that God is the created world is of course extremely vague. To be at all helpful religiously, this part of the hypothesis needs to be specified by a more concrete interpretation of just what this world is. It is far more important to specify this "part" of the divine character than to specify the sense in which God is Source; indeed, the way to make that more specific is to specify that of which God is the source. From the perspective of this vague hypothesis, it would seem equally plausible to specify God's identity in the world by the metaphors of Maya, the dance of Shiva, the Absolute aspect of the Mahayana One Mind, or the Incarnate Logos.

Third, God is the very activity of creating. That activity has no form or nature of its own except that of the determinations created. If the traditional Christian story is correct in the main, and the Christ is the redeeming perfection of fact and norm, then the central or paradigmatic character of the creative activity can be called "the mind of Christ." But this historical characterization cannot be made until a proper Christology has specified the speculative hypothesis and independently justified itself. From the standpoint of the hypothesis, the creative activity has the character of its product, just as the action of a human has the character of what it does. But whereas human action always proceeds in part from antecedent potentialities, giving it a nature that, in part, must include the past in present action, the activity of ontological creation has no such character stemming from the past.

On the other hand, one of the more universal or transcendental products of creation is the determinate metaphysical character of creation itself; and within this character, the activity serves as the mediator linking the source and the product. The source could not create the product without the creative activity. The product could have no being without the creative acitvity. The creative activity could not end in its determinate product without the (otherwise) indeterminate source, because its own determinate nature as creative activity would need to be created. The creative activity could not be the activity or expression of the source without issuing in the determinate world, for otherwise there would be no creating.

The creative activity is related to the world and to the source in ways strikingly parallel to the Holy Spirit as understood in trinitarian theology. Of course, trinitarian theology is equally expressive of the experience of Jesus and is based on a Christology which will not be investigated here. What already has been investigated in the previous section, however, is how the creative act seems to be like the Holy Spirit, when specified by a cosmology that is otherwise attractive in the public discussion.

We may now suggest that what the Christian tradition has called the Holy Spirit is both a plausible category for interpreting the ontological dimensions of experience, as revealed in the discussion of cosmology, and a coherent symbol within a speculative notion of God as Creator. We have not inquired, however, into the nature of the intellectual strategy of treating the Holy Spirit according to the hypotheses of the speculative conception of God and the philosophical cosmology. Is it not an arrogant impiety to "reduce" the concrete witness of Christians about the Spirit to a matter of hypotheses?

III. The Holy Spirit As a Speculative Problem

The Holy Spirit traditionally can be identified in a variety of matrices. According to the New Testament, the Holy Spirit has a historical identity: It expressed divine commentary on Jesus' baptism, for instance, and appeared at the day of Pentecost. The Holy Spirit was identified by Jesus as part of his promise; the Spirit sent by God after Jesus' death has a quasi-historical identity. Then there is the Spirit that manifests itself with potential universality in the life of the communities of Christians, a Spirit with a capacity for pervasive or multiple location. The Holy Spirit also has been looked to as a tester of personal spirits and as an interpreter of Scripture and doctrine.

Along with all these relatively concrete matrices for identifying the Holy Spirit, there is also the conception of the Holy Spirit as divine, as part of God, or as divinity itself. This matrix has its own special complications, joining and unifying a wide variety of relatively concrete identities of the Holy Spirit and connecting all these with other things that should be said about God. The proper matrix for conceiving the Holy Spirit as God is speculative theology. Because speculative theology (or speculative philosophy dealing with God) has not been practiced popularly, it is important to say something about it, to provide a new vantage point for reflection on the previous discussion.

Speculation is the attempt to envision the whole of one's subject matter. Envisagement requires a selection of the important elements to be kept in view, as distinct from the relatively more trivial elements that can be dropped from sight. The important elements are articulated in categories which indicate their bearing upon one another in logical, causal, and all other ways that make for the importance in question.

Speculation thus has two directions of movement. One is from the relatively chaotic welter of experience to the systematic categories, articulating what is important in experience. The other is from the systematic categories back to experience, now as interpreted by the categories. Both movements are necessary and are implicit in any genuine speculative endeavor. Speculation has frequently been identified as only the move away from experience to the systematic categories. Sometimes it has even been identified as logical thinking *within* the system of categories. But the categories themselves are vague and do not articulate what is important *in experience* unless the move from the categories to the experience of the subject matter is made as part of the systematic thinking. The systematic categories construed according to a formal structure might be identified as a speculative "system." But "system" as adjectival to speculative *thinking* refers to the responsibility for moving from experience to the categories, and from the categories to experience, each move reinterpreting and correcting the other.

What is the relation of the system of speculative categories to the experience which constitutes its subject matter? There are five points in regard to that relation which also indicate the role of speculation in public inquiry.

1. The system of categories collectively, and the categories individually, are *hypotheses* about the subject matter. The subject matter could be simplified and articulated in a variety of ways, perhaps, and it is hypothetical whether any given categorial simplification is the best. Since the categories are hypothetical, certain formal requirements obtain—namely, that they be consistent and coherent.

The move from experience to the categories does not proceed according to any logical rules but is what Peirce called "a guess at the riddle" (1935:311-39). The categories therefore must be relevant to the subject matter, although judgments about relevance can be made only after the articulation of the categories. With a history of speculation, the guesses are "educated." The historical dialectic of systematic answers to basic philosophical and theological answers provides a rich background for any contemporary speculator, and there are sufficient standard moves to indicate the general advantages and disadvantages attending various types of categories.

A hypothesis, although imaginatively produced as a guess, must be internally articulated in order to be made applicable to experience. Again, there are no rules for the preliminary parsing of speculative categories. But the end product of the analysis of categories ought to be an articulation in logical form, so that the categories are expressed in what logicians call "well-formed formulas." Once the categories are articulated with formal precision, it is possible to make logical deductions from them.

At its best, a hypothesis can be very plausible. To discover how plausible, one deduces experiential consequences that should follow if the hypothesis is true, and then one tests to see whether the hypothesis is applicable as specified to experience. A hypothesis can never be certain. It can never be a deduction from experience, because experience does not provide well-formed formulas from which it might be deduced; "geometrical" thinkers such as Spinoza did not deduce their theories from experience but from some allegedly indubitable, logically well-formed first principles. Nor can speculative hypotheses ever become certain, even by having 100 percent plausibility, although concrete particular doubts may be removed, at least for the time being.

2. A hypothetical system of speculative categories is logically *vague*. As a logical notion, "vagueness" does not mean fuzziness. It means that the proposition that is vague is insufficiently determinate to specify the objects to which it refers and that it requires supplementary propositions to identify those objects. For instance, the proposition "Someone is about to die" is vague because it does not specify *which* person. The proposition "Things are going well" is vague because it does not specify which things and because it is quite compatible in our ordinary language with "Some other things are not going so well."

"Vagueness" contrasts with "generality." A proposition is general if it refers to a class and is determinate as to which individuals it refers to in that class. "All men are mortal" is general because it refers to anything that is a man.

Hypotheses, as described above, may be general or vague. (Or they may be particular.) Scientific hypotheses aim to be general so that they can be tested by particular critical experiments; a hypothesis about electrons that is vague as to what counts as an electron would be difficult to test. Speculative hypotheses, however, should be vague. A speculative hypothesis about God for instance, cannot refer to particular experiential manifestations of divinity unless there are intermediate interpreting hypotheses. These intermediate hypotheses might be historical accounts of God in human affairs; they might be interpretations of religious experience, of a divine grounding for moral judgment, or of a

Is God GOD?

whole host of other interpretive strata. And since the interpreting hypotheses themselves may be vague in their own way, the set of hypotheses that relate speculative systems to concrete experience might be hierarchically ordered, partially overlapping, or historically contingent in their relations, following the saga of hermeneutic development.

3. One advantage of vagueness in speculative hypotheses is that it directs attention to the various positive tasks in specifying the hypotheses so as to determine objects. The hypotheses *necessarily* must be supplemented by interpretive propositions arising from considerations *other than those directly forming the speculative hypotheses*. Most particularly, if God is hypothesized to be the creator of the world, then further interpretive theories about just what is created, how creation takes place, the difference between divine creation and intraworldly causation, and many like issues must be developed before the creator-hypothesis determines God. Furthermore, these midrange interpretive theories might not be consistent with one another. For instance, the creator-hypothesis might be made specific by claiming that the cosmos created is an Aristotelian substance world. Or it might be claimed (as in section 1 above) that it is a process world. Let us suppose that these midrange hypotheses are incompatible. They cannot both be true. And the one that is preferable cannot be deduced from the supervening vague creator-hypothesis, for the creator-hypothesis is true if either (or some other) midrange hypothesis is true. The probation of the claims of the midrange hypotheses must be made on their own terms, according to criteria appropriate to the middle range. And in fact, there are many midrange hypotheses involved in specifying a vague hypothesis, and they have many kinds of connections.

Because it is logically required that vague speculative hypotheses be specified positively, the diverse religious traditions and the incompletely congruent strains within single traditions necessarily have potential contributions to make to the inquiry about God *from the speculative standpoint*. If the hypothesis is properly vague, then *any plausible positive interpretive experience of God must be capable of specifying it.* The truth of that specifying religious statement must be made out on its own account; it cannot be derived from the vaguer hypothesis; neither can it be falsified by the vaguer hypothesis.

Proponents of a midrange position have no immediate reason to fear that the speculative hypothesis would prejudice the plausibility of their position. If their position is a possible specification of the vague hypothesis, then it has been demonstrated to the public community to be at least a possibility. The Christian claim, for instance, that God created the world *ex nihilo* is not obvious to everyone even as a possibility, and the speculative creator-hypothesis would show that it is a possibility. In the short run, if the speculative hypothesis does not show the midrange claim to be a possibility, then there is a fault in the vagueness of the speculative hypothesis. In the long run, of course, it might be found that it is impossible to arrive at any speculative hypothesis that shows a midrange view or a particular religious claim to be a possibility; it also might be found that the speculative hypothesis which receives overwhelming support from many other areas of experience is incompatible with a hypothesis that does allow for the possibility of the less vague position. But this only amounts to saying that the particular religious position is simply found to be implausible in the long run, a fate to which any interpretation of anything is liable: It may be unable to sustain itself in public inquiry.

4. Another advantage in vague speculative hypotheses is that they lay the foundation for testing the universality of proposals required for public inquiry. Let us suppose that a vague hypothesis about God is specified in each of the directions proposed by the major theological traditions (this is by no means an easy matter, but let us suppose it can be done). Whereas the presentations, in terms internal to each of the traditions, are somewhat incommensurable with one another, as specifications of a vaguer speculative hypothesis, it would be possible to see how they relate. They might be complementary, irrelevant to each other but compatible, or contradictory and irreconcilable; perhaps the traditions relate to some degree in all these ways. For instance, it might be

discovered that the Buddhas of Mahayana, the avatars of Hinduism, and Jesus the Incarnate Logos are overlapping and compatible models of divinity in human affairs, but that the Christian claim that Jesus is the exclusive or supreme figure is incompatible with the rest. This discovery by itself does not say that the Christian claim is right or wrong—only that it is incompatible with the rest. With a properly vague but variously specified speculative hypothesis, it is possible to locate in public inquiry some of the issues that otherwise are hard to find.

Furthermore, in conjunction with the possible specializations, awareness of the problem of developing an adequate speculative hypothesis serves as a regulative principle of public inquiry. Speculative hypotheses are potentially universal—capable of illustrating any religious claim that can sustain its plausibility. And it may generally be supposed that any tradition with massively interpreted experience of the divine, which has sustained itself through a long period of its own internal responses to affairs, is plausible in its main contentions.

5. The truth conditions for a speculative hypothesis now can be summarized. A hypothesis is true if, in the judgment of an infinitely critical community of inquirers, the following conditions hold:

(a) the hypothesis is formally consistent and coherent, and
(b) the hypothesis is dialectically superior to alternate hypotheses on formal grounds, and
(c) the hypothesis can be compatibly specified by all true claims of lesser vagueness (however the truth of those claims is established), and
(d) some plausible claims of lesser vagueness do specify the hypothesis, and
(e) the plausible claims are incompatible specifications of the hypothesis, no other speculative hypothesis satisfying (a) through (d) would make them compatible, and the hypothesis could be consistently specified by a world-range of claims compatible with the falseness of one side of the contradicting plausible claims.

If a speculative hypothesis is supported by the specification of a plausible view which in time comes to be implausible, the hypothesis is not necessarily falsified. But it requires plausibility from elsewhere, and it must be specifiable by whatever view becomes plausible in the stead of the first. Otherwise the speculative hypothesis must be altered. Of course, the history of thought has shown that the plausible speculative hypotheses which have functioned in partial ways to constitute the background for public discussion have themselves developed through the dialectic of inquiry. There is no reasonable expectation that any speculative hypothesis, however attractive today, will have much staying power. But this does not denigrate its usefulness to present public inquiry whose positive existential needs must be met for our own discussion.

The Holy Spirit is a speculative-specified problem in the following way. In the tradition of Christian theology, the Holy Spirit has been an integral part of the conception of God, and it in turn has been specified by various particular identities of the sort mentioned at the beginning of this section. The previous sections have presented a vague speculative hypothesis about God as creator of everything determinate, and a somewhat less vague speculative cosmology specifying the creation theory, which on independent grounds interprets the main domains of experience in the twentieth century. It was argued that a certain economic trinitarian view from the Christian tradition specifies the hypothesis of God in ways that reinforce and elaborate the cosmology, with special relevance for the notion of the Holy Spirit. The speculative hypothesis suggests that God is present in the world as Creator through the Holy Spirit, and it specifies the hypothesis with the Christian tradition. It is now possible to see, in part at least, how this conception of the Holy Spirit is an enlightening interpretation of central experiences and is a contribution to the public inquiry about God. It remains an open, but opened, question whether the historic and symbolic associations of the notion of the Holy Spirit are publicly valuable, or whether they remain limited in worth to the Christian tradition.

IV. God and the Holy Spirit in Public Inquiry

The "problem of God" is a public question for our period,
formulated in a variety of related ways. What is God's nature?
Is there a divine element in experience? Is there a divine word
for us? Can spiritual practices have spiritual (rather than
merely technological) results? Is there an unconditional
standpoint of moral judgment on human affairs? Is there an
unconditional dimension of things generally? Is there a
meaningful unconditioned ground for the world? A meaningful unconditioned goal?

Inquiry into the problem of God must reflect the public
context of the discussion if it is to be serious. This normative
thesis stems from a logical observation. Inquiry into the
problem of God deals with God and related matters as the
subject matter about which it seeks to discover some truth. To
put forward an affirmation, however hypothetically, requires
that it be presented in such a manner that the evidences for its
plausibility are potentially accessible to the other interested
inquirers.

One must stress the *potential* accessibility here in order to
do justice to the profound particularity of cultivation involved
in deep experience and skilled, wise thinking; not everyone
has the capacity or preparation to inquire critically into the
validity of quantum mechanics, the veracity of Wallace
Stevens' poetry, the integrity of the Arab-Israeli negotiations,
or the spiritual depth of Buber or Merton. Moreover, it is
always necessary to acknowledge the indefinite ambiguities of
the rhetorical context of dialogue; most inquiry is taken up
with clarifying questions and with making explicit the
associations and suppositions brought to the discussion.

But *if* one puts forward a proposal about God in the public
context of inquiry, then one must make it and its evidence
potentially accessible. "Evidence" here refers not only to
experiential critical variables and rational proofs, but also to
the cultural and linguistic context of interpretation, the
motives behind the proposal, and the potential of all these for
further critical examination. Part of the purpose of a public
proposal is that, when grasped from the perspective of all the

evidence, it will be "evident" to all inquirers that the subject matter is as proposed.

Not to make it potentially accessible is to say that the proposal is "true for those in privileged position X." This, however, is to change the subject matter of the proposed hypothesis. For "true for those in privileged position X" means "Those in privileged position X consider the proposal true." The latter clause is not about the subject matter—God—but about those in the privileged position. It is one thing to note that some inquirers do not have access to the evidence: In this case the proposal cannot be asserted as completely true, but only potentially true. It is another thing to assert the proposal to be true for those in a privileged position: This is to change the subject covertly.

The logical argument sketched in the previous paragraphs is not without controversy. It might be objected, for instance, that with all the talk about evidence and dialogue for the clarification of meaning, "truth" means "provable within an actual community with a common language (for practical purposes) and a common, steady sense of what counts as proof, good evidence, argument, and so forth." Some philosophers of science have put the point this way (Putnam, 1978:lect. l, 2): " 'Electrons exist' is true" means " 'Electrons exist' is provable in L," where L is a language spoken by a properly qualified community. In L_1, a different language within a different community, "Electrons exist" is not provable and therefore is not true. Since all inquiry takes place in some language or another, there is no language-neutral inquiry about electrons. Therefore we cannot inquire whether electrons "really exist" but only whether they are provable in L, L_1, L_2, and so on. There is no truth concerning electrons, but only truth in L_x. There are, in fact, no electrons to be referred to except through the references whose publicity is language-specific.

Few scientists accept that analysis, since they are interested in electrons. They treat the above observation as true for theories, but not for the discourse of scientific inquiry. Theories may be altered or traded off according to evaluative considerations which characterize rationality within the community of investigators and which are broader than any theory or finite set of theories. The language-specific theory of truth, however, is taken far more seriously within religious discussions where it is used to protect the integrity and irrelevance of religious traditions. Because the language-specific (or religious tradition-specific) theory of truth is taken seriously within theology, it is important to argue against it if one wants to assert the notion of public community of inquirers suggested earlier (see also McClendon and Smith, 1975).

Inquiry within a tradition, if the tradition is living, is always partly normative for that tradition. Inquiry often implies recommendations about what to value, what to believe, and what to do in order to achieve the excellence of the tradition, and over the course of time this constitutes change. Such inquiry supposes that there are criteria to judge what is worthwhile within the tradition—criteria that are not completely bound to any finite section of the tradition; for if they were, there could be no claim that "M is worthwhile," but only that "M is regarded as worthwhile according to the criteria of the tradition at privileged moment X." To say that moment X is privileged is to define the tradition as nonliving beyond that moment.

Furthermore, stating the theory that truth claims are specific to languages or to traditions presupposes a theory of reference and truth contradicted by the theory asserted. One may attempt to get around this argument with a theory of levels or "orders of discourse," allowing that propositions that are false on the lower level may be true on the higher. But at which level are the propositions religiously significant? Suppose the first-order proposition is "Jesus is the Christ," and the second-order proposition is "Jesus is the Christ for Christians, but not for Jews." Can one say that only the first-order proposition has religious significance and that this significance is rich enough to quicken religious life? There are several ways to respond to this question.

1. The dogmatic way is to read the second-order proposition as being really on the first order, translating roughly as follows: "Jesus is the Christ, as the Christians know, and the

Jews are mistaken in not believing that he is." If this is the beginning of the inquiry rather than a possible conclusion, the dogmatic reading fails to respect the integrity of the alien inquirers and thus reduces to the second-order point that Jesus is merely the Christ for Christians.

2. A social-scientific way reads the first-order proposition as exhaustively contained within the second order, translating as: " 'Jesus is the Christ' is something one believes because one is a Christian, and if one is a Jew, one believes the contrary." The "because" here says that there are no first-order evidential justifications for the belief—only sociological explanations. But this position is false if a participant in the inquiry holds a belief for reason of evidence or, more strikingly, changes belief and sociological affiliations because of evidence.

3. A theologically inquiring way to respond to the first- and second-order observations is to transfer the religious significance of the first up to the second, and potentially beyond. This way translates as follows: "Although Christians believe that Jesus is the Christ, the fact that (other) Jews who also had access to the same material believe the contrary makes the whole situation problematic." The situation of religious belief is therefore regarded as in the middle of inquiry. Inquiry may settle on the view that Jesus is the Christ, or it may come out the opposite. Most probably, the inquiry will redefine the religiously significant terms so as to transcend the controversy; but perhaps not, and a general conversion to one position will take place.

The topic of this paper can now be set in the context of this long postlude. How does the conception of the Holy Spirit contribute to the public inquiry concerning God? The notion of the Holy Spirit is at once a historical artifact developing through centuries of Christian thought, a philosophical concept defined through various theological controversies, and a symbol pointing beyond that which its meanings explicitly describe. Can it contribute to our understanding of God? This is not the dogmatic question, What should Christians believe about God as Holy Spirit? What Christians should believe about God as Holy Spirit is what *anyone* should believe, and that depends on the validity of the notion of the Holy Spirit, however understood in its proper historical context.

The key to the contemporary worth of the notion of the Holy Spirit lies in the speculative development of its conceptual form. The historical and symbolic aspects of the notion are of course much broader than the speculative conceptual component. And the conceptual element by itself perhaps has little if any religious significance. But a proper respeculation of the conceptual form can render those other elements viable and valuable for contemporary inquiry into the question of God.

A final reflective question can be posed about the Holy Spirit as God. Within the Christian tradition, the Holy Spirit has often been conceived with a historical dimension. The Spirit was to have been sent by Jesus to guide us to the end. And the thesis has sometimes been urged that we are now, or soon will be, or must wait for, the historical dominion of the Spirit. Since we now live in an age when many of the normative characteristics of the community of public inquiry have come to consciousness, it may well be said that God is most clearly present in the immediacies of that inquiry and in the norms of justice entailed by it. No longer is the authority of the transcendent Source of creation recognized beyond what shows itself immediately in public inquiry. No longer do historic events of revelation carry authority in themselves apart from the Spirit's testimony that consists in the way things stand in public inquiry.

But is the presence of the Spirit in public inquiry sufficiently numinous to be spiritually transforming? Even when the Spirit is understood as an indissoluble part of the Trinity, is this sufficiently numinous? Perhaps the age of the Spirit does away with religiously powerful symbolism. Perhaps public inquiry in not numinous except for those engaged in more individual spiritual practices of prayer and meditation. Whatever the answers to these questions, testimonies to the Spirit's numinous divinity are present in the Spirit's own operation.

Notes

1. Within the technical details of process cosmology, elimination of the process God requires that one develop alternate categories for solving the problems that Whitehead solved by suggesting that God supplies the lure which provides an original subjective unity to any occasion. To defend a creationist theory of God, as I do, requires one to show how divine creation enters the creative process, a topic discussed in the present essay.

2. Not appreciating this distinction, Whitehead was led to treat God as a being within the cosmos, and his principles for understanding the cosmos itself are mere empirical generalizations that do not account self-referentially for themselves. See Whitehead (1929) and Neville (1980).

References

Cobb, John B., Jr.
  1965. *A Christian Natural Theology*. Philadelphia: Westminster Press.

  1969. *God and the World*. Philadelphia: Westminster Press.

Ford, Lewis S.
  1970. "The Viability of Whitehead's God for Christian Theology." *Proceedings of the American Catholic Philosophical Association* 44:141-51.

  1972. "Neville on the One and the Many." *Southern Journal of Philosophy* 10/1 (Spring): 79:84.

Hegel, G.W.F.
  (1807) 1977. *(Phaenomenologie des Geistes.) Phenomenology of the Spirit*. Trans. A. V. Miller. Oxford: Oxford University Press.

McClendon, James Wm., Jr., and Smith, James M.
  1975. *Understanding Religious Convictions*. Notre Dame, Ind.: University of Notre Dame Press.

Moore, Harold F.; Neville, Robert; and Sullivan, William
  1972. "The Contours of Responsibility: A New Model." *Man and World* 5/4 (November): 392-421.

Neville, Robert
  1968. *God the Creator*. Chicago: University of Chicago Press.

  1969. "Creation and the Trinity." *Theological Studies* 30 (March): 3-26.

  1972. "A Metaphysical Argument for Wholly Empirical Theology." *God: Knowable and Unknowable*. Ed. Robert J. Roth, S.J. New York: Fordham University Press.

1974. *The Cosmology of Freedom*. New Haven: Yale University Press.

1978. *Soldier, Sage, Saint*. New York: Fordham University Press.

1980. *Creativity and God*. New York: Seabury Press.

Peirce, Charles S.

1935. *Collected Papers of Charles Sanders Peirce*. Vol. 6. Ed. Charles Hartshorne and Paul Weiss. Cambridge, Mass.: Harvard University Press.

Putnam, Hilary

1978. *Meaning and the Moral Sciences*. London: Routledge & Kegan Paul.

Richardson, C. C.

1958. *The Doctrine of the Trinity*. Nashville: Abingdon Press.

Smith, John E.

1961. "Is Existence a Valid Philosophical Concept?" *Reason and God*. New Haven: Yale University Press.

Whitehead, Alfred North

1929. *Process and Reality*. New York: Macmillan & Co.

About John B. Cobb, Jr.'s Essay

How does a book *end* if its role is not to settle everything but only to report on work in progress? One possibility is to look back to the point from which we began; another is to point to the far horizons ahead. The present essay by John B. Cobb, Jr., does both, and is thus somewhat fitly the final one.

In his own terms, John Cobb raises questions which were put in another way in the general introduction. There we asked, Is God GOD?—that is, is the concept of God with which present-day theologians and church members operate, properly representative of that which it is meet and right to worship, serve, and trust—namely, GOD? John Cobb speaks instead of "ultimacy." He points out different ways to conceive of ultimacy in human civilizations and notes the ways different ultimacies have or have not been seen as that which humans must worship and trust. So one can ask, Do any or all these concepts of ultimacy (God) properly conceive that which is indeed ultimate (GOD), and which as such must be trusted and worshiped?

Yet unlike the other essayists, Cobb's focus here is not upon Christian theology, though that is always in the background, but upon Oriental religion, especially upon Japanese Pure Land or Amida Buddhism. Analyzing this, he is in a position to argue that the traditional understanding of Buddhist thought as atheistic is not final; there is in the tradition a strong if obscure witness to an ultimacy worthy of worship and trust. And this, if true, is a matter of great interest to Christian theologians.

Thus Cobb's is an essay in comparative theology; it represents a move in contemporary religious studies across a long-forbidden barrier. The cautious rule that one *theologizes* within one's own tradition and only *reports* on the beliefs of others, is transcended. No doubt that was a wise caution when the only transreligious tactics were either to consign outsiders to the devil or to pronouce blandly that "all religions have the same message." But comparative theology, as it is done in this Cobb essay, is too complex a task for such summation.

Many will recognize John Cobb as a foremost process theologian, whose *Christian Natural Theology* (1965) is a definitive application of the process thought of philosopher Alfred North Whitehead (1861–1947). While the present essay avoids many of the technical terms of that philosophy, one can recognize Whitehead's analysis in the rejection of substance metaphysics (section 1 and elsewhere). But Cobb has typically pressed on beyond Whitehead and Charles Hartshorne (b. 1897) to develop a constructive Christian theology creatively related to his own Protestant heritage, while in *Christ in a Pluralistic Age* (1975), he began to raise the Christian/Buddhist questions pursued here.

We may wish to question his development of both Christian and Buddhist thought. For example, does the Western Christian conception of ultimacy *as Cobb represents it here* adequately allow for a real creation, intact and integral, such as argued for by Karl Barth (1886–1968) and such as Paul van Buren attempts to justify in this present volume? And does the Buddhist claim (as Cobb relays it) that the connection between emptiness and compassion *cannot* be merely psychological (since on the Buddhist view, when Emptiness is experienced the psychological self ceases to exist) entail a fallacy? Cobb doesn't say. Yet detail aside, the project represented here by a major theologian is surely of intense intrinsic interest.

It also is interesting, finally, to note the connection

between this essay and the first, Thomas Altizer's "The Anonymity of God." Both Altizer and Cobb are deeply influenced by Eastern thought. Both deal with a sense of absence, Nothing, Emptiness. Their conclusions seem to be in profound tension. Are they indeed?

10. The Buddhist Witness to God

John B. Cobb, Jr.

There was a time not very long ago in our Western history when the question, Does God exist? seemed quite clear. In journals of philosophy today, there still appear articles which assume this situation. Those who like to disprove the existence of God find it helpful to their cause to suppose that the terms of the question are quite unproblematic. Sometimes believers in God accept the proposed definitions and engage in defense of the existence of One who possesses all the specified characteristics.

From the perspective of both modern Christian theology and the history of religions, however, most of these discussions seem incongruous. The God whose existence is debated is only vaguely related to what is meant by "God" in Bonhoeffer or Tillich or Hartshorne or Ebeling or Pannenberg. The concept under debate is difficult to correlate with anything in Hinduism, Buddhism, Taoism, or Confucianism.

It is, of course, quite legitimate to ask whether the affirmation of God by Augustine, by Thomas Aquinas, by Luther, or by Schleiermacher is philosophically or religiously warranted. The same question may be asked of Bonhoeffer, Tillich, Hartshorne, Ebeling, or Pannenberg. Strictly speaking, we can assume that the answer *must* be negative in many cases, since the accuracy of one account would count against the truth of most of the others. If we turn to the history of religions and consider all the entities that have been named by words that are sometimes translated as "God," the mutual inconsistency of the "gods" in question is even more manifest.

As long as there are those who use the word "God" positively and seriously and who try to give fresh accounts of what they mean, those who wish to deny God can do so finally only by engaging each new affirmation. Yet one must sympathize with the atheist who finds this requirement unreasonable. Surely there is some way to formulate key features of what is at stake in the discussion of God so as to allow a more general critique, even if such a critique can never be decisive for all serious and thoughtful uses of the word.

The discussion clearly is most important in relation to the great religious ways of humankind, and especially to Judaism, Christianity, and Islam. It is widely recognized in these traditions that concepts of God are varied, and yet it is assumed that many of these are concepts of GOD. This indicates that the word "God" has some meaning which the concepts intend to evoke but which is not fully captured in any concept. This meaning can be approached through examination of what it means experientially to believe in God and what it means to deny God.

Two central aspects of what it means to believe in God are to worship and to trust in a very fundamental way. People who change their belief structure in ways that lead to continued worship and trust are likely to think that they have come to a new understanding of God. People who change their belief structure in ways that make worship and fundamental trust seem inappropriate are likely to understand themselves as having rejected belief in God. Although there are exceptions to these generalizations, I propose to conduct the discussion about the existence of God in these terms.

Accordingly, in this paper I identify the question of the existence of God with the question whether worship and fundamental trust are appropriate responses to reality. Is true or final reality such that its deepest understanding leads to worship and trust? This question has its ambiguities, and it does not capture what is centrally important in *all* talk of God, but it does orient the investigation more fruitfully. For most people to whom the question is important, if reality is such that worship and trust are appropriate, then either reality as such or some unsurpassable aspect thereof may appropriately be called God.

To formulate the question in this way is not to favor either

believers or unbelievers. Both answers are plausible.
Inasmuch as hundreds of millions of people have trusted and
worshiped, the burden of proof is on the unbeliever to show
that this is inappropriate. But inasmuch as the dominant
modern world-views do not include anything apparently
worthy of fundamental trust or worship, the burden of proof is
at least equally on the believer.

The question can be pursued in many ways. One that seems
particularly interesting and fruitful today is through the
investigation of Buddhist experience and thought. Buddhism
is interesting because it clearly deals with experience at the
deepest and most fundamental level, and yet it does not
generally associate that level with the idea of God as One who
is to be worshiped and trusted. It is, on the one hand,
profoundly religious, and on the other, in its usual orthodox
interpretation, nontheistic. The existence of Buddhism
constitutes a special challenge to the believer in God.

Buddhism is a complex movement, and I will make no
pretense of dealing with all its forms here. My discussion will
be restricted to Mahayana Buddhism, as I have come to
understand it through Japanese Buddhists. Their exposition is
in terms of ultimacy, and it opens the way for us to consider
whether Buddhist experience at the ultimate level provides
evidence for or against the existence of God.

Before dealing with the Mahayana account of ultimacy, a
modern Western problem must be faced. The very notion of
ultimacy is vague and unclear to many in the West, and
recently, dominant philosophical schools have questioned its
meaningfulness. Hence, section 1 of this paper discusses the
meaning of ultimacy and the way it has been approached in
East and West. Section 2 deals specifically with the Buddhist
experience of ultimacy. Section 3 discusses the correlation of
Buddhist experience with Christian belief in God.

I

The human mind restlessly seeks explanations of what it
finds in its world. Often it is satisfied, provisionally, with
explanations that give an immediate account of the phenome-

non in view. We learn that a plant produces flowers to attract
bees. But such an explanation also raises many other
questions. Aristotle classified these questions in a way that has
been useful in subsequent Western reflection. The explanation just mentioned is a final cause. If we ask instead for the
physicochemical processes which produce the flower, we will
be seeking the efficient cause. If we ask for the mathematical
formulas which describe these processes, we are seeking
formal causes. And if we ask of what the flower and the bee and
the chemicals are composed, we seek the material cause.

Answers to any of these questions not only point to the need
for questioning along other lines but also raise further
questions along the same line. If the flower is produced to
attract bees, we ask, Why does the plant need to attract bees?
If the answer is in terms of pollination, we ask, Why is this
important? Then there remains the question, Why does the
plant aim at reproduction? Reflection along these lines leads
to answers that no longer apply with any specificity to a
particular plant, or to plants alone, but to all living things and
perhaps to nonliving things as well. It leads, in short, in the
direction of ultimacy. Aristotle himself sought ultimacy in this
direction, and his answer was his doctrine of a supreme
perfection which moved all things and was itself unmoved.
For Aristotle, as for much of Greek thought, ultimacy in the
line of final causes was inseparable from ultimacy in the line of
formal causes.

Other cultures have sought ultimacy in other directions.
Modern science was based on a shift of attention from final
causes to efficient causes. Every event is explained by
antecedent events, which in turn are explained by events that
precede them. Some philosophers and theologians argued
that such a series could not be infinite and that some initiating
event must be ultimate in the line of efficient causes. The
difficulties with this argument brought considerable discredit
on the whole quest for ultimacy, at least insofar as it was
associated with a doctrine of God.

As science advanced and became "purer" it became more
formal. Less and less attention was paid to particular efficient

causes of particular events, and more and more to the forms manifest in all similar processes. Progress in science came to be the discovery of forms of such generality that the many diverse formulas descriptive of particular ranges of phenomena could be-seen in their unity. The drive of science toward ultimacy in the direction of form has been checked by acute problems in quantum mechanics and in the reconciliation of quantum and relativity theories, but there is no reason to suppose that the aim at ultimacy will disappear.

In the West, the quest for ultimacy in final, efficient, and formal causes has usually been associated with religious feeling. "Ultimate reality" has often been used almost as a synonym for "God." This has led to confusion even when final, efficient, and formal ultimacy are in view. It is particularly confusing when ultimacy is sought in the line of material causes. Since this has been the primary direction of the Indian quest for ultimacy—in sharp contrast with the Greek—I will develop this at somewhat greater length.

Science begins with ordinary perceptual objects and analyzes them into their chemical and physical components. At one time it was believed that this analysis came to its end in what were, accordingly, called atoms. But at that point the question was asked, at least implicitly: Of what are these atoms composed? Some answer was required, if atoms were not to be conceived as mere forms or human ideas. The answer assumed by science was that the atom was a unit of *matter*.

Of course, matter could never be found as such. Only atoms could be found, along with larger objects composed of atoms. But the belief that atoms were units of formed *matter* shaped scientific expectation and theory. It turned out that these expectations and theories were partly false, but that, of course, does not imply that the doctrine was meaningless.

One element in the falsity was the locus of the atom. What scientists called an atom turned out not to be an atom in the philosophical sense. It was composed of subatomic particles. This was a factual error, which in itself did not invalidate the materialist answer to the question about ultimate reality. But the other element of error was that the subatomic particles turned out not to behave in the way that units of matter would behave. The question then arises: Of what are *they* composed?

One possible answer is that they are composed of still smaller units, but unless this is supposed to be an infinite regress, at some point we return to the question of ultimacy. Of what are the least units composed, if they cannot be conceived as units of matter? Today the answer might be matter-energy. Alternatively, it might be suggested that the particles should be viewed as abstractions from the energy field. My opinion is that these answers still reflect the background of materialist thinking and that more radical answers are needed. But for our present purposes the development of an adequate answer is not at issue. The important point is that ideas about the ultimate continue to give direction to experiments and to affect the structure of the mathematics that are developed to interpret the evidence.

The quest for ultimacy in India has been more religious than scientific. The question is not so much about what is objectively experienced as about the human subject of experience. What, ultimately, is my being? The meditational disciplines and modes of reflection through which answers have been sought have been just as rigorous and demanding, in their way, as have been the disciplines of modern science.

The major tradition of Indian orthodoxy has answered the question in terms of Atman. The ultimate "I" is discovered to be very different from the empirical or phenomenal "I." It is wholly beyond all forms and hence beyond any characteristic or boundary that could differentiate it from the "I" of others. Indian saints and sages testify that the existential realization of themselves as Atman liberates them from all selfish concerns within the phenomenal world.

The question which led to this discussion of ultimacy is whether reality is such that worship and fundamental trust are appropriate. Scientific ideas of the ultimate in the line of material causes seem, superficially, to be irrelevant or negative. Even if matter is ultimate, it would be odd to worship or trust it. Matter-energy and energy field are not, in any apparent way, more promising. In general, the West has assumed that the question of ultimacy posed in *this* way is not the religious question.

In the East, however, since the quest for ultimacy through the subject is religious, the question as to whether the Atman is God is a serious one. That the identification is possible is supported by the conviction that Atman is Brahman, since Brahman is the ultimate religious concept. But whether Atman, or better, Brahman, is God is difficult to determine; for believers in Brahman have subtly different concepts which affect whether worship and trust are appropriately directed to Brahman. In general, when worship and trust are chiefly in question, the direct focus is a divine being, rather than Brahman as such. Hindus may worship a variety of such divine beings. But all these beings are forms or manifestations of Brahman. It can be said that it is Brahman who is worshiped in and through all these manifestations, and this suggests that, indeed, Brahman is God. On the other hand, when Brahman is conceived *as such*, the proper response is not worship as much as the quest for the realization of self as Brahman. Worship is one means of pursuing this quest, but such worship is directed to some manifestation of Brahman, which, in the highest realization, disappears. Hence, it seems that, although Brahman may be approached as God, in the final realization, Brahman is not God. It is the manifestations of Brahman that are gods, and their reality, while important in every penultimate perspective, is relative.

Brahman is beyond all distinctions of good and evil, creator and destoyer. This indicates that much of what biblical religions have conceived as divine goodnesss, in which humans can fully trust, is not finally to be asserted of Brahman. Yet Brahman also seems to be the source, the ground, and the power of all being, evoking the wonder and praise that are expressed in worship. Hence the ambiguity as to whether Brahman is God remains.

Buddhism retained the insight that the ultimate is beyond good and evil, but it rejected the idea of a source, a ground, or a power underlying the world of experience. *Nothing* underlies. The ultimate is not Brahman but *Shunyata*, Emptiness. The gods are just as empty as are worldly goods. There is nothing to which it is appropriate to be attached, even Emptiness.

The Buddhist goal is the realization of the Emptiness of all things, and especially of ourselves. There seems to be a numinous quality to this realization, and there is no question that it is a transformation of existence experienced as of utmost worth. There are Christians who wish to identify this ultimate with God, even though it is apprehended as Emptiness. They point to the language of emptiness and nothingness that is found in reference to God in the Christian tradition as well. Some Buddhists, also, are willing to allow the use of the word "God" in this way.

Undoubtedly there are definitions of "God" in terms of which Emptiness is God. Specifically, if "God" is defined as the ultimate, and the ultimate turns out to be Emptiness, then it follows that Emptiness is God. But precisely this consequence shows that the definition of God as the ultimate is itself of questionable usefulness. This essay is based on a different fundamental definition of God: that which is appropriately worshiped and trusted. If we ask whether Emptiness is to be worshiped and trusted, some of the ambiguity we found with respect to Brahman remains. But on the whole, in the strictest and purest formulations of Buddhism, worship and trust are not the appropriate relations to Emptiness as such. If there are gods, they are empty, but Emptiness is not God.

That the ultimate, understood as the *what* of all things, as *what* I ultimately am, is not God, should not be surprising. Our thought of God is shaped by Greece and Israel. In neither is God conceived as the ultimate material cause. It did not occur to Aristotle that human beings could find blessedness through realizing themselves as instances of ultimate matter. Indeed he did not press to any ultimate in this direction. It certainly did not occur to Aristotle that the material cause should be worshiped and trusted.

The biblical view of God is different from Aristotle's, yet Christians were not wrong in seeing and developing affinities. In the Bible, God creates the ordered world out of chaos, the formless, the void, or nothingness. There is no reflection in regard to this material cause, but the classical theological tradition was correct to deny to it any substantial reality.

It is precisely the Emptiness of which Buddhists speak.

In the biblical-Christian tradition, knowledge of our grounding in nothingness may prevent us from supposing that our material cause is an evil principle; it may keep us humble; and it may remind us of our complete dependence on God for our lives and for all that enriches them. But no more than Aristotle, did biblical writers suppose that blessedness could be found through realization of ourselves as instances of this primordial nothingness! The whole attention is directed to the One who redemptively creates an ordered world out of the void.

Viewed in this light, it is puzzling that Christians should ever have come to identify God with ultimate reality in the sense of the *what* of all things. This seems to have come about in two steps. First, theologians and philosophers were not satisfied with the void as the material cause of all things. Their sense of the substantial character of the world required something more "material." In the Aristotelian tradition, this became prime matter. God was no longer conceived, as in the Bible, to have created the ordered world out of the void. An intermediate step was needed in which God created matter as something contrasted with the void, or nothing. This matter became the substance underlying all physical things, established by Descartes as the foundation and the dilemma of modern physics and philosophy. The entities that make up our world are not forms of the void but forms of material substance.

Second, Thomas Aquinas had clearly recognized that actual things cannot be conceived as merely the union of passive matter and abstract forms. Things *exist*. They have being. The act of being cannot be analyzed in terms of matter and form. It is *sui generis*. Thus *esse* is affirmed as the most fundamental principle.[1] It is the new conception of what things most fundamentally are. They are instances of *esse*. But it could not be recognized that *esse* is the ultimate material cause, since a purely passive matter was required by the substantialist assumptions shared by virtually the whole of Western thought. *Esse* was not a passive substance but pure act, or act as such. That *esse*, rather than being added to form and matter as an additional principle, should replace matter as the answer to *what* things are, could not be recognized until in the later course of philosophy and science the concept of material substance had been dissolved. Only recently has it been possible to see the affinity of *esse* as the act of being, with energy as such viewed as the material cause of all things.[2]

In the meantime, however, *esse* had been identified with God. Obviously the intention was not to think of God as the material cause, since that role was left to material substance. As long as material substance was affirmed, *esse* appeared as somehow external to the matter to which it gave being and hence, as the creative act of giving being. The relation to the biblical God is then apparent, and the identification understandable. But when the idea of substantial matter is recognized as an illusion, and when *esse* is seen as the deepest answer to *what* things ultimately are, this identity with the biblical God breaks down. The biblical God is *not* the void out of which the ordered world is created, however dynamically that void is conceived. Nor is this void, even when recognized as the pure, formless act of being, the object of trust and worship.

While under the spell of the identification of God with *esse*, Christians discovered the deep affinities between *esse* and Brahman and Emptiness. Since the understanding of *esse* had been deeply affected, not to say distorted, by its identification with God, Christians tended to find Brahman and Emptiness inadequate accounts of the ultimate reality they knew as *esse*. But since they believed that *esse* is God, they also tended to the view that Brahman and Emptiness are names of God. In general, therefore, the Christian encounter with Hindus and Buddhists has been premised on the false assumption that the ultimate reality so profoundly experienced in the East, when truly and adequately known, is the Christian God.

On the other side, few Hindus and Buddhists who have gone deeply into their own distinctive experience have been persuaded that Christian orthodoxy provides a satisfactory account of what they have realized. Only in those mystics inspired by the Thomistic identification of God and *esse*, especially in Meister Eckhart, do the Hindus and Buddhists find affinities to their own experience. These affinities lie in Eckhart's realization of his identity with *esse* as Godhead, rather than in his mystical relations with the personal God.

My argument thus far has been that (a) the quest for ultimacy, in the sense of *what* all things fundamentally are, is meaningful and important; (b) ultimate reality in this sense is not the object of trust or worship and is not what was meant by "God" in either Greece or Israel; and (c) the confusion of God with ultimacy of this sort was occasioned chiefly by the Western assumption of a material substance, which prevented Thomas Aquinas from recognizing in his discovery of *esse* the true answer to *what* all things most fundamentally are.

This does not answer the question with which we began. It only prepares the way for asking it more clearly. If the ultimate material cause of all things is not an appropriate object of worship and trust, is there something else that is?

II

The question can still be approached in many ways. When we are clear that for Greece and Israel, God was not ultimate material reality, we can ask again, What feature of reality led to worship and trust? It would then be possible to inquire whether this response was based on a false interpretation or whether today also this feature of reality can be discerned as appropriately eliciting worship and trust.

This essay pursues a different approach. In Mahayana Buddhism, we have an understanding of reality and of the appropriate response to it in which worship and trust in the biblical sense are not encouraged. The most orthodox teaching argues against the presence in reality of anything to which one should give oneself in this way. Yet worship and trust appear as powerful forces within Buddhism. Does this provide evidence that some feature of reality as humanly experienced *is* worthy of such response? The dominant orthodox answer is that worship and trust have psychological value when insight into reality is not developed but are not appropriate to reality as adequately apprehended. I propose to examine the acceptability of this answer.

There is no doubt that much of the "worship" at Buddhist temples is little more than superstition, with no inner connection to Buddhist teaching. People in Japan, for example, seek worldly benefits from one or another of the Buddhas, or seek to assure that the spirits of their ancestors will be peaceful and hence will not disturb their living descendants. This is not worship and trust in the sense that warrants correlation with God. At a higher level, Japanese Buddhists of all degrees of spiritual insight express reverence and veneration for all human greatness, and especially for the Enlightened Ones. This, too, is different from what biblical traditions mean by worship and trust.

More relevant to our inquiry is the language used in Buddhist teaching about the *Dharmakaya*. The *Dharmakaya* is the "body" of all Buddhas—that is, it is what is embodied in all enlightened experience. That, in turn, is nothing but *Shunyata* or Emptiness (in Japanese, *Kū*). When the talk is of Emptiness, the emphasis, quite properly, is upon complete formlessness. That is, the ultimate has *no* character whatever, because its different instantiations can have *any* character whatever. It is completely neutral. It is as instantiated in the atomic destruction of Hiroshima as in the love of parents for their children. Emptiness is completely beyond all duality, including the duality of good and evil.

At the same time, the realization of Emptiness is the realization of wisdom and compassion. This is affirmed on the basis of factual evidence. There is no *a priori* reason to suppose that my realization of myself as completely empty would lead me to wise compassion for others rather than to indifference. But in fact, in Mahayana Buddhism, the testimony that Enlightenment results in wise compassion is universal.

This cannot be treated as a contingent psychological fact. The Buddhist analysis does not allow us to suppose that becoming compassionate is merely the psychological result of a person's realization of Emptiness. The Buddhist doctrine of

No Self *(Anatman)* entails that when Emptiness is realized, there is no psychological person to be affected by the realization. The true self *is* the Emptiness. It is the realized Emptiness that is compassionate. This has led Buddhist writers of many schools to speak of the *Dharmakaya*, that which is embodied in the Buddha, as wise and compassionate.

There is an inner tension in Buddhist thought at this point. On the one hand, the *Dharmakaya* as ultimate is completely beyond all forms, including wisdom and compassion. On the other hand, it is wisdom and compassion that are realized in the embodiment of the *Dharmakaya*. Hence the characteristics of wisdom and compassion cannot be simply denied to the *Dharmakaya*.

The standard Buddhist solution to this problem is to distinguish the *Dharmakaya* (in Japanese *Hosshin*) from the *Sambhogakaya (Hōjin)*, or body of bliss.[3] It is the *Sambhogakaya* rather than the *Dharmakaya* as such which is wise and compassionate. The *Sambhogakaya* is the form taken by *Dharmakaya* for the sake of the salvation of sentient beings.

Especially in the Pure Land tradition, another distinction is made. This is between *Dharmata Dharmakaya (Hosshō Hosshin)* and *Upaya Dharmakaya (Hōben Hosshin)*. The former is the *Dharmakaya* as such; the latter, the *Dharamakaya* in its expedient form. Shinran, the leading teacher of the Pure Land school in Japan, recognized that these two distinctions were the same: The *Sambhogakaya* and the *Upaya Dharmakaya* are identical.

The implication of these distinctions for most Buddhist thought is that the *Dharmakaya*, as wise and compassionate, is less fundamental, less ultimate, less religiously important than the *Dharmakaya* as such, which is beyond all forms including wisdom and compassion. This is a bias or judgment that lies deep in the Buddhist tradition. Yet Mahayana Buddhism as a whole is most moving and convincing in its account of the actualization of wisdom and compassion in those who are enlightened. That this state is subordinate to another is the most theoretical, the most questionable, the least verified Buddhist doctrine.

In the Pure Land tradition, the *Sambhogakaya* or *Upaya*

Dharmakaya is called Amida. Amida, then, is ultimate reality *as* wise and compassionate. People are encouraged to put their faith in Amida and to turn their attention away from the effort to realize, through difficult practices, the *Dharmakaya* as such, the ultimate that is beyond all form.[4] In this way Pure Land Buddhism tends to renounce the general Buddhist subordination of Amida to ultimate reality as such, as far as practical and religious matters are concerned. On the other hand, most Pure Land teaching suggests that this focus on Amida is a concession to human weakness, and it accepts the theoretical subordination as its encompassing context.

In Shinran we find the strongest tendency to center everything in Amida. The general subordinationist rhetoric and imagery is not entirely overcome, but it plays a secondary role in his thought and faith. Amida is ultimate *for us*, and this is the only ultimacy that matters. Faith in Amida is not a secondary type of religious life; it is its essence.

Now we are ready to ask our question again. Is Amida, as understood by Shinran, appropriately worshiped and trusted? Here the answer must be affirmative. According to Shinran, we are saved by faith in Amida's graciousness. Amida is not merely one Buddha among others, worthy of reverence and veneration, for Amida also names the ultimate as fundamentally characterized by wisdom and compassion. In relation to Amida, it is appropriate that reverence and veneration pass over into fundamental trust and worship.

Finally, it is important to recognize that in referring to Shinran, we are not speaking of an isolated Buddhist figure. We are speaking of the man from whose teachings arose one of the largest Buddhist denominations in Japan. Although the purity of his doctrine has not always been preserved by his followers, his authority is rarely questioned. Indeed his authority for his followers is more analogous to the authority of Paul for Christians, than to that of Luther or Calvin for Lutherans and Calvinists. If it is correct to say that Shinran taught the existence of God, then it follows that much of the most vital Buddhist life in Japan during the past seven centuries has centered on belief in God.

III

Section 2 showed that although Buddhism is officially nontheistic, Buddhist experience pushes in the direction of acknowledging that the ultimate material cause is primordially characterized by wisdom and compassion. There are Christian theologians, such as John Macquarrie, who have understood God as "being as gracious."[5] Buddhist experience has driven Buddhists, despite doctrinal resistance, to affirm God in this sense. This character of Buddhist experience is significant evidence that there *is* in reality that which warrants trust and worship and is appropriately called God. But this conclusion moves against the dominant Buddhist view which theoretically subordinates this form of ultimate reality to that which is beyond all forms. Let us consider this problem further through the language of Alfred North Whitehead.

The ultimate as such, Emptiness, or the *Dharmata Dharmakaya (Hosshō Hosshin)*, Whitehead calls creativity.[6] This is *pratitya-samutpada*, or dependent origination (in Japanese, *engi*). It is wholly beyond all forms, the ultimate answer to the question concerning *what* I am or *what* anything is. For Whitehead, the *Upaya Dharmakaya (Hōben Hosshin)* is creativity as primordially characterized. Although creativity as such is apart from all forms, its actualization is always affected by an order among possible forms. This order is not random or neutral, but is decided by a primordial *eros* toward the realization of values—that is, by a primordial wisdom and compassion. Whitehead calls this the Primordial Nature of God. Through this divine envisagement, creativity acquires the primordial character by virture of which some Buddhists name it Amida.

Few Buddhists engage in speculative explanation of the source of forms and the reasons for the primacy of wisdom and compassion. This may be because the Buddhist tradition has never encouraged attention to forms. On the contrary, Buddhists have been impressed by the fact that forms are always limitations, and they have sought to transcend all limitations. Further, the idea of form has been bound closely to the idea of spatial shape as in the Japanese notion of *katachi*.

Western history, in which philosophy and mathematics have progressively abstracted the notion of form from that of spatial shape, has not yet had much effect on Buddhist thought. Buddhist speculation rarely goes farther than the insistence that the formless expresses itself in forms or that forms arise from the formless.

Whitehead, on the contrary, was a mathematician-philosopher in the Western tradition, much of whose lifelong thought focused on the understanding of forms. The forms he considered were very far removed from mere spatial shapes. Although he, too, knew that forms are always limitations, he stressed that limitation is the price paid for actuality and value. For him the questions of the source of forms, and especially of the order among forms as they function in the world, are fundamental.

From their common grasp of ultimate reality as primordially characterized by wisdom and compassion, most Buddhists turn their attention to ultimate reality beyond all characterization, whereas Whitehead turns his to the "principle of limitation" which provides the character. These two directions are characteristic of Eastern and Western thought respectively. Stated in this way they appear as two legitimate options, neither of which should claim superiority over the other. If that is true, then there is no reason deeper than cultural tradition for the subordination of Amida to Emptiness as such or to the *Dharmata Dharmakaya*. A religious subordination is certainly possible, and the history of Indian religious traditions displays its profound achievements. But it is equally possible to turn the most searching religious attention in the other direction. It is for this reason that, despite the subordinationist context in which Amida is viewed in most of Buddhism, Amida as understood by Shinran can be recognized as God.

Both the understanding of Amida by Shinran and the understanding of God by Christians have moved between two poles. Amida or God may be identified either as creativity (*Dharmakaya* or Emptiness) as primordially characterized or as that which primordially characterizes creativity. To think of Amida or God in the second way introduces the note of interpretation or speculation, which most Buddhists and most contemporary Westerners try to minimize. Nevertheless, since it is the mode that is dominant in our Western traditions, it is important to view this possibility also from the perspective of Buddhist experience.

The realization of Emptiness is at once the realization of *pratitya-samutpada* or dependent origination *(engi)*.[7] Dependent origination is the emergence of a new occurrence or momentary experience through the coalescence of all else—that is, it is empty of any being, substance, or form of its own. Even when it has coalesced it achieves no existence in itself, for in the moment of arising it also perishes, to become part of that world whose coalescence produces other entities. In this vision all reality is present in every entity, and every entity pervades the whole. No one entity is identical to any other, but no entity exists apart from or over against other entities. This nonduality is not monism, however.

The Emptiness that is realized is the absence of all form and structure of one's own. One is, in each moment, what one becomes through the coalescence of all things. For this reason, Emptiness is also Fullness; it is not the absence of all experience, but the perfection of all experience. It is letting go of the illusions that distort the way the world is perceived and allowing each entity to be just what it is, to contribute just what it has to contribute. The emotional accompaniment to each constituting element becomes just what is appropriate to that element, neither more nor less. All discrimination is transcended. This means that the response of one who is enlightened flows out of allowing each element in the coalescence to play its proper role.

We have noted that the more fully one realizes Emptiness or attains Enlightenment, the more fully one is characterized by wisdom and compassion. To explain this, we must recognize that Emptiness or *Dharmakaya* as ultimate reality has a primordial character. This can only mean that among the elements coalescing in every new entity, there must be one primordial actuality, which, when allowed to play its appropriate role, contributes wisdom and compassion to every entity.

The wisdom of the enlightened person is not a matter of vast information, but the ability to act appropriately in the concrete situation apart from any rational calculation of consequences. It is the spontaneous grasp of what is needed for the sake of others. This implies that what is derived from the primordial actuality is a directivity toward the appropriate act, the resistance to which is removed through Enlightenment.

Stated from the other side, there is a primordial actuality, an element in every coalescence, whose character it is to form that coalescence toward the appropriate expression of wisdom and compassion in its particular situation. Since all the elements in every coalescence are themselves empty, this primordial actuality is also empty. But Emptiness when it is realized means freedom from all restriction on being filled. The primoridal realization of Emptiness that provides orientation to all other entities toward appropriate embodiment of wisdom and compassion can best be conceived as a perfect coalescence of everything else—of all possibilities as possibilities and of all actualities as actualities. This primordial coalescence is so ordered as to provide relevant direction to all other actualities insofar as they are empty of all that impedes its appropriate effectiveness.

Although the language we have been using is more Buddhist than biblical, the inference from the primordial character to that actuality which provides the primordial character is more typical of Western modes of thought. Also the conclusion, that there is a primordial actuality whose effective working in the world is always toward wise compassion and compassionate wisdom, moves toward the biblical vision. The primordial actuality in question is certainly worthy of total trust, and the attitude of worship is entirely appropriate. The fact that it, too, is an instance of Emptiness or dependent origination in no way subordinates it to Emptiness or dependent origination as such. Hence there is no question but that we are speaking of God.

Clearly, there is no proof in all this of the existence of God. There is, however, a bold claim. This claim is that the experience of Enlightenment, to which Buddhists attest, witnesses to the reality of God. Most directly, it witnesses to the primordial characterization of ultimate reality as wise and compassionate. On examination it witnesses, usually unintentionally, that there is a wise and gracious primordial actuality by virtue of which ultimate reality has this character.

Notes

1. This position was first developed by Thomas Aquinas (1949).
2. The identity or near-identity of *esse* and energy in its most general contemporary usage is recognized by Macquarrie (1966:99, 103, 182).
3. The doctrine of the three Buddha bodies is succinctly summarized in Ingram (1977:83).
4. Something of the force of Shinran's concerns can be appreciated by reading the booklet of passages recalled by his disciple (1977).
5. Macquarrie more frequently identifies God as "holy being." However, the explanation of his meaning focuses on graciousness (1966:79).
6. See Whitehead (1978:7, 31).
7. For an excellent account of Emptiness, see Streng (1967).

References

Aquinas, Thomas
  1949. *On Being and Essence.* Trans. Armand Maurer. Toronto: Pontifical Institute of Mediaeval Studies.

Ingram, Paul O.
  1977. *The Dharma of Faith: An Introduction to Classical Pure Land Buddhism.* Washington, D.C.: University Press of America.

Maquarrie, John
  1966. *Principles of Christian Theology.* New York: Charles Scribner's Sons.

Shinran Shōnin
  1977. *Tannisho: Lamenting the Deviations.* Trans. Taitetsus Ueno. Honolulu: Buddhist Study Center.

Streng, Frederick J.
  1967. *Emptiness: A Study in Religious Meaning.* Nashville: Abingdon Press.

Whitehead, Alfred North
  1978. *Process and Reality.* Corrected ed. by David Ray Griffin and Donald W. Sherburne. New York: Free Press.

About the Contributors:

William P. Alston is professor of philosophy at Syracuse University. He is the past president of the Western Region of the American Philosophical Association. In addition to his widely used textbook *Religious Belief and Philosophical Thought* (Harcourt Brace), he has written a number of books and essays in the areas of the philosophy of mind and the philosophy of language. His books include *Philosophy of Language* (Prentice-Hall) and, with Richard Brandt, *Problems of Philosophy* (Allyn).

Thomas J. J. Altizer has taught since 1968 in the English Department and the Program of Religious Studies at the State University of New York at Stony Brook. One of the leading representatives of the death-of-God theology of the 1960s, his most recent books are *The Self-Embodiment of God* (Harper & Row); *Total Presence* and *The Descent into Hell* (Seabury).

Paul M. van Buren is professor of religion at Temple University. Well known for his *Secular Meaning of the Gospel* (Macmillan), his latest book is *Discerning the Way* (Seabury), the first of a four-volume systematic theology.

David Burrell, C.S.C., is past chair of the Department of Theology at the University of Notre Dame. His most recent books include *Aquinas: God and Action* and *Exercises in Religious Understanding* (Notre Dame Press).

John B. Cobb, Jr., has taught since 1958 at the School of Theology at Claremont and Claremont Graduate School and is director of the Center for Process Studies. His publications include *The Structure of Christian Existence* (Seabury); *A Christian Natural Theology* and *Christ in a Pluralistic Age* (Westminster Press). His serious studies of the relation between Christianity and Buddhism began as a fellow of the Woodrow Wilson International Center for Scholars in 1976.

Charles Davis has taught since 1970 at Concordia University,

Montreal, Canada. His most recently published books are *Body as Spirit: The Nature of Religious Feeling* (Seabury) and the text of the Hulsean Lectures, *Theology and Political Society* (Cambridge University Press).

Gordon D. Kaufman is the Edward Mallinckrodt, Jr., Professor of Divinity at Harvard University. He has served as president of the New England chapter of the American Academy of Religion and also of the American Theological Society. His recent books include *God, The Problem* (Harvard University Press), *An Essay on Theological Method* (Scholars Press), and *The Theological Imagination*, forthcoming (Westminster Press).

James Wm. McClendon, Jr., is professor of theology at Church Divinity School of the Pacific. His recent books include *Biography As Theology* (Abingdon) and, with James M. Smith, *Understanding Religious Convictions* (Notre Dame Press). He is currently at work on *Ethics*, Volume 1 of a three-volume systematic theology.

Robert Neville is director of the Program in Religious Studies at the State University of New York at Stony Brook. His most recent books include *The Cosmology of Freedom* (Yale University Press), *God the Creator: On the Transcendence and Presence of God* (University of Chicago Press), *Soldier, Sage, Saint* (Fordham University Press), and *Creativity and God* (Seabury).

Axel D. Steuer has taught at Princeton University, Swarthmore, and Haverford colleges and is presently chair of the Department of Religious Studies at Occidental College in Los Angeles. His published essays focus on the implications of philosophy of mind for theology and ethics.

Beyond the
Cake Sale

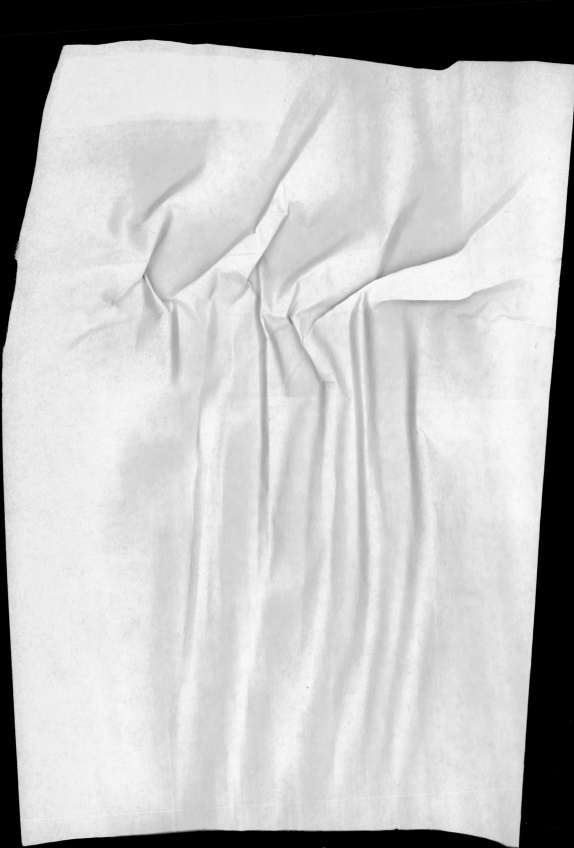

Beyond the Bake Sale

The Ultimate
School Fund-Raising Book

Jean C. Joachim

ST. MARTIN'S GRIFFIN ⚜ NEW YORK

BEYOND THE BAKE SALE: THE ULTIMATE SCHOOL FUND-RAISING BOOK. Copyright © 2003 by Jean C. Joachim. All rights reserved. Printed in the United States of America. No part of this book may be used or reproduced in any manner whatsoever without written permission except in the case of brief quotations embodied in critical articles or reviews. For information, address St. Martin's Press, 175 Fifth Avenue, New York, N.Y. 10010.

www.stmartins.com

Book design by Donna Simsgalli

Library of Congress Cataloging-in-Publication Data

Joachim, Jean C.
    Beyond the bake sale : the ultimate school fund-raising book / Jean C. Joachim.—1st ed.
    p. cm.
    ISBN 0-312-30483-8
    1. Educational fund raising—Handbooks, manuals, etc.
I. Title.

LC241 .J63 2003
371.2'06—dc21   2002031899

10   9   8   7   6   5   4   3

For

Larry, David, and Stevie Joachim

and Andee and Chuck Bram

A successful school creates and nurtures a sense of community that encourages a collaborative effort on the part of all its constituencies toward the ultimate desired outcome of the development of intellectually capable, well-prepared, and confident students and contributors to society. At P.S. 87, fund-raising plays an important role in achieving this goal.

—STEVEN PLAUT,
FORMER PRINCIPAL AT P.S. 87

Contents

Acknowledgments xi

Introduction xiii

1. The Basics   1

Fall Events

2. The Pledge Drive   17
3. The Wrapping Paper Drive   23
4. School Photos and the Magazine Drive   28
5. The Halloween Harvest Festival   34

Winter Events

6. Dances, Friday Night Pizza and a Movie,
   Kids' Holiday Shopping Day   47
7. The Auction   58

Spring Events

8. Car Wash, Handyman Day, Art Show   93
9. The Book Fair   101
10. The Just Kids Street Fair   108

Year-Round Events

11. The Flea Market   143
12. The Ultimate Bake Sale   156
13. Candy Sales, Sports Equipment Exchange
    Day, Alumni Club, School Store   165
14. Tapping Corporate America   174

Final Thoughts

15. Idea Bank   189
16. Creating New Ideas and Getting
    Volunteers   197

*Important Phone Numbers and
Web Sites*   *207*

Acknowledgments

Many thanks for help and support to:

Elizabeth Beier, Leslie Berger, Jane Buckley, Katherine Charapko, Joyce Eisman, Diana Finegold, Judy Gehrke, Dave Gibson, Greg Goldstein, Catherine Harding, Jeanne Kerwin, Anne Murney, Dee Rieber, Sydnie Ronga, Steve Russo, Regina Ryan, Kim Mogul Wright.

Introduction

This school fund-raising story begins at P.S. 87, an award-winning public elementary school on the Upper West Side of Manhattan. Fifteen years ago, P.S. 87, a school with a dwindling population in a marginal neighborhood, was reborn. A special principal, Naomi Hill, and a group of pioneering parents who believe in public education got together to create a strong learning environment for kids.

While Ms. Hill recruited the best teachers she could find, the parents raised money to meet the school's needs and support special programs. Together they forged an unbeatable alliance. Working together to raise money and improve the school, they created a strong sense of community, too. Word of the renaissance at P.S. 87 traveled to parents in districts all over the city. Soon the enrollment swelled to almost 1,200 students from kindergarten through fifth grade.

As the enrollment grew, so did the needs of the school. Private schools could boast of impressive computer labs and excellent libraries. The P.S. 87 parents got to work and raised $40,000 to create a complete computer lab and $50,000 to pay a top librarian and stock the library with new books. Now the funds raised at P.S. 87 each year pay for the art program, science enrichment, a guidance counselor, classroom supplies, sports equipment, copiers, and much more.

Incredibly, the strong alliance forged between school administration and the parent association survives to this day, through several principals and many new parents.

I have been a proud member of the fund-raising team at P.S. 87 for the past ten years. We traditionally used trial-and-error at P.S. 87 because there was never a "how-to" book on school fund-raising available. Now there is. The information in this book comes from our experience at P.S. 87 and from other successful school fund-raisers across the country. It's been time- and school-tested, and I hope it will help you set up a fund-raising program for the first time or increase the amount of money you raise for your school.

The Basics

Money, Money, Money

"At 87, fund-raising has been elevated to an art that connects students, families, and staff. Fund-raising at P.S. 87 serves as a community builder. It brings together families and staff and provides vehicles for parents to be part of and contribute to their children's education. A clearly articulated vision of the goals of fund-raising, as well as accountability and demonstrated evidence of how the proceeds both directly and indirectly benefit students, is at the core of the program."

—STEVEN PLAUT, FORMER PRINCIPAL AT P.S. 87

The fund-raising events and activities in this book reflect fifteen years experience and fifteen years of making money and fifteen years of saving money. We have made plenty of mistakes in our fund-raising efforts, but we never got discouraged. I have learned that it takes a year or two to really get an event to run smoothly. You have to have patience, be creative, listen to other people, and be open to suggestion. We started small with bake sales and grew over the years to huge events that made up to $60,000. But it didn't happen overnight.

If you are just starting out, your school or parent association may not have much cash. Some of the events described in this book require money to pay for things up front, like food for an event, or a rental hall for your auction. In each chapter that has an event or activity that requires a significant outlay of cash, we have created a special section at the end called "Just Starting Out?" This section outlines ways to start the event that don't require much money. We have stripped the event down to the basics that are necessary to get it going. As your financial reserves grow, you can add on any of the additional, more costly activities.

A RESERVE FUND

I can't stress enough the importance of putting some of your profits aside to form a reserve fund. At P.S. 87 we created a healthy reserve fund over the years for a rainy day. There have been times when we had to dip into that fund and were so grateful that it was there. When we did dip in, we worked hard to replace the money. A reserve fund is essential to any fund-raising plan that is going to grow and be a stable source of funds for school improvement year in and year out.

If you save half the money your parent association earns, you will quickly build a reserve fund. It was always our goal to have a year's budget in our reserve. So if we expect to take in $200,000, which we do every year, then we need to have $200,000 in reserve. You can accomplish this by budgeting to spend only half of what you make. Put the other half in a special fund that earns interest so the money will grow over time.

If you need more money during the year, have a quick and easy fund-raiser, like a bake sale, instead of dipping into the funds you have put away. This is the only way you will have enough money to throw a major event that requires a significant cash outlay. Save your money for a rainy day and build your financial power.

THE BASICS YOU NEED BEFORE YOU START FUND-RAISING

Successful school fund-raising requires solid support systems, like:

1. a widely-read school newsletter that goes home to parents;
2. good relationships with the teachers and the administrative staff, including the secretaries and other support staff in the office;
3. active, reliable class parents;
4. a school handbook spelling out dates and regular fund-raising events for the year;
5. an up-to-date school phone directory; and
6. a school Web site.

1. School Newsletter

Our school newsletter, the *BackPack News*, has been around for fifteen years. It is a four-page newsletter, 11" × 17" folded once, printed in black on colored paper and issued weekly. By printing black ink on colored paper, we get the excitement of color but pay for only one-color—black—printing, which is much less expensive than four-color printing. Our regular features in the *BackPack News* (*BPN*) are:

- principal's column
- parent association president's column
- schedule of upcoming events
- classified ads

This invaluable tool is also important for publicity for upcoming fund-raising events. We request and thank volunteers, publish the success of our events, request donations, and let the parents know about changes in the school in the *BPN*. It's a big job to get the newsletter set up. But once you have settled on a format, type style, basic departments and a logo, it's not so difficult. We have a stable of different people who construct the *BPN* from parent submissions. Every week a special packet folder is placed in the school office for newsletter submissions. Each week the editor picks up the folder on Thursday afternoon. If you can get ten people with computer access to agree to edit and type four editions of the newsletter, you'll have the year covered. Sponsorship should cover the cost of printing the newsletter. Sponsors receive acknowledgment and a large ad in the newsletter.

The parent association pays for printing of the *BPN*. But we defray the cost by selling sponsorships to advertisers like summer camps and insurance and real estate agents. For a few hundred dollars, a business can reach more than five hundred families. If you have just a few people selling sponsorships at the beginning of the year, you can run a newsletter cost-efficiently.

In the school office every Monday morning, a parent volunteer counts out the correct number of copies for each class and puts them in the teachers' mailboxes. The teachers distribute the newsletters to the kids to take home every Tuesday. The deadline for submissions is Thursday if handed in on paper, or Friday by e-mail (since it doesn't have to be typed in). Classified ads are free to all P.S. 87 parents. Nonparent classified advertisers pay $25 per ad. Help-wanted ads are also accepted free of charge. Ad length is determined by space availability, a decision determined by the editor of the week.

2. A School Web Site

A school Web site is extremely valuable as a tool to disseminate information. You will have a technologically savvy parent in the school who can construct the school Web site for free. Some teachers put their homework assignments on the Web site. That way, if children are absent or their memories are unreliable, the parents can access the homework assignments and make sure the children are getting it all completed on time.

A really efficient school Web site can contain the school newsletter, too. You can also sell advertising on the Web site.

3. Good Relationships with Teachers

Our parent association makes it a point to support and acknowledge teachers. The teachers are the lifeblood of our school. Most of our PA funds go to support our teachers and improve the school environment for our children. Teachers' help with fund-raising is vital. It's the teachers, not the parents, who hand out the forms and information for our wrapping-paper and magazine drives. In fact, it is the teachers who:

- collect fund-raising forms
- create class projects for the auction
- create class booths for the street fair
- create a quilt to be sold at the auction
- offer to take children out for breakfast or pizza as an auction prize
- bring their classes down to bake sales and book fairs
- disseminate the *BackPack News* every week

And, of course, in addition to those and a thousand other things, they teach our children. So we do everything we can for the teachers.

On parent/teacher conference nights, throw a potluck dinner just for the teachers. In the evenings, the teachers are too busy with conferences to go out for dinner. Supply delicious, homemade food in the cafeteria so the teachers don't have to go hungry.

We give free tickets to the auction to the teachers. Many teachers prefer to stay home with their own families than to spend Saturday night with the parents of the kids in their class, but still, the gesture is warm and inclusive.

We allocate class funds from our fund-raising for every teacher. Our classroom funds provide $200 for each teacher or a $400 fund for a new teacher or a $300 fund for a teacher who is changing grades. The teachers decide how to spend the money. However, receipts are required for each expense. All expenses are submitted to the treasurer for approval.

We also make sure to honor special requests from the teachers. Nancy Goldstein, an excellent third grade teacher, appealed to the PA board one year for money to print a book of P.S. 87 children's poetry, open to all the children in the school. The expenditure was approved and a stunning book was produced.

Robin Ulzheimer, a fifth-grade teacher, won a grant to create a reading garden. When the money fell short before the garden was finished, the PA provided the additional funds to complete the project.

In our newsletter, we publicize many teachers' wish lists for supplies, furniture, appliances, and books for the classroom. Our parents fulfill as many wishes as they can.

We host an appreciation breakfast for teachers every year.

And those are just some examples. A good relationship between the PA board and the teachers is essential. Ask your board to come up with eight ideas for showing teacher appreciation. Pick two or three and make them happen. After all, everything we do is about supporting the classroom, the teachers, and creating the best classroom experience possible for our children.

The same attitude holds true for the administrative support staff in the office. I don't know how many times I've needed help from Anne Murney, Annie Nelson, or Emily Paxinos our school office administrative staff, and they have been there every time.

From opening the locked PA closet door, to copying, to helping me locate a teacher, a child, or a parent, not to mention letting the PA keep all kinds of flyers, the *BPN*, auction donation forms, and everything else needed for fund-raising in the office. Auction and street-fair donations get dropped off there, too.

It is impossible to stress enough the importance of having the office staff on your side. So make it clear you appreciate them. Buy them a cup of coffee or a doughnut now and then. Remember to say please and thank you.

4. Class Parents

Class parents are parents who volunteer to be responsible for parent association coordination with other parents in their child's class. We usually have two class parents per class. They are essential to successful school fund-raising. Class parents help out with field trips, straighten up in the classroom, and coordinate collecting for the teacher gifts at holiday time and the end of the year, too.

But class parents are also an important part of school fund-raising because they represent personal communication. Class parents call other parents or speak with them face-to-face at play dates, morning drop-off, or afternoon pickup at school. Class parents enable the school fund-raising efforts to reach right into each classroom to pull volunteers or donations and generate activity. Class parents become part of the parent network.

Usually the teacher selects two parents who volunteered from his or her class to become the class parents. These people are responsible for making sure that school fund-raising is being supported in their class. They are the ones who decide, frequently in collaboration with the teacher, what the class booth at the street fair will be. The class parents are the ones who contact the parents in their child's class and urge people to donate to the auction. The class parents are the ones pushing the wrapping-paper sales and magazine drive. The class parents make sure the teacher gets a book wish list to the Scholastic Book Fair or the school day at Barnes & Noble.

Class parents create a phone tree by dividing their class list into four or five columns and listing people vertically. Then the class parent calls each parent at the top of a column, and each parent then calls the parent beneath him or her on the phone tree with the same message. Using a phone tree means that every parent, with the exception of the class parent, only has to make one phone call, and everyone in the class has been reached quickly and efficiently.

5. Staff Relations

Successful school fund-raising requires the help of the school staff. From administrators to custodians, you will need everyone to pitch in. Go out of your way to build bridges, include and acknowledge the school staff.

I can't run a bake sale if Benny the custodian doesn't get the big tables set up and the extension cord for the coffee machine. I'm stuck if Al doesn't bring the giant garbage cans with lots of extra bags for my rummage sale. Many cooperative teachers have let us use classrooms to make coffee or store excess stuff. Office staff members have made copies and kept track of deliveries. Remember that without the support of the principal and assistant principals, you won't be able to do anything in the school at all. You will need all the support you can get.

6. Handbooks

There are three kinds of handbooks that will help you with fund-raising: a parent or school handbook, a new-teacher handbook, and a community resource handbook.

Parent / School Handbook

This handbook is a collaboration between the administration and the parents' association. A good handbook should inform the parents of all the rules and regulations regarding their child's new school. In addition to basics like admonishing the parents to bring their children to school on time, the handbook also outlines the fund-raisers planned for the school year. You will need only two people to create the handbook: one who knows the school inside out and one who can type. They can even be the same person. Once a handbook is produced, it can be used for years with only minor changes.

Either the PA or the school can print the handbook and distribute it free to the new parents. Distribute it to new teachers, too, to get them acquainted with your activities early in the year. Ours is printed on three-hole paper so parents can keep it in a binder.

You can make the handbook whatever you want it to be. Here is what P.S. 87 has done, which might be a place to start.

1. A mission statement. We use the mission statement from our school leadership team and then add a paragraph about what makes us special, including our logo and slogan: One Family under the Sun.
2. A section on admissions, physical exams, list of all types of staff (by position rather than by name).
3. A resources and facilities section, including a floor plan of the school. This section includes brief descriptions of:
   - library
   - P.S. 87 Science Resource Center
   - youth garden

   This section sets up some of the special facilities that are provided by the PA so that when donations are requested, people already have some idea where the money they contribute might go.

4. A curriculum section, provided by teachers and the administration.

5. A brief section on kindergarten including the orientation period and a description of a typical day to make the new kindergarten parents feel more at ease.

6. A section on assessment, standardized testing, and frequently asked questions, zeros in on common parents' concerns.

7. The parent association section, which starts with the PA board, school-wide committees, and finally fund-raising.

   • This chapter details the annual fund-raising events and the month or season they take place in.
   • We also include the following:
     Year-round fund-raising activities, like schoolpop.com and AT&T Points for School programs, A+ America/ Spring Free Technology for Schools program, Box Tops for Education.
   • Teacher and parent association wish lists
   • The flea market (see Chapter 11)
   • A pie chart showing the distribution of PA funds.
   • Arts-in-Action—This is a program paid for and run by the parent association that brings trained parents into the classroom to teach curriculum-based art lessons.
   • Parent Network Committee
   • Class parents

8. After-school program—Included is a brief description of our after-school program that includes sports, clubs, homework helps, and creative activities.

9. School rules.

Community Resource Handbook

The Community Resource Handbook began with questionnaires to incoming kindergarten parents about their skills, jobs, and hobbies. Soon it became apparent that we needed the resources of all the parents in the school. So a questionnaire was created to gather information about abilities, experiences, professions, and hobbies and was distributed to all the parents in the school.

A handbook was compiled from the questionnaires dividing parents into groups, like music, marketing, carpentry, writing, police, sewing, covering the diverse skills of the parents. The handbook was distributed to the teachers and put in the library. The teachers had a ready reference of whom to contact if they needed a bookshelf built, or a short lecture to the class on the stock market.

The book was extremely popular and became a resource for fund-raising, too. With this book, you can locate parents who have lighting experience to help with your haunted house, or who work for Fortune 500 companies if you need a specific donation, or who are professional actors to perform as storybook characters for your street fair.

Put your questionnaire in the first issue of your newsletter. Form a committee to gather this information and publish a community resource handbook.

7. The School Directory

It's impossible to run successful school fund-raising without this tool. The school directory should list all the students by class, with alphabetical cross-referenced listings in the back. We list a cross-reference with parents who have different last names from their children in the back, too.

We also list all the names of the members of the parent association board and their phone numbers and e-mail addresses. We list all the important numbers for the school, like the office, the guidance counselors, and the nurse.

We sell advertising in the directory to cut down on the printing cost and so we can distribute the directory free to all families. Consider charging a dollar for a second copy.

The directory is where everyone goes to call for volunteers or donations. You can't run programs or your child's social life without it. The biggest problem with the school directory is getting it out quickly.

> To get your directory out at the earliest possible date, start the directory at the end of the year. Get next year's classes from administration and begin the directory during the summer. In the fall, you'll just have to add kindergarten classes, a few new students in other grades, and make a handful of class changes. This will speed up delivery of the directory.

Phone Trees

A phone tree is a class list broken up into columns of names. You can usually fit four columns on a page. Each column has a student and parent lined up underneath. Then the person at the top of the column calls the parent directly underneath to pass along information, ask for volunteering, or ask for donations. Then that person makes one phone call to the person underneath her name, and so on. Eventually everyone on the list gets called and each person only had to make one phone call. Here is what it looks like:

Edna Brown
146 Chestnut Street
Edison, NC

Mary Brown
Kevin Brown
344-7988

↓

Gary Barrett
422 Elm Street
Rhonda Barrett
Glenn Barrett
324-6659

↓

Tiffany Cassel
112 Magnolia Lane
Clara Cassel
Michael Cassel

Once you have these support systems in place, you're ready to beginning planning your first fund-raising events.

"Eagerly awaited events such as the magazine drive in the fall, the auction in late winter, and the "Just Kids Street Fair" in the spring, to name but a few, mark the passage of the school year as surely as any academic calendar. The benefits that accrue to students transcend the material improvements to their school. Children develop an appreciation for the priority that education represents for their families as well as perceiving their school as a community that is the basis of the formation of lifelong relationships and friendships."

STEVEN PLAUT, FORMER P.S. 87 PRINCIPAL

Fall Events

· · · · · · · · · · · · · · · ·

The Pledge Drive

What is a Pledge Drive?

A pledge drive is a plea for money—like Jerry Lewis's Muscular Dystrophy Pledge Drive telethon on Labor Day—but through the mail instead of on television. During Jerry's telethon, people pledge or promise to donate a specific amount of money to be sent in at a later date. Our pledge drive letter asks for immediate donations to our parent association for use in the school.

HOW DOES A SCHOOL PLEDGE DRIVE WORK?

Mail a letter from the parent's association president to parents asking for donations of money. Our letter describes what the funds will be used for and how money has been spent in the past. You can ask for a specific amount. P.S. 199 asks for $300. Pick an amount that isn't too high or too low.

Get the best copywriter parent volunteer you can to write the solicitation letter. The letter should explain why the money is needed and specifically where the money is going. We use a pie chart to show what percentage of our fund-raising goes to each program. Usually it's 33 percent to the library, 20 percent to the art program, five percent to science enrichment and so on.

Mail the pledge drive letter along with the summer mailing from your school so the school instead of the parent association picks up the postage. If your school doesn't do a summer mailing, perhaps you can encourage them to start one.

Enclose an addressed reply envelope in your mailing. It doesn't need to be postage paid. The reply envelope will increase response and will ensure that the response goes to the correct person at the correct address. Usually pledge drive money ought to go to the treasurer. But if the treasurer is on vacation in August when the replies start coming in, have the donations sent to the PA president or another responsible board member.

Ask people to give what they can. Public school parents usually come at all income levels. Be sure your letter is not too demanding and does not make the lower-income parents in your school feel badly if they cannot afford to contribute much or at all. Point out that there are many ways to contribute, such as donating time to run a class booth at the street fair or donating a cake, cookies, or brownies to a bake sale.

VOLUNTEERS

This event brings in the most money with the least number of volunteers. Volunteers for the pledge drive must be able to work during the summer, as the first mailing goes out in August. You need only a chairperson and about three volunteers including the treasurer, to:

- write copy
- have the letter copied and order the envelopes
- get the mailing out (can you get help from school staff?)
- keep track of and post response

SECRETS TO INCREASING PLEDGE DRIVE REVENUE

Recently, P.S. 87 hit on a magic formula for our school that took the pledge drive revenues up from $30,000 to over $85,000 in one year. Here it is:

1. Credit Card option.

    Get a merchant account with MasterCard, American Express, Discover, and Visa for the pledge drive. You can get a merchant account from the bank where you have your PA account. This makes it *much* easier to get donations. You can offer a payment plan where the parent donor's credit card is charged a specific amount indicated by the parent each month for three or six months. If a parent wanted to donate $300, but not all at once, you could be authorized to charge their credit card $50 per month for six months. This makes it easier for some parents to give more money. Credit cards cut down on bounced checks, too, saving your PA time trying to get those checks made good and saving your PA the high cost of those returned-check charges from the bank.

2. Timing.

    Timing is very important. At P.S. 87, we have been doing the pledge drive for years, and always mailed in December, figuring—like many nonprofit companies—that year end is a time when people scramble to make tax-deductible contributions before the IRS deadline. But when it came to contributions to our particular school, we were wrong. Mailing in December, our pledge drives never brought in more than about $30,000. Perhaps the mailing gets lost in the deluge of holiday cards and end of year commitments.

    We now mail on August 15, before the school year begins.

    Mailing early while people are excited about and anticipating a new school year is key. Get contributions from parents before they become disenchanted with their child's teacher or something else occurs that might turn them off the idea of donating money.

    Mail early to new kindergarten parents who have gotten used to paying huge preschool fees. A onetime contribution of $300 may seem paltry to people who have been paying $500 or more per month for preschool. Get to them before they become used to school being free.

3. Ask for a specific donation amount.

We request a minimum donation of $300. If every family were able to donate $300, we wouldn't have to do any additional fund-raising at all, we say in our letter. Of course we don't get $300 per family, as there are many families in our community who can't afford to donate even $50. But we get enough from those who can donate to push our pledge drive up and up.

4. Make a connection with new families before they enter school.

Our parent association board members contact kindergarten and other new parents before the school year begins. We welcome them with personal letters or phone calls from board members, and a picnic just for new parents, board members, and their children. Welcoming new parents helps to reduce their September anxiety by making them feel like a part of our special community even before they walk in the door.

Kindergarten is more daunting to every member of the student's family than people expect. When new parents come into our school, they feel a little overwhelmed by the size of the school and the tight-knit PA. A friendly hand extended before the year begins is welcomed by these parents and makes them more comfortable with us right away. It makes them more generous, too.

We also have a new parent breakfast outside in the kindergarten yard on the first two half days of school. This gives the parents an opportunity to hear from members of the PA board and to meet experienced parents and ask us questions. The breakfasts really help these parents to make the adjustment to "real" school. We have sign-up sheets for eight PA committees, from library to technology to fundraising, to capture volunteers early. This gives us an opportunity to get parents, who will be in the school for six years, involved and volunteering early on.

5. Incentives.

One year we kept a running bar graph in the lobby of the school showing which class had raised the most money through the pledge drive. We also published a list of the names of donors, but not the amount donated, in the school lobby. We gave a pizza party to the class whose parents donated the most money. Think of simple but public incentives that could work in your school.

6. Write thank-you notes.

This job should be the responsibility of the administrative vice president or the secretary of the PA board. Thank-you notes are an excellent way to acknowledge donations and make new parents feel appreciated right away. Handwritten is best, but if you don't have time, use a printed card with real signatures and a word or two. Timeliness is important.

7. Mail Again.

The same pledge drive letter mailed again can produce more donations. Or write a new letter telling your parents how much you still need to raise to meet your goal. Don't mail the second letter until the end of October, to give parents time to respond to the first letter. Be sure to mail before Thanksgiving. You don't want parents' generosity to be short-circuited by the financial burdens of the upcoming holidays.

8. Have a table at parent/teacher conference night.

We set up a table, (really only a desk) with a volunteer and a sign to collect any pledge drive money anyone wants to give on the spot. Be prepared to take credit cards at that table, too. This is ideal as you have all the parents in the school marching in and out during conferences.

9. Organize an ice cream or pizza party for the winning class.

HOW MUCH MONEY WILL YOU RAISE?

It is hard to predict response to the pledge drive. Our school, at 950 students, is very large. Yet when it was larger, over 1,100, we actually raised less money. The pledge drive may fluctuate because of economic conditions as well as the mix of families in your school. Whatever you raise through a pledge drive is usually considered gravy since it didn't involve much in the way of volunteers or time compared to many other events. In our best year so far, the pledge drive has produced over $85,000.

Timeline • • • • • • • • • • • • • • •

Beginning of June (end of previous year)	find volunteer copywriter
Middle to end of June	finalize copy
July	order printed reply envelopes
	get letter copied
	get thank-you notes ready
August	add letters to school mailing
	mail
	begin to get donations
Beginning of October	mail a second letter stressing how close you are to your goal, and what more is needed

The Wrapping Paper Drive

What is a Wrapping Paper Drive?

Several companies that manufacture wrapping paper and holiday items have created programs that give schools or parent associations a percentage of the revenue from sales made through the school. We have sold wrapping paper from different companies in the past with varying results. Some of these companies are:

5 Star fund-raising: www.fivestarfundraising.com

Genevieve's: 1-800-842-6656

Kathryn Beich: www.kathrynbeich.com

QSP Reader's Digest: 1-800-561-8388

Resource Solutions: www.resourcefundraising.com

Sally Foster: www.sallyfoster.com

These companies prepare everything you need to run a successful wrapping-paper drive, including a catalog with actual paper samples and order forms. It is important to stress that the children should *not* be out selling wrapping paper door-to-door by themselves, as it is not safe. A parent or another responsible adult should always accompany children.

Each company works in a different way and may offer a different percentage to the parent association or school. Select the company with the right product mix for your school population and the highest percentage donated to the school. Sally Foster offers 50%. QSP Readers' Digest offers up to 50%. Most offer up to 50%.

For several years we used Sally Foster exclusively. The paper was exceptional, but the bookkeeping was so complicated that subsequent fund-raising chairs were turned off by the enormous outlay of time the accounting took.

One year we offered two catalogs from two different companies—one was Sally Foster, exclusively wrapping paper, and the other was Genevieve's, offering wrapping paper, gifts, ornaments, and other items. This combination worked well although it was a little confusing, because there were two catalogs, more choices, two forms to fill out. The chairperson had to keep orders straight for two companies instead of just one.

Later we reluctantly gave up Sally Foster and used Reader's Digest exclusively. We had the best sales ever and made the most money. A catalog combining wrapping paper with other holiday gift items might work best at your school. Speak with different companies and pick the combination of items you think will work best with your parent body.

The company will send you all the catalogs and forms you need. Remember to get extras. We always have parents who lose the catalog or want to give one to "Aunt Martha" to sell to her office staff, so we order about a hundred extra. Offices are a great place to make sales: be sure to suggest that your parents tap their colleagues to benefit your school.

HOW DOES THE WRAPPING PAPER DRIVE WORK?

The chairpeople and two or three volunteers get together and count out the proper number of catalogs for each classroom. A volunteer delivers the catalogs in a plastic bag right to the classrooms. Teachers disseminate the catalogs and collect the orders.

When the orders start coming in the teacher puts them in the plastic bag and hangs it on the outside knob of the classroom door. Then the chair or other volunteers can pick up the orders from the bags without disturbing the class.

Leave the plastic bag there two weeks beyond the order due date for the teacher to add more orders, or put a box in the school office for people to put orders in. Some people don't want to send orders in with young children. It's easier to collect very late orders from a box in the school office. Instruct people through a notice in your school newsletter to drop orders in the office after a certain date.

A group of volunteers processes the orders as they come in. If you wait until they are all in, you'll be inundated. Starting early gives you time to gather information missing from order forms before you're snowed under with orders.

Allow four weeks for this process from start to finish. About a month or more after you have completed all the paperwork and sent the check to the wrapping paper company, the wrapping paper is delivered. The company sends each order complete and already boxed so you don't have to do anything but distribute it.

Inform all the parents that the wrapping paper has arrived. We make an announcement in the *Backpack News*, our newsletter, and put up signs at the school and in the schoolyard announcing the arrival of the wrapping paper. Keep all the orders in a gymnasium or on the stage in the auditorium, because you will need a lot of space. The parents or caregivers must come and pick up their orders since many orders are too heavy for children to carry home on their own.

Volunteers check off each parent's order as they pick up their wrapping paper. Do not have more than three or four people handling this job since you need to keep excellent records to be certain that all orders are delivered to the proper people and that none disappear.

Timing is very important. Contact wrapping paper companies by June to set up your holiday program. The company will create a timetable with you. You must get this launched and orders submitted in time to have the wrapping paper back before Thanksgiving. After that, parents panic that it won't arrive in time for the holidays. You must have the paper distributed to the parents before the Thanksgiving break.

VOLUNTEERS

You need to have someone to chair this committee. Two chairs are even better. The chairs need to set up a chain of command. You will need volunteers for the following activities:

- counting out and distributing catalogs
- collecting orders
- tabulating orders and filling out paperwork for the wrapping paper company
- supervising distribution of orders
- troubleshooting incorrect orders

The number of actual volunteers you need will depend upon the size of your school. About five volunteers should be enough for a big school. A smaller school with 300 students or less can get by with only two volunteers.

SECRETS TO SUCCESS

Time your deadline carefully. You want the maximum return but have a limited time frame. The best way to handle the deadline is to keep the real set-in-stone deadline to yourself. Give out a first deadline that is ten days earlier than the final one. Then give two extensions. We find that about 30% of our parents don't hand anything in until the last minute. Giving extensions works best to bring in the maximum number of orders. Set your deadlines according to the reliability of your own parent group.

Put reminders of the deadlines to sell wrapping paper in the newsletter. Create flyers for the teachers to insert in the students' backpacks to remind parents to sell wrapping paper and get their orders in on time.

Run contests for the most wrapping paper sold per class and offer a pizza or ice cream party for the class with the highest sales. Have a bar graph in the school lobby charting the progress of each class. Suggest that grandparents also get in on the act and sell to their friends.

HOW MUCH MONEY WILL YOU RAISE?

Our school is big—950 students. In 2001 our wrapping paper drive netted about $25,000. The wrapping paper company should give you an idea how much money a school your size can expect to earn.

Timeline

May the previous year	select wrapping paper company
By September 20	distribute catalogs
To be determined by company	process and send in orders
Before Thanksgiving	distribute orders to parents

JUST STARTING OUT?

This is a good fund-raising event to try if you are just starting out since you don't need to lay out money in advance.

School Photos and the Magazine Drive

School Photos

WHAT ARE SCHOOL PHOTOS?

Every elementary school I know takes photos of every school class. The parent association gets almost half the total revenue from these photos to add to our coffers. But we've added a new twist. Since we have many families whose children graduate to middle schools and high schools that may not have school photos, we have created a Family Photo Day in addition to the regular School Photo Day.

Family Photo Day takes place on a Saturday. Anyone can come and get in the picture: mom, dad, baby sister, even the dog. There are many families who prefer to have one photo with all their children instead of separate photos for each. This also saves money, as the family only has to pay for one set of photos instead of one for each of several children.

Photo packages range in price from $20 to $35. As the price increases, the number of items—photos, magnets, bookmarks—also increases. Family Photo Day helped to generate more income because families that might have turned down three photos will pay for this one.

HOW DO SCHOOL PHOTOS WORK?

You need to have permission to use the school on a Saturday. Send out flyers in advance to the parents. Put a reminder in your school newspaper. Put up posters around the school. When you have a list of all the families who paid in advance for family photos, set up a schedule. Allow ten to fifteen minutes between families. Stress to the parents that they need to be on time. Word-of-mouth is the best way to find a photographer. Call other schools or parent associations until you find one that is satisfied with their photographer. The Yellow Pages won't be able to recommend the most reliable. Reliability and photo quality are more important than having the lowest price.

We always have school photos and Family Photo Day in the fall. Fall photos mean that people will have them in time for the holidays to send with greeting cards or frame as gifts for grandma and grandpa.

Unless you have a huge turnout, you should be able to handle family photos in one day. Be sure to have many disposable combs and a mirror on hand.

Photos must be completely paid for in advance. If the photos turn out terribly or get messed up in some way, you can schedule a retake day. Collect in advance because there will be people who change their minds about their pictures, and the parent association will be stuck paying for those.

VOLUNTEERS

Often the photographer comes with one or two assistants. You will probably only need two to four volunteers during the day on Family Photo Day to help the photographer's assistants. The photographer should run the show.

You may need one or two volunteers to get flyers out to the parents and collect the money before the picture day.

SECRETS TO SUCCESS

Family Photo Day is our secret to extending school photos and increasing the revenue. We also offer one other special feature.

We make sure that every child in school gets a photo of the whole class, whether they can pay for it or not. The parent association picks up the tab for those few class photos that families can't pay for. Being able to extend a helping hand in this area is one of the many benefits of spending so much time raising money. The families who can't pay really appreciate having class photos for their children.

HOW MUCH MONEY WILL YOU RAISE??

Our big school raises about $6,000 on school/family photos.

Timeline • • • • • • • • • • • • • • •

End of previous school
year (May or June)   select a photographer

You will be assigned a date from your photographer since he or she keeps a tight schedule on school photos, a major bread-and-butter event for the photographer. Make sure that he or she schedules you in time to get the photos back before the holidays, allowing for retakes.

JUST STARTING OUT?

This is a good event for you if your school is just starting to raise funds because there is no cash up front required by the photographer.

The Magazine Drive

WHAT IS A MAGAZINE DRIVE?

A magazine drive is similar to a wrapping paper drive in that parents and kids sell magazine subscriptions to their friends, family, and neighbors. Again, do *not* let your children go door-to-door without an adult.

Certain companies process magazine subscriptions for a profit and share a percentage with schools. The companies provide all the forms you need, including complete lists of magazines and the special prices they are offering for subscriptions or subscription renewals. Renewals may be easier to sell than new subscriptions. Sometimes the companies also sell CDs and music cassettes in addition to magazine subscriptions.

The best company to use for this is:

QSP Reader's Digest: 1-800-561-8388.

HOW DOES A MAGAZINE DRIVE WORK?

There is a huge selection of magazines covering many special interests, like woodworking to more general publications like *Time*, *Newsweek*, and *Woman's Day*.

You will receive all the materials you need to get and process orders from QSP. The publicity is all yours. You will be responsible for setting up a time frame for running this fund-raising event.

Follow the same procedure used for the wrapping paper drive, the catalogs of magazines and other products are counted out and delivered to the classrooms. The teachers distribute them to the students, who take them home in their backpacks. Orders are returned to the teachers, who turn them over to magazine drive volunteers or class parents. The chair of the drive tabulates the orders with any help he or she requires, and sends everything in to the company . . . and that's the end of the work. This is a no-brainer because there is nothing more to do after taking orders, and absolutely no products to distribute and no follow-up. The processing company forwards the subscription lists to the publishers, who send out the magazines, while the company itself sends CDs right to the purchaser.

The magazine drive doesn't have to operate under the same time constraints as the wrapping paper drive—it's not a seasonal event. You can extend the deadlines more than you can with the wrapping paper drive.

This magazine drive doesn't have the dazzle of the wrapping paper drive or the Halloween Festival, but it brings in quite a bit of money and requires much less work than other events.

VOLUNTEERS
The magazine drive can be carried off with a minimum number of volunteers. You'll need help with:
- disseminating the catalogs
- collecting orders
- tabulating orders

That is not much help compared to other events. In fact your chair can probably run this event by herself or himself.

SECRETS TO SUCCESS
There are not too many secrets for this event. You can provide incentives, like a pizza or ice cream party, for the class selling the most magazine subscriptions. You might also keep a sales bar graph in the school lobby. This event usually runs itself, so you don't need to do much to get the desired results.

HOW MUCH MONEY WILL YOU RAISE?
Since our school is so big, we had major expectations. Before we moved the pledge drive to September, the magazine drive contributed as much as $12,000 to our income. With the pledge drive taking center stage at the same time as the magazine drive, it has reduced our magazine drive revenue to about $8,000. You've got to sell a lot of cupcakes to make that much money, so we keep this going, even if it isn't as much fun as other events.

Timeline • • • • • • • • • • • • • •

End of previous school
   year (May or June)   contact the company

   Run your schedule based on the company information. They will
tell you when to expect materials and when to have the orders in.

JUST STARTING OUT?
This event makes a good first fund-raising event if your school is
just starting out since you don't have to lay out money in advance.

The Halloween Harvest Festival

What Is a Halloween Harvest Festival?

Our Halloween Harvest Festival is like an indoor street fair with food, music, dancing, games, and a haunted house. All the kids and many of the parent volunteers come in costume. The Halloween Harvest Festival can replace traditional Halloween activities. It provides a safe place for our children to celebrate this wacky holiday to the max. Our Halloween Harvest Festival takes place in the evening on the Friday closest to, but always before, Halloween, and is one of the liveliest events of the year.

HOW DOES THE HALLOWEEN HARVEST FESTIVAL WORK?

Our Halloween Harvest Festival evolved from the Harvest Festival, which was like a small autumn street fair with no real theme. The original Harvest Festival was a huge amount of work. Enthusiasm waned, we had a hard time finding volunteers, and the financial return kept shrinking.

One year our terrific PA president, Sydnie Ronga, suggested that we change the Harvest Festival to incorporate Halloween. Everyone loved the idea.

We made several changes, taking the festival indoors to the

gym, hallways, cafeteria, and stairwells from outside in the yard where we were vulnerable to the whims of the weather. We added music and dancing in the gym and a scary Halloween haunted house, created in a side stairwell (if you don't have a stairwell, use a room with a door at each end to manage traffic flow.) We added a bake sale, face painting, games in the hallway, and an admission charge. And of course everyone came in costume. It became a huge hit.

A successful Halloween Harvest Festival can consist of the following:

- haunted house
- hot dogs, soda, and bake sale (see "The Ultimate Bake Sale," Chapter 12)
- hired (or volunteer if you can) DJ with music and dancing in the gym
- free ice cream or soda with $5 admission
- face painting and games in booths or at tables in the hallways next to the gym and cafeteria
- Keep the festivities restricted to specific areas.
- grab bags (This year we are adding Halloween grab bags to the mix. The grab bags contain inexpensive small Halloween toys and candy bought through catalogs like U.S. Toy and Oriental Trading and mixed up in brown paper lunch bags, with no two bags carrying exactly the same items. They will cost us about 50¢ and we will sell them for $2 each. We are making 150 bags, which will sell out quickly because the kids love them.)

We put the music in the gym and the games in the hallway just outside. The cafeteria is a good place for the hot dogs, soda, and bake sale.

Believe it or not, the best place for the haunted house is a side stairwell. This allows children to enter from one floor and leave from another, avoiding crowding. Also, using the stairwell does not mess up any teacher's classroom. If there are windows in the stairwell, open them to keep the area from getting too hot. If you don't have a stairwell—many modern schools are on one floor—use a classroom or other room with a door at each end. This allows you to have one door as an entrance and one as an exit. Using two doors prevents traffic problems and keeps the children moving.

We don't do much with decorations except in the haunted house, since decorating can eat up your expense budget and the kids and parents come "decorated" by wearing costumes. We always schedule this event on the Friday before Halloween, unless Halloween is on a Friday. It starts at 6:00 P.M. and is finished by 9:00 P.M.

We sell hot dogs and soda for a dollar each. And the bake sale is amazing. I don't think I've ever seen so many cupcakes in my life, and the decorations are incredible. Halloween brings out the artist in all the cupcake donors. Using icing, candies, sprinkles, and anything else edible, the fabulously decorated cupcakes show witches, or pumpkins or goblins, or swirling combinations of orange, black, and white. Each batch is an example of the wonderful creativity of children brought out by this holiday.

We like to have rock 'n roll music usually with a DJ and a good boom box. Hire a teenager to take care of the music. After all, what would a Halloween Festival be without dancing to "The Monster Mash" in the gym?

We are very fortunate to have a professional lighting designer, Phil Sorenson, in our parent body. His lighting techniques and creative input have helped the haunted house team. But you don't need professionals to have a fantastic haunted house. Kim Mogul Wright, a member of the team that created the first haunted house, gives this advice:

- Buys lots and lots of black fabric. Use it to cover walls and objects in the room you are using. In the dark, the black fabric gives the illusion that the room is empty. Then you can create your own scary scenes in front of the dark backdrop.

- Dress everyone in black. Buy scary masks or make up the faces of your adult and older child volunteers to be scary creatures like Dracula, ax man, Frankenstein, or other monsters. Your only limitation is your own imagination.
- Hold a lit flashlight under your chin to create a spooky look.
- Use lots of props, like fake spiderwebs, a cleaver, and chains.
- Buy a sound-effects tape of eerie noises, like creaking doors.
- For a graveyard effect, create fake tombstones, build a fake coffin, and have someone rise up out of it.
- Make a papier-mâché head using an inflated balloon as the base. Paint it to look ghoulish. Use green olives with pimentos for eyes.
- Use only black lights. They make everything white glow in the dark.
- Hang string to break against the kids' faces in the dark.
- Put stuff on the floor, like bubble wrap that makes noise when stepped on.
- Set up a wire and pulley system so you can send a homemade ghost sailing out of nowhere into the light.
- Paint empty eggshells with Day-Glo paint to make scary eyes.
- Hang up scary critters like skeletons, bats, spiders, ghosts, black cats, and witches, that move or have eyes or mouths that move.
- Buy scary rubber hands, or stuff rubber gloves.
- Record your own tape with scary laughs, screams, and creaking hinges.

You can hang scary things, like glow-in-the-dark skeletons and fake body parts, from the ceiling. Create shadows and keep it dark. Spring out of the darkness to scare the wits out of the children. The big kids get a real kick out of that. Remember that older children in the haunted house need adult supervision.

Two cautions: When the younger children come through the

haunted house, we try to notify everyone so they can tone down the performance. Also, use white or glow-in-the-dark tape to tape a trail or guideline on the floor for children to follow. Save what you buy to use again the following year, that helps to keep expenses down and in a few years you will have a treasure trove of Halloween fright gadgets and supplies.

You can charge $1.00 or so for each time through the Haunted House, on top of admission which can be as high as $5. The admission price can include a hot dog, piece of pizza or soda, too.

Games run the gamut. Face painting is popular, especially for children who don't come in costume. Ring toss, ping-pong ball toss, temporary tattoos, and jewelry making are just four examples of the many, many indoor games and activities you can set up at tables quickly and easily. Game booths take more time to create. Start early.

Publicity is very important in order to recruit volunteers and get donations of baked goods, as well as getting people to attend. Advertise in your school newsletter and in the neighborhood as well by putting up posters in local store windows. Put up posters throughout the school. With all the concern for children's safety surrounding Halloween, many parents are looking for alternatives to trick or treating for their children. A Halloween festival is a safe, fun way to enjoy the occasion. You should attract people beyond your own school.

Security is very important. You must make sure that nothing in the school is damaged. One year a very concerned parent, Steve Russo, invested in some wide rolls of plastic. He put the plastic over the artwork on the walls in the halls. This ensured that all the artwork on display was unharmed.

You'll also need to keep children confined to specific parts of the building, with your own security guards—or volunteer parents— to keep people out of off-limits locations. We like to pay our after-school security staff to handle security for the Halloween Harvest

Festival. We pay three guards $50 each for the whole event. Remember that security is very important. If the building is trashed or artwork or class work on the walls destroyed, the principal will be reluctant to let you use the school for this event again.

Try these booth ideas:

Mask-Making: Decorate plastic half-masks from the store with glitter, feathers, and stickers. Make your own masks out of cardboard and string or paper bags.

Milk Carton Crash: Knock down half-gallon milk cartons (with the tops cut off so they can be stacked) with tennis balls.

Bean Bag Toss: Toss homemade beanbags into a witch/ghost/ Frankenstein's mouth. Make the witch or monster out of sturdy corrugated cardboard. Cut a generous hole for the mouth to make it easier.

Weird Nails: Use green or black nail polish and nail stickers and glitter to make spooky fingernail designs.

Cupcake Decorating: This is always popular. Use Halloween-colored icing in orange and black and Halloween candies.

Pin the Tail on the Donkey: For Halloween, use a Pin the Tail on the Black Cat or Pin the Broom on the Witch. Recruit the best artists in your school to draw the figures.

An admission charge covers the cost of a DJ and music. We give everyone a free dish of ice cream or a soda for the admission price. Collect right at the door. Then, also at the door, sell tickets for everything else, like hot dogs, haunted house, and games. Keep access to cash limited to just two or three trustworthy people. I never thought that money would disappear in a school, but sad to say, it does happen. The best way to guard against stealing is by using tickets for everything except admission. Keep all the cash in one place. Even the bake sale table can use tickets. Our treasurer or assistant treasurer monitors the cash at every event. This consistency provides a safeguard against theft.

VOLUNTEERS

You will need a lot of volunteers to run this event. Start with a chairperson and committee heads. I suggest the following committees:

food—with two subcommittees: bake sale and hot dog/soda
music
haunted house
games
publicity
security
admissions/tickets

Each committee chair should be responsible for recruiting his or her own volunteers. But the event chair should help by recruiting and deploying volunteers where they are needed most.

Don't plan to have one person handle a booth alone all evening. Everyone wants to have a good time. Make sure you have enough people helping and taking turns so everyone can dance in the gym and enjoy a hot dog and cupcake.

SECRETS TO SUCCESS

What really makes this event special is the attitude of everyone involved as well as the haunted house. The parents really get excited about this event and that enthusiasm is contagious.

Many other schools and organizations have Halloween parties, but our haunted house takes the party to another level. It is the hit of the evening. The line to get into the haunted house is always long and children have to be dragged away to go home at closing.

Music is also something unique to our Halloween Harvest Festival. I've been to many Halloween parties and never seen one that included a DJ and dancing in the gym. This provides a safe place for the children to be active and work off some of the sugar they have taken in at the bake sale table.

Our grab bags are unique and best-sellers at every event. I will go into more detail about grab bags in the chapters about the auction (Chapter 7) and the street fair (Chapter 10).

HOW MUCH MONEY WILL YOU RAISE?

Our old original Harvest Festival was producing only $1,500 when we made the changeover. In its first year the Halloween Harvest Festival produced $5,000. By 2001, revenue had increased to about $6,200. This is not our biggest moneymaking event, but it sure is a big "fun" raiser.

Timeline

End of previous school year	line up chairperson and committee heads
	secure the date with the school
	arrange for DJ and music
September	meet with committee chairs and map out locations and plan activities

End of September	secure volunteers for each committee
First week of October	purchase all grab bags items and decorations*
Week before the event	stuff grab bags
Few days before event	purchase food
Day of event	create haunted house

JUST STARTING OUT?

This event requires some money up front for haunted house supplies.

- Sell tickets in advance to get some cash for food and supplies.
- Try to get haunted house supplies donated from local stores.
- Ask parents to contribute or even just lend supplies they may have, like old black fabric or Halloween decorations from holidays past.
- Ask a few parents to purchase supplies and be reimbursed after the event.
- Get the event sponsored by a store or civic organization.
- Because you are charging admission, you will have cash to pay the security guards and the DJ at the end of the evening.
- Skip the hot dogs and just have a bake sale.
- Ask the people doing grab bags to lay out the money for the small toys in advance and reimburse them when the event is over.
- Have games only at the fair. Games don't usually require much in the way of supplies. For example, knocking down empty milk cartons with a tennis ball is a great game that requires only a few dollars to set up and run.
- Find a teenager or rock 'n roll music buff parent who is willing to be your DJ for free.

*Oriental Trading may have a special advance purchase Halloween catalog they mail in July. You may get free shipping, and you will save a lot of money by buying your supplies from this early catalog. You can reach them at www.orientaltrading.com.

Make sure your publicity is strong. Include posters in key loca-tions in your community, like store windows and pediatricians' offices as well as in school and in your newsletter. If you are asking people to lay out some money in advance, you need to be sure that you will have a big enough turnout to be able to pay them back after the event and clear extra revenue for your coffers.

Winter Events

• • • • • • • • • • • • •

Dances, Friday Night Pizza and a Movie, Kids' Holiday Shopping Day

Dances

You can create a dance for any reason at any time for any age group. A dance is a classic event that can be put together easily at the last minute. Here are three examples of dances that are easy to run successfully.

SOCK HOP

What Is a Sock Hop?

A sock hop is a dance with a 1950s theme. You play 1950s music and the kids come dressed in 1950s outfits.

Costumes

The girls wear "poodle skirts," felt circle skirts with a cutout—the poodle was popular—glued on. Poodle skirts are usually done in pastel colors and worn with color-coordinated sweaters and ankle socks. But any version of a skirt and top that has a '50s look will do. A ponytail is the easiest '50s hairstyle, but a pageboy also qualifies.

The boys slick their hair back with gel or mousse into the closest version of a DA (duck's ass) as they can get. They roll up the sleeves on short-sleeved shirts or even T-shirts and wear tight pants.

Music/Dancing

Music from Bill Haley and the Comets, Fats Domino, Elvis, and others is readily available. Parents can teach kids how to do the Lindy or the jitterbug, the most popular dances at that time.

You don't really need poodle skirts or ponytails to have a successful sock hop. Just assorted '50s music, some food, and a group of kids ready to dance is enough to have a great event.

What Does a Sock Hop Entail?

Pick a date for the hop that allows you at least three weeks to complete preparations for the dance with ease. Secure the rights to use your gymnasium. In New York City we have to pay a custodial fee to keep the building open beyond the normal hours. Then you need to find a DJ. This can be a professional, but you have to pay about $100 for a DJ, sometimes more. It would be better to get a few parents together who have collections of '50s music and ask either a parent or a teenage sibling to be the DJ. You can give a teenager $10 or $20 for their time, or just reward them with free pizza, soda, and cupcakes. A parent DJ should do the job as a volunteer and not charge anything.

Try new dance themes like:

1. Wearing clothes backwards.
2. Coming in pajamas and nightgowns.
3. Western theme with country music.
4. Hawaiian theme with colorful shirts, grass skirts, and fake flower leis.
5. Black and white theme. Where everyone dresses only in black and white.
6. Sports theme.

7. Valentine theme.
8. Square Dance.

Food is important. Since we do not have access to the school kitchen when we have a dance, we usually offer a slice of pizza or a can of soda to the parents and kids as part of the price of admission. If you can use the school kitchen, then you can have a potluck or make and sell other food, like hot dogs. Have a bake sale, too.

Put time limits on the dance. We start at 6:30 and throw everyone out at 9:30. For older children in middle or high school, you can start later and keep the kids until 10 or 10:30 P.M. on a Friday or Saturday night.

You must have monitors or chaperones. Hire teachers or get parent volunteers. Pay parents if you have to, but security is mandatory. Restrict the kids to one or two floors or sections of your school at the most and be firm. You must protect the building from rampaging and overactive kids. A few rolls of clear plastic about four or five feet wide can be put on the hall walls to cover and protect artwork. Even though we told parents that they could not just drop their kids off and leave, some did anyway. Children without any parental supervision can go wild with the sugar from the cupcakes and the provocation of the music. Most kids are fine, but two or three troublemakers without parents can do damage.

Publicity is easy for this event. If you have a school newsletter, put notices in two weeks in advance and again one week in advance. Posters around the school are excellent too. You can also hand out fliers at morning school drop-off and at school dismissal time.

VOLUNTEERS

Dances need fewer parent volunteers than other events. A committee can consist of one person for this event, but a minimum of two is advisable.

You will need:

1. a small publicity committee
2. music committee
3. security committee
4. decoration committee
5. food committees: pizza and soda committee and baked goods committee
6. someone to check the rules and regulations of being in the school at night. Don't forget a cleanup committee.

SECRETS TO SUCCESS

We charge $5 at the door for everybody, adult or child. This is to pay for the pizza and/or soda, and the DJ, if you can't find a parent to do the job.

We sell baked goods, too. We sell them cheaply, 50¢ for a cupcake and so on, so as not to make it an expensive evening. But we get a lot of donations of baked goods and we do quite well. Baked goods can also be thematic, like poodle-decorated cupcakes, polka dots or other '50s images on cookies or cupcakes.

We don't decorate the gym. Decorations are expensive and the colorful theme clothes seem to add decoration enough. Middle and high school dances require decoration. Perhaps a decoration committee could get decorations donated by families to avoid adding to expenses. Have older kids make decorations for their dances. Or get some brightly colored balloons and helium and float bunches of balloons in several places.

Try to form a special relationship with the local franchise of a pizza chain like Domino's. Domino's supports our local school groups and our scout troops as well. Domino's gives us pizza at a reduced price because we are a school. That enables us to clear more money by reducing our expenses. Don't be afraid to ask for freebies or discounts. A good relationship with your school helps to sell more pizza for your local pizza parlor. In a franchise, speak with the manager. In a mom-and-pop shop, speak with the owner.

Publicize any retail outfit that gives you a break and encourage families to frequent those restaurants or stores that contribute to your school.

We buy soda at the price club. Maybe you can go to the big beverage warehouse vendors. Get everything as cheaply as possible. Free is even better!

We always schedule our dances on Friday nights. This seems to be the best night since most families are looking for fun family activities for Friday nights before the more heavily scheduled core of the weekend sets in.

HOW MUCH MONEY WILL YOU RAISE?

We have made as much as $6,500 on a school dance, although our first dance only made $3,500. It takes a few times to work out the kinks and maximize your profits.

Timeline • • • • • • • • • • • • • •

Three weeks ahead	select a date and okay it with the school
	appoint committee chairs, decide on food
Three–two weeks ahead	hire DJ and security guards
Two weeks ahead	start publicity

One week ahead	negotiate with pizza/soda company
	order food and drinks
Day of Dance	put up plastic protection on walls
	put up Stop signs to keep kids in
	designated areas

DANCE VARIATIONS

You can throw several dances per year, but be sure to change the theme to spur enthusiasm. Our two most successful dance theme variations are the Valentine's Day Dance and the Square Dance.

Valentine's Day Dance

This theme offers almost limitless ideas for cupcake and gym decorations. It also allows for a broader range of music. A Valentine's Day Dance in the dead of winter can really pick up everybody's spirits.

Square Dance

This dance theme, which lends itself to a country and western motif in both baked goods (do you know how to make a shoofly or sweet potato pie?) and gym decoration. One benefit of a square dance is that the caller tells everybody what to do, so kids—mostly boys—who might be shy or don't know how to dance can dance right along instantly.

Also, as with a circle dance, square dancing sometimes doesn't require a specific partner. Even if you do have a partner, it isn't as intimate as a slow dance. One drawback is that you must hire a caller, which can be expensive and possibly be hard to find in your area. Maybe a parent in your school would volunteer to be the caller. Advertise the need for this position in your school newsletter. Square dances make for a lot of laughter as you allemande right instead of left and the whole dance gets thrown off. The square dance was our first successful dance at P.S. 87.

Other possible dance themes might include: St. Patrick's Day, May Day, Sadie Hawkins (girls ask the boys—for older children) Day, Folk Dance, First Day of Spring, or any special occasion happening in your school.

JUST STARTING OUT?
You can have a dance without all the expense by:
- having potluck food instead of hot dogs and pizza
- use a volunteer as DJ
- getting a corporate sponsor. Maybe the senior class would like to sponsor the dance, which means that the parents of the seniors would chip in and pay the dance expenses. That wouldn't cost much.
- Don't get anything you have to pay for in advance. Pay the DJ, pizza, and soda out of the proceeds at the door.

Friday Night Pizza and a Movie
WHAT IS FRIDAY NIGHT PIZZA AND A MOVIE?
Friday Night Pizza and a Movie at school was invented to combat the winter blahs and answer the eternal Friday night question, "What are we going to do tonight?"

WHAT DOES FRIDAY NIGHT PIZZA AND A MOVIE ENTAIL?
In the school, on Friday nights in January, February, and March pizza is served at 6:30 P.M. and we show a kids' movie in the auditorium at 7:00 P.M. Popcorn, soda, and chocolate milk are sold for $1 each at intermission. When possible we offer baked goods for sale. The evening winds up around nine, depending upon the length of the movie.

You don't have to use really current movies. We started by showing *Spaceballs* and *The Wizard of Oz*. You can't rent movies to show because of the legal restrictions of showing a rented movie for profit. But you can use videos you own. Comb the parent body for video suggestions. You can use a big screen TV and a VCR, or projector and screen.

We charge $10 per person. This includes the pizza, a drink, the movie, security, and the cost of renting the school. We don't make much money, this is more of a community builder, but over time, the small profit will add up. In the meantime, the parents and kids have a wonderful time being together. Try to make an arrangement with a local pizza establishment for a special low price for the pizza since you will be ordering every week.

VOLUNTEERS

This event doesn't require many volunteers, but you do need people each week. Our fund-raising vice president appealed to the parent association board to have at least one board member there every week. You will need a food committee and a movie committee and security/building committee to be certain that security people are present every week and that you have permission to use the building every week. A publicity committee of one is probably enough since once this begins, there will be word of mouth and you only need to post the upcoming movies in your school newsletter and place a few posters reminding people what the movie is that week. Of course you will need a cleanup committee, too. But that should be an easy job.

SECRETS OF SUCCESS

We screened our first movie for sixty people. That's quite a turnout. One of our secrets is that we allowed parents of children in third grade and up to just drop their children off and leave. This became a wonderful way for the parents to let the kids have an independent experience safely. Of course it also becomes an opportunity for the parents to run out to dinner without paying a baby-sitter.

We also bought a long square carnival-style popcorn machine. With this machine we can make very professional popcorn and sell it cheaply and produce some additional income. You can also use a microwave and microwave popcorn instead.

HOW MUCH MONEY WILL YOU RAISE?

We raised almost $4,000 dollars after two and a half months. Your profit depends upon how much you can charge, how high attendance is, and how low a price you can negotiate for the pizza. Some movies will pull more people than others and it takes time to discover what movies work the best. After a month or so, you'll know more what kind of movies to show. But this is more about building community and providing a service than it is about raising money. Everyone has a blast.

Here is a list of movies that would be appropriate to show at Friday Night Pizza and a Movie and should appeal to both boys and girls:

Homeward Bound (both 1 and 2)

Beethoven (1 through 4)

Andre

Free Willy (1 and 2)

Air Bud

Dunstan Checks In

Dr. Doolittle (1 and 2)

Spy Kids

The Incredible Journey

That Darned Cat (2 only)

I'll Fly Away

Milo & Otis

The Goonies

The Santa Clause

Jingle All the Way

Miracle on 34th Street (the original only)

Snow Day

Alaska

Sandlot

The Princess Diaries

Timeline • • • • • • • • • • • • •

This event does not need much advance preparation.

Beginning of the school year or as soon as possible	secure the right to use the school
In December	select the first three movies
In December	start publicity

Additional movies can be selected during the first three weeks. Publicity should be ongoing.

Holiday Shopping Day for Kids

WHAT IS A HOLIDAY SHOPPING DAY FOR KIDS?

This is a Saturday where the school is open only to children shopping for Christmas or Hanukkah gifts for their families. The parents buy, make, or donate items that would be appropriate gifts. The children then come to school with a few dollars in their pockets and buy whatever they feel they want to give as gifts. The items must be priced reasonably so the children don't have to spend too much money. The money used to buy the gifts goes to the school or the parent association.

HOW DOES KID'S SHOPPING DAY WORK?

You need to have parents in your school who can make and donate lots of things or who are willing to buy and donate lots of things to make this fund-raiser work. Try a gift-wrapping table. For 50¢ you could wrap each gift. This works if someone is willing to donate lots of wrapping paper.

First find your donors. If you think you have enough, proceed to selecting a day and starting your publicity.

VOLUNTEERS

You will need parents to shepherd the children through the sale and parents to make change and wrap gifts. The number of volunteers you need depends upon the size of the sale and the number of children buying.

HOW MUCH MONEY WILL YOU RAISE?

This event can raise anywhere from $100 to $1,000, depending upon the size of your school and the size of your sale. This is not so much a fund-raiser as it is a fun day and a lovely service for kids, teaching them the joy of giving.

Timeline • • • • • • • • • • • • • •

Two months ahead	line up donors and volunteers
One month ahead	start publicity, get wrapping paper donations

The Auction

> Write up all the procedures you use for the auction and put
> them in a loose-leaf binder to hand to the auction committee
> chairs the following year. This will save a lot of meeting time
> and duplication of effort.

The auction is one of our biggest events of the year. We consider it
the party for the parents, no children allowed. It takes place in the
evening and most people dress up. At the auction many items and
services are sold, much wine is drunk, delicious food is eaten, and a
huge amount of money is raised.

What Is an Auction?

An auction is a gathering where people bid against each other for
donated goods and services. Two types of auctions take place during
the evening: live and silent. The live auction is where one person stands
up and auctions things off one at a time and people in the audience raise
their hand or numbered paddle to signal their bids for the items.

A silent auction is where the actual item being auctioned off—
or a description of the item printed on a piece of paper—is available for viewing and people write down their names and their bids
for the item on the paper.

Of course the item always goes to the highest bidder. People have to pay that evening for items they have won at the auction. Payment is usually made by cash or check. These days, we are accepting credit cards, too, since schools are eligible to get merchant accounts from major credit card companies and banks. Get MasterCard and Visa merchant accounts through the bank where your parent association does business. The bank can instruct you how to fill out all the necessary forms. You should receive checks from MasterCard, VISA, Discover, or American Express directly.

Adding credit card option will make your auction more successful and checkout will move faster.

WHAT IS THE PROCEDURE FOR RUNNING A SUCCESSFUL AUCTION?

Running an auction is a big project. Here are the first steps you need to take to get started:

- Put together your auction committee. This will consist of the following committee heads:

    space
    food
    publicity
    silent auction
    live auction
    auctioneers
    decorations
    grab bag
    local canvassers
    bazaar table
    setup
    catalog
    cleanup
    raffle

banking

tickets

- It is best to have auction co-chairs running the event because there is too much work for one person.

- Set the date for the auction early. We like to do it on a Saturday night in March, when there are no school vacations and no other big fund-raising events to get in the way. Inform the parent population right away of the date you select so they can reserve the date and put it on their calendar.

- Have donation forms printed up in triplicate with different colors for each sheet. You need one copy for the donor (yellow), one copy for the winner (white) and one copy for the auction committee to keep records (pink).

- Find a location for your auction. We used to use the school, but the auction got too big. Then we moved it to the New York Historical Society, but the auction still continued to grow. We finally ended up in a cavernous church giving us the space we need for each part of the auction, plus food, chairs, a bar, and decorations. As you would for any special event, book the room well in advance. This requires an estimate of the number of attendees at your auction. Our peak year we had over 600 people, but we have a big school of 950 kids. You will probably have to put down a deposit to hold the date for your space. See the "Just Starting Out" section that follows to get an idea of how to have an auction without this expense.

- Find a caterer who will do a light, attractive meal, or grazing with finger foods for a low rate. Maybe you can find a caterer among your school parents who would do it for cost. Ticket prices should cover the food, if possible. Most years, the tickets just broke even on the cost of the meal. Our tickets are now $20 per person. Considering that this includes dinner, it's not a bad price. But $15 or less is better if you can do it and not lose money. If you raise the price, give away a glass of wine with each ticket, if possible. It is essential to get the wine donated; then you can sell it for $2 or $3 per additional glass and make money. A high price for wine will make it too expensive for your parents. You want to be sure the attendees have plenty of money to spend on auction items.

- Come up with a theme. We usually do this by selecting someone to honor at the auction. When we honored our special art teacher, we had a wonderful built-in theme of artist's palettes and paintbrushes to use for invitations. Honoring a local political figure who has done things for your school is a good way of saying thank you. You may also increase your number of attendees because your politician's friends, relatives, and political connections will have to attend, too.

  Additional auction themes you might consider using are:

  Black-and-White Ball

  Honoring art in the school

  Honoring a district leader: the mayor, principal, teachers, local political figure

  Spring theme with lots of fresh and paper flowers

  Country western theme

  Mystery theme

  Honoring great parent volunteer, PA president, outstanding custodian, gym or music teacher

  Author's night: invite authors; theme is books and reading

  Dedicated to raising money for the library, science lab, computer lab

  Elegant dessert and champagne dress-up

  Beach motif / Hawaiian night

  Midnight in Paris

    Sunny Spain or Mexican night with appropriate music
       and food
    Art Gallery: using the kids' art
    Safari/Wild Animal/Jungle theme
    Bird watchers or just birds theme
    Dogs or Cats or Dogs and Cats theme
    Alpine theme

- Give free tickets to your teachers. We do this every year even though only a handful of teachers actually come. It is a nice payback for all the wonderful things your teachers do all year long for our children. Don't be upset if teachers don't come. Saturday night is time off for them and some may be afraid that parents are going to corner them and complain, whine, or ask about their children all evening.

- Print up attractive invitations. Send them home in the children's backpacks to avoid paying expensive postage.

Live auction

This is the biggest event of the evening. The live auction comes after everything else is completed, including dinner. We grab the attention of our audience through about 34 items or packages. Too many more than that and you will lose people's attention. The items in a live auction are the biggest, most sought-after, most expensive items you have. All the live auction items are written up in detail in our auction catalog.

Sometimes live auction items are solo—a pair of courtside tickets to a Knicks game, for example—and sometimes they are "packaged," grouping theater tickets, dinner for two, and a limousine together. Our auction team creates packages by sorting through all the donations and putting things together creatively.

For example, if someone donates the gym at a local church,

then a birthday party package would be created that would include: the gym, a donation of cupcakes from one family, goodie bags from another family, and two hours of basketball instruction for two teams from the gym teacher. Voilà—a basketball birthday party package for the live auction. While those items separately might not generate high bids, a complete basketball birthday party could go for several hundred dollars at our auction.

When we get an airfare donation and a swanky hotel or condominium donation we create dream vacation packages. A package like that can go for $2,000 or $3,000 at our auction.

Other packages might include tickets to the symphony, babysitting services, dinner, and a limousine, or tickets to a sporting event plus a signed hockey stick and baseball cap. Making up packages for the live auction is fun and creative.

Silent auction

This is where you put items and services that cannot be used or packaged for the live auction. Often they will command a lower price than live auction items. You can use a large number of silent auction items, many more than in the live auction, as people will gravitate to the type of items they are interested in. The more items, the better you'll do. Even if silent auction items go for less money, it is all pure profit for the school. Divide your donations into categories, such as:

1. Tickets—concerts, plays, sporting events
2. Class projects—This category was invented by our terrific teachers. Our class projects include lots of creative ideas, like decorated shower curtains or sheets or pillow cases or murals, gift baskets of items donated by parents of a particular class or bought with funds raised from a bake sale.

3. Educational—Any courses you can get donated from any educational institution are good. Classes in pottery or creative writing are good, too.

4. Services (Consulting)—Request donations of: wills from lawyers; computer installation; room painting; furniture assembly; bookcase built to order; dog walking; baby-sitting; ironing; extermination; errand running; chiropractic exam; massage; manicure; pedicure; three hours with a professional organizer; estate planning; ninety minutes of PC troubleshooting; computerized tax preparation; home decorating; court reporting, architect walk-through; graphic design of letterhead, business card, and envelope; the list is endless.

5. Day camps/camps—Approach a day camp or sleep-away camp for either a free week, month, or a discounted price.

6. Lessons—Almost any parent in your school can offer some sort of lesson. Here are a few examples: cooking, computer software, piano or other musical instrument, skiing, ice skating, dance, painting, ceramics, photography, singing, speech and language screening for adult or child, drama coaching, swimming lessons, tennis lessons, soccer coaching, basketball coaching, baseball coaching, origami, calligraphy, knitting, crocheting, sewing, and so on. Sometimes a free lesson will pique interest enough to generate a new student for your donor. Use that carrot to sell your parents on donating lessons.

7. Equipment—computers and extra equipment, photography equipment, new tools, art supplies, small kitchen appliances. Everything must be brand-new. Save used items for the white elephant sale at your street fair (see Chapter 10).

8. Books—This category is tricky. If you have single books, put them on the bazaar table. But collections of books, like the four craft books donated by my friend, B. J. Berti, at Book-

of-the-Month Club, do better as a set. One year I also got four cookbooks. We put these two sets in the silent auction and sold them as a set of four craft books and a set of four cookbooks. Instead of getting $5 per book, which is what we would have gotten at the bazaar table, we got $80 for each set of four books, and the bidding was hot and heavy.

9. Jewelry, clothing, and accessories—Get jewelry donations from local shops and from parents in your school who make jewelry. Get handmade knit and crocheted clothing. We always have the most original jewelry made by parents and the bidding is good for these one-of-a-kind pieces.

10. Tutoring—This category is like the lesson category but more specifically for academic subjects. Teachers and expert parents offer tutoring on all subjects from science to Spanish and especially that new math that seems to trip up many parents. People will bid high for tutoring to help their children.

11. Music—This category is similar to the book category in that bigger bids are generated if your donations are packaged. Robin Ahrold, a parent in the music business, donated a collection of fifty CDs by various groups he works with. That collection sold very well. My friends at Musical Heritage Society donated wonderful hard-to-find collections, like Beethoven's sonatas, which sold for $80.

12. Software—Offer everything from business software to computer games. We had incredibly competitive bidding for the *Mad Magazine* complete collection on CD-ROM. Although it was selling on the Internet for $49.95, it sold in our auction for over $100!

13. Memberships—This includes country clubs, gyms, golf courses and anything else that requires a fee to get in.

Most of our local gyms offer free one-week trial member-ships. A country club might offer something off on their initiation fee or free use of the pool for two weeks.

14. Artwork—This is a broad category. We have sold fabulous paintings by really talented artists who are also parents in our school. Several of these paintings went for over $1,000. One year one of our artists made masks of several different people, painted them in exotic colors and attached whimsical ribbons on them. They were beautiful and sold out quickly. Anything interesting, unusual, or original can be sold. Look around. You probably have artists in your parent body that you don't even know about.

15. Uniquely your school—lunch with, breakfast with, museum visit with, at the movies with any classroom teacher, librarian, music teacher, gym teacher. A great item that we put in our live auction because it does so well is Principal for a Day. You can expand that to include assistant principal, librarian, gym teacher, music teacher for a day, if you have cooperative staff.

16. Health & Beauty—acupuncture, haircuts galore, free exam & pair of eyeglasses, bike rentals, beauty makeover, day at spa, hair cornrowing

17. House & Home—free exam at vet clinic, messenger package service, five hundred copies at a copy shop, free cell phone with one-year contract, quilts and afghans, pet shop gift certificate, moving company gift certificate

---

Buy or wrangle a donation of unfinished furniture and have a well-known artist or your child's class paint/decorate it and auction it off.

18. Memorabilia—Vintage photos of famous people, collectible dolls, autographed soccer ball, basketball, baseball, even autographs of famous people
19. Special parties—custom cake to feed fifty, jewelry-making party, gingerbread house–making party, church space rental, gym rental, dinner with famous author (or other person) or the mayor, origami party
20. Tickets—Tickets to rehearsals (ballet, soap opera, play), Disney World, Universal Studios, taping of a TV show, sporting events, local theater, even movies (ten tickets feels substantial)
21. Miscellaneous—Firehouse tour, radio or TV station tour, tour of sports stadium

---

Stores that are closing might be good places to hit up for donations. One carpet store in our neighborhood that was moving donated a beautiful oriental carpet that went for $800 in our live auction.

If you are looking to chain stores like Home Depot or Talbot's for donations, you have to go to their national/corporate headquarters. This takes a long time, so plan ahead.

Make sure all items are legitimate and that there are no strings attached. For example, we wanted to sell a sleepover birthday party in the gym. This would have been a great item and would have generated terrific competitive bidding. But the Board of Education said we couldn't do it. Check things like that before accepting an item.

Make certificates for donations from the Auction Contract that donors have filled out. Certificates look official and provide the information needed for the winner to get in touch with the donor to receive the item or service purchased at the auction. You can get nice certificate paper from Staples or Paper Direct on the Internet at www.paperdirect.com.

Bring extra blank bid sheets for on-the-spot donations that are too small to go into the live auction.

Bazaar table

The bazaar table is a place to put all the items that cannot become part of a live auction package and won't sustain enough bidding or a high enough price to go into the silent auction. This is the table with the low-price items. Some examples of bazaar table items are: new housewares; single books (preferably hardback); accessories like matching scarf, hat and gloves; new baby clothes; new knick-knacks; new videos; single CDs; or software.

Mystery Certificates

Gift certificates to be sold individually like dinner for two or $15.00 worth of dry cleaning are a big hit. You know that the value of what you bought will be higher than what you're paying. Attach the gift certificates to helium-filled balloons. For a mystery theme, attach them to mystery books. For an art theme, tape the certificates to cardboard artist palettes you made. We divide these up into mystery certificates that sell for: $10, $20, $30, $40, and $50. Sometimes we eliminate the $30 category. That depends upon what your donations are. Each mystery certificate should sell for at least $10 less than the value of the certificate being sold. If you have any

$5 or $10 gift certificates or items, put them together. If the buyer doesn't get a good value, he or she will be unhappy. After all, auction mentality often says why pay $20 for a $20 gift certificate?

Here is a sample of the type of items that belong in this category:

a bottle of wine of your choice from the local liquor store
shoe repair gift certificate
gift certificate to florist or nursery
five or ten free video rentals from video store
haircut for kids
gift certificate for dry cleaning
deli gift certificate
shoe store gift certificate
laundry gift certificate
hardware store gift certificate
music/book store gift certificate
candy store gift certificate
lunch at local restaurant
brunch at local restaurant
dinner at low-price local restaurant
pet shop gift certificate
pizzeria—one pie gift certificate
pharmacy gift certificate
toy store gift certificate
supermarket gift certificate
art gallery gift certificate
bakery gift certificate
take-out food gift certificate
fish market gift certificate
Mary Kay gift certificate
paint store gift certificate
membership at local museum
three-month health club membership

museum guest passes
personal trainer
dinner at your home
one-year subscription to a magazine

Parents can donate many of the items in the balloons. A parent who doesn't know what to donate can buy a gift certificate to any store or shop and donate that, or buy a magazine subscription to donate. The balloons are very popular because everyone knows that they will get a great value and usually these are the first things sold out at the auction.

GRAB BAGS

Usually I think of children when I think of grab bags (see "The Supreme Street Fair" in Chapter 10). But the idea for these auction grab bags for women came about by accident. I was having breakfast with my friend Jane Buckley the year she was auction chair to discuss her new ideas for the auction.

Jane wanted to give away bags of promotional things, like free certificates and product samples from companies sponsoring the auction, to all the attendees. That's a great idea and a good way to promote sponsorship. She also considered selling space in the promotional bags for people who were not sponsors in order to give samples and discount coupons to hawk their merchandise.

I had been in charge of grab bags for kids at the street fair for the previous five years. Those grab bags were filled with donations of all sorts of promotional items, from key chains with bank logos to baseball caps from various companies.

Even though I heard promotional bags, I mistakenly thought she meant grab bags. It was then that we got the idea of selling women's grab bags filled with promotional goodies and samples for women.

We were lucky enough to have several parents connected to cosmetics companies in our parent association. We got the most fabulous donations from Avon, Estee Lauder, and Yves St. Laurent.

We were able to put together terrific bags containing lipstick, powder, lotions, eye makeup, jewelry, perfume, nail polish, and other small items. We sold them for $5 each. The first year these bags were sold slowly as they were new and no one really knew what to expect.

They were packaged in brown paper lunch bags, so no one knew what was inside. But that did not make them very attractive. Even the fabulous Yves St. Laurent perfume samples in the most exquisite package ever only prompted people to buy a hundred fifty of the three hundred bags we made.

The second year we only made one hundred and fifty bags. They sold better, but it was hard to get rid of the last fifteen or so. The third year, we made one hundred and fifty bags, but packaged them in beautiful small Avon blue-and-white shopping bags and they flew off the table. We had people so disappointed that the bags were sold out that we increased the number of bags to two hundred bags the next year. They sold out in an hour. Here is what we put in our grab bags for women:

lipsticks
nail polish
eyeliner pencils
mascara
rings, bracelets, necklaces, earrings
fake flowers
discount coupons for photo finishing
compacts
watches
makeup bags

creams of all sorts

scents and perfumes

bubble bath or shower gel samples

Remaindered cosmetics and perfumes are great. Or go back to Jane's original idea and turn the grab bags into promotional bags for local or national merchants to use to distribute discount or free trial coupons and free product samples. Stores and manufacturers might even pay a promotional fee to have samples distributed to the parents in your school.

For our cosmetics grab bags, we charge $5, a great bargain. For strictly promotional bags you probably can't charge as much. But spending $2 for a bag full of free opportunities at local merchants may be the right way to use grab bags for your school.

If you can't get nice small shopping bags at the local discount store, you can get them from Oriental Trading. Go to their Web site: www.orientaltrading.com to order the bags directly or to order a catalog and place your order by phone. Grab bags make great Mother's Day gifts.

50/50 raffle

This is a very special raffle that we don't use at any other function. Unlike a usual raffle, it involves no prizes at all. Instead, money is the prize. A 50/50 raffle ticket offers a chance to win half of the money collected from the sale of the tickets. If you sell $1,000 worth of tickets, the winner collects $500. This is especially effective at the auction because most of the time the winner turns around and spends the $500 in cash on auction items.

This is a very easy raffle to conduct since tickets are only sold at the auction and there are no prizes involved. All you need are the tickets and good publicity. Announce the raffle several times over a loudspeaker or microphone during the auction.

SETTING UP THE BIDDING

Assigning opening bids:

1. Make them low enough to get things started.

2. An opening bid is not the value of the item. Explain that to donors, who worry that a low opening bid is a negative comment about their donation. If people want something, they will bid high for it. One of the staff members at Job Path offered her services as a personal trainer. (Job Path is a nonprofit organization that finds jobs for people with developmental disabilities.) We put the item in the silent auction and started the bidding at $25, not certain if people would want this or not, and we wanted to make it easy to get the bidding started. The session went for $185!

3. Making low opening bids serves another function. If you have an item that you are not sure will sell, and it's a product made by a parent or a service donated by a parent or teacher and you are concerned that the donor will be upset and hurt if no one bids on the item, a low opening bid allows a friend to bid on it or for the auction committee to put in a starting bid, using money generated by the auction to win the item.

   This is so important. People's feelings can be seriously hurt or they can feel a sense of public humiliation if their special blanket, picture, or offer of advice is left on the table with no one bidding on it. Be sure to have a plan to bail out these generous folks and you will always have donors. Even if you buy the item or service, you don't have to use it. But your donor will feel that he or she did their part.

4. Bidding increments for silent auction items should be $5, $10, $15, or $25. For the live auction, bidding increments

of $25, $50 or even $60, should be used. Give the auction-
eer leeway to do whatever he or she feels is right for the
moment. Sometimes, if an item is hot, you want to use a
$50 or $100 increment to get the bidding high quickly.

If an item is not going well, the auctioneer may want to
use a lower increment of only $25 or even $15 to keep the
bidding alive and try to milk the item for as much as it can
generate.

When coming up with a minimum or opening bid for
silent and live auction items price the item at less than half
of what you estimate the retail value to be. Start with 40
percent of retail and if that's too high, come down. For
example if a haircut in a salon would be $40, the minimum
bid for this item should be $15. For a two-hour estate plan-
ning session, which might cost $250 on the outside, price it
at $60 for the minimum bid.

Also consider how desirable an item may be. The more
desirable, the higher the minimum bid should be. For less
desirable items select a minimum bid as low as 75 percent
off retail.

Remember that you want to sell *everything*. Any money
you can generate from a donation is pure profit, even if it is
much less than you anticipated.

> - Start to selectively reduce the minimum bids of silent auction
>   items that are not receiving any bids about 40 minutes after
>   silent auction begins. You may want to slash the opening by
>   half to get the bidding started. If the items are not going, you
>   priced them too high.

THE AUCTION CATALOG
An Overview

The catalog, a Xeroxed numbered list of all the auction items except bazaar table items, is an important selling tool. Since there are no pictures, the catalog describes all the silent and live auction items in enough detail to make them enticing. List all the donors in the catalog, so it also becomes a place to give recognition to everyone who made a donation. The timing of the catalog is important.

You should get the catalog distributed at least a week before the auction, so people can see in advance what's being auctioned off. I always go through the catalog and make check marks next to the items I am interested in bidding on. That way I can be focused at the auction and get what I want.

Put the most prized and expensive items in the live auction. Select the two live auction items you think will generate the most bidding. Put one of these items first and one last, to keep people there until the end. The opening bid should be much higher for live auction items than for silent auction items. Be aware that some people may have feelings about their donations ending up in the silent auction instead of the live. They may be angry and feel unimportant. It is necessary to explain in advance that decisions to put donations in live or silent auction are not made based on the person but based on where the committee thinks the item or service will generate the most money. Sometimes you might have to put something in the live auction to appease a big donor. Don't worry about it. Just do it and be happy.

CREATING PACKAGES

Sometimes packaging things will bring in more money than having the items sell singly. You can make more live auction items that way, too. For example, package two theater tickets plus a dinner plus one or two nights at a hotel. You may be able to get as much as $400 for that, which is more than the combined total each item would bring in if auctioned alone.

Package a fabulous hike with an experienced guide with a local hotel and a meal at a good restaurant in the same area. Package golf, tennis, or riding lessons with a local hotel and maybe a meal. Package airfare with a hotel in an exotic location for a spectacular trip.

CATALOG TIMING

Donors tend to be "last-minute Louie"; so there will always be additional items that come in after the catalog has been printed and distributed. To answer this problem, we come out with an addendum as late as two days before the auction to give people an updated list. Even that may not be correct because if something really wonderful comes in the day before the auction, you're going to use it. You can even accept great items at the auction.

We send the catalog home in the backpacks of the children whose parents have bought tickets in advance. Some catalogs are also available at the auction for people who decide to pay at the door.

CATALOG COPY

The catalog should be fun and have some tongue-in-cheek selling copy. But don't forget that you need to have a good, brief description of everything that comes with a package. Be accurate, even if something is not so great. You don't want bidders to be disappointed. Try to find an advertising copywriter among your parents who will write your catalog copy for free.

BANKING

The Role of the Treasurer

Treasurers are most important in this event. The treasurer and assistant treasurers should make the round of all the places where cash is being taken, like the bar, the grab bags, the bazaar table, the people selling the raffle tickets, and collect money from them periodically. Do not leave people with big wads of cash throughout the evening.

Remember, some tables may need change during the course of the auction. At the grab bag table, we're always in need of fives and tens since so many people pay with twenty-dollar bills.

The treasurers can be enormously helpful by bringing change to people running tables or the bar. When you unload cash to the treasurer be sure to get a receipt indicating how much money you have turned over. If the treasurer can't do it on the spot, and most can't, as they are much too busy, ask them to deliver the receipt when they bring you change.

You need to keep track of how much money your booth or table is making and to have a written confirmation of how much money you have turned over to the treasures. This is just a simple safeguard to protect against confusion and misunderstandings.

Banking is a big job. You will need one banker for every 50 people, with a minimum of four. We need about ten people. Our auction draws about five hundred attendees and auctions off over three hundred items in the silent auction alone. If your auction is smaller, you may not need as many people in banking, but be sure to have enough. People don't like to wait in long lines to check out.

There are two basic banking methods: computerized or paper (manual). I will discuss both ways here. If you have someone who can handle a computer and owns a program like Excel that can create reports, then computerized banking may be the way to go. If you don't readily have someone who can do that, then use the paper or manual way. If you choose the manual method, you will need several big cartons to keep alphabetized auction vouchers and folders in—one for each attendee by paddle number. Here are the steps for banking *before the auction:*

1. As vouchers with donations come in, they are given an item number and entered on a spreadsheet, in Excel or a database program that can produce reports, such as Access. Include all the information on the voucher and don't forget the retail value. The retail value is important so buyers can deduct any amount in excess of the retail they paid for an item from their taxes as a charitable contribution.

2. When the auction catalog is written, it becomes a shortened version of the spreadsheet.

3. Tie registration to banking. Each registrant gets a paddle number. Those same paddle numbers must also be in the system tied to the name, address, and phone number of the person attending.

4. Bring a laptop computer with all the information, spreadsheets, and so on to the auction.

Be prepared for creative ideas from the auctioneer. Say the bidding is hot and heavy on a weekend house on the Italian Riviera in the live auction and the donor decides to be generous and offer a second weekend for the losing bidder. This is great for the auction, but tough to handle for the banking people who now have to create a whole new item and put it in their database and award it to the proper bidder. Designate one volunteer to communicate any changes in the live auction to the bankers.

At the auction: print each silent auction item on a sheet that has a duplicate or two carbon copies attached. This is necessary because when the silent auction bidding is closed, the sheet collectors take the top sheet to be organized by item number whether you're doing electronic banking or by paddle number in the paper system.

The bottom sheet is left on the tables, so that bidders can see what items they won.

1. Once the silent auction is over, the name and paddle number of the winning bidder must be entered into the system. Be very careful *not* to transpose the paddle numbers and winning bids or someone might find himself or herself being charged $437 for a lunch with the music teacher she never bid on! Sheet collectors sort the top bidding sheets by item number for computerized banking or by paddle number for paper banking.

2. You should need only one data entry person. If the data is well organized, one person can handle the job. Using only one person will cut down on the number of mistakes like double entries. Once the data is entered, a report can be printed and then the appropriate vouchers can be pulled and put in each folder by paddle number so that when people come to check out and pay for the items they won, everything is in one place.

3. If you're using the paper method, you'll need three to five people pulling silent auction vouchers and putting them into folders. This can be a complex process and our school's Steve Russo, who ran banking for at least two years, recommends using the paper method for your first auction. Using the paper method makes it easier to completely understand the process.

4. Use your electronic report for bill preparation. Group the silent and live auction items by paddle number. Pull the certificates/envelopes for the items people won and put them in a folder marked with the winner's paddle number. Create a bill totaling all the items won and add it to the folder. Pass the folder to the cashier. You will need three to four people to pull certificates and envelopes. You will need about five people matching up certificates and envelopes with the correct folders

and handing them to the cashiers. Use only two to three of your most trusted parents as cashiers taking money, especially cash. The majority of our parents pay by check or credit card.

> Your voucher pullers will have to work like madmen to pull all the vouchers to get bills ready for those leaving after the silent auction. You have more time if you start pulling the bills for those who have remained for the live auction.

> The two biggest crunches are right after the silent auction closes and after the live auction. Try to close banking for half an hour right after the silent auction. This will give you time to gather all the items and set up bills and make paying run much quicker and smoother.

Reconciliation:

1. This is done after everyone has paid and gone home except you!
2. Count out your cash and give it to the treasurer. We like to do this more than once during the evening so that the money does not sit in one place too long, tempting fate.

> In our parent association closet, we have a special safe that can take deposits and keep them secure without being opened up. There is a big slot in the top and the deposit drops into a drum. You rotate the handle and the deposit is dumped into the body of the safe. If you have a setup like this in your school, deposit cash in the safe regularly so it doesn't get stolen lying around.

Keep track of all the receipts for cash you turned over to the treasurer.

3. Keep a record of each and every check and credit card. Your bill forms should have a carbon copy for the PA so you can keep track of the payment information.

4. Check and see who won items and didn't pay for them or didn't pick them up at all. There will always be someone who couldn't wait on line because they had to get home to the baby-sitter. An electronic system is ideal for this step as it can run a report of all unclaimed items.

5. A paper system is more complicated since it involves collecting the vouchers, envelopes, and actual items still left, and sorting them out by paddle number.

6. Next you will need to make calls and collect money. You will become a mini collection agency. Most people do pay up. If anyone says that they no longer want an item they won, let them off the hook. You can offer the item to the number-two bidder. If the number-two bidder doesn't want it, try number three. If you can't sell it to any of the bidders, sell it through your newsletter, at another event, or give it to a really hardworking volunteer or deserving teacher as a reward. It really isn't worth it to try to force the winning bidder to pay for something he or she doesn't want. People get carried away and sometimes make mistakes. Be generous about it. Out of an average 250 to 300 silent auction items only 10 to 15 usually will have to be collected.

VOLUNTEERS

Have a floater or two who can get drinks or food for workers like the masseurs, the palm reader, and the people manning the grab bag and bazaar tables. Floaters can relieve people to go bid or go to the bathroom. Floaters can solve problems, and locate the auction chiefs in any emergencies.

Each committee needs volunteers. Here is a suggested breakdown by committee:

- location—Location selection should be done by the chairs of the event.
- sponsors—The chairs usually find auction sponsors, but you can have a subcommittee handle this job.
- food—This committee needs to find a good caterer who will do all the serving in addition to supplying the food. You will still need people to remove plates, unless you can talk the caterer into doing that, too, for the same price.
- publicity—One or two good people are enough.
- auctioneers—You will need three to four auctioneers; if you hire a professional you only need one.
- live auction—One person to work with chairs creating live auction packages. Two spotters to call out and record paddle numbers of winning bidders.
- silent auction—Two people to make up silent auction bidding sheets. Four people to collect and sort bidding sheets after bidding is closed.
- bazaar table—One person to price items and three people to sell at the table at the auction.
- grab bags—One person to solicit donations. Two or three to make up bags. Three to sell bags at the auction.

Hiring a professional auctioneer who is paid on a percentage basis will increase the amount of money you will take in, but might not be as much fun as a parent volunteer.

Have some entertainment at the very end of the auction, like live music, or old gold records to entertain people while they are waiting on line to pay.

- decorations/setup—Combine this committee with the setup committee. The two decorating committee chairs design and purchase the decorations and the setup volunteers put everything in place. You will need about five volunteers for this combined committee.
- local canvassers—This committee needs a large group of volunteers. For best coverage you will need ten to twelve canvassers unless you live in a small town. Canvassers are volunteers who solicit donations for the silent and the live auction by asking retail stores, restaurants, and local businesses for contributions of items or services.
- setup—Make this part of the decorating committee.
- cleanup—The staff at our current location provides cleanup for a small fee. This is an excellent way to handle cleanup. The parent volunteers are tired at the end of the evening and there are too many loose ends to take care of at the end of the auction to be hassled by cleanup.
- banking—At a professional auction, the attendees leave their credit card imprint at check-in when they pick up their paddle. That way, at the end of the auction, the banking people just add up their purchases and put it on the credit card and the buyer only has to look over the charges and sign the credit

Here are some suggestions for selecting people for the various banking jobs. People who do well under pressure are best for data entry and sheet separators.

The people pulling items will have to work quickly together. Select your people well: people with a sense of humor and who thrive under a bit of craziness do really well with this job. The best personality type for cashiers is the orderly type.

card slip. This makes checkout very fast. We have always waited to add everything up at the end and take cash, checks, or credit cards when the auction is over. Of course, people can leave early, but those who stay to the end usually end up waiting for at least twenty minutes in line to get checked out.

- donations—We send out auction donation voucher forms with a Xeroxed suggested donation instruction sheet attached. We request that all donations be mailed or delivered to the school office. We store the auction items in school closets, empty offices, or the basement of a volunteer.

- Tickets—This committee only needs a few volunteers. You need two people to sell tickets in advance and two people to sell tickets at the door. After the first two hours of the auction, everyone has arrived and this position is no longer needed.

- The biggest group of volunteers is the donors. You need as many of them as you can get. People can donate more than one item, too. The more items you have the more productive and fun your auction will be since more people will be able to go home winners.

Decoration

Make things elegant: beautiful tablecloths, sleek bags for grab bags, soft lighting, and color-coordinated decorations. A special-occasion surrounding promotes good feeling and may encourage higher bidding.

Use a coat rack and clips to display large items, like quilts and afghans.

Have a card, a designed computer printout or photograph to display for each service offered: A picture of the donor with a resume that explains the person's qualifications makes the item seem substantial. For example, we had a picture of Elizabeth Wolff and her résumé to show her Julliard schooling and experience to back up her offer of a piano recital, at the Job Path auction. Display brochures of hotels where rooms are offered. Show the work of a photographer who is offering a photo shoot or video of your next party.

Balloons are easy inexpensive decoration. Get silver or gold and black balloons and helium and bunch them up with a cluster at each table. Balloons lend a festive air to the room and the sophisticated colors will make the display feel special.

Timeline • • • • • • • • • • • • • • •

This is the ideal timeline. You can put an auction together in a shorter time frame, especially if you hold the event at your school.

One year ahead	select the site and put down a deposit
Five months ahead	select committee heads
Four months ahead	recruit volunteers for the committees
Three months ahead	start publicity
	set up banking software spreadsheets
	committees swing into action
	begin requesting donations
	as donations come in, begin data
	processing by putting donations up

	on computer (even if you will use paper for creating bills)
Two months ahead	design and print invitations
	design decorations
	design catalog cover
	continue data processing
One month ahead	pile on the publicity
	increase pressure for more donations
	begin putting parents' information up on computer
Three weeks ahead	make live auction packages
	determine what goes in silent auction
	start catalog copy
Two weeks ahead	print catalog
One week ahead	distribute catalog

ACKNOWLEDGMENT

Saying thank you is always important in fund-raising, but never more so than for the auction. Although you don't need to send thank-you notes to the parents, you will need to send them to all companies that contribute, especially if you want to ask for those contributions again the next year. If your school is large, this will be a big task and you may need a committee just to be in charge of issuing thank-you notes.

The easiest way to acknowledge a donor is to send a thank-you note when each donation comes in. This will keep one person busy for a few weeks. Mailing notes at receipt is a lot less daunting than attempting to send out three hundred thank-you notes the day after when everyone is exhausted and tired of hearing about the auction. Set up the notes in advance with return address and an opening or closing paragraph that you can use for each note. That way you only have to personalize one short central paragraph where you mention the actual donation.

Make a list of each item on an Excel or Lotus sheet, including the contact name, address, and phone number. Check each one off when the thank-you note goes out. This list will be very handy the following year when you want to solicit the same donors again.

NEW IDEAS

Make your auction an entertaining event by adding fun activities, such as massages, a palm reader, games or games of chance. Hire actors to dress up as palm readers. Parent massage-therapist volunteers can bring their massage chairs and set up. They can charge $10 for five minutes. (You will need at least two massage chairs since this will be a very popular addition to your auction.)

Games like pick-a-number, darts that break balloons, ring toss with nice donated prizes can raise money and make your event more lively.

Set up adult games, like darts or ring toss or pick-a-number. Offer nice prizes like leather change purses, CD holders, small kitchenwares, paperback books, CDs, pocket calendars, memo pads, address books, journals, small pocket tools, and other little items. The pick-a-number game works this way. One person picks a number from one to ten and then writes it down on a slip of paper. Four people on the other side of the table pay $2 or $3 to guess the number. Each one picks a number, no two the same. The winner gets a prize.

For ring toss, players land three rings on spikes set up on the floor and win a prize. Charge $5 a try ($1 per ring tossed). Or put together a darts game with exploding balloons. Children are not the only ones who like to play simple carnival games. Games will lend a sense of fun to the event—just don't have too many to overwhelm the auction or keep people from visiting, eating, and bidding!

Sell tickets to those special booths to avoid having too much cash floating around. For our massage tables, palm reader, and grab bags at the Job Path auction, we sold tickets at a central table. Then each special service simply collected the correct number of tickets required, for example: two $5 tickets for a massage, one for a palm reading, and four for a grab bag.

JUST STARTING OUT?

You can have a fine auction and raise lots of money even if you're just starting out. Here are some suggestions for schools just beginning to get their fund-raising off the ground and who don't have a lot of money to spend:

1. Have the auction in the school. You won't have to pay a big space rental fee. Have the food and silent auction in the cafeteria and the live auction in the auditorium or the gym, with chairs set up and standing room at the back.

2. Have a potluck dinner instead of charging admission. Get food donations from local restaurants, or tastings from several restaurants who want to become known in your area.

3. Solicit donations from local restaurants and other merchants for free goods or services. Dinner for two or lunch for four will bring in money in a silent or live auction.

4. Ask for donations of goods and services from the parents in your school. Persuade people to really think about it; everyone has something they can offer. For Job Path, I donated three cooking lessons. The auction doesn't have to be all about things but can involve services, too. Parents might consider donating:

    cooking lessons

    dinner for two at their house or delivered to your house

    one month's dog-walking service

dog bath and brushing

lawn mowing for a month

snow shoveling for a month

errand running for a month

power tools lessons

make your own bookshelf (birdhouse, toy chest, etc.) with a carpenter

tutoring your kids for a month

two Saturday nights of baby-sitting

piano or any other musical instrument lessons

sewing lessons

knitting/crocheting lessons

homemade afghan

homemade quilt to order with your fabric selections

three hours of word processing or editing or résumé writing

picking up your kids at school every day for two weeks

tennis, golf, swimming, or riding lessons

bridge, gin rummy, pinochle, bid whist, or poker lessons

planting, weeding, harvesting in your garden for two weeks

car service to wherever you wish for a day or transport your kids

class projects created in school

The list is endless!

5. Have a small but wonderful and creative live auction. You might consider getting the following donations from parents and local businesses:

week or weekend at someone's vacation home

lunch with a local celebrity

membership at a local club or camp

displaying your art at a local art gallery
a beautiful piece of art donated by a local artist
art done by the kids in school
dinner for two or four donated by a local restaurant
two nights donated from a nearby hotel
tour of a television or radio station
tour of a newspaper plant or candy factory

And on and on. It all depends upon what is available in your community and what resources your fellow parents have.

AND DON'T FORGET . . .

- Bring blank certificates to be filled in for anything that's missing or forgotten or for donations that are made on the spot.

- Hold a post mortem meeting to discuss what worked and what didn't work at the auction. Getting everyone's opinion can help to make things smoother and more profitable the next year.

Spring Events

. . . .

Car Wash, Handyman Day, Art Show

Car Wash

This event is easy for schools on a campus. Having a circular drive-way on the campus is also helpful. The children and their parents wash cars for $5 per car.

WHAT IS A CAR WASH?

You will need several hoses with nozzle controls, buckets, extra-large sponges, plenty of old towels or a huge supply of paper towels, garbage bags, mild soap—I like to use dishwashing liquid—and plenty of energetic children. Make sure you have several places where you can connect hoses. One hose will not be enough and will slow things down considerably.

You will also need a warm day, because everyone involved in this will be soaked to the skin by the time the event is over. I recommend planning this event in September when it is still warm or May, if the weather is warm enough where you live. The problem with June is that many schools get out early, before it is really warm enough to be wet comfortably. Also, in June people are pretty worn out and are looking forward eagerly to the summer break. The kids are champing at the bit to get out of school. It is hard to organize any fund-raising activity.

Set up a "path" where cars can enter and where they will

leave. You will need a parking lot that has an entrance and an exit so cars can move through and make room for more cars. This can be done in the city if you get a permit to use the block your school is on. You can have cars coming in at one end of the street and exiting, clean as a whistle, at the other. Safety is an important issue. Make red Stop signs and use tape to mark the stop lines in key areas, like the payment booth, wash, dry, and rinse areas too. Make 5 m.p.h. speed limit signs and place them where drivers can see them.

Divide your path into four sections: waiting area, washing area, rinsing area, and drying area. People don't want to wait for long, so you need to have plenty of volunteers to move cars through. The waiting area is where you take the money. Give the largest amount of room to the washing area to keep things moving quickly. Keep the drying and rinsing areas small, since those functions take the least amount of time.

You will need several big signs. If you intend to have this event every year, then it is worthwhile to invest in large banners advertising the car wash. If you don't have the funds to buy two big banners this year, make big signs by hand using poster paper. Five dollars is a reasonable amount to charge, and making change is easy. There is very little monetary outlay here, except for the signs—just some soap and paper towels. If you think you can get $10, go for it!

Schedule the car wash on a Saturday in the afternoon, when the sun is the strongest and the air is the warmest. Lunchtime to late afternoon is a good time to run a car wash, since you'll catch many cars out running errands. Four hours should be enough to discover how it will work for you. That is enough time to soak and exhaust everyone involved.

Try to get your car wash mentioned on local radio. So many people listen to radio in their cars that it is the perfect medium for car wash advertising. It might drive some impulse traffic to your car wash. Call the community affairs or program directors of your local radio stations. For mention in your local newspaper, go to their Web site and under the "contact us" section, you will find instructions for submitting information about your upcoming community events.

VOLUNTEERS

You will need to have managers, publicity people, and lots and lots of workers: washers, rinsers, dryers, and people to take the money. Divide the day into crews of people who will work for one hour. For a four-hour event, you will need four crews. Each crew could consist of one money taker, six washers, two rinsers and two dryers. Figure out in advance how many cars you can get into your space to wash at one time.

Washing will require at least two people per car, one on each side. Rinsing can be one person per car and drying will require two per car, again one on each side. That will tell you how many people you will need for each crew.

You will need volunteers to make sure drivers are obeying all the stop signs and proceeding slowly. Choose a volunteer for each stop sign. Have alternates ready to give them a break.

SECRETS TO SUCCESS

If your school is located near a main drag or highway, you will have a better chance of attracting more cars. If you are located off on a side street somewhere so that people will have to drive out of their way to get to you, it will be harder to attract customers. Put banners on the main streets with arrows leading to your car wash.

One way you can boost the number of customers is to align yourself with a civic organization. If you can get the sponsorship of the Rotary, Elks, Lions, or other fraternal organization, you will get the word out and increase your number of customers dramatically. A fraternal organization may also make a small donation or pay for your banners as part of their sponsorship. Perhaps a store, or even a gas station, will sponsor your event. Look for members of these organizations among your parents or grandparents to provide initial contact. Or call your local organization and ask for the name of their community liaison.

You might consider charging $5 for wash only and $10 for wash and dry. Add waxing to increase your revenue if you have enough volunteers. If you do add waxing, sell coffee and cake to waiting car owners to boost your profits. This will bring in more money and move your lines along faster.

HOW MUCH MONEY WILL YOU RAISE?
You can raise several hundred dollars if you have help in generating publicity, and are well located near a busy street. If you get sponsorships, that will mean more money, too.

Timeline • • • • • • • • • • • • •

End of previous year	pick date, plan event, get volunteers, get sponsors
A week before event	start heavy-duty publicity

Handyman Day

This event, where kids get paid for doing odd jobs, is probably best used for middle and high school rather than elementary school. You could have a Handyman Day for just the upper grade in elementary school. Check with your PA board about insurance regulations. Make sure you won't have any liability problems. *Extremely important: do not send a child to anyone's house alone.* A minimum of two children should be together to go out for chores. Assign an adult to check up on the kids periodically to make sure everything is okay. Outdoor chores are best, but some inside tasks are okay in appropriate households. This is an important safety feature and cannot be overlooked.

The event involves kids doing all kinds of chores for money that is donated to the school. Spring is a good time to have this event. Fall is good, too, as there is so much leaf raking going on. If you are nervous, schedule the event in the fall and only for outdoor chores. Then, if it's a success, you can plan a spring event. Here is a basic list of chores that can be done by teenage kids:

cutting the grass
whitewashing a fence
painting furniture
washing a car
weeding
dog walking
dog brushing
dog bathing
hedge clipping
garden planting
leaf raking
baby-sitting
errand running—cleaners, grocery store, shoemaker, drugstore, hardware store, stationery store
spring cleaning
lifting, hauling, and carting
taking large items to the local dump or recycling center

You will have to make up your own price list according to the job or by the hour.

Also, be careful when choosing the children who do the jobs. You don't want anyone who is irresponsible or out of control to be in a position where they can inflict damage on someone's property.

This event is easier to do in the suburbs or the country than in the city, and it really works best in a smaller community. But in the right environment, this is a great event; it's fun for the kids and gets them acquainted with responsibility. The kids have a great sense of accomplishment after an event like this.

VOLUNTEERS
You will need a small group of parents and a large group of kids. Parents need to be the ones who get the job requests on the phone and dole out jobs to the appropriate children. Also, parents need to drive around and drop in on the kids at work to make sure everything is going well and there are no problems.

If the kids are too young to drive, make sure you have a few parents manning cars to ferry the kids around to do errands for people.

SECRETS TO SUCCESS
Get the word out to senior citizens and people with disabilities who could use a hand with outside work or heavy lifting and hauling, which is ideal for teenage boys.

Be sure the parents of your teenage volunteers know what is happening. Perhaps they would like to be involved, too. You will need at least twenty volunteers, and perhaps more, depending upon how many work requests you receive. Publicity will be key to the success of this event.

Here, too, as with the car wash, you might want to get a fraternal organization involved. Perhaps they would like to sponsor the services for senior citizens and people with disabilities. So your school would be paid by the fraternal organization and the senior citizens and people with disabilities would receive the service free. There is something wonderful about an arrangement like that. In fact, if you can get enough corporate sponsors, you can turn

Handyman Day into specifically a Help Senior Citizens and People with Disabilities Day, with the school receiving the money from the sponsor and the kids providing the services.

HOW MUCH MONEY WILL YOU RAISE?

This is very hard to predict, as there are so many variables: how many people call with jobs, how many kids volunteer, and even the weather. Give yourself a year or two to figure out how much to charge, work out the problems, and overcome obstacles to making this event a big success. In fact, you might want to run this event in both the fall and spring. That way you will be able to fine-tune the event sooner.

Timeline • • • • • • • • • • • • • •

Several months before event	find corporate sponsors
Three weeks before event	start publicity. Put signs in as many store windows as possible
	try to get a short piece in your local newspaper about the event
	get publicity on the radio
	use your school newsletter
	put up posters in key areas around town

The Art Show

The art show is one of our finest days at P.S. 87. The walls are loaded with the most incredible creativity I've ever seen. The Arts-In-Action Director, who writes the curriculum and conducts the art program for the school, is an exceptional artist and child-centered teacher. She works magic with the children on a miniscule budget.

WHAT IS AN ART SHOW?

Artwork from all the classes is mounted by parents and hung on the walls outside the classrooms. We don't really use this as a fundraising opportunity. But we always need money to fund the art program since it is paid for exclusively by the parent association at our school.

Every class does art. If your teacher could have one or two lessons involving art where he or she put away the work and the parents came in and mounted the artwork on black construction paper and hung it outside the classroom, you would have an instant art show. There are a few twists you can add to your school art show that would make such an event a small fund-raiser.

At the art show you can sell frames for the artwork, champagne or wine, or even turn it into a dinner with pizza and soda, and charge for the refreshments. Even a bake sale at the art show would be fine.

The art show is another magnet to bring in every family in the school. You can set up a pledge table at the front door, too. Or have a raffle with the money going for more art supplies in the school.

Have a "special donation" or grant sign-up sheet for parents. Special donations could include paper, paints, or even gift certificates to art supply stores or catalogs.

The Book Fair

What Is a Book Fair?

A book fair is a sale of children's books through one company that takes place on the school grounds, through a mail order catalog or even on-line for a "virtual" book fair. Book fairs promote reading and boost literacy.

We have an on-site book fair put together by the publisher Scholastic Books. Scholastic carries both their own books and books from 150 other publishers. They are the leader in book fairs; they deliver more than 140,000 fairs worldwide. You can reach Scholastic on-line at www.scholastic.com/bookfairs.

Scholastic has the best selection of instructional nonfiction and reference books, including some books on parenting. Some of the books seem to be a few years old, not the newer books that have just been published. The books may be remainders, leftover books that didn't sell, which may generate more money for the book company because they can buy them more cheaply.

Book fairs do not require any money up front and so they are ideal as fund-raisers for schools just starting fund-raising programs.

HOW DOES AN ON-SITE BOOK FAIR WORK?

The book company brings portable aluminum bookcases that fold together, so the books can be safely stored at night in the school. The books arrive in boxes. Our volunteers set up the shelves with books according to age, reading level, or grade level in the school lobby. Scholastic gives us other items to sell, too, including book-marks, CDs, writing equipment, software, and posters. Although their service leaves something to be desired, because we can't always get the books we want and getting supplies replenished quickly is not automatic, they are the most knowledgeable and sophisticated at providing product for these "literary festivals" that we've come across. The percentage discount the school gets depends upon the plan or tier you select or agree to with the publisher.

In smaller communities, the smaller publishers who offer book fairs, like Troll and Chinaberry, might be more appropriate. Troll and Chinaberry only offer mail order catalog or on-line book fairs, no on-site fairs. Chinaberry offers free shipping if your fair generates more than $300 in sales. Their mail order catalog *Book Fair* offers large credit percentages in lieu of discounts, if you prefer. For example, you could sell over $1,600 worth of books and choose to take a 20 percent discount, giving your PA $320 in cash; or with the same sale of over $1,600, you could choose to take 35 percent of the total sales in merchandise, giving you $570 in books and other merchandise. The last option might be better than cash for your school if your goal is to restock your library. You can reach Chinaberry on-line at www.chinaberrybookfairs.com and Troll at: 1-800-454-TROLL (8765). They are open Monday to Friday 8:00 A.M. to 5:00 P.M. EST.

There are other creative alternatives in setting up a book fair.

Approach a local bookstore to set up a fair at the school, giving a percentage to the school. This might work more like our Barnes & Noble Night (see Chapter 14). Perhaps some combination between the traditional Scholastic book fair and the Barnes & Noble Night would work best for your school.

This year in the spring, our chair, Leslie Berger, decided to settle for 25 percent of the cover price instead of 35 percent because she wanted a better selection of books and not just paperbacks as we had previously had. With this tier, we also got games and other items to sell that added to the fair's success. We found that the newer books and hardback books brought in higher sales.

If we sell over a certain amount, we will receive vouchers that can be cashed in for books. We usually receive vouchers that we turn over to our librarian to use to select books for the library. Speak with your rep about book selection, replenishing sellouts, selling tips and ideas. Get the best service possible.

Be careful when you select your representative at Scholastic. The right rep can help you get a better selection of books and get better service with reorders. We reorder books that have sold out while the book sale is in progress. That way we can capitalize on a book's popularity. Scholastic picks up the leftover books and other items when the fair is over. The school is not responsible for unsold books or other items.

WHAT ARE THE STEPS FOR AN ON-SITE BOOK FAIR?

First you must get in touch with the publishers who provide these traveling bookstores. [The most experienced book fair publisher is Scholastic, although both Troll and Chinaberry offer book fairs.]

Examine all the possible purchase discount tiers or plans they have, select the one that is right for your school, and make a deal.

Book selection is key to the success of the fair. "Our parents always look for Caldecott, Newberry, and Coretta Scott King Award—winning books," our book fair chair says. Although the book selection is done by Scholastic, take an active roll and request certain books you know will sell to your parents. Perhaps your librarian or experienced teachers can help you select books.

SCHEDULING

Schedule your book fair for a day or evening when you know parents are going to be in the school. For example, if the kids are putting on a huge school play, have the book fair during the run of the play. Set it up in the school lobby. Parents can browse before or after the show and during intermission.

Schedule your book fair to coincide with your science fair or art show. Schedule your book fair before or during a basketball or other sporting event that takes place in the gym. You can build a really big fair by scheduling the book fair right before Christmas and adding some games in the gym, with a bake sale and pizza in the cafeteria.

We have two book fairs each year, one in November during the fall parent/teacher conferences and one in March during the spring parent/teacher conferences. Parent/teacher conference night is the most popular time to schedule a book fair. Make sure you lock in your date early as the publisher may be swamped with book fairs at that time.

All the parents in the school pass by our fair on their way in and on their way out of school to meet with their child's teacher. Not all the parents buy books, but we get higher sales because we are right there in front of people and it's hard to walk away without buying something. Our November sale comes just before Christmas, so we also get holiday purchases and multiple purchases, too, boosting sales.

Through the years we have kept stretching out the length of the book fair. At first we held it for just two days, during conferences. In fact it started when conferences did, which was one half day and the next full day. Gradually we kept adding days as we discovered that people kept buying books. Now our fair lasts an entire week. We make as much as $8,000 and gather lots of books for our school. Having the book sale for a week allows teachers to sign up to bring their classes down to the sale so the kids can buy books of their own choosing. We post a sign-up sheet in the school office for teachers to bring their classes to the fair. Remind teachers to tell parents which day their child is coming to the fair, so the kids have money to buy books.

Publicity is vital. You must get the word out to your parents that you're having the fair and where and when it is being held. Promote the sale in your school newsletter. Put up signs both in the school and on the front door, send flyers home in the children's backpacks.

VOLUNTEERS

If you can find a parent who loves books and is knowledgeable about them, grab him or her and hope that they stay with this job for a long time. Keeping someone to chair this event for more than one year is important so you don't have to reinvent the wheel every year. Also, the person chairing the event will find volunteers and those volunteers will come back time and time again. So it will be easier to run a smooth, profitable event if you have an experienced chair and volunteers returning to run the event.

Pull in two volunteers for each shift. Volunteers answer questions, help people find books, and keep an eye on the cash box at the same time. If you run five shifts each day, you will need ten volunteers per day. If you run the book fair for five days, you'll need at least fifty volunteers. The chairman of the event should also be there most of the day, every day if possible.

SECRETS OF SUCCESS

One secret is to have the book fair on conference night. It is the only time during the year that every single parent comes to the school.

This may not be true in your school. Perhaps other events draw more parents, but in our school, conference nights reign supreme.

Another idea we use to help stock the classrooms with books is to have teachers create wish lists of books they want to have in their classroom. The event chair can get a list of the books that will be available to the teachers in advance. Then the teachers pick the books they want for their classrooms. We publicize the fact that wish lists for the classrooms will be available at the sale and that the parents just have to look at the lists and choose whatever they want to contribute.

We take bright-colored plastic bins and put the teacher's name on the front. Then the actual books on the list are stacked in the bins with the lists on paper. As a parent buys a book, they move it to the back of the stack behind the paper list or a cardboard marker. This way, parents know which books have already been bought and which are left to buy.

To encourage the purchase of books for the classroom, we give the parents a small stick-on bookplate for each book they buy. They can put their child's name on the plate and stick the plate inside the book. This way everyone will know that you have given books to the classroom and your child will garner a little status for having contributed.

We also ask the librarian to create a wish list and use book-plates for the books on that list, too.

We are one of the few schools that runs book fairs twice a year. Most schools run them in the fall, right before the holidays. But our chair says that it's harder to get the best books then since all the schools are doing this at the same time. She said that we made more money in the spring because we were able to get a better selection of books than we got in the fall.

HOW MUCH CAN YOU EXPECT TO RAISE?

Book fairs are not the biggest moneymaking events. Our on-site book fair makes about $3,000–$4,000 net per fair. If you're not doing much in the way of fund-raising, the book fair may produce even more for your school. In our school, book fairs frequently have to compete with other fund-raising activities or happen just before or after other activities, taking away somewhat from the book fair.

This is a fairly uncomplicated event to produce that requires no dollar outlay up front. Parents understand the need for books in school. At least you won't get the people who don't want to buy baked goods because they're fattening giving you excuses at the book fair, and we get a lot of new books in the classrooms and the library.

Timeline • • • • • • • • • • • • • •

End of previous year, or right at the start of school	select your publisher and lock in a date
Beginning of school year	recruit fifty volunteers
One month before the fair	put the book fair on the calendar in your school newsletter remind volunteers
Two weeks before event	get wish lists from teachers start heavy-duty publicity in school newsletter make signs sign up volunteers to specific shifts
One week before event	send home flyers in backpacks put up signs put out sign-up sheet for teachers to schedule their class visit to the fair

The Just Kids Street Fair

The street fair at P.S. 87 has grown into a major event over the last fifteen years. We lay out $10,000 to $15,000 in advance of the fair for expenses, like rides, food, banners and equipment. Many schools don't have the resources to do a fair this size. If your school is in this boat, be sure to check out "Just Starting Out?" at the end of this chapter. It will give you a scaled-down version of the street fair and point out features of the fair that do not require financial outlay.

The auction is the party for the parents, the street fair is the party for the kids. It is a totally child-centered event with rides, food, game booths, secondhand books, toys, games, clothes, housewares, music, and much more produced as much to have fun as to raise money. Planning, organization, and volunteers are essential to having a successful street fair.

How Do You Create a Street Fair?

A street fair starts with the parent association getting a permit to close the street for one Saturday each year. If your school has a campus, your fair will be a school fair and may not involve public streets. You can also set up in a football field, a gym, the cafeteria, or a spare parking lot (if you still have enough space left for cars to park). Check with your city or town hall to see if you need a permit to conduct the fair. You may need a restaurant permit from your city or town to cook and serve food. This permit details the required temperature of the grills and the safe handling of food by having workers wear gloves and so on.

Insurance coverage is important. Before you have your street fair, make sure that the school's insurance company adds a rider to cover the street fair. Ride providers should have their own insurance, too. Be sure to ask about that and see some proof of insurance.

We always schedule the street fair for the first Saturday after Memorial Day weekend. This is the biggest event of the year and involves more people than any other event in the school. Almost everyone plays some part in the street fair. It is P.S. 87's finest moment.

We take over the street and fill it with fun, magic, rides, surprises, games, laughs, food, and just plain glee. Use all the space available to you. We have three yards of our own and a middle-school yard across the street that we get permission to use.

We fill our big yard with class booths, while the smaller playground has storybook characters wandering about, and the kindergarten yard has food and picnic tables for eating as well as music. The petting zoo and trackless train are located in the middle-school yard. On the street we have outside vendors hawking their wares.

CORPORATE SPONSORSHIP

Corporate sponsorship is a very important part of making a street fair a big moneymaker. A street fair has some fixed expenses such as huge banners, costume rentals for the storybook characters, food, rides, promotional materials, and more.

For two years Chase Manhattan Bank sponsored our street fair. They gave our school $2,000 and we put "Sponsored by Chase Manhattan Bank" on our banners, flyers, and everything. They have a community affairs budget with money to donate to local community projects every year. The trick is to get your request, in writing, to the right person early in the year, before their budget is totally allocated to other events. Often banks will spend money to create goodwill in their communities.

Also try fraternal organizations, big local stores, brokerage firms, law firms, and any other large, successful businesses in your neighborhood. Sponsorship adds a lot of money when you see that so much of what you make on the street fair is composed of many, many very small sums. Hard work and a sponsorship will take some of the pressure off and really boost your profit by minimizing outlay.

Also try to find sponsorships for specific booths. One year, The Pet Bowl pet food and supplies store sponsored our petting zoo. You might have an easier time finding a store or local business that would be willing to put up $300 to sponsor a ride for your fair or a manicure shop that might be willing to donate $150 toward supplies for a manicure booth. Specific sponsorships like this give you the opportunity to have some booths or happenings that you might not have been able to afford otherwise.

The fair can be put together in an endless variety of ways to match your community's interests and to keep it fresh every year. Here is what makes up our fair:

CLASS BOOTHS

Class booths have games or activities invented by each class and put side-by-side in a big blacktopped yard behind our school. We have thirty-one classes in our school, and thirty-one booths in our yard. Sometimes all the classes in one grade will unite and do something big. For several years, the entire fifth grade ran the petting zoo instead of having several individual class booths.

Class parents collect money from the other parents in their

class to buy supplies and prizes for the class booth. Depending upon the type of booth you have and the size of your class, contributions from $2 to $5 per child are usually enough to fund the booth prizes.

One year our street fair chair decided that our class booths needed a creativity boost so he started a contest within the school for the Best Class Booth at the fair. He offered a pizza and ice cream party for the winning class. The results were terrific and we had more new class booths that year than ever.

Here are some examples of class booths:

cupcake decorating

doughnut eating—where doughnuts are hung by string and two kids compete to see who can eat the whole doughnut first, without using hands. This booth is ideal for corporate sponsorship by Dunkin' Donuts or Krispy Kreme.

ring toss—toss rings onto rubber spikes

knock down the milk cartons with a tennis ball

kids jeopardy

guess-the-item—put household items in a pillowcase, blindfold the child, and have them guess what things are. Use things like: fork or spoon, bar of soap, small candlestick, candle, crayon, chalk, pencil, toothbrush, nail file, and a quarter.

wheel of chance

face painting

penny toss—toss pennies in small cups that float in a big tub of water

magnetic fishing—fish using a magnet on a string tied to a stick. The kids can make cardboard or paper fish (with metal paper clips through their noses) with numbers on them that correspond to prizes.

temporary tattoos

manicures with nail stickers

SnoCone stand

lemonade stand

popcorn stand—rent or buy popcorn-making machine

create your own sand art

dunking booth—our wonderful former principal, Steve Plaut,
has cheerfully agreed to be the object in the dunking booth
for the last few years. He's a good sport about it, too. It's a
good idea to have several people volunteer for this booth
so each one can be relieved to dry off and warm up a bit.

All the games booths offer prizes. We usually get the prizes
from the U.S. Toy Catalog or the Oriental Trading Company Catalog. Find these catalog companies on-line at www.ustoy.com and
www.orientaltrading.com. Sometimes discount stores also have
good inexpensive small toys to use as prizes.

If you decide to pick out the prizes yourself, remember to select
ones that appeal to both boys and girls. Here are some ideas for prizes
that appeal to both sexes: Pencils, rulers, compasses, magnifying
glasses, tattoos, small plastic animals, fortune fish, tiny notebooks,
palm-sized games, individually wrapped candy, plastic Dracula teeth.

What's most important is that every child receives some sort of
prize at the booth. Make the games easy or have different prizes for
different levels of achievement. My favorite booth is one where you
knock down the milk cartons with a tennis ball, a game you must put
in a spot with a fence around it or you'll be chasing tennis balls all
day. It's a very simple booth that does not require much preparation,
but it's always very popular because kids love to throw things.

We only charge two tickets for our booth and draw lines on the
pavement with chalk to show where the kids should stand. We keep
moving kids up until they knock down the milk cartons. Everyone
coming to our booth gets a prize. As a result, we always have a line
of kids waiting at our booth.

Try to keep the prices low at the class booths. Our sand art booth, where kids create art by layering different colored sand in a small bottle, is the most expensive since the sand and bottles are expensive. The cheaper the booths, the more activity you will get and the more tickets you'll sell.

Another thing the committee chair running the class booths needs is a well-drawn map of the yard, the gym, or wherever you plan to put the booths. Draw a floor plan and give each class booth a spot. Don't put booths with candy in a sunny spot. Then on the day of the fair, each class can come to you and see where their booth should be set up and there won't be any confusion.

How do you get all the classes to comply and put together a booth? We use the class parents as the motivators. They are responsible for getting a class booth up and running. Sometimes the teacher likes to get involved and she or he will have the kids make the banner for the booth or maybe even parts of the booth itself in class. Sometimes we have classes that just cannot get it together and don't participate. That's not the end of the world since we have so many classes that do participate. This is one area where the creativity of your parents and children can really run wild.

We usually charge from two tickets (for the milk carton booth) to five tickets (for sand art) and the tickets cost 50¢ each. One hint to making your class booth really popular: the better your prizes are, the better the turnout at your booth will be.

THE MAZE

This idea got started when we had a parent who owned a moving company and donated huge boxes to the school. Someone came up with the idea of using the boxes to make a crawl-though maze and put it in the middle of our big yard during the street fair. Architect parents drew complicated plans and a crawl-through maze was fashioned out of the wardrobe moving boxes. The maze had a few breakthroughs or openings so the children could pop their heads out or parents could look into them for a lost child.

The maze was one of the most popular attractions of the street fair. For two tickets, kids disappeared for five minutes and crawled around in the dark like babies. When the kids of the parents who donated the boxes finally graduated after ten years at the school, we all mourned the passing of the maze.

GRAB BAGS

Although grab bags have been covered somewhat in the Harvest Festival chapter, the street fair is the major grab bag event where we make and sell 500 grab bags. They are so popular that they sell out before 3:00 P.M. That means that we sell about 125 bags per hour!

The contents of these grab bags are made up mainly from donations from corporations and parents who work at companies that have premiums. For example, our parent Kim Estes at the Environmental Protection Agency gives us EPA pencils or small boxes of four crayons every year. McDonald's donates five hundred toys to us every year. Time Warner donates a box of about two hundred individual servings of microwave popcorn. We have gotten key rings from Chase, pens from Empire Blue Cross, and mouse pads from the Children's Museum.

Insurance companies always seem to have giveaways. Fifty or a hundred of these can really help your grab bags. A past P.S. 87 parent gave us hundreds of fabulous reversible caps that were black on one side with the logo of the Sci Fi channel and white on the other with the logo of the USA Network. We were able to give one out with every bag. These caps drove up grab bag sales and we sold out in record time.

One parent who works for Colgate got us toothbrushes and little toothpaste sachets. I also attend the Premium Incentive Show where I pick up samples of all kinds of things. If you go on the last day to a show like that, some people are happy to donate a lot so they don't have to pack it up and cart it home. Kids love all this little stuff, even if it isn't toys.

I always get a good donation of temporary tattoos from California Tattoo at the Premium Show. Sometimes we get terrific small items donated from the gift shop of the Museum of Natural History. One year, The Gap donated five hundred small backpacks. Truly amazing!

When donations aren't quite enough, order from U.S. Toy or Oriental Trading. I have frequently bought small magnifying glasses, American flag pins or miniature Tootsie Rolls, items that would be good for boys or girls.

Try to mix up the bags and make them all a little different. It's better when you have one hundred of this and seventy-five of that because it's easier to vary the bags. Buying assortments from the catalogs is great. If the bags are all identical, why would anyone want more than one? We sell three, four, five or more bags to one child because each one is a surprise and a little different. Repeat buyers make your school more money.

We usually charge $2—or four tickets—for a grab bag. So if your child goes wild and has to have three bags, it's only $6. If you've collected some items that are too big to fit into those lunch bags, do not despair. Make "special prize" tickets out of neon-colored paper for the oversized items and put them in the grab bags. Write the name of the item on the prize ticket.

At the street fair we ask the kids, "Did you get a special prize ticket? Look inside." This really drives the multiple sales. Kids keep coming back, hoping for special prize tickets. The more special prizes you have, the better. It's not even the prize itself that most kids are after; it's the *winning* of the prize that is so important. It really seems to make kids feel special to win something. Grab bags only need to be put together one or two days before the street fair.

We stuff brown paper lunch bags with our donated goodies and staple them so that the contents don't fall out and kids can't peek in them and choose based on the stuff they see.

We load the brown bags into huge sturdy black plastic garbage bags and store those in the PA closet until the morning of the fair. With five people to help stuff the bags, the task goes along quickly and should be complete in about three hours.

For the grab bag table, we use three long tables joined together in the shape of a U. The three tables work best so you can store the grab bags under the tables and pull them out when the supply on the tables gets low. Special prizes need to be kept behind the table and out of sight.

Manning this table is the best job in the street fair. I have people who come back year after year to do this job. To see the look on the faces of the children, the excitement, the anticipation, the joy, the wonder, the happiness is just great. Our street fair is about the kids, so when we get a child who doesn't have enough tickets or even no tickets, we give them a bag anyway.

STORYBOOK CHARACTERS

Rent costumes and get actors or hams among your parents to volunteer. Dress up as the Cat in the Hat, Raggedy Ann or Andy, Curious George, Stuart Little, Pippi Longstocking, or any popular children's storybook characters you can rent or make costumes for. Have the characters circulate among the people at the fair, playing with kids, posing for pictures, and lending a festive air to the event. Costume rental for the storybook character is money out the door, but they add so much fun and surprise to the day they are worth it.

SECONDHAND ROSE

This is a great section to sell all the white elephants that our parents can haul into school. From toys to china, from sporting equipment to board games to kitchenware, these tables are close to a garage sale.

Storage is the biggest problem with this booth. Our school has a second, smaller gymnasium that we commandeer for the street fair the week before. We manage to squeeze all our books, clothes, and white elephants into that room. You will need volunteers to price all the items beforehand and throw out anything broken. Group the items by type; all china items in one place, all board games together, all small toys together and all kitchen items together. Put small items of about the same value in a box or basket and put one price on the basket.

Be prepared to haggle. It's better to sell everything you have even at lower prices than to have to throw out or give away anything. Your mission should be to turn everything into cash.

BOOK TABLE

This is the most amazing section of the street fair. We frequently make $3,000 at the book table because we have such fantastic donations. We get used children's and adult's books from our parents, but we also get terrific contributions of new books from publishers. If you can drum up this kind of contact you can clean up in the book department. Check your parent body for someone who works for a book publisher or bookstore.

Divide up the books into children's and adults'. In the adult section, divide the books into hardcover and paperback. Then divide into categories the mysteries, biographies, cookbooks, parenting, science fiction, romance, how-to, coffee table books, and so on.

In the children's section it can be helpful to pull books of a series together, like all the Nancy Drew in one place, the Babysitter's Club in another. Parents are often looking for more books like their children's favorites.

We used to charge $1 for hardback and 50¢ for paperbacks, but with all the brand-new books, we've raised our prices. New books go for various prices up to $5. Same old low prices for the second-hand books. As the day wears on, we drop our prices so we can move more books. You don't really want to have to haul all those heavy books somewhere after the fair is over.

At the fair at P.S. 9 on West 84th Street in New York City, they offer a shopping bag for $5 to fill with all the books that fit in. It's a great way to get rid of books, especially during the second half of the fair.

MASSAGE

If you have a professional massage therapist among your parents, or a pro who is willing to donate his or her services for a day, set up chairs at the street fair and offer a massage. Charge $10 for ten minutes. This is one of the most popular booths and will always be busy.

SECONDHAND CLOTHES

Secondhand clothes are a big draw at our street fair. We get mounds and mounds of clothing donated every year. Running the second-hand clothes table is a big job. We ask that people donate only gently used clothing, but of course you get clothes you wouldn't put on your dog. Have a group of volunteers sort through the clothes. They separate them in big bins for men, women, boys, and girls. They also discard any clothing that is in bad shape.

As a bonus for doing this thankless task, the head of this committee usually lets the sorters select a few items to buy before the fair.

We tried having a presale for all the parents in the school before the fair but it didn't really work for two reasons: it was a lot of extra work getting people to cover the sale in the lobby the day before the street fair, using up good volunteers before the event, and having all the best clothing pulled out before the fair reduced interest in the clothing booth and diminished sales the day of the fair.

You will need coat racks, hangers, and lots of plastic or paper bags. Hang up as much as you can so the clothes will be easy to look at and will take up less table space. The better the display, the more the clothing will sell. Group clothing by gender, and for kids, as much by size as you can, with infant and toddler sizes separate from the larger sizes.

Separate male and female clothing and group by type of clothing. For example, blouses together, pants together, dresses together. This not only makes it easier for the potential buyer to find what they're looking for but also makes a more appealing display.

Be ready to haggle here, too. The object is to get rid of the clothing, turn it into cash. Be willing to accept a lower price. The bag-of-books idea works here, too. As the fair wears on, you might offer an all-you-can-stuff-in bag of clothing for $5.

SCHOOL TABLE

At the fair we have a P.S. 87 table. This table serves many functions. It is where the raffle tickets are sold. It is where P.S. 87 Street Fair T-shirts are sold and it is the table that disseminates material about our school, and has veteran parents available to greet incoming kindergarten parents.

This central table is where everything originates and where you can find the PA heads most of the day. We send an invitation to the street fair to the incoming kindergarten parents and direct them to this table. The incoming parents find it welcoming to be able to talk with current parents face-to-face.

We always have a raffle with terrific prizes. We sell the tickets at the school table but we also have roving raffle sellers hawking tickets throughout the fair. Typical raffle prizes are bicycles, televisions, and even dinner for two at a popular restaurant. The raffle can raise $500 pretty quickly and with very little fuss.

We create special street fair T-shirts with our logo of "One Family under the Sun" in Spanish and English every year. These colorful shirts sell quickly. One year we used a design from a student in a design-the-T-shirt contest. We buy our T-shirts fairly cheaply, at about $3 per shirt, and sell them for $5 for kids and $10 for adults. Look for a local T-shirt silkscreen printer to get a good price, or find one online. Try www.epromos.com.

Use iprint.com or a similar service on the Internet to print your T-shirts using four-color art. If you use them, you will need to call and negotiate a special rate if you plan to print more than two hundred shirts. The rate posted on their site is for a maximum of two hundred T-shirts. We printed one thousand. Be tough and get a low price.

We use specially designed P.S. 87 T-shirts, sweatshirts and sweatpants to raise money for scholarships to Nature Camp, a fifth grade trip. There our markup is higher as we need to raise several thousand dollars for this trip. T-shirts are only one fund-raiser among several earmarked for Nature Camp scholarships.

FOOD

Food is a big part of the fair and is provided in several ways:

The Grill

We set up a grill to cook hot dogs and hamburgers. Rent an "industrial-strength" 3' × 6' grill instead of something small and flimsy. We also sell cold soda and water. Get your supplies at the discount beverage stores. To sell beer you need a special liquor permit. We had a keg of beer.

Bake Sale

We have a bake sale with mostly homemade goodies from our parents. For the street fair we approached local bakeries and received some donations of loaves of special bread such as peasant bread and whole grain bread. These loaves were big sellers and made us more money than street fair bake sales had in the past.

Multicultural Buffet

Our multicultural committee goes all out for the food for the street fair. They start cooking in the school cafeteria kitchen on Friday night. In our kindergarten yard, they set up several long tables for food and picnic tables for diners. We buy the food and have parents prepare it. But if you can get donated food, as you would at a potluck dinner, you'll make more money. We rent professional-size chafing dishes from a local caterer for our steaming pans of Jamaican chicken, beans and rice, and homemade chili.

The exotic foods send enticing odors wafting through the air. This is the best advertising, as the wonderful smells bring in hungry families. We charge $5 for a plate and people fill them up along the buffet line as they wish.

One year Dave Gibson did the street fair with no co-chairs. To handle the food situation, Dave rented or bought everything he needed, including grill, charcoal, lighter fluid, hot dogs, hamburgers, buns, chafing dishes, lemonade containers, lemonade, napkins, silverware, condiments, and plates from a caterer. It cost a lot, but at 7:00 A.M., all these wonderful supplies just arrived and Dave could put his attention elsewhere. It may cut down on profits, but if you're stuck find the easiest way to get it done.

MUSIC

We get a few parents who are musicians to agree to play for an hour or so at the street fair. We set them up in the kindergarten yard where the food is being served so people can listen while they eat. Everything from country music to cool jazz works well. Having the music in the yard means that we can use the electric outlets in the kindergarten classrooms by opening the windows and plugging in the electric guitars.

Music attracts people to your fair and to the food stands; it's a great advertisement that a fun time is being had somewhere. Keep the music at the proper level, though, so people can sit and listen without being blasted out of their seats. Also, if the music is too loud, it drowns out necessary talking at booths and friendly conversation.

RIDES

Rides are big attractions at any street fair, but the rides are expensive to rent. You may not make a profit on the rides unless you have corporate sponsorship for them or charge higher prices. But rides do attract customers to the fair, so they are worth it. Some years some of our rides have made money, like the swing, trackless train, and castle-bounce. Rides that take more kids are more likely to make money. The rock-climbing wall, which only took two kids at a time, was a money loser.

The best places to locate companies that provide rides for fairs are your local yellow-page telephone book under "amusements" or "rides," and on the Web search for amusement rides.

Some amusement companies will not charge for a rented ride if the fair is rained out. This is a very important feature to look for when you select a ride company. With rides costing from $500 to $2,500 each (in New York City) it's crucial insurance to have a company that will give you a credit for a rain date.

Most of the companies charge in advance. Some may get paid when they deliver the ride. When selecting rides, please take into account the space you plan to use for rides. Get the dimensions in advance for each ride you're interested in, including the height. Height is important if there are any trees in the area you will be using for rides.

You can't wait until the day of the fair when the rides are delivered to discover that a ride doesn't fit into a space earmarked for it. You need to have a floor plan with accurate dimensions and then sit down and plot out the places the rides will fit in.

Also you will need to know if a ride needs electricity so that you can locate it near a good plug. If a power source isn't available, rent rides that come with generators. Rides are powered by either gas generators or noisy electric fan generators. Check with your company to find out the electrical requirements. If they are bringing a fan generator, ask how noisy it is. Many fan generators are as noisy as a lawn mower. This may distract from the enjoyment of the ride, so a gas generator may be preferable.

Rides are delivered on large trucks. Make sure that you know when the truck will be arriving and that you have mapped out a route for the truck that will be clear when it arrives. If you will have vendors, make sure their goods are not blocking the path of the rides truck.

Select rides that have room for a lot of kids at once as opposed to rides that can only be for one kid at a time. For example, the castle-bounce—that big inflated thing that looks like a castle and that kids climb on and bounce around for a while—can take about eight kids at a time whereas a ride like the rock wall can only be climbed by one child at a time. Figure eight kids at $2 per child is $16 for about five minutes. Times ten for an hour, allowing for getting-on-and-off time, and you could make $160 per hour. The rock wall, with one child for five minutes, even at $5 per child, is only $50 per hour.

For the castle-bounce you will make about $800 for a five-hour fair, while you will make only $250 on the rock wall. Charge for the rides at a projected breakeven. Figure out how much you have to charge by the price of the ride and the number of hours the fair will be open. That should give you what you need to charge people to break even or make a profit.

Our most popular rides have been:

The castle-bounce—I love this ride because the kids get tired out while you sit on a bench, relaxing and recouping.

The trackless train—This little ride can take several children at one time. The magic of trains is always a winner with kids.

The swing—This ride can take about twenty kids at a time so you can make a lot of money. Kids love to swing. After fifteen rides, the swing has covered its cost.

The giant slide was very popular and a magnificent ride, but it cost $2,500! Still, there was always a line waiting to get on and the sheer height and size of the ride drew attention from the neighboring streets and attracted a crowd.

David Letterman's Velcro wall—The kids put on a Velcro suit and bounce on a trampoline, flinging themselves at a Velcro wall, where they will stick!

Make the most of the rides by placing concession stands adjacent to where the lines for the popular rides will be. My friend, Steve Russo, who has handled our rides for nine years, says this is how Disney World makes so much money. Cotton candy or lemonade or hot dogs or cookies being sold next to the line of a popular ride will do well. Check with your ride companies and get a date when you have to book the rides. In New York City, we need to book the rides a few months in advance. In other communities the lead time may be different. Remember that when you book, you will need to pay a deposit.

Planning involves selecting ride companies and rides, choosing appropriate spots to put rides where they will fit easily and leave room for a line of children waiting to get on, and lining up enough volunteers to run rides if there are not sufficient staff from the ride company.

Usually the ride company will provide one person to run the ride—such as the engineer to drive the train—and that's all. You will need to check and make sure that a person who knows how to work the ride will be included as part of your deal and then you need to get busy rounding up volunteers.

Better to plan to have too many parents helping on the rides rather than not enough. So if it is your first year, round up as many parents as you can. You can offer the running of a ride to a class instead of a class booth. This works well with our fifth grade where some of the parents are burned out from years of fund-raising. Running the ride is an easy solution to keep them involved.

Some rides need more volunteers than others. For example, the trackless train needs several volunteers to handle getting the children on and off the train. Each car on the trackless train has a little door. Parent volunteers need to be there to help children off the trains and help other children on the train. Don't leave this up to parents of kids riding as they will swing their children right on ahead of others and it will be chaos. We know about that because the first year we didn't have enough parents and it was a disaster. The trackless train is one of the most popular rides we've had. It cost us about $650 and we took in $1,200 on the ride.

Set up time slots of one hour for each ride and get at least two volunteers for each time period. That way if someone doesn't show up, at least you will have one volunteer, and time to recruit another. If people know that they only have to put in an hour, it will be easier to get them to volunteer. If one-hour time slots don't work, try half an hour. Half-hour time slots will require more supervisers but if it gets people to step up to the plate and volunteer, do it.

One year we offered a $20 "bracelet" for kids that would allow them to ride all the rides as many times as they wanted. You may not be able to charge quite as much in your community. An unlimited-ride bracelet can reduce arguments with kids who may want to go on rides again and again, and at $2 per ride the parents may have to put their foot down.

Rides are a blast; the little kids really love them. They can be moneymakers, either directly or by boosting attendance. Either way, they add excitement to your fair.

VENDORS

Years ago, we made a fortune on vendors. We don't have as many vendors now, but vendors are essential to a good fair and a very easy way to make money.

Vendors are outside merchants selling items not related to the school or the fair. The school makes money by renting space in a special spot allocated to vendors. Charge by the space; we charge $50 for a small space, and up to $80 for a large space.

Vendors must operate under certain restrictions. Do not accept vendors with alcohol. Do not accept any food vendors, except perhaps an ice cream truck. Food vendors compete with your own food booths. Do not accept any other vendors that compete with products you are selling, such as books or secondhand clothes.

Do not accept vendors who sell seriously overpriced merchandise. Several years ago, my son, David, bought a Pokéman card from a vendor at our street fair for $10 before I had a chance to see what he was doing. The same cards were selling for $2 in stores. That vendor was not allowed back to the fair in subsequent years. You don't want your customers to be cheated by a vendor. Create a contract with vendors specifying what items they cannot sell. For example, we don't allow vendors to sell those poppers that explode when kids throw them on the ground.

Some vendor items that should do well and complement your fair are jewelry; baskets; sheets and towels; kitchen gadgets and supplies; pet supplies; new clothes, especially socks and accessories; baby items; leather goods; furniture; soap and perfume.

You might want to solicit nonprofit organizations to put up vendor booths, for example the local ASPCA or animal shelter, volunteer firehouse, local museum for memberships, and other local charities. Offer these groups a special, lower nonprofit rate for the space. You might contact the local fraternal organizations, especially if they are sponsoring your fair, and give them a booth for free.

Where to find vendors? Usually when you have fairs with good attendance, vendors find you. But you can go out and solicit. I remember being part of a team that hawked at other fairs and flea markets and passed out flyers about our own fair that stated who was going to attend, how many people we were expecting, and the names and phone numbers of the volunteers who were handling the vendor booths at the fair. This got a good response, and I was there to answer any questions these vendors had about the fair and to hand the flyer only to vendors whose wares were appropriate to our fair.

There is also a magazine in our area that covers flea markets and fairs. We took out a small ad. You might advertise in a local pennysaver newspaper, or other local newspaper for vendors. Money from renting space to vendors is the easiest money you'll make at the fair, so give it a good push.

Designate a setup area for vendors. We run our own booths in the schoolyards so we put the vendors in the street. Draw a floor plan of all the space available for vendors. Plot out a special space for vendors that will get traffic, not someplace off to the side or out of the way. If the vendors don't sell anything, they won't be back the next year. On the other hand, if they make money, you can count on their coming back the next year without your having to solicit. So be helpful and give them good space.

Divide your vendor spot into ten- or twelve-foot spaces and number the spaces. One space costs $50 to rent. Vendors who need more room can buy two spaces, perhaps for a discounted price of $80. You will need to draw or mark out the spaces and the numbers on the ground in the area you've allocated to vendors.

We do this with neon-colored removable tape that we put on the curbs the day before the fair. In the past, some chairs used spray paint, but after the fair was over, the street had to live with the spray-painted numbers and it made the people on the block angry. The tape has to be pulled off after the fair, but you should be able to find a few kids willing to help pull it off during cleanup.

Keep a written record of the spaces, numbers, and which vendors you've allocated to which spaces. Notify the vendors in advance, if you can, as to which space they have received. Then they can just come and set up without trying to find you during the chaos of setup before the fair. Don't place vendors selling similar merchandise next to one another.

NO-PARKING COMMITTEE

This is the thorniest part of the vendor booth plans. If cars are parked where you plan to have booths, it will be a huge problem. If you are using actual city streets, then you will have cars parking there. You need to put up signs early in the week to alert drivers that there is no parking on the day of your fair. We also put signs in the building lobbies on the street, asking tenants to please move their cars on the day of the fair.

Recently someone got a brilliant idea. Instead of just asking people to move their cars, we are offering the building tenants the opportunity to park their cars in the middle schoolyard for the whole day for a fee of $10. In New York, all-day parking is very expensive, so this is not only a bargain but also a no-hassle way for people living on this street to handle parking their cars.

We always close the street off with police sawhorses or neon orange tape wound around garbage cans around midnight. Even though we're not supposed to close the street that long before the fair, no one has ever stopped us. I'm convinced that closing it early has kept cars from parking in the dark where they can't read the No Parking signs on the trees.

We also put leaflets on all the cars parked in the street. Getting the street cleared of all but two or three cars is a victory. Plan your vendor spaces with the idea that you may lose a few spaces to people who refuse to move their cars. Have a few extra spaces tucked away for an emergency.

PETTING ZOO

You should be able to locate a petting zoo through a local pet store or veterinarian. Try to get this attraction sponsored by a pet store or a local fraternal organization.

You will need to block out a sizable area in the shade for your petting zoo. Find out from the owners how big the zoo is and how much space they anticipate needing. Do not put the animals in the sun, as everyone will suffer.

You will also need plenty of volunteers to guide the kids and fetch water for the animals and their trainers. A petting zoo is a big draw. If you have a sponsor, you can make a lot of money on a petting zoo. If you have to pay for it yourself, it may lose money or break even, because a petting zoo is expensive. But it will increase attendance significantly.

All the younger kids love a petting zoo. You need volunteers to make sure that the kids behave appropriately with the animals so no one gets hurt. Also, you need to have something to keep them happy in line. And you will need someone to clean up at the end of the fair after the animals have gone. A petting zoo makes an ideal class booth for two or more upper-grade classes.

One essential you can't forget is either antibacterial hand wash or towelettes for the kids. After all, many kids will go straight from the petting zoo to a food booth, and need to have clean hands.

INSIDE EVENTS

Even though our fair is always the first Saturday after Memorial Day, and the weather is usually beautiful, we always schedule a few events inside the school auditorium to capitalize on the space. Since we have to pay a fee for the custodians on Saturday anyway, why not use the school, too?

We usually put on a play or a puppet show during the fair. We may have a talent show, where anyone can get up and sing, dance, make funny faces, do impressions or stand-up comedy. Sometimes we have a concert with a musician from our parent body, or a performance of the school band. We don't schedule a lot of events inside, but a few are welcome and add to your sales and the fun of the fair.

SECURITY

Security is terribly important at the fair. There is a lot of money floating around. Besides the ticket booth, which is fairly secure, there is money at all the food booths, the Secondhand Rose, secondhand clothes, books, and PA table, not to mention vendors. We have a plainclothes security team headed up usually by a board member, or perhaps the husband of the street fair chair. Any responsible person from the parent association will do.

Although we have a volunteer running security, we hire men to be part of the security team. Gym teachers, school aides, even teachers will make great security guards. We hire professional security men at $75 per day to augment our parents and teachers.

Professional security guards get paid after the fair, when you will have the funds readily available.

We invested in a set of really good high-powered walkie-talkies so we can keep in touch with security. We have at least three roving security men assigned to a territory. You will need security at each end of the fair and one or two people roaming through the crowds and checking in regularly at the booths that take in money.

Part of the security job is to make sure the children are safe. Since we close the street to traffic, the kids run around on their own. We feel that the environment is very safe. But security people need to watch the crowds and make sure that the children are safe. So far we have never had a problem.

I like to believe that because there are so many parents there, the kids are being watched over by thousands of eyes, that if someone unsavory were talking to my son, Stevie, someone who knew me would intervene or come and let me know.

You also need to have security people inside the school. Our inside events all occur on the first floor, so security people keep everyone off the other floors to protect the school. Even the bathrooms are on the first floor. You must keep the school open so people can use the bathrooms, anyway, even if there are no events going on in the school. Once you open the school, you need security to keep vandals at bay. You also need to keep the school safe from thieves.

BANKING

Here is a banking system that works well if your treasurer and assistant treasurer are available to work the fair. Having two treasurers is a good idea as it spreads out the workload and keeps people honest. Every hour, the treasurer makes the rounds of each booth where money rather than tickets changes hands. At the booth, the treasurer counts the money earned that hour and takes most of it, leaving some for making change. The treasurer then gives a receipt to the person working in or in charge of that booth stating the amount of money turned in and the time.

Hourly money pickup helps keep down risk of loss or theft. It is not good for the people handling the booths to have too much money at any time. This invites trouble. The person working at the booth gives the receipt to the person in charge of the booth who can keep track of how much money was earned by adding up the receipts.

Only the treasurers should handle the money. Open up a class-room in the school and count the money there. If you don't have a safe, perhaps you can convince the principal or other school official to lock the money up in his or her desk or office.

Do not take any money home from the fair. You can come back the following week and pick up the cash and deposit it, when no one will know how much money you have and it is safe to travel with the money. We net over $30,000, so the treasurers need to lock up the money and go home empty-handed at the end of the fair so they can be secure.

We sell tickets good for the class booths, the maze and the grab bags at a table in the middle of the big yard. Tickets may also be used for food and rides. This keeps most of the cash in one place, reduces the hassle of making change, and cuts down on loss and theft.

PUBLICITY

Publicity is extremely important for any street fair. The street fair needs to have maximum attendance to be really profitable because the money you are making is in such small increments: 50¢ here, $1 there, $2 elsewhere. You need to have as many people as possible pass through your fair to make the most of all the work everyone puts in and to generate a handsome profit.

Create press kits with brightly colored folders containing flyers with all the pertinent information regarding the fair, such as time, place, and rain date which can be the following week. Include pictures of previous fairs if you have them. If not, remember to take pictures of this fair so you can use them for the press kit next year. Include sheets with information about your school, the breakdown of the student body, and the activities that the money will go to support. Put a black-and-white picture of your school on the top of the sheets with school information.

If you have an art director in your parent body, recruit him or her to design the flyers and information sheets so they look professional.

Send the press kits to all the local newspapers, magazines, television stations, and radio stations. Write several thirty-second radio announcements and add them to the press kits going to the radio stations, who usually announce community events on the air.

Put up posters in local stores and shops. Send home notices in the backpacks of all the students in the school. Put up on the school a huge banner that can be made out of a sheet and poster paint, or on the school fence where passing cars can see it. Emphasize the time and date of the fair on the banner.

Put up small posters in: the library, pediatricians' and other doctors' offices, dentists' offices, the hardware store, the fire station, the police station, the train station, the post office, the grocery store, the video rental store, and anywhere else you feel people who would come to the fair might be.

Send your press kits to the media at least two months in advance. Magazines should get the kits three months ahead, if possible.

CLEAN UP AND MAKE A DONATION
AT THE SAME TIME

When the street fair is finished, there will be a surprising amount of stuff left over. Clothes, books, housewares, games, toys, and other white elephant stuff will remain. It is a shame to throw all this stuff out.

One year we called the Salvation Army and alerted them that we would like to donate all our leftover things and they came and picked it all up. What a relief! Any nonprofit organization, the ASPCA or local animal shelter, a homeless shelter, a church, any organization that needs clothes for people or has a secondhand shop can use your leftovers and will give them away or sell them to support their organization.

Call in advance and make arrangements. Double-check and make sure that they are coming, confirm the time they are coming and the location. This will make cleanup a much easier job.

AND DON'T FORGET . . .

Rent tables and chairs for your street fair. You need so many long tables, one for each class booth, and several for other booths. The grab bags alone need three or four tables. And chairs are needed for every booth, too. It's much easier to rent them. They'll get delivered and you just have to set them up and then they pick them up. Chair and table rental is a necessary expense.

You will need a cleanup crew. This is the toughest job to fill. At the end of the fair, everyone is exhausted. We usually snag a few parents to knock down and pack up the tables, but we hire a cleanup crew. We hire the Doe Foundation, a local organization that provides work for jobless and homeless men and women, to bring in people to make the yard and street "broom clean" at the end of the day. It's amazing to see that an hour after the fair is over, it's as though the fair was never there. You must leave not only public areas but any common areas borrowed from your school in excellent condition.

JUST STARTING OUT?

If your parent association or school doesn't yet have funds for expenses, here is how you can start up your own street or school fair without big expenses:

1. Use class booths that are not expensive, like the knock-down-the-milk-cartons-with-a-tennis-ball, and others that only require inexpensive prizes that can be funded by small parent donations. Have as many class booths as possible. Class booths and a bake sale is the way P.S. 87 started out with its first street fair over fifteen years ago.

2. Get as many small corporate sponsorship donations as you can. Even if a company only donates $50 or $100 it can be put together with other small donations to fund one ride or something else you want for your fair.

3. Make fifty or one hundred grab bags out of secondhand small toys donated by parents if you can't get new items donated.

4. Create your own storybook characters by using home-made costumes and extensive makeup or face painting instead of renting expensive costumes.

5. A "store" to sell secondhand books, toys, and housewares doesn't require any outlay of money. Make these booths as big as possible. Price the merchandise as low as necessary to sell as much as possible and generate more cash.

6. Have one or two massage chairs if you have parents who can do that in your school. Otherwise approach professionals and ask if they would work the fair and split their proceeds with the school.

7. Have a school table. Create a modest raffle using second-hand bikes or donations of televisions, mixers, CD players and so forth in great condition for the raffle.

8. Try for corporate donations to create a modest number of T-shirts, perhaps fifty or one hundred to be sold at the fair.

9. Use a borrowed or donated small grill for hot dogs and hamburgers. Take up a collection to buy the food.

10. Skip the hot food and just have a bake sale at your first street or school fair. Get all baked goods donated. Hopefully they'll all be homemade; those sell the best.

11. Skip the multicultural buffet unless you can get donated food and equipment. Perhaps one or two restaurants would like to sponsor tastings, where people pay a modest fee and receive tastings of several different kinds of food. This can be a good marketing tool for a restaurant, getting its samples out to the public. Make sure the restaurant will be responsible for bringing all utensils and plates.

12. You can still have music if you have a parent in the school willing to play for free. Music helps to attract and build crowds, which means more business for your fair.

13. Get one or two sponsors together to sponsor one $300 or $400 ride. One ride will be enough the first time. You can add more rides each year as your attendance grows.

14. You can have vendors. Make your flyers in the school, using the school copy machine to save money. Remember that vendors bring in money and don't cost anything.

15. Inside events can still take place if the school produces them or someone volunteers to put on a show. Make the inside event a spelling bee, or a vocabulary or math competition. That creates involvement and doesn't cost anything, except for a modest prize.

16. Security is still mandatory. Try to get corporate sponsorship

from a security company, or at least a donation of one security man.

VOLUNTEERS

This event chews up more volunteers than any other event in the school. You need probably a hundred volunteers if you are producing a full-scale fair. If you're just starting out, you'll need fewer. Here is a basic list:

1. two overall chairs for the event
2. committee chairs:
   food (with the following subcommittee chairs: grill, bake sale, multicultural food)
   class booths
   rides
   security
   banking
   publicity
   corporate sponsorship
   grab bags
   secondhand clothes
   books
   white elephant
   vendors
   cleanup
   school table
   raffle
   inside events
   storybook characters
   petting zoo
   the maze
   T-shirts

Each committee head will have to establish how many volunteers they need. You will need the majority of the school to get involved one way or another, even if it just means baking a pan of brownies or manning the class booth for an hour. The success of this event is composed of small contributions by a great many people. That's one of the secrets that makes this event such fun and creates a family feeling at the school. No one is left out of a street fair.

SECRETS TO SUCCESS

Grab bags are one of the secrets. Unusual class booths, great publicity, lots of parent participation, excellent food, and great rides all combine to make this fair a big success. Give a free T-shirt to every committee head, and start T-shirt sales in school two weeks before the fair.

HOW MUCH MONEY WILL YOU RAISE?

The amount of money you take in depends upon several factors:

1. the weather: rain or the threat of rain will drive away customers
2. the amount of publicity
3. the amount of class participation in creating class booths
4. school spirit

We have raised more than $30,000 net after expenses. But we have a big school and we have been putting on a street fair for a long time. Smaller schools will raise less. But considering the amount of fun had by all, a street fair is always a hit.

Timeline • • • • • • • • • • • • • • • •

Because our fair takes so much time to plan, we have it in the spring
so we can get an early start on planning and setting up volunteers.
Set a date a year ahead if you can. We always have our street fair on
the first Saturday after Memorial Day.

As far in advance as you can	pick the date
	file for your permits: if you need permission to close a street, serve liquor, or cook and serve food, get those permits filed in advance
Beginning of school year	apply for corporate sponsorships
	begin vendor recruitment
Four months ahead	have a planning meeting with your committee heads to identify problems and brainstorm solutions
	reserve rides
	gather raffle prizes
	decide on storybook characters and make costume arrangements
Three months ahead	line up all volunteers needed
	hire security people
	find and hire petting zoo
	select design for T-shirts
Two/three months ahead	get publicity out to all relevant media
	order T-shirts
Two months ahead	plan all food and make shopping lists
	ask for grab bag donations from parents
	send letters to companies asking for grab bag donations
	have raffle tickets printed up

	advertise in school newsletter for parent vendors
One month ahead	order additional grab bag items
	assign vendors slots
	gather materials for school table
	assign locations for class booths
Three weeks ahead	post sign-up sheets for donated food
Two weeks ahead	start publicity
One week ahead	make up grab bags
	organize donations for secondhand books, clothes, and toys
One night before	make the food that can be made in advance

Year-Round Events

. . . .

· · · · · · **11** · · · · · ·

The Flea Market

Over fifteen years ago, a small, enterprising group of parents of
P.S. 87 students and graduates came up with a new idea that has
grown into a huge business that supports four schools today. They
saw an opportunity to start a flea market in the yard of their children's middle school on Sundays. How did they see this? Well, to
be quite honest the flea market was really started by vendors who
snuck through a hole in the fence and set up shop. They were selling there for two years before the parents noticed and decided to
take over and start a real flea market.

There was opposition from the local residents, who resented
the noise early on Sunday morning and the loss of parking spaces.
They also expressed distress at the mounting load of garbage that
grew with the market. A greenmarket was added to the vendor
mix, which helped to mollify the local residents, who were now
more willing to quiet down and buy beautiful fresh vegetables and
fruit trucked in from the farm right to their block. The farmer's
market participation was really key to winning over the local residents and to the long-term success of our flea market.

What started as a volunteer-run fund-raiser making a few dollars grew, until it grossed $10,000 a month. Now, under profes-
sional management, the flea market is a huge operation that makes
several hundred thousand dollars per year. The rapid growth of the

flea market meant that it could no longer be run by volunteers. So we hired a professional manager to take over.

In the beginning, the parent volunteers would carry tables, chairs, and other paraphernalia out to the yard where the market was. They would collect fees from the vendors, count the money, do the bookkeeping, and administer all the paperwork. At the end of the day, they would once again carry the tables and chairs back into the school building, do the sweeping, and collect the garbage. Without the participation of the parents of both schools, the market would not have survived because there were not enough volunteers from only one school to get everything accomplished every week.

Fairly quickly the parents realized they needed to hire a manager, and they did. Even so, they still needed to recruit ten to fifteen parents *each week* to work every Sunday of the year. It was an enormous task. With two schools, there were many more parents to recruit from. The flea market parents expected that all the parents in the school would devote two or three Sundays per year to the flea market. However they couldn't count on a steady or consistent bunch, so employees were hired. Still, all the bookkeeping, legal, and administrative functions were done by parent volunteers.

One part of this plan that is so wonderful for the schools is that the money being raised does not necessarily come out of the pockets of the parents. The flea market thrives on neighborhood traffic and buyers who come from all over the city, not just the parents of the elementary and middle school children.

This fund-raiser makes more money than all the other fundraisers combined. But it's so big it has to be professionally run. Be sure to consults an accountant and an attorney when you start setting up your school flea market. Why? There is a danger that the money from the flea market that flowed into the parent association, which was considerable, would be considered as nonrelated business income and would therefore be subject to federal, state, and local business income taxes. That would put a serious dent in the profits from all that hard work and ingenuity.

On the advice of tax counsel, the parents had a for-profit corporation known as GreenFlea, Inc. created to operate the flea market in order to protect the tax-free transfer of money from market operations to the parent associations. The creation of the Green-Flea Corporation allowed money to be paid tax-free to the Middle School 44 PA as a royalty. Because of all the hard work in setting up and running the market initially that came from P.S. 87 parents, the P.S. 87 PA was made a shareholder, too, and would receive 20 percent of the proceeds under the terms of a separate contract between the M.S. 44 and the P.S. 87 parent associations.

This will all be much less complicated if you have only one school involved in your flea market. But you may wish to pull your district schools together to create and run a central flea market or you may benefit from joining up with just one other school. You'll have to share profits, but you'll also have a much larger pool of volunteers to draw from. Here is how you start a flea market of your own.

What Is a Flea Market?

A flea market is a group of people selling goods—from jewelry to fresh vegetables—to the general public set up in an area like a big schoolyard or parking lot. Frequently the vendors can offer lower-priced merchandise than traditional retail establishments since they are not paying rent each week but only a small fee to the owner or operator of the flea market space.

HOW DO YOU SET UP A FLEA MARKET?

First, you have to have a schoolyard or parking lot as well as some space inside the school, like a hallway and the cafeteria, to expand your market and to use for bad weather weekends. The school has to have a great location where it will draw shoppers from across the community, not just the parents from the school. A flea market cannot survive week after week with only the parents buying. Just as in any real estate transaction, location is everything. A flea market does not cost much to start, so it is ideal for a school just beginning a fund-raising program.

Think of your flea market as a new mall being constructed. Would there be enough shopper traffic in the neighborhood? Is the school located near downtown? Is it in a neighborhood with lots of people doing errands and out on the streets on the day you will be running the market? If the answer to these questions is no, don't give up. Perhaps you don't have enough traffic to run a flea market fifty-two weeks a year, but how about two or four times a year? How about only during holiday times? Could you run a flea market in November and December for holiday shoppers and again in April and May for Mother's Day and Father's Day? Think creatively and be flexible and open to the ideas of others.

Not sure if a flea market could be successful at your school? Test it out. It doesn't require much of an investment other than time to try it out. To test a market and get an accurate reading on whether or not a flea market will work, you must run for at least five or six weeks in a row, maybe longer. One or two weeks will not give you enough information to decide whether your flea market will be a success. What if you have rain or snow for one or two weekends? You also have to allow enough time for the word to get out that the flea market is there and that the merchandise is good.

Take time to figure out what will work best for your school. Be honest about the retail potential of the site. If the retail potential isn't good, consider testing a smaller format: fewer vendors, three times per year.

If you are successful you will need to hire a manager. Remember that parent volunteers are not only hard to come by but their children graduate from the school and they move on, taking their knowledge and experience with them. If you hire a good manager, he or she will be there year in and year out.

Find out from your principal who you have to contact to get permission to use the school on weekends. At Middle School 44 in New York City, we have to pay a permit fee, which covers the time-and-a-half salary of the custodian who must be there to open the school, clean up after the market, and close the school.

Draw a map of the total area available to you and carve it up into separate spaces. Assign rental cost to each space based on the size of the space and its location in the market. Or offer the spaces as singles or two spaces together as doubles, which may be more appealing for vendors who need larger spaces, like farmers. Each vendor rents space in the market. The flea market makes money on the space rental.

Why doesn't the flea market take a percentage of the vendor's sales? Wouldn't they make more money that way? Not necessarily. There are several compelling reasons why a good flea market doesn't provide space on a percentage basis:

1. It would be impossible to document what was sold and how much money the vendor made from sales each day.
2. Would you take your percentage on the gross sales or net, (sales less the cost of goods and expenses)? How would you determine the net for all the items sold?
3. Giving space on a percentage-of-sales basis means the flea market would be making an investment in the vendor, or rolling the dice, taking the chance that the vendor has the right goods, displayed well and priced right for sale. Taking that kind of chance without having any control over the items sold and at what price could be a disaster. There are simply too many variables to keep track of.

4. The bookkeeping would be a nightmare and would have to be done at the end of each day before the vendor leaves so you can collect your share. This would be impossible if you have five vendors or more.

5. The flea market would be hurt if the weather turned bad or the flow of buyers went down for a week.

Instead of accepting any risk with the vendors, a well-run flea market just charges a flat fee, depending upon the size of the space. Make the fee reasonable to keep the market profitable so that vendors return to the market to sell every week. The flea market will really make its money on vendors who come week after week.

Give a discount to vendors for repeat business. Make special offers, like rent for three consecutive weeks and get the fourth week free. This is especially good if you are just starting out. Even if you're not, if there is any space left that you're not collecting money for, you will do better to make a few dollars on that space than to make nothing. So try a standby offer for parents in the school only: if you come for last-minute space you only pay $25 instead of $50 if there is space available. Then the leftover space may get rented, but it won't be in as strong a location as the $50 space. Be creative and keep testing offers to see which ones bring in the most response from vendors. Be careful not to stress the remaindered space because you may have vendors who pull out and just wait for remaindered space, thus leaving you to sell too much space at half price.

Be careful about raising the rent for space. You need to keep new vendors coming in. If the rates get too high, you may be bringing in the wrong type of vendors, ones selling merchandise that is too high priced for your crowd of shoppers. Antique and craft vendors will draw more crowds and more repeat customers than displays of new merchandise or gimmicky gadgets.

Low rents allow for vendor consistency. Having the same vendors every week is important for shoppers. I get all my family's athletic socks and apples from the vendors at our flea market. I don't want to come back and find that when we need socks, the vendor is not there. Other shoppers will feel the same way. My children mourned when the little china-animal lady retired and they could no longer visit her table on Sunday studying the new tiny china creatures and begging me to buy one.

If you're charging too much, you'll hear about it. Complaints from the vendors will be an indication that your prices are too high. It is more important to have a high occupancy percentage than it is to make the maximum on each rental. Aim for an occupancy rate of over 65 percent each week. Steady rental customers are the best way to make money. Don't be greedy by trying to get the highest price possible for vendor space. It will backfire and you will find yourself with an empty flea market.

We don't offer a monthly vendor discount. Instead we have peak and off-peak season pricing. Also, any vendor who rents thirty-four times per year pays the lowest average rent. Only the people renting in the best season—usually holidays, spring, and fall—pay more.

Give space free or at half the rent for community organizations such as the Girl and Boy Scouts, ASPCA, dog and cat rescue groups, not-for-profit theater groups, soup kitchens, and other organizations that are trying to raise money for the homeless. This will bring you both goodwill in the community and a whole new group of shoppers.

> Reserve a table for the parent association each time. You can sell baked goods or just have a white elephant sale.

ORGANIZATION

A successful flea market can grow quickly and become too big to be run by volunteers. The Greenflea, which is the flea market started by P.S. 87 and M.S. 44 parents, bids on the flea market business in the school space controlled by the school district office just like any other vendor. The Greenflea employs a small but savvy and hard-working staff.

But before you grow, you have to start out with volunteer power. Here is a list of what has to be done each week so you can divide up the tasks to work efficiently:

- By Wednesday you will be receiving calls from vendors to reserve space. You can use an answering machine to take vendor reservations rather than man a phone full-time.
- You need to have a chart and/or drawing of the space that you can write on each week so you can keep track of who is renting which space that week. You may want to start out on a first-come, first-served basis on space until you have a steady stream of reliable vendors renting space. Greenflea started out renting on a first-come basis. But that is a little difficult for vendors as people start lining up at 6:00 A.M. to get a spot. But until you know who is reliable, this is the best method of renting out space. Then you will not be sitting with space unsold because someone reserved space and didn't show up. You may have turned down someone reliable because you erroneously thought you were sold out, which means lost revenue.
- You need to keep track of each and every vendor and collect cash the day of the flea market for the space. Do not accept

checks or money orders. Too many checks bounce. It also encourages thieves or con men to come in and rip you off, passing you bad checks. Cash makes it much easier. You will need at least two people to collect and count the cash to keep everything honest and make sure that no cash disappears.

- You will need strict guidelines on handling money. Your manager should be responsible to ensure that there is no payroll padding, like paying one person twice for the same job. You will need an experienced bookkeeper or accountant to help you set up the financial picture correctly and put safeguards in place. Put out the word among the parents in your school for professional help.

- You will need liability insurance no matter the size of your flea market. If someone gets injured, your market can be wiped out financially if you don't have insurance. Insurance is based on the size of your business. Try to find a reputable insurance broker in your parent body. You need to keep excellent records and show up for your insurance audit. Our manager saved $20,000 in insurance payments just by going to the audit and finding an error. If you have employees you will need workmen's compensation insurance in addition to liability insurance.

- Hire a manager who has managed before. Your flea market is no time for someone to learn on the job. You will need a manager who can hit the ground running and get your flea market up and bringing in revenue quickly, efficiently, and correctly.

- You need to advertise to bring buyers to the flea market. Start with your school newsletter—it's free.

- You may need to advertise in the beginning to attract vendors. After you have been up and running for a while, vendors will find out about your market from word of mouth.

Offer vendor slots to the parents in your school first at a very low rate to get started. You'd be surprised at how many people practice a craft that they want to sell, or who would just like to set up a lemonade and homemade cookie stand.

- You will need an advertising budget. Advertise where you will reach the most people. Place ads in newspapers near the garage sales pages. Many garage sale addicts love flea markets, too. Advertising can also include signs in the local supermarket and hardware store windows. Put up posters at school and houses of worship. It is very important to attract as many buyers as possible. Don't overlook neighboring towns for advertising. When you have a big crowd of buyers, the vendors will seek out your flea market and you'll really be in business.

Buy a few dozen large folding tables. You can rent them to vendors who don't have tables and don't wish to make that investment or don't have a place to store a big table. Store the tables in the school. All vendors rent tables and chairs from us because we rent them so inexpensively. We started with thirty tables and we have four hundred now. Table and chair rentals generate $25,000 to $30,000 per year, which more than pays for the personnel to handle the tables. Table rental service makes it much easier for beginners to become vendors at our market.

DON'T FORGET
- You will need the help of the custodian. Be nice to him, address him courteously. Treat him with respect. Give him

a gift or card at holiday time and always remember his birthday.

- You will probably need permission from the principal of the school where you are holding the flea market.

- Just as in every other real estate transaction, location is paramount. Only start a flea market if your school space gets lots of traffic from people other than parents at the school—for example, if your school is on a street that leads to a supermarket, movie theater, mall, or house of worship.

- If your school doesn't get that much outside traffic, consider running a flea market on a more limited basis, either quarterly, monthly, or only during holiday times, like Christmas and Mother's Day.

- Provide both outdoor and indoor space. Outdoor space usually works best as people can see the tables and the goods, but indoor space is extra space and may be key during bad weather.

- Get local farmers to bring in fruits and vegetables. The greenmarket is the backbone of our flea market. It draws people from all over to buy the choice produce trucked in so fresh that the grocery stores can't compete.

- Hire staff to double as both security guards and cleanup crew. You will need at least two people and maybe more, depending on the size of your flea market.

- Track monthly payments of vendors and keep excellent records for the state. Special income-and-expense-reporting requirements may be imposed on your flea market by your state.

- Start a vendor hotline and take reservations on Monday and Tuesday. On Wednesday, call each vendor to give them their assigned space for the market. We used to do a lottery for space on Saturday or Sunday morning. But that reduced the number of vendors. We had long lines and we ran out of space, creating angry vendors; which is not good for business. The first-come, first-served method that we tried also didn't work since early arrivals tended to be vendors selling junky merchandise. The most successful flea markets keep some control over the type of merchandise sold. Don't allow just anyone who has money to come; be choosy picking which vendors you sell space to. In the long run it will improve your profits and build a solid reputation among buyers who will be confident that they can find good merchandise at your flea market.

Hint: Leave the area you are using as spotless as possible. You will lose permission to use the space if there is garbage piled up on Monday morning. Don't rely on the school custodian to take care of cleanup. If he doesn't do a good job, it reflects badly on your operation.

Offer discounted vendor space to teachers.

Price space rental very low to begin with. A good level for us in Manhattan is indoor space at $45 to $50 for the day, since there usually isn't as much traffic indoors as there is outside. Try $80 to $100 for a prime space outside. If you're just starting out you might charge only $25 per space. You can always raise your rates as the market grows. But if you're priced too high, vendors won't make enough money to come back again.

Special offers are good, especially when you are starting out:

- Offer vendors a free week if they come three weeks in a row. Get four weeks for the price of three!
- If you have a full-time vendor, one who is there every week, you might want to offer a lower per week rate.
- Offer a special monthly rate to those who rent every weekend. Since you will be doing the work, and paying your staff whether you have rented ten spaces or one hundred spaces, it may make sense to lower your rental prices in the beginning to fill up the market.

The most important goal is to have all the spaces rented, even if the rates are low. This way you will make the most money, be able to pay your staff, keep going, and build a reputation.

As the market gets established and you have regular shoppers, you can raise the space rental rates and vendors will gladly pay the higher prices if they are consistently selling merchandise and making money.

12

The Ultimate Bake Sale

It seems as if every school from the beginning of time has had a bake sale. P.S. 87 has raised as much as $1,500 at one bake sale. Our bake sale operators are truly experts.

How Does a Bake Sale Work?

There are two basic kinds of bake sales that require two different types of plans: the in-school and the out-of-school bake sale. The in-school bake sale takes place during the school day, starting early and finishing up by the end of the after-school program, around 5:30 P.M. Those sales are usually held for some specific cause, such as raising money for a class or grade trip or for library books or classroom supplies.

The out-of-school bake sale might still take place in school, but is directed toward nonschool buyers, for example a bake sale during Election Day, whether school is in session or not. We also have a bake sale in the flea market yard on the night before Thanksgiving because so many people come to see the Macy's Thanksgiving Day Parade balloons get inflated right down the street from our schoolyard. We also have bake sales at our dances, the Harvest Festival and the street fair. Look for a special event in your community that brings out potential customers who will be in a festive mood and ready to buy cupcakes, cookies, and brownies.

> You could have a themed bake sale: a pumpkin/mince pie and cranberry bread bake sale right before Thanksgiving.

THE IN-SCHOOL BAKE SALE

An in-school bake sale takes place before, during, and after school. The buyers are parents, teachers, and the students. Here are some tips to make the in-school bake sale a success:

- Kids will buy store-bought baked goods that adults will not be as eager to buy. For example, Entenmanns's chocolate chip cookies, priced at two for a quarter, sell well to kids at the in-school bake sale, but don't sell well at the out-of-school sales that appeal mostly to adults.

- Besides baked goods, candy, chips, pretzels, other snacks, soda, and water may sell well. Send parents to the nearest discount store or warehouse club to buy huge containers of individually wrapped candy, like Twizzlers, and sell them for a dime each or two for a quarter. Items selling for only a dime allow everyone at the school to buy something at the bake sale without it being a big expense. Full participation is good not only for the morale and self-esteem of the children but it generates income and good feeling at the same time.

- Make sure you have plenty to sell. Running out of merchandise will kill your bake sale fast. Send a volunteer out to buy more to sell when donations get low and you'll generate money all day long.

- Start the sale early, about half an hour before school starts. You will reach all the early parent and teacher arrivals.

> Sell bagels with butter or cream cheese to the early birds.

- Place your sale strategically to reach the most people. We use the lobby of our building, where many students and teachers pass through on the way to the classrooms in the morning.
- Arrange for teachers to bring their classes down to the bake sale, one class at a time. We post a sign-up sheet on the office door for teachers to pick a time to bring their class down for ten minutes or so for the kids to buy goodies.
- Publicize the bake sale not only to those from whom you are requesting donations but also to everyone in the school, so every kid can bring money to school. Most younger children don't carry money to school, so you need to remind them to bring 50¢ or $1 for the sale.
- Charge lower prices than you would for an out-of-school bake sale. For the in-school bake sale, brownies and cupcakes are 50¢ a piece. For an out-of-school bake sale, selling mainly to adults, brownies and cupcakes are $1.

If a child approaches me to buy something and he or she doesn't have enough money, I'll sell it to them for whatever they have. If they don't have any money, I let them select something small to take with them for free.

- Be sure to get the word out to all the parents. You will need two parents per hour to help run the table. The same parents can cover several hours. Everyone should make some contribution or other. Promote your goal. Parents are more likely to contribute when they know what the money is being raised for.
- There are several ways to safely handle bake sale cash. Deposit the cash in the school safe frequently. I don't like to keep more than about $50 in change and low-denomination

bills with me at the bake sale. If you don't have a safe, you can send a reliable parent to the bank several times during the day. Store cash that comes in after banking hours in the principal's office. This will cut down on loss and theft.

OUT-OF-SCHOOL BAKE SALE

We have bake sales that are directed to nonschool adults and children a few times a year, depending upon local events. We put on a bake sale for every primary and regular election. Since all the voting for our district is done in our school, we are guaranteed a large group of adult buyers traipsing by our tables.

ELECTION DAY BAKE SALES

- Set up early. I try to get the table up and running before 8:00 A.M. as there are many people who vote before going to work. If you start setting up at 6:30 A.M., you will be all ready by 7:30 when people start arriving.
- Sell coffee, especially in the morning. Our PA owns a huge coffeepot that makes fifty to a hundred cups. I try to get this up and perking early as it takes half an hour to forty-five minutes to make the coffee. Coffee sells well, especially to people who won't buy baked goods because of dietary restrictions. We sell the coffee for $1 a cup. That really isn't much more than you pay elsewhere, and less than Starbucks. Try to get a coffee donation from Starbucks or a local coffee roaster or supermarket in exchange for promoting where the coffee came from. This will increase sales. Otherwise go to a discount store where you can get a gigantic can of coffee for the best price.
- Sell only homemade baked goods. The one question I get repeatedly at the Election Day bake sales is, "What's homemade?" Even if your prices are higher than those at the in-

school bake sale, they are still lower than a bakery's prices and the items are probably twice as good. People love to buy homemade baked goods.

- One exception to store-bought goods is Krispy Kreme donuts. Everyone loves these doughnuts and will buy them no matter what. We are lucky that Krispy Kreme has a special deal for schools and sells us the doughnuts at almost half price so we can make a nice profit on them. Is there a company like this in your neighborhood? We run out and buy fresh Krispy Kremes with the proceeds of the sale when we get low on donated baked goods. This will keep the sale going.

- In the evening continue to sell coffee, but add cold soda and water, which sell well with an adult crowd, too, especially with people watching their calories or cholesterol. Everyone can buy a bottle of water for $1 and feel like a contributor to your school. Water and soda should be bought at a discount store or a beverage outlet. Borrow a giant garbage can from a custodian, line it with a triple layer of thick garbage bags, fill it with ice, and add the drinks. Profits from drinks add up quickly.

- Concentrate your selling during peak hours: 7:00 to 11:00 A.M. and 3:00 to 8:00 P.M. If there's not much traffic, it wastes volunteers to man the table if there are almost no sales to be made. Pack things up loosely and stow them under the table so you can open up again quickly after lunch.

- Presentation is important, especially for the out-of-school bake sale. Use tablecloths, attractive serving platters, paper napkins and paper plates.

- Whole cakes are best in the out-of-school bake sale. I have occasionally sold an entire cake in one fell swoop. But even if you don't, cakes generate a good profit. If you slice a cake up into ten pieces, and sell each one at $2, you will raise $20 from each cake donated. There are a greater variety of cakes than cupcakes, where decorations usually take the cake! Homemade angel food cakes have always been one of our top sellers. But you can have lemon cakes, bundt cakes, coconut cakes, pound cakes, and of course chocolate cakes. If you sell cakes, don't forget plastic forks. Ask for donations of paper goods and plastic utensils from parents who don't have time to bake anything.

- Pie works great by the slice or by the whole pie. When we offered sweet potato pies, the first one flew off the table; I could hardly cut and serve the pieces fast enough.

- In the morning, we sell bagels and cream cheese with coffee. These are perfect items for parents who can't bake to

> Sell cheap raffle tickets with a beautiful, large homemade cake as the prize.

donate. Bagels sell quite well to people who don't want to make another stop on their way to work. We also sell homemade muffins in the morning. Corn or blueberry do well, or throw in mini chocolate chips and make chocolate chip corn muffins, a big seller. Any breakfast pastry is also a surefire hit.

- Use kids to help sell. On major election days, when school is out, running a bake sale table gives the kids something positive to do with their time that is also fun. Adults respond well to the children at the table and their presence makes your customers feel more connected to the school. And, all adults like to see children working for things instead of just expecting handouts.

- Try homemade sandwiches during lunchtime at an Election Day bake sale. A voter stuck on a long line that's eating up his lunch hour is a captive customer for a convenient and well-priced premade sandwich.

SPECIAL-OCCASION OR THE-NIGHT-BEFORE-THANKSGIVING BAKE SALE

- We conduct a bake sale in the schoolyard the night before Thanksgiving because that is when we have the Macy's workers inflating the mammoth balloons for the parade the next day. There are thousands of people milling around trying to get a look at the balloons before the parade and watching them being inflated. Every community has special events that bring people out in droves. Plan your school bake sale to coincide with a special event such as town Christmas caroling, or an Easter parade or Memorial Day parade or Fourth of July festivities and fireworks.

> Our school bought a popcorn machine and at the Night-before-Thanksgiving bake sale we sold bags of popcorn for $1.

- We also sold hot cider and hot chocolate along with our hot coffee. The hot chocolate and cider far outsold the coffee.

> For our Thanksgiving eve sale, we had a table of nothing but pumpkin pies. Sell seasonal specialties so you can save people a trip to the bakery or the trouble of making it themselves.

SECRETS TO SUCCESS

Buy big containers of giant pretzel sticks, or small individual boxes of pretzels, boxes of individual packages of cookies at a discount store and sell the individual packages for 50¢ or 75¢ each.

When you get low on baked goods, pretzels, chips, or whatever you're selling, go out and buy more supplies, such as bags of cookies or a box of doughnuts, from a local store with the money you're making on the sale. At two cookies for 25¢, you can still make money dividing up a bag of store-bought cookies. This keeps you in supplies all day and helps to cover the bare spots, when supplies get low— between people dropping off those precious homemade goodies.

Advertise your purpose for the sale. At the Election Day bake sale we received donations of $5, $10, and $20 when people were told that we were raising money to pay for paraprofessionals in kindergarten classrooms.

VOLUNTEERS

Have the children from the class or grade that is raising the money help to sell the baked goods. This gives the kids a chance to practice their math and learn to make change. They feel like part of the process and will ensure that their family donates something to the sale.

You will need two kinds of volunteers: parents who will supply you with baked goods to sell, and parents who will be at the sale and run the booth. You will need two volunteers at the booth at all times since there is much to do with wrapping purchases "to go", getting forks, and counting out change.

Timeline • • • • • • • • • • • • • •

This event can be thrown together in a week if you do the right publicity and have a good group of parents who will bake, but three weeks ahead is a preferable time frame. If you have a bake sale every year at the same time—like an Election Day bake sale—then start publicity early to remind people.

Three weeks ahead	start publicity
	start soliciting donations
	send home sign-up sheets and flyers with kids in their backpacks
Two weeks prior	reserve tables with the custodian
	send out reminders to parents
	publish in school newsletter
	put up posters
One week prior	solicit donations from bakeries, doughnut shops
	remind parents to bake
	shop at discount stores and beverage wholesalers
	put reminder in newsletter
Two days before	put up poster reminders around the school
Day before	arrange for extension cords, etc. for coffee machines
	arrange for ice and garbage cans
	gather paper goods donations

13

Candy Sales, Sports Equipment Exchange Day, Alumni Club, School Store

It seems that every organization that needs to raise money—from schools to scouts—sells candy. P.S. 87 resisted the urge until 2002, when our financial needs grew fast—we had to pay for paraprofessionals in five kindergarten classrooms that were cut from our budget by the district. We tried everything we could to boost our fund-raising efforts.

What Is a Candy Sale?

There are several different kinds of candy sales, run through a variety of candy companies. The school buys boxes of candy bars for 50¢ per bar and sells them to the public for $1 per bar, netting a 100% profit.

HOW DOES A CANDY SALE WORK?

Find a company that is set up to do candy sales. We used QSP, the same company that helped us with our wrapping paper and magazine drives.

Sally Foster also sells candy to schools and there are other companies that can be located on the Internet. QSP is on the Net at www.qsp.com, or you can reach them by phone, toll free: 1-800-561-8388.

QSP, like other companies, has several different candy offers for schools with a varying number of bars and type of candy. We selected a Hershey collection provided in large boxes containing fifty-two candy bars each. The price from QSP was $25 for fifty-two candy bars. We got two bars free as a bonus. So when each candy bar from that box is sold for $1, the school will net $27. An order of $800 worth of candy (or thirty-two boxes) gets you free shipping. Most companies offer free shipping.

This fund-raiser is fine for schools just starting out, since there is no up-front cost. QSP sends you the candy and an invoice. You pay when you sell the candy.

Most candy sales are done in the fall, when people are most enthusiastic. We do ours in the late winter/early spring, and we did fine. Many of these sites also offer candy and other products to sell for fund-raising:

www.allstarfundraising.net

www.awardfundraising.com

www.ezfund.com

www.fivestarfundraising.com

www.kathrynbeich.com

www.lollies.com

www.lollipops.com

www.northvalleyfundraising.com

www.officialfundraising.com

www.resourcefundraising.com/candy/html

www.smithfundraising.com

SECRETS OF SUCCESS

We suggested to parents that a box of chocolate bars was a great reward at the office, and those parents handed out the fifty-two bars to employees. We also had parents who took the boxes to the office and sold tons there.

HOW MUCH MONEY CAN YOU RAISE?

We made almost $4,000 on our investment. This is a fund-raiser you can start small and build.

VOLUNTEERS

Another nice part of this fund-raiser is that it doesn't chew up a lot of volunteers. You only need about three people to have a candy sale fund-raiser.

Timeline • • • • • • • • • • • • • •

Two months ahead	decide on the company you want to use and the type of plan you want
One month ahead	Order the candy and start your publicity

CAVEAT

This fund-raiser works particularly well when the kids sell the candy. Do not under any circumstances send your children out to sell the candy by themselves. If you want them to sell it, they must be accompanied by an adult. No door-to-door sales without a grown-up along.

Sports Equipment Exchange Day

This is strictly an in-school event. Sports Equipment Exchange Day is a day when parents can donate their children's old, outgrown sporting equipment to the school and buy secondhand sporting equipment, which other people's children have outgrown at a really good price. What could be better than to keep up with a child's growing feet by picking up a pair of Roller Blades for $10 to $20? A secondhand baseball mitt might sell for $5 or $10.

This sale serves two purposes: parents can get rid of all that old sporting equipment cluttering up their homes, and parents with younger children can outfit their kids for a lot less money than new equipment would cost.

HOW DO YOU RUN SPORTS EQUIPMENT EXCHANGE DAY?

First you need to get your donations in the school. Start publicity early—you might emphasize that Exchange Day is a perfect opportunity to encourage kids to try out a new sport inexpensively. Publicize to both donors and potential buyers. You will need to provide a place to store donations. Allow parents two weeks to bring in all donations.

Plan on a day or two to sort and price everything. Try to sort the equipment by size, by sex, and by sport to make purchasing easier. Schedule your sale to stretch over several days to give people every opportunity to buy the equipment.

Have a plan for the equipment that is not sold. Charities like the Salvation Army will pick up the leftovers. Or if you have room, you can store leftovers to sell at another school event, like your street fair or Halloween Festival.

VOLUNTEERS

This event need not involve too many volunteers. You need a committee divided into donations and reselling. The donations group finds the storage space and sorts and prices the equipment. The resale group does the publicity, sets up the sale, and runs it. The resale group should also make arrangements to get rid of the unsold equipment.

The receiving group need not be bigger than three people. The resale group should probably be six or seven parents.

HOW MUCH MONEY CAN YOU RAISE?

You can make anywhere from $500 to $2,000 depending upon the size of your school and the zeal with which your student body pursues sports.

Timeline • • • • • • • • • • • • • • •

This event can be done on short notice. But be sure to tell the parents way ahead so they will remember to save the old and outgrown sporting equipment instead of giving or throwing it away.

Six months ahead	inform parents of your intent
Two weeks ahead	ask parents to bring in used equipment
	inform parents when the sale will take place

NEW TWISTS

You can take this same concept and try it with books and toys, too. Have parents bring in books their kids have outgrown and resell them to parents with younger children. Donate leftover books to the school.

You can also try this concept with clothes. Have parents bring in outgrown clothing and resell to parents with younger or smaller kids. Give away unsold clothing.

Alumni Club

I am a member of the first Alumni Club at P.S. 87 so I don't have much to say yet that is based on experience. I expect that I will make mistakes and learn what to do and how to do it. Here is our plan:

1. Establish an annual (or semiannual) one-page, two-sided newsletter just for alumni, called *Alumni News*. Our news-

letter will include important news about the school, for instance which teachers are still at the school, where some recent grads have gone and what they are doing, issues that affect the schools like budgets, physical changes to the school like the revamping of the library, all the details of the reunion, and any new events planned for the year.

2. Plan a reunion. There is one month when not much is happening at the school—February. The fund-raising chairs have given me a date in February and we are planning a reunion. The reunion will have pizza and soda in the cafeteria and dance music in the gym for the kids and wine, cheese, and other finger foods in the lobby for the parents. We plan to charge admission of $10. We will also have a table to take donations for the school. The reunion will be a fund-raiser for the school. We will also have a table where people can "join" the alumni club for $5 and receive another newsletter or two about the school.

What Is a School Store?

The school store is an area in the school designated solely for selling merchandise displaying the school logo and school colors.

PROCEDURE

The school store can make money all year long if you have enough people to run it and reorder supplies. Try opening just one day a week at first. If you have enough volunteers, increase the number of days per week that the store is open when it begins to make money. You will need capital to start the store since you have to buy items and pay in advance of selling. Items for the store can be ordered from companies that personalize products. Try epromos. com, or look up other companies on the Internet or in your yellow pages.

Some items you might sell in the school store include:

pens

pencils

book covers or protectors

notebooks

binders

backpacks

flashlights

umbrellas

pencil cases

funky erasers

mugs

key chains

sweatshirts

T-shirts

caps

Some online companies that provide personalized products are:

www.customprinting.com

www.epromos.com

www.gopromos.com

www.iprint.com

www.logo-it.com

www.promotionalpencils.com

www.suzannepens.com

www.tagdesigns.com

www.thediscountprinter.com

VOLUNTEERS

You will need several volunteers to man the store on the day(s) you are open. Have two volunteers for each shift. If your store is very small, one will do, but it's always better to have two people handling cash. You will also need a committee head who orders products and keeps the books to track expenses and income. Create your own catalog and price list and distribute to everyone.

SECRETS TO SUCCESS

Although we don't have an actual, physical school store because there is no space in our school, we do sell items with our logos on them, like T-shirts and mugs. One secret is to have a table selling imprinted items at the school fair. Another is that we save half our profits for our reserve fund. This gives us the capital we need to purchase more items. Set up your store on a big cart you can keep in a school closet. Call it out out for sporting events, bake sales, book fairs, and conferences.

HOW MUCH MONEY CAN YOU RAISE?

This depends upon how much you can invest and how long it takes to sell all the items. We make about $1,500 on T-shirts alone. But we have a big school and we advertise for months. This is a school business you can grow slowly and profitably.

Timeline • • • • • • • • • • • • • •

Try to have your designs ready to go by the beginning of the school year. The earlier you order merchandise, the sooner you can begin selling.

JUST STARTING OUT?

You need money to start a school store, but you can start small. Even just $100 collected from parents $5 at a time can get you started. Try to find a corporate sponsor to kick in $200 to $500 to start your store.

Negotiate with your suppliers for either a reduced price or extra merchandise for your order. Get prices from competing companies and play them off each other until you get a price you can afford.

Pencils might be the best place to start as you can buy them so cheaply. At www.rwpencil.com I found imprinted pencils at $19.25 per gross (144 pencils) which is about 13¢ per pencil. This is just imprinting, not a logo, but for about $50 you could have two or three gross of pencils and start selling them at only 25¢ apiece and you'd soon be making a profit. Search the Web for more imprinted-product companies or check your yellow pages. Reinvest your profit by buying more products and your business should flourish.

14

Tapping Corporate America

With money for schools getting harder and harder to find, more parents are turning to the corporate world for help. Smart marketing people are finding many different ways to encourage purchase or trial of their company's products by reaching out to schools. These companies are willing to reserve a small amount of the profits as a payback to those schools. More and more companies are jumping on the school fund-raising bandwagon every year. Some smart people are inventing companies to support school fundraising and making money themselves doing so. Following are some companies with excellent school fund-raising promotions that are very easy to bring to your school.

Schoolpop.com

Schoolpop.com is a Web site that serves as a portal to other Web sites. In other words, you click on schoolpop.com and you will see links to other popular companies' Web sites. Schoolpop.com makes money for schools by getting a percentage of the sales made by parents who bought from a Web site they went to from a link at schoolpop.com. Schoolpop then passes along part of their percentage to participating schools that promote the schoolpop.com Web site.

Schoolpop.com started in early 1999. Although they haven't

been around for long, they have survived the dot-com shakeout and have signed up over 23,000 schools. Schoolpop.com has participating schools in every state, but tends to be a bit stronger in small towns that don't have so many retail outlets of the stores they link to. Schoolpop.com has 300 participating merchants with at least 250 being on-line. They even have grocery stores participating.

Schoolpop can survive on a small percentage because the volume is so high. Schoolpop.com has given over $5 million to schools since 1999.

Schoolpop.com's fund-raising magic is available to all schools: public, private, and parochial. Although they deal with mostly K–12 schools, they are open to accepting preschools and other children related services, like the scouts, as long as it is a nonprofit organization.

Schoolpop.com has links to many Web sites like: amazon.com, llbean.com, landsend.com and others where you can buy merchandise. You can find over one hundred company names and logos on the schoolpop.com Web site.

Register with schoolpop.com on-line to have the royalties from your purchases credited to your school. The registration is easy to set up. First, register your school on-line if it's not already registered. Then you register yourself and select your school. Once you are registered with schoolpop, go to their Web site, click on the link to the company you are interested in and then buy through that company's Web site. A percentage, which varies from company to company, of the purchase you just made will go to schoolpop.com and a large percentage of that will go to your school. It's amazing how fast this can add up. The only additional work you have to do is remember to go to the schoolpop Web site first before you purchase. It is very important to get this information out to your parent body. It is a completely painless way to make money for your school.

Schoolpop.com even offers this service for purchases made not on-line but actually at some grocery stores and local merchant establishments. With grocery stores and local merchants, you may have to get them signed up first. Schoolpop and your school get a small percentage of whatever purchases you make at that store only by using the credit card you have registered with schoolpop.com. Even small percentages when tallied frequently from a large number of people can add up quickly.

If you go to the site, click on merchants, and put in your zip code, you can get a list of the local merchants in your area that are hooked up with schoolpop.com. When you shop at the registered stores with the credit card you registered with schoolpop.com, your school will receive a percentage of your purchase.

How much can you raise from schoolpop.com? That depends upon how much you promote it. You will get back whatever you put in. If you only have one or two participating parents, then you might get as little as $150 or less. But according to schoolpop.com, one school recently made $10,000 in a single quarter! Our school has done well. We've made over $1,000 in one year from schoolpop.com.

Adopt-a-Classroom

Adopt-a-Classroom is a nonprofit organization that harnesses the resources of the community and the Internet to support educational experience. Jamie Rosenberg, the founder of Adopt-a-Classroom, is a lawyer who saw teachers reaching into their own pockets for classroom supplies and started this remarkable organization. He realized the tremendous need in classrooms today for supplies that are not budgeted for.

Rosenberg found donors willing to sponsor classrooms with donations of $500. Rosenberg then gave up his corporate life to run Adopt-a-Classroom, a program benefiting schools.

HOW ADOPT-A-CLASSROOM WORKS

To be eligible to receive Adopt-a-Classroom supplies free, a teacher must apply directly on-line. Principal approval is also required. Then the teacher waits for Adopt-a-Classroom to find a partner willing to "adopt" them and contribute $500.

Rosenberg offers a catalog of school supplies. The teacher selects up to $500 of whatever he or she needs from the catalog and orders it through the Adopt-a-Classroom Web site: adoptaclassroom.com. Adopt-a-Classroom buys the supplies and has them shipped to the teacher. This is a onetime offer. The entire $500 worth of supplies must be ordered all at once.

Adopt-a-Classroom tries to match donors to classrooms in their area so the donors can visit the classrooms and see the results of their generosity.

Adopt-a-Classroom also receives funds to run the company from unrestricted contributions from foundations, businesses, and individuals, and makes money to defray expenses by negotiating with suppliers for volume discounts. The difference between the $500 and the discounted price becomes the income of Adopt-a-Classroom. For example, if your teacher, Jenny Smith, ordered $500 worth of pencils, markers, special paper, and glue, the Adopt-a-Classroom would negotiate with the supplier to get the supplies for $450 instead of $500. So the $50 difference between what the donor actually wrote a check for and the real cost of the supplies shipped to Jenny Smith becomes the income of Adopt-a-Classroom. That is a terrific way to cover expenses of the company without taking anything away from the sorely needed classroom supplies.

Adopt-a-Classroom will only deal with teachers, not parents or parent associations. So you need to publicize this wonderful bonus to all the teachers in your school. The teachers and principal must go to the Web site, adoptaclassroom.com, to apply for the stipend.

WHAT DOES THE TEACHER DO?

1. A school gets selected for this program by just applying on-line. Donors can target their donation to be earmarked for a specific school. If the donor does not specify a particular school, Adopt-a-Classroom will pick the school from the schools registered on the Web site. Their aim is to provide support for the most needy schools.
2. You must be a public school established before August 15, 2001. The teacher must have a valid e-mail address since all communication is done through e-mail.
3. The teacher registration form is easy to fill out. This is a new program that is growing. Get your teachers registered and ease some of the fund-raising burden on your parent association.

Box Tops for Education

One of the first corporate programs to support education, this combination of charitable contribution and product promotion is an excellent and easy way to get some extra money for your school.

WHAT IS BOX TOPS FOR EDUCATION?

General Mills has printed the Box Tops for Education logo on over 330 products. This seasoned program has raised money for more than 60,000 K–8 schools nationwide. The schools have earned over $50 million in donations. Here is the participating products list: Almond Oatmeal Crisps, Apple Cinnamon Cheerios, Apple Cinnamon Oatmeal Crisps, Basic 4, Berry Berry Kix, Boo Berry, Brown Sugar and Oat Total, Cheerios, Chex Morning Mix, Cinnamon Grahams, Cinnamon Toast Crunch, Cocoa Puffs, Cookie Crisp,

Corn Chex, Corn Flakes Total, Count Chocula, Country Corn Flakes, Fiber One, Franken Berry, French Toast Crunch, Frosted Cheerios, Frosted Wheaties, Gold Medal Raisin Bran, Golden Gra-hams, Harmony Vanilla Almond, Honey Nut Clusters, Honey Nut Cheerios, Kaboom, Kix, Lucky Charms, Milk 'N Cereal Bars, Multi-Bran Chex, Multi-Grain Cheerios, Nature Valley Granola, NesQuick, Oatmeal Crisps, Para Su Familia, Raisin Bran Total, Raisin Nut Bran, Reese's Puffs, Rice Chex, Team Cheerios, Trix, Wheat Chex, Wheaties, Wheaties Energy Crunch, Wheaties Raisin Bran, Whole Grain Total, Yoplait yogurt products, Betty Crocker products, and Lloyd's Barbecue Buckets.

HOW THE PLAN WORKS

1. Buy General Mills products from the above list.
2. Save the Boxtops for Education logo by cutting it off the top of the box.
3. Turn the box tops in to your school coordinator.
4. Count and bundle them and send them to General Mills by the deadline, usually around March 30.
5. General Mills will send you a check! The box tops are worth 10¢ each. But when you have hundreds of people saving box tops over the course of many months, it adds up. Our school has received at least $500 every year from this program. An enrolled school can earn up to $10,000. The school can spend the money any way it pleases.

Register your school on-line at www.boxtops4education.com and get started today.

BOX TOPS BRANCHES OUT

The intelligent folks at Box Tops for Education have expanded their fund-raising program to include a percentage of on-line shopping.

Just like schoolpop.com, if you start your on-line shopping trip at Box Tops for Education and click on any of over 100 Web shopping sites, including amazon.com, eddiebauer.com, and petsmart.com, your school can get up to 10 percent of each on-line purchase—up to $10,000 per school per year—at no cost to you in either time or cash.

Box Tops takes fund-raising one step further. To continue their profit-making and additional contributions to your school, Box Tops for Education has gone even further than any other company and come up with the Box Tops Visa Card. You can apply for this at the www.boxtops4education.com site. There is no annual fee and a low APR. Call 1-800-227-9605 to apply.

Once you get your Box Tops Visa card, 1 percent of every purchase you make with that card will be donated to your designated school—up to $10,000 per school per year.

General Mills and Box Tops have made it very easy to make money for your school with very little effort.

Campbell's Soup Labels for Education

The Campbell's Soup Company seems to be the originator of "school donation for proof-of-purchase" as they have been running their program for twenty-eight years. The Campbell's Labels for Education (TM) program has been giving schools free educational equipment in exchange for labels from various Campbell's products. Your school can receive free supplies of all kinds by saving up Campbell soup labels and sending them in. Details are on their Web site, www.labelsforeducation.com. Or if you forget, you can access them through the Campbell's Soup Web site, www.campbellssoup.com.

HOW DOES IT WORK?

You need to have everyone start saving labels from the following eligible Campbell's products: Campbell's bean products, Chunky

soups, Campbell's condensed ten-ounce soups, Campbell's condensed twenty-six-ounce soups (family size), Campbell's Healthy
Request soups, Campbell's Healthy Request tomato juices (forty-
six-ounce), Campbell's low-sodium soups, Campbell's ready-to-
serve soups (can), Campbell's Select soups, Campbell's Soup to Go
(tub), Campbell's Tomato Juices (ten-ounce, forty-six-ounce),
Campbell's Simply Home soups; Franco-American Gravies;
SpaghettiO's and Pasta; Pace Salsa; Picante and Picante Con Q;
Prego Pasta Sauces; V8 Vegetable Juice; Healthy Request; Splash
juice drinks; Pepperidge Farm breads, croutons, rolls and stuffing,
cookies, crackers, Goldfish crackers, frozen garlic breads, cakes,
turnovers, dumplings, puff pastry and phyllo dough; Swanson
broths and poultry.

Bonus labels can be obtained from two products:

- Earn ten bonus labels when you save the UPC label from any
  specially marked Campbell's Supper Bakes Meal Kit.
- Earn five bonus labels when you save the front label from
  Franco-American SpaghettiOs A to Z's.

One catch seems to be the high number of labels needed to get
merchandise. For example a pedestal Globe for the classroom
requires 4,250 labels. But the incredibly long list of products with
qualifying labels may make this easier than it seems. I couldn't
believe how many products we use that were on that list.

The list of products you can get for your school is on the Web
site. It might be a good idea to search the list for specific items to
spur the drive. It's easier to save up labels when you know what
you're saving up for. In fact, each class can make their own wish list
and the parents can get to work gathering labels from family and
friends to meet the goal. Publicize the drive often with small
reminders in your newsletter. Have a "deposit" box handy in the
school lobby and office. Ask teachers to collect them in the classrooms.

Retail On-site Fund-raising Events

P.S. 87 NIGHT AT BARNES & NOBLE

This is something new created for our school by a former fund-raising chair, DJ Shepherd. DJ negotiated a special relationship for our school with Barnes & Noble through their community affairs director at the local bookstore. With DJ's keen understanding of how dependent local stores are on community traffic and her persuasive abilities, she arranged with the community affairs director to have a P.S. 87 Night at Barnes & Noble. It was a huge success. Here is how it works.

- The school and the store agree on an evening to have the event.
- The store makes a deal on the percentage of the gross receipts the school will receive and how that will be calculated. At Barnes & Noble, they fly balloons from the registers they have selected to count for the P.S. 87 portion. Out of five registers upstairs they might designate two or three for P.S. 87 and out of three registers downstairs, one or two.
- The school promotes the day exhaustively for weeks before the event. We frequently get a date in the fall, before Hanukkah and Christmas. We try to convince our parents to do all their holiday shopping at Barnes & Noble on our special day. Our fund-raising co-chairs came up with a great new twist, especially for the parents who could not make it to the event. They offered to go and buy gift certificates at Barnes & Noble for the parent who could not attend. The revenue from the gift certificates counted toward our percentage. I know one family that bought $500 in gift certificates and then did their holiday shopping at their leisure. What a great idea.

- The store allows us to have parents at the store, handing out flyers informing the other, non-P.S. 87-parent customers that if they check out at the designated registers, they too can contribute to your school. This was so successful that one year, Barnes & Noble had to open another register to accommodate the flood of customers who had just become fund-raisers.

- Select the volunteers you have at the store carefully. You don't want anyone who will not be grateful for what is being done and anyone who will raise a ruckus. This is the fastest way to get the whole program canceled. Find people with pleasant, positive personalities. Encourage people to explain very briefly about the register and then add a boost for the store. I always say, "Corporate America giving back, isn't it wonderful!" People really respond to that kind of promotion from the parents.

- Be grateful to the store and show it: I have walked into our Barnes & Noble and gone up to the manager and told him that I was there shopping instead of buying at Amazon.com because Barnes & Noble supports P.S. 87. They really need to hear that their generosity is creating terrific customer loyalty and added sales for the store.

- We have made as much as $10,000 in one night with this event. It was such a huge success that when DJ went to work for the school district, she continued her relationship with Barnes & Noble and to this day the store rotates the schools who are allowed to have a night there because of her ingenuity. This program affects many schools. She also has one designated for the school district. Funds from that evening can be parceled out to specific needs on a school-by-school basis.

Fast Food

Our local Burger King has a special program open to schools, scouts, and similar organizations. We created a P.S. 87 Night at Burger King. Call around to the local franchisees of national food chains and present this innovative idea to the owner or manager.

HOW IT WORKS

Burger King agreed to give a percentage of the gross from receipts collected in boxes marked for P.S. 87 on a particular night from 5:00 P.M.–8:00 P.M. We did lots of publicity and got as many fifth grade parents and caregivers to show up as possible.

We had three boxes marked for our school, plus a sign we made and placed on the counter. Burger King allowed us to gently solicit from other customers and ask for their receipts. We had a wonderful time. The whole evening was like a school or class potluck with no one cooking and no one cleaning up. We made only $300, but it was very easy and pure profit.

Go into any store or restaurant in your community—especially those known to be popular with your students—and arrange to have a special night there for your school. Let the restaurant or store pick an especially slow night so you can increase their traffic and total receipts. Do lots of publicity. This opportunity to join hands with retail establishments to increase their sales while making money for your school is just opening up. Joining fun with fund-raising is an unbeatable combination.

Target Targets Schools

Target stores have a special fund-raising offer. If you get a Target Visa or Target Guest Card, Target will donate an amount equal to 1 percent of your qualifying Target Visa or Target Guest Card purchases at Target stores or on-line at www.target.com. You can pick the school (K–12 grades) where you want the money to go to. Target sends the money to the school twice a year.

More than 114,000 schools across the country are participating in this program. The program is available to any public, private, or parochial school from grades K–12.

HOW DO I GET STARTED?

To sign up your school, call 1-800-316-6142. If you already have a Target Visa or Guest Card and want to designate a school, you can do so either on-line or call 1-800-316-6142. You can apply for a Target Visa or Guest Card on-line at www.target.com.

AVON

Avon has a special fund-raising plan through their local representatives.

Avon has many products to choose from. Their holiday catalog is a big seller. You can have average orders of $20 or more.

There is minimal paperwork and no door-to-door selling with an Avon fund-raiser. Your school can earn between 30% to 40% of the sale as profit. And the profits will roll in as little as three weeks.

Your local Avon rep will take you through the entire process and handle much of the work.

Avon is a nationally known company. Their products come with a money-back guarantee. Their products are diverse and are good for all family members.

You can get in touch with a local rep through their national Web site or through www.avonrepnetwork.com/fundraising.html. or E mail the U.S. fundraising manager, Sandy Booth, at sandy.booth @avon.com.

Final Thoughts
· · · · · · · · · · · · · · · ·

· · · · · · · ● 15 ● · · · · · · ·

Idea Bank

Following is a list of miscellaneous ideas. Pick one that works for
you and make it happen:

1. *Holiday Parties* Use any holiday such as May Day, Cinco
   de Mayo, President's Day (Washington & Lincoln), or
   Valentine's Day to have a party and charge admission.
      Make a potluck or order pizza and soda and charge an
   admission fee. Add a bake sale and a few games and you
   have a fund-raiser. Remember to negotiate with your
   pizza provider to give you a special rate. Domino's once
   donated pizza to a Boy Scout Awards Night because they
   valued the business from our scout families. For years
   Domino's was the only place our family bought pizza.
2. *Flea Market Table* Have a table for your school at the flea
   market and sell white elephant items donated by the parents.
3. *White Elephant Store* Have a secondhand or white elephant store in the basement of the school, just as many
   churches do. Run it during the school year.
4. *Crafts Fair* Have a craft fair in the school just before
   Mother's Day. Offer crafts made by parents and children.
   Donate half the proceeds to the school and half to the

maker of the items. Or donate 60 percent and keep 40 percent, whatever works for your school.

5. *Avon Calling*   Get an Avon representative in the school to donate half her commission percentage and have an Avon Week in the school with the Avon lady taking orders and giving half her proceeds to the school.

6. *Candy*   Sell candy at the flea market.

7. *Parent/Child Sporting Events*   Have a father-daughter volleyball game or a father-son basketball game or a teacher/student game or a parent/student tournament in the school. Charge a small participation fee. Serve food and have a bake sale at the event. Get corporations or fraternal organizations to sponsor so you can sell T-shirts commemorating the event and give out trophies to the winners. Keep the rest of the money for the school.

8. *Movie Theater Night*   Get a movie theater to give your school a special discount price on tickets. Or rent an entire theater and have a school night at the movies. Sell tickets at regular price and keep the difference for the school.

9. *School Play*   At a school play, ask for donations, have a bake sale, sell popcorn and drinks.

10. *Cash-In on Kindergarten*   Put kindergarten parents in charge of an easy event with an experienced parent as co-chair to get the kindergarten parents involved quickly.

11. *Join Forces with the Girl Scouts*   Make a deal with the Girl Scouts. Make an arrangement where kids sell Girl Scout cookies in the school for $3 per box; $2 go to the Girl Scouts and $1 goes to the parent association.

12. *Concerts for Cash*   Any famous parents in your school? Any musicians? The classical musicians in our new kindergarten class got together and put on a concert in the school auditorium. They raised almost $5,000!

13. *Stand-Up Fund-raiser* Have a stand-up comedy night. With good publicity you will attract aspiring comedians, who are always looking for an audience. Or have a kids' stand-up comedy night. Charge $5 admission.

14. *Halloween Village Art* Hold a Halloween window-painting contest. Get local merchants to donate the use of their windows or use the windows in your school. Get kids to sign up to paint their own imaginative Halloween designs in water-based poster paint on the windows. Judge the windows and give out awards. Get a $10 registration fee from each child. Can't find prize donors? Give cash awards from the proceeds instead.

   This event takes place every year in Rye, New York. The local schools do not sponsor it, but the wonderful artwork is up for several weeks, keeping the Halloween spirit alive.

15. *Shovel Snow for Dough* Plan in advance to have a snow-shoveling day when your area's first snowstorm hits. Then, when it snows, you will be ready. Send middle and high school kids out to shovel driveways and shovel out cars. Charge $15 for a driveway and $5 to dig out a car.

16. *Sell Wrapping Paper in Your Flea Market* Right after Thanksgiving, contact your wrapping paper company or search for wrapping paper on Google.com. Most companies have leftover wrapping paper for sale at a huge discount in the fall. Sell the paper in December, long after your seasonal wrapping paper sale is over. This idea requires money up front. See if you can find a sponsor if your school doesn't have the funds.

17. *Wine and Cheese Tasting* Get donations from local liquor store or winery and gourmet cheese store. Charge $10 and make this an evening or late afternoon event. This idea

comes from the British International School of Brussels (Belgium) PTA.

18. *Fashion Show*   Have children or adults, or both, design and sew their own clothes and throw a fashion show. Provide donated refreshments. Charge $5 admission. This idea comes from the St. John's School, in the United Kingdom.

19. *Cook Book*   Create your own cookbook using recipes from the parents in your school. There are companies on the Internet, like www.fundcraft.com, that can produce a cookbook for your school.

20. *Domino's Pizza Week*   Make arrangements with Domino's Pizza that on five special nights if people ordering mention the name of your school, Domino's will donate 20 percent of their order to your school. The James Daly School in Montgomery City, Maryland, has pioneered this idea.

21. *Cookie Dough Tubs*   Schools in Austin, Texas, gave us this fund-raising idea. Sell frozen tubs of The Chippery cookie dough. Just thaw, scoop, and bake. Each three-pound tub makes ninety-six cookies with no fuss. To see all the different types of cookie dough you can sell for your school, just click onto www.thechippery.com. Their on-line catalog will take orders and answer questions, too.

22. *Pancake Breakfast*   If you can commandeer your school cafeteria and kitchen, a pancake breakfast will be fun and raise funds at the same time. This idea came from the Parchment, Michigan, PTA.

23. *Dog or Cat Show*   Let children enter their pets. Have special ribbons for pet tricks. Make sure everyone gets a ribbon. Charge a $5 entry fee. Have a cat or dog "parade" where everyone can participate and an audience can applaud and cheer.

24. *Talent Show/Joke-Telling Contest*   This can be for parents and children alike. Charge $5 admission and award prizes. Make sure everyone gets a participation ribbon.

25. *Craft or Quilt-Making Contest or Fair*   Award prizes for the best crafts or quilts. Charge an entry fee or a small admission fee to view the crafts. At the end of the show, sell any crafts the maker wants to donate to the school.

26. *Walkathon*   Get sponsors, from your boss to grandma, to give $5 per mile walked. Conduct the walkathon with parents and children, or just children alone. You can raise money and get into good shape at the same time.

27. *Readathon*   Suggested by the Parchment, Michigan, PTA, a readathon is the same as a walkathon, only sponsors pay per book read. This is a long term project, but you can create excitement and keep track of reading as it progresses. Also this one is great for getting your mind in good shape.

28. *Pumpkin-Cooking Contest at Thanksgiving or Halloween*   Charge an entry fee for all edibles made with pumpkin. From pies to casseroles, let your parents and kids run wild. Sell the entries after the judging.

29. *Quiz Show*   Conduct a Jeopardy-type game contest between parents and teachers, teachers and teachers, teachers and students, parents and students, or any other combination. Charge admission for those who wish to watch. Sell baked goods at intermission. This idea comes from the St. John's School in the United Kingdom.

30. *Start a Vegetable and Flower Garden on School Property*   Let the kids plant and tend a small garden. Sell the vegetables and flowers at their own roadside stand when all is ripe and in full bloom.

31. *Your School's Day at the Ballpark*   Approach a local minor league (or major league) baseball team about having a

"day" for your school, when 20 percent of the box office receipts would go to your school.

32. *Art Show and Silent Auction*   A silent auction of donated artwork, a free kid's art activity area, and a show of over one hundred of Portland's artists, including a student gallery, coupled with some light fare from a local bakery or the parents make up the Buckman Elementary and Da Vinci Arts Middle School's Art Show & Tell in Portland, Oregon.

33. *Photo Sales*   The enterprising parents at Oliver Middle School in Broken Arrow, Oklahoma, sell photos of memorable occasions, like awards ceremonies. Select a few gifted photographers from your parent body and do the same. Sell photos from the school play, graduation, class picnics, and other special school occasions.

34. *Discount Cards*   In Sumter, South Carolina, a favorite fundraiser is selling buy-one-get-one-free cards that are applicable to local merchants. Call Win Win Discount Cards at 1-800-394-6946 to find out about discount cards in your area.

35. *Entertainment Books Make Money for Schools*   In Austin, Texas, selling entertainment discount books to parents, grandparents, friends, aunts and uncles, and neighbors raises needed cash for their schools. Call Entertainment Books at 1-800-933-2605 to find out how you can get this fundraiser going in your school.

36. *Redeem Tyson Products for School*   Tyson Project A+ is a label-redemption program that can earn your school up to $12,000 per calendar year. Just clip and save the labels of specially marked packages of Tyson products and redeem them for 24¢ cash to use any way your school wants.

37. *Raise Money from Your Child's Artwork*   Original Works (1-800-421-0020) professionally reproduces your child's artwork onto a variety of high-quality products they can wear and share. Makes a great fund-raiser.

38. *Art for School's Sake*   Turn your child's original artwork into colorful greeting cards or T-shirts to raise money for your school with Kidoodlez—A Child's Adventure in Drawing (1-800-455-4449).

39. *Fido Gets into the Act*   Raise money for your school by selling pet treats. Pet Treat Companies (1-815-943-8144) gives your school a 50 percent profit on pig ears and other goodies for cats and dogs.

40. *Keep Warm and Raise Money*   Have throw blankets custom designed for your school by Liberty Logos (1-888-829-0280). Use your school colors, mascot, or logo. Finished size is 54" × 72". Perfect for a cold-weather fund-raiser.

41. *More Great Cookie Dough and Human-i-tees*   Check out Bake & Co. at 1-800-535-2253 for other great fund-raising products, like cookie dough and beautiful T-shirts from Human-i-tees.

42. *Looking for Just the Right Cookbook Company for Your School?*   Check out these companies:
    Walter's Cookbooks—1-800-447-3274
    Cookbook Publishers—1-800-227-7282
    National School Cookbooks—1-800-426-9827
    G&R Publishing, The Cookbook Specialists—1-800-383-1679
    Rasmussen Company—1-800-665-0222

43. *More Cookie Dough Companies*   Looking for just the right cookie dough company? Try one of these:
    Grandma Corbi's Homemade Cookie Dough—1-888-JCORBIS

Chef-Co. Gourmet Fund-raisers—1-800-960-2014

Classic Cookie—1-877-933-5444

44. *More Web Sites to Try*   Check out fundraising.com or ezfundraising.com (1-800-991-8779).

45. *Walk for the Arts*   Joseph Estabrook School in Lexington, Massachusetts, has a walk-for-the-arts to raise money. They also have a talent show.

46. *Fifth Grade Barbecue at Estabrook School*   Have a grade sponsor a barbecue to raise money.

47. *Market Day in Illinois*   An Itasca, Illinois, woman, Trudi Temple, started with day trips from suburban Illinois to Chicago's farmers' markets. Make a deal with local farmers' markets to come and sell for a fee in your school parking lot. A win/win situation: fresh, healthy food for all and money for the school.

48. *Bye-Bye Summer Sale*   Have a secondhand kids' summer clothes sale in your school in October. People can donate shorts, T-shirts, summer dresses, and bathing suits that will be too small to wear next summer. They can buy summer clothes in a larger size ahead of time very inexpensively. This sale shouldn't deplete donations to the spring street fair where families donate outgrown winter clothes.

49. Make a deal with a nursery to sell Christmas trees in the school parking lot on weekends. Get a flat fee or a percentage of sales.

Creating New Ideas and Getting Volunteers

Brainstorming New Ideas for Your School

Your most important resource is the intelligent, creative, devoted, hardworking parents and teacher body at your school. You will be surprised who will come up with the best ideas. A brainstorming session can help to get your fund-raising off the ground.

Run a brainstorming session just as a business would; after all, fund-raising is a nonprofit business. Here is what you need to conduct a productive brainstorming session:

1. a large room you can occupy for at least four hours.
2. a huge pad of paper, an easel, and plenty of colored markers.
3. chairs and table, preferably round so there is no "head," which often stifles people from speaking up.
4. food—hungry people are more argumentative. Once we started bringing food to the PA board meetings, much of the arguing stopped.
5. a board member with good or at least legible handwriting to chair the session or preferably two members: one to lead and one to write.
6. creative people who are not afraid to speak up. When parents are part of the planning and idea-generating process

they are more likely to "own" the results and volunteer to move ideas forward.

You will not need many rules, but one is mandatory: no one is allowed to shoot down or criticize any idea. All ideas are acceptable and all ideas shall be heard. If you allow people to criticize or cut off ideas, before long no one will open their mouth to contribute anything and your meeting will be fruitless.

The meeting leader should be a strong person with a positive approach who can direct the meeting while still being open to new ideas. The leader should come in with some general topics to start off the session.

Every new idea gets written on the pad. The leader asks people to expand on each idea. He or she must lead the process when response is slow or people are shy. Call on people if you have to. Write down all the expansions on each idea and then tear off the sheet and clip, pin, or tape the sheet to the wall.

As the meeting progresses, the sheets will start to fill up the walls. The leader needs to assign ideas for follow-up to people in the meeting. When the meeting is over, the follow-up people take the big sheets with them. It's great if you can have a secretary in the meeting writing everything down or taking notes on a laptop so you have a record of all the ideas in another place in case someone's dog eats the big sheets or they fail to follow up.

Follow-up is key. Without follow-up a good idea is just a piece of paper. The fund-raising chair is responsible for all follow-ups. You have a chance to make the person who came up with the idea head the committee to flesh out the idea and find a way to make it work. Jump on the opportunity at the end of the meeting to assign a committee to each person who is taking home a big sheet. Try to convince the people who contributed to the big idea to be on the committee to make it happen. People will work harder to make something they conceived of successful.

VOLUNTEERS

Which brings me to the subject of volunteers. Fund-raising events happen only because somebody volunteers. Some people work tirelessly for our school for years, others only bake a cake or supervise a class booth for an hour. Whatever the amount of time, the volunteers are the lifeblood of fund-raising.

HOW TO GET VOLUNTEERS

There are many ways to bring in volunteers. Here are a few that work for schools across the country:

1. Post sign-up sheets on bulletin boards around school.
2. Have class parents call parents in their class or use the phone tree to save time.
3. Advertise the need for volunteers and describe the job thoroughly in your school newsletter.
4. Ask every volunteer to bring a friend who may also volunteer to the next meeting. We have a group of women who are friends who love to come and do the grab bags every year.
5. Have a special welcoming meeting on the first day of school for the new kindergarten parents. At this meeting have board members and committee chairs speak briefly about what they do. Have sign-up sheets for the new parents to volunteer.

KEEPING VOLUNTEERS

Once you have volunteers, it is very important to keep them. Getting volunteers is hard, you need to use patience, rewards, and acknowledgment to keep volunteers coming back. It's so much easier to have smoothly running events when you have experienced people at the helm.

Volunteers who feel a sense of gratification and appreciation will come back to volunteer again. Following is a list of basic do's and don'ts when managing volunteers:

1. Trust your volunteers. That means you shouldn't look over the shoulder of every volunteer to make sure he or she is doing a perfect job. I remember wanting to do this when I was making grab bags. Was this lady putting the right stuff together? Was the other lady putting too much stuff in one bag so we'd run out too soon? I made myself crazy.

   Finally I realized that the feelings of my volunteers were more important than having every bag perfect. So I stopped watching so closely and trusted that they would do a good job. Of course the bags sold out quickly, as usual; and I have an ongoing crew of ladies who like to put together the grab bags because they are respected and treated well.

2. Try to make volunteering fun. Have a few laughs, tell jokes, or relate funny stories while you work. Bring food, even if it's only a bowl of pretzels to nosh on while working. A volunteer who has a good time will come back.

3. Acknowledge and appreciate. Remember to use words of praise with your volunteers. Telling people they are doing a great job really makes them want to come back and help again. Volunteers are hard to get so you must treat them really well.

4. Be positive and praise often. Criticism just tears people down and drives them away. Be positive and cheerful. Everything doesn't have to be perfect.

5. Be a good listener. Be open to new ideas and ways of doing things. People who think their way is the only right way often

end up doing everything by themselves. No one wants to work with a dictator. Besides, you never know where a good idea is going to come from. Don't shut people down with a negative attitude or you'll find yourself working alone.

6. Listen to your volunteers. When a volunteer complains that he or she needs help with a job, or additional tools, listen and be prepared to act. Either find someone to help her or him or else you jump in and help. A volunteer who feels ignored, overworked, burned out, or overwhelmed will not come back to volunteer again.

Reward your volunteers. Here are several ways:

1. Throw a volunteer appreciation breakfast. A few urns of coffee, some juice, and bagels with cream cheese are not expensive. Being invited to an appreciation breakfast will really make your volunteers feel special. Make sure to go up to each and every volunteer and say thank you.

2. Publish lists of volunteers for all your events in your school newsletter. Seeing your name in the school newsletter is a real boost. People will begin to see the same names over and over and a person's status in the school will grow. Not to mention the fact that you know who doesn't mind volunteering and you can call people on one thank-you list to volunteer for another event.

3. Purchase a "badge" of volunteering. One year we bought little apple pins that had "P.S. 87 Volunteer" plus the year on them. The pins were like tie tacks, cute and colorful. We thought the pins were too small to mean much, but boy were we wrong! Everyone who volunteered wanted that little pin. It was a real prize, a sign of giving and belonging. And they cost us only $1 apiece. You can find premium

companies on the Web or in the yellow pages that will produce pins like that for you, or many appropriate premiums
can be bought ready-made. Some companies are: iprint.
com, epromos.com, and gopromos.com.

4. Publish a list of volunteers on poster paper and hang it in
the vestibule or office of the school. Having your name on
this list is a real badge of honor.

Keeping volunteers is all about recognition, appreciation, lis-
tening, and laughing together. That's what makes all this fund-
raising so special.

Have fun with your school fund-raising. It's a great experience
to get involved in your school. Be creative, laugh, and have a great
time. The parents at P.S. 87 have made an enormous difference in
the school and in the educational experience for their children. Our
kids know that we care, because we are there.

Budgeting

Part of the job of raising the money is learning how to spend it.
Creating and following a budget is an important part of running a
parent association. You need to prepare a budget, present it to your
parent association, and have it approved by a majority vote.

The budgeting process starts with the creation of a budget
committee. This should include at least: your treasurer, PA president, and fund-raising chair. Members of other important committees, like enrichment, who may be in charge of spending much of
the money you raise, should also be on the committee.

The budget committee meets during the summer months to
prepare a budget. The budget is presented to the parent body at a
PA meeting as early in the school year as possible. Nothing can
begin until that budget is approved.

WHAT IS A BUDGET?

A budget has two parts: income and expenses. Make a list of the estimated income from your fund-raising for the coming school year and a list of estimated expenses for the coming school year.

Once you've had some successful fund-raisers, you need to have a well-thought-out plan for the expenditure of the money. The first thing you do is take half the money and put it in a PA savings account. It will earn interest while remaining untouched. If you place half your earnings in savings, before long you will find that you have a reserve fund growing nicely. Then when you need to lay out money in advance you can borrow it from the reserve fund, if necessary. The reserve fund is essential. If you spend every penny you make you will be unable to grow, as you will not have the necessary funds to lay out in advance for important, growing events that are expected to bring in lot of money. We started a reserve fund because we will lose a lot of money if it rains on our street fair.

Every committee head who wants money for expenses should either be at the budget meeting or give his or her plans, in writing, to someone who will be at the meeting. It is not enough to say, "I want two thousand dollars for the health and safety committee." You will need to have a spending plan ready to explain, and preferably in writing to pass out to all the members of the budget committee.

Plan on budgeting some money to be spent at the principal's discretion and some to allot to teachers. Meet with the principal and discuss what he or she would like to do if they had more money. Allocate what money you feel you can toward his or her school enrichment plans.

We have a teacher's fund. Every year every teacher gets $200 to spend on classroom supplies. For new teachers the amount is $400. This allocation is actually spent by reimbursing teachers who spend the money and submit invoices/bills to the PA. Please be prompt with reimbursement to the teachers. They do not have deep pockets to finance the enrichment of your child's classroom.

The treasurer needs to keep a close eye on expenditures or your committees and even principals and teachers can go over budget by accident. Both the president and the treasurer of the PA should approve each principal and teacher reimbursement. Never budget your expenses to exceed your income. But you can budget to have money leftover and not spend everything you raise.

This can become an "opportunity budget." An opportunity budget is money set aside to be available if some wonderful special opportunity should present itself to your school that no money has been previously allocated for. For example, a traveling opera comes to town. Your principal makes a deal for the opera to perform at a cut rate for the children in your school. But it will cost $500 and the principal has already spent his discretionary fund. With your opportunity budget, you have the money to take advantage of this special event.

The budget should be re-examined in January. You will have had one or two fund-raising events by then and will have some idea if you have raised more or less than you budgeted. Some committees will not spend their full allotment—their budget can be reduced—and some may need more. In January you can revisit your earlier plans and make adjustments and move money around as is necessary. Make sure to present the revised budget to the parent association for approval.

Your budget is your most important guideline. It will help you to focus your fund-raising efforts on specific needs, which may inspire people to give more money. For example, if you are raising money for a new piano, music-loving parents might give more money than they would for a general fund-raiser. It will also tell you how well you're doing and where the most important school needs are.

Keep an open door for teachers. Some wonderful ideas were created because our parent association was open to funding special projects. One teacher and her class created a reading garden using grant money and PA funds. Another teacher created a school-wide poetry book with funds from the PA.

Remember that as a member of the board of your parent association, you have a financial obligation to be responsible for the money that comes through your treasury.

Contact Me

Please share your fund-raising travails and triumphs, or ask me questions at my Web site www.beyondthebakesale.com.

Important Phone Numbers and Web Sites

WRAPPING PAPER

Sally Foster:www.sallyfoster.com

QSP/Reader's Digest:1-800-561-8388 or www.qsp.com

Genevieve's:1-800-842-6656

5 Star Fundraising: www.fivestarfundraising.com

Kathryn Beich:www.kathrynbeich.com

Resource Solutions: www.resourcefundraising.com

MAGAZINES

QSP/Reader's Digest: 1-800-561-8388 or www.qsp.com

BOOK FAIR

Scholastic: www.scholastic.com/bookfairs

Chinaberry: www.chinaberrybookfairs.com

Troll:1-800-454-TROLL (8765)

KID'S GRAB BAGS

The Oriental Trading Company: www.orientaltrading.com

U.S. Toy Company: www.ustoy.com

T-SHIRTS

    iPrint: www.iprint.com

    ePromos: www.epromos.com

CANDY SELLERS

    QSP/Reader's Digest: 1-800-561-8388 or www.qsp.com

    www.resourcefundraising.com/candy.html

    www.lollipops.com

    www.lollies.com

    www.allstarfundraising.net

    www.smithfundraising.com

    www.northvalleyfundraising.com

    www.fivestarfundraising.com

    www.officialfundraising.com

    www.awardfundraising.com

    www.ezfund.com

    www.officialfundraising.com

    www.kathrynbeich.com

SCHOOL STORE/LOGO ITEMS/PREMIUMS

    www.iprint.com

    www.epromos.com

    www.gopromos.com

    www.logo-it.com

    www.customprinting.com

    www.uscolorprint.com

    www.promotionalpencils.com

    www.thediscountprinter.com

    www.suzannepens.com

    www.tagdesigns.com

CORPORATE WEB SITES

schoolpop.com

Adopt-a-Classroom: www.adoptaclassroom.com

Avon Representative: www.avon.com or www.avonrepnet
work.com/fundraising.html

General Mills Box Tops for Education: www.boxtops4
education

Box Tops VISA Card: 1-800-227-9605

Campbell's Soup: www.labelsforeducation.com or www.
campbellssoup.com

Target Stores: 1-800-316-6142 www.target.com